STUDIES IN DANTE

FOURTH SERIES

STUDIES IN DANTE

FOURTH SERIES

TEXTUAL CRITICISM OF THE 'CONVIVIO' AND MISCELLANEOUS ESSAYS

BY

EDWARD MOORE, D.D.

HON. D.LITT. DUBLIN

CANON OF CANTERBURY; HON. FELLOW OF QUEEN'S AND PEMBROKE COLLEGES, OXFORD;
CORRESPONDING MEMBER OF THE ACCADEMIA DELLA CRUSCA; FELLOW OF THE
BRITISH ACADEMY; FORMERLY PRINCIPAL OF ST. EDMUND HALL, OXFORD, AND
LECTURER ON DANTE AT THE TAYLOR INSTITUTION, OXFORD, AND BARLOW
LECTURER ON DANTE AT UNIVERSITY COLLEGE, LONDON; AUTHOR OF
'CONTRIBUTIONS TO THE TEXTUAL CRITICISM OF THE DIVINA
COMMEDIA', 'TIME-REFERENCES IN THE DIVINA COMMEDIA'
(REVISED AND ENLARGED AS 'GLI ACCENNI AL TEMPO
NELLA DIVINA COMMEDIA'), 'DANTE AND HIS
EARLY BIOGRAPHERS', AND EDITOR OF
THE OXFORD DANTE'

HASKELL HOUSE PUBLISHERS LTD.

Publishers of Scarce Scholarly Books

NEW YORK. N.Y. 10012

1968

First Published 1917

HASKELL HOUSE PUBLISHERS Ltd.
Publishers of Scarce Scholarly Books
280 LAFAYETTE STREET
NEW YORK, N. Y. 10012

Library of Congress Catalog Card Number: 68-29737

Haskell House Catalogue Item # 220

Printed in the United States of America

PREFACE

THE revision of the proof-sheets of this volume had been all but completed by Dr. Moore at the time of his death (Sept. 2). What little remained to do (including sundry additional notes, and the compilation of the list of editions, editors, and commentators of the *Convivio*, the list of emended passages in the text of the *Convivio*, and the index) has been done by myself,[1] with the approval of Dr. Moore's representatives and of the Delegates of the Clarendon Press. This I feel would have been in accordance with Dr. Moore's own wishes. We had worked together at Dante in informal partnership for more than five and twenty years. I had read the proof-sheets of this volume, as I had done those of the three previous volumes of *Studies*; and I had been in constant communication with him throughout the progress of the work up to within a day or two of his death.

The contents of the volume speak for themselves; but I may be permitted to express my satisfaction, which will be shared by every serious student of Dante, that Dr. Moore was able to complete the highly important series of studies on the textual criticism of the *Convivio*, which constitute nearly half the volume, and represent the outcome of his collations, through a long series of years, of corrupt passages in the text in the thirty-three known manuscripts of the treatise.[2] The majority of the resulting emendations (numbering close on fourscore)

[1] Such few additions as I have made in the notes are enclosed in square brackets.

[2] It may be mentioned in this connexion that the valuable manuscript of the *Convivio* (designated M in this volume) which belonged to Dr. Moore, and is described by him on pp. 130-1, has passed by his bequest, together with a manuscript of the *Divina Commedia*, to the Bodleian Library, which now possesses two out of the three manuscripts of the treatise at present in this country. The third is in the library of the Earl of Leicester at Holkham. There is a fragment in the British Museum. Of the remaining twenty-nine, two are in the Bibliothèque Nationale at Paris, and the rest in various public and private libraries in Italy.

have been embodied in the text of the *Convivio* as printed in
the third edition (1904) of the *Oxford Dante*; but owing to
the fact that the scheme of that work excludes anything in the
shape of an *apparatus criticus*, they have had to be introduced
sub silentio.   These studies constitute as it were the *pièces
justificatives* of the emended text.   Of the other articles, three,
namely, 'Dante's Theory of Creation,' the 'Introduction to
the Study of the *Paradiso*,' and 'Sta. Lucia in the *Divina
Commedia*,' are now published for the first time.   The re-
mainder are reprinted, with due acknowledgement, from various
periodicals, namely, 'The Tomb of Dante' from the *English
Historical Review*, 'The Battifolle Letters,' and the notes on
'The Almanac of Profacius,' and on 'Two Proposed Emendations in Dante's *Epistola VI*,' from the *Modern Language
Review*; and the note on 'Dante in Northern Latitudes,' from
the *Academy* (under the editorship of Mr. J. S. Cotton).

It would be out of place here to attempt an estimate of
Dr. Moore's work as a Dantist; suffice it to say that his
intimate acquaintance with the whole range of Dante's writings,
his attainments in the many fields covered by his subject, his
acute yet cautious critical judgement, his sound scholarship,
and indefatigable industry, gained him a European reputation,
which was recognized by his election, among other distinctions, as a Corresponding Member of the Accademia della
Crusca, and as a Fellow of the British Academy.   That he
was invariably courteous in controversy, though a hard hitter
on occasion, will be admitted even by those with whom his
differences of opinion were most pronounced.   That he was
ever ready to place his knowledge and resources at the disposal
of a fellow-student, and that he was ungrudging in his acknowledgement of help received, none has better reason to know
than the writer of these lines.

PAGET TOYNBEE.

Fiveways, Burnham, Bucks.
September 28, 1916.

NOTE

I HAVE adopted in this as in my last volume of *Studies* a simpler method of reference to the *Summa* of St. Thomas Aquinas, which I hope will be found convenient, but it needs explanation. That Treatise is divided into five main divisions, known as Pars Prima, Prima Secundae, Secunda Secundae, Tertia, and Tertiae Supplementum. These are indicated as I, II^1, II^2, III, and III Suppl. Each *Pars* is subdivided into *Quaestiones*, and these into *Articuli*. The general plan of each Article is (1) a statement of the subject; (2) the view of opponents with their arguments under distinct heads; (3) a general *Responsio*; and then a separate *Responsio* to each of the opponents' arguments. The 'Questions' are here given in small Roman numerals, and the 'Articles' in Arabic numerals. The letters r, r_1, r_2, r_3, &c., refer to the general or the separate 'responsiones' above described. Thus a full reference such as II^2 xcvi. 3. r_2 would mean that a quotation was found in the Second Division of the Second Part, Question xcvi, Article 3, and in the answer to the second argument of the opponents.

I must also again warn my readers that my references to Scriptural quotations apply to the Vulgate, as the Version used by Dante himself. Not only does the numbering of most of the Psalms differ from that of our English Version, but sometimes also the division of verses in other Books is different, and especially in the Apocrypha. A variation in the Latin and English Translations may sometimes cause a reference to the English Version to appear irrelevant or mistaken. I repeat this warning, as I have occasionally received kindly meant but mistaken suggestions for corrections in the Scriptural references of my previous volumes.

E. MOORE.

CONTENTS

LIST OF ABBREVIATIONS

Ant. Trans.	*Antiqua Translatio* of Aristotle.
Aq.	Aquinas (see note on p. vii).
Arist.	Aristotle.
Aug.	St. Augustine.
Bisc.	Biscioni (see List of Editions, &c., of the *Convivio*, No. 5).
C.D.	*De Civitate Dei* of St. Augustine.
Conf.	*Confessiones* of St. Augustine.
Edd.	Editions.
Edd. Mil.	Editori Milanesi (see List of Editions, &c., of the *Convivio*, No. 8).
Ep.	*Epistola* (of Dante).
EV.	English Version of the Bible.
Frat.	Fraticelli (see List of Editions, &c., of the *Convivio*, Nos. 10, 12).
Giorn. Arcad.[1]	*Giornale Arcadico* (see List of Editions, &c., of the *Convivio*, No. 11).
Giul.	Giuliani (see List of Editions, &c., of the *Convivio*, No. 13).
Greg.	St. Gregory.
P. Lomb.	Peter Lombard.
Ped.	Pederzini (see List of Editions, &c., of the *Convivio*, No. 9).
Pert.	Perticari (see List of Editions, &c., of the *Convivio*, No. 7).
RV.	Revised Version of the Bible.
Sentt.	*Sententiarum Libri* of Peter Lombard.
Tomm. e Bell.	*Dizionario* of Tommaseo e Bellini.

Misprinted *Accad.* on p. 79.

LIST OF EDITIONS, EDITORS, AND COMMENTATORS OF THE *CONVIVIO*

Referred to in the article on ' Textual Criticism of the *Convivio*'.

[COMPILED BY DR. PAGET TOYNBEE.]

1. *Convivio di Dante Alighieri Fiorentino.* Firenze, 1490.
2. *Lo amoroso Conuiuio di Dante: con la additione* [1]: *Nouamente stampato.* Venetia, 1521.
3. *L'Amoroso Convivio di Dante, con la additione, & molti suoi notandi, accuratamente reuisto & emendato.* Vinegia, 1529.
4. *L'Amoroso Convivio di Dante, con la additione, et molti svoi notandi, accuratamente revisto et emendato.* Vinegia, 1531.
5. *Prose di Dante Alighieri e di Messer Gio. Boccacci.* Firenze, 1723.
   [Edited by Anton Maria Biscioni. ' Convito di Dante Alighieri ' occupies pp. 53–210.]
6. *Serie di Aneddoti.* V. Verona, 1790.
   [Edited by Giovanni Jacopo Dionisi. Contains (pp. 146–62) ' Nuovi significati e vocaboli nell' opera detta il Convito'.]
7. *Saggio diviso in quattro parti dei molti e gravi errori trascorsi in tutte le edizioni del Convito di Dante.* Milano, 1823.
   [By Vincenzo Monti. Part iv contains numerous emendations in the text of the *Convivio*, proposed by Giovanni Jacopo Dionisi, Giulio Perticari, Gian Giacomo Trivulzio, and by Monti himself.]
8. *Convito di Dante Alighieri, ridotto a lezione migliore.* Milano, 1826. (60 copies only.)
   [Edited by Gian Giacomo Trivulzio, Vincenzo Monti, and Gian Antonio Maggi (usually referred to as ' Editori Milanesi'). This edition was reissued (under the editorship of Angelo Sicca) at Padua in 1827.]
9. *Il Convito di Dante Allighieri, con note critiche e dichiarative di* Fortunato Cavazzoni Pederzini Modonese e d' altri. Modena, 1831.
10. *Convito di Dante Alighieri ridotto a lezione migliore, colle illustrazioni del Marchese Trivulzio e del Sig. Pederzini.* Firenze, 1834. 2 vol.
    [Edited by Pietro Fraticelli (see No. 12).]
11. *Nuova Centuria di Correzioni al Convito di Dante Allighieri proposte da* Carlo Witte. Lipsia, 1854. (150 copies only.)
    [With regard to the title ' Nuova Centuria di Correzioni ', Witte notes (on p. 41): ' La presente Centuria di correzioni si è detta *nuova*, perchè sin dall' anno 1825 più di cento altre correzioni al Convito, da me proposte, uscirono alla luce nel *Giornale Arcadico* di Roma.

---

[1] This apparently refers to the summary of contents prefixed to the treatise, which is lacking in the *editio princeps*.

Sessanta ne furono—con espressa citazione, o tacitamente—adottate, oppure commendate dagli illustri Editori Milanesi. Quattordici si riproducono ritoccate nel presente opuscolo. Oltre a venti correzioni, passate sotto silenzio nell' edizione di Milano, tuttora mi sembrano giuste, e per tali cerco di provarle nell' *Appendice* sottoposta. Il resto oramai da me stesso è giudicato erroneo, o certamente dubbio.']

12. *Il Convito di Dante Alighieri e le Epistole, con illustrazioni e note di* Pietro Fraticelli e d' altri. Firenze, 1856.

[This forms one of the volumes of *Le Opere Minori di Dante* published by Barbèra. It has many times been reprinted. The latest edition is the ninth. The seventh, which Dr. Moore appears to have used, is dated 1893.]

13. *Il Convito di Dante Allighieri, reintegrato nel testo con nuovo commento da* Giambattista Giuliani. Firenze, 1874. 2 vol.

14. *Tutte le Opere di Dante Alighieri, nuovamente rivedute nel testo da* Dr. E. Moore. [Con *Indice dei Nomi Propri e delle Cose Notabili compilato da* Paget Toynbee.] Oxford, 1894. [The *Oxford Dante*. 'Il Convito' occupies pp. 237-338.]

15. *The same.* [Seconda Edizione.] Oxford, 1897.

[With corrected title-page, and sundry corrections in text and index.]

16. *Tutte le Opere di Dante Alighieri, nuovamente rivedute nel testo dal* Dr. E. Moore. Con *Indice dei Nomi Propri e delle Cose Notabili compilato dal* Dr. Paget Toynbee. Terza Edizione, più estesamente riveduta. Oxford, 1904.

[In this, the latest, edition of the *Oxford Dante*, the title of the treatise has been corrected throughout from *Convito* to *Convivio*.[1]]

---

[1] Except in Conv. I. i. 102 ; ii. 2 ; x. 2, where 'Convito' has been left unaltered by inadvertence.

STUDIES IN DANTE

I.

TEXTUAL CRITICISM OF THE *CONVIVIO*

(i) CONDITION OF THE TEXT
(ii) DISCUSSION OF SELECTED PASSAGES
(iii) LIST AND BRIEF DESCRIPTION OF THE MSS. EXAMINED

(i) ON THE CONDITION OF THE TEXT

THE text of the *Convivio* has come down to us in a very unsatisfactory state. Many passages are deplorably confused and corrupt. It is much easier to account for this than to remedy it. The subjects discussed in this Treatise are often abstruse and technical. They deal with 'things unattempted yet' in the 'Volgare,' Latin having been thought hitherto the only suitable medium for such subjects. Again, the prose style of Dante is still rugged and often obscure, though showing a very great advance on any writers that had preceded him, such for example as Ristoro d'Arezzo, Ricordano Malespini, and others. Hence the 'limae labor' of modern editors in order to remove such ruggedness as may still remain is wholly out of place. Its effect is not to restore what Dante himself wrote, but by so-called 'improvements' to depart further from it. One might as well attempt to revise Tacitus into the style of Cicero, or Lucretius into that of Virgil.

With actual corruption of the text, when either no intelligible sense is left, or one obviously inappropriate is presented, the case is different. Under these circumstances we can feel sure that we have *not* got what Dante wrote, and our aim must be, if possible, to recover it. The large amount of such corruption is, under the circumstances already described, the natural result of the offhand and amateur criticism of copyists, unhampered by conditions of rhyme and metre, or by knowledge of the subject. But it may be doubted in the case before us whether the text has suffered more from the blunderings of copyists or the misplaced assiduity of editors. The chief offender in this respect is Giuliani. The liberties which he has taken with the text are almost incredible, unless one has had special occasion to compare it with MS. authorities. Giuliani simply rewrites sentences that he cannot understand, or misunderstands, and in the latter case he has sometimes made alterations that totally pervert and obscure Dante's real meaning [1]. Now when a sentence is evidently mutilated or defective, merely to supply *something* without any evidence or any reason, except that it gives some likely sense to this passage, is not criticism, but rather a sort of ' missing word competition.'

The method which I have adopted is simply this. To set down first the MS. evidence so far as it was attainable. Then, if no sense could be made out of it, even allowing for ruggedness of expression, to introduce the *minimum* of change possible by means of which some tolerable sense could be elicited. With this further proviso, that only such changes should be thus admitted as could be justified by well recognized critical principles applied to the MS. evidence, or supported by parallel instances. Finally, in a few extreme cases, when it seemed absolutely necessary to propose the addition or omission of words in order to secure any suitable sense, such additions or omissions have been distinguished by appropriate symbols [2], so that the reader may be aware of the change, and form his own judgement as to its necessity.

The notes which follow are strictly no more than ' contributions ' to the revision of the text. They are fragmentary and unsystematic, but may still, I hope, prove useful as materials for the work of future students. My

---

[1] See especially note on III. v. 154. But several other instances of this will be found in the passages discussed later.

[2] See *Oxford Dante*, p. 239.

general plan was to make a selection of passages of special difficulty, and to collate them in all available MSS. Unfortunately these collations have been spread over many years and made at irregular intervals. Thus my list of passages has naturally been increased as time went on, but it was rather a small one at first, so that the MS. record is very incomplete for some of those passages that have been added later. Otherwise, I have myself examined more or less (unfortunately in some cases 'less' rather than 'more') *all* the existing MSS. of which I can find any trace[1], except one, viz. the Venice MS. marked *F*. This was away on loan on the occasion of my visit. But through the kindness of the librarian of the Biblioteca Marciana (Dr. Coggiola) I have obtained a record of the principal passages in that MS. also. Dr. Witte in his *Nuova Centuria di Correzioni* refers to a MS. belonging to himself and another belonging to Baron Kirkup, but in the absence of any description of them, and being unaware what became of them after the death of their owners, I have not reckoned them, since it is possible they may be identical with some of those now in the list I have given. Moreover the information given by Dr. Witte is very scanty and occasional, and touches comparatively few of the passages here selected.

I have been able, I believe for the first time, to collect and present in the following pages the evidence of *all* the known MSS. in a certain number of selected passages. In a few cases the corruption of the text seems beyond remedy, since all the MSS. repeat with dull monotony the same unmeaning collections of words. Happily such desperate passages are not very numerous, since in many cases, by a comparison of the *different* blunderings of several MSS., some clue may be discovered as to the causes of error, and so the steps may be retraced with more or less confidence to the probable original. This, however, is evidently a case where the strictest curb must be placed on the inevitable (and only

---

[1] If any of my readers should find or hear of any other MSS. of the *Convivio* than those found in my list (*infra*, p. 118), I should be very grateful if they would send me such information.

too tempting) process of conjecture, and the conditions and limits of its employment must be most carefully laid down and jealously guarded.

When I was honoured in 1892 by the Delegates of the University Press with the task of preparing the text of the *Oxford Dante*, in regard to the ' minor works,' it was only proposed that I should recommend the best existing text for reprinting. It was then that I discovered in regard to the *Convivio* the utter untrustworthiness of all the existing texts owing to the enormous intrusion of conjecture to which (happily) its authors proudly called attention in their notes. As far as possible I got rid of such confessed intrusions *ipso facto* as self-condemned, but I had very slight *apparatus criticus* to guide me to anything better. There were only known to me two MSS. in England, but both happily in Oxford, one in the Bodleian, and one most fortunately acquired some years ago by myself. Further than that, I had only occasional records, in the notes chiefly of Fraticelli and Giuliani, of the readings of a few MSS. in Rome and Florence which they had consulted. Since that I have made a point of examining (more or less) every existing MS. of which I could find a trace, in number 33[1]. When I say ' more or less,' I mean, in the first place, that it was only possible to examine a *selected list* of passages ; and in the next place that whereas the complete list of such passages ultimately amounted to about ninety, it was compiled gradually (as already explained) by additions made from time to time, so that in the MSS. consulted earliest some of the passages were not included. Some of these omissions have been supplied since by the kindness of others. I hope that the materials here collected will prove useful to students who will be able to carry the work much further. But meanwhile I feel some confidence that even now they afford the means of making several rectifications of the text within the limits of the passages dealt with. Many other passages too may be reclaimed (as I hope has been already the case in the case of

---

[1] For the case of a MS. belonging to the Library of St. Mark, vide *supra*, p. 3.

the *Oxford Dante*) from the distortion to which they have
been confessedly subjected by successive editors, or from the
corrupt condition to which in some cases dependence on the
text of only one or two MSS., rather casually chosen, has
necessarily condemned them. It must be remembered that
anything like a complete critical revision of the text, even in
thirty-three MSS., is beyond the power of any single student.
It would be the work of some years, and would demand the
collaboration of several hands. Also the task of collating
even isolated passages is extremely laborious in the case of
a prose work, of which many of the chapters are very long,
and in MSS. many of which do not number the chapters,
while in some even the divisions of the chapters are very
obscurely or not at all indicated.

The following from Browning (*Men and Women*) very aptly
describes such a task as this :—

> 'But by the time youth slips a stage or two
> While reading prose in that tough book he wrote,
> (Collating and emendating the same
> And settling on the sense most to our mind)
> We shut the clasps and find life's summer past!'

It is only natural that the text of the *Convivio* should be
much more depraved than that of the *Divina Commedia*.
For the copyist, being untrammelled by conditions of rhyme
or metre, and being thus in a position of greater freedom and
less responsibility, the variations both of accident and design
would be far more frequent. But, further, even as compared
with such a work in prose as the *Vita Nuova*, the *Convivio*
is at a further disadvantage. The subject-matter of the
former is much more clear and generally intelligible, whereas
that of the *Convivio* is often so technical in detail, and so
abstruse in thought, as to be practically as meaningless to
an ordinary copyist as if he were transcribing a table of
logarithms. The tediousness and want of interest in such
a job would tend to the multiplication of blunders, especially
such as omissions due to ' ὁμοιοτέλευτα.' The *De Vulg. Eloq.*
in this respect offers in many places a close parallel to the

Convivio, and there also we meet with a text exhibiting somewhat similar conditions of confusion.

Besides therefore the *general* causes of textual corruption which I have discussed in my work on the *Textual Criticism of the Divina Commedia*, there are others which *specially* apply to a work of the nature of the *Convivio*, which will now be briefly indicated.

1. The chief of these, and one which occurs with extraordinary frequency in the *Convivio*, is the error arising from 'ὁμοιοτέλευτα.' That naturally plays a very small part in a metrical work. I might illustrate this by scores of examples, but it will be enough here to give references to a few prominent cases which will be found among the passages discussed later[1]. The discussion of II. i. 20 *seqq.* should be specially referred to.

2. In MSS. of the *Convivio* we sometimes meet with sentences consisting apparently of a mere jumble of words without meaning or construction, though the same words in a rearranged order may give a satisfactory sense. One can only compare the phenomenon to the disaster known to printers as 'pie[2],' and the process of reconstruction to putting together the pieces of a Chinese puzzle. Such confusion could scarcely occur except in prose works, and even there only when the subject-matter is so abstruse or technical, or the copyist so dull, that he would not expect or 'presume' to understand what was written. Enough for him that he has rendered in the aggregate his 'tale of words.' I have found

---

[1] e.g. I. v. 101 (p. 25); I. vii. 11 (p. 26); II. v. 89 (p. 43). The following is a curious case of superfluous *addition* from ὁμοιοτέλευτα (*omission* being naturally the more usual result). At II. ii. 33 H reads '*dalla parte* dinanzi continuamente, e l' altro *dalla parte* | dinanzi continuamente e l' altro dalla parte | della memoria di dietro.' Also at IV. iii. 32 H omits the words in square brackets, 'si ha due membri : il primo è la variazione dell' opinione [dello Imperadore : il secondo è la variazione dell' opinione] della gente volgare,' thus depriving the 'due membre' of any meaning.

[2] It seems an especially common source of error in my MS. and in H. A good instance of this will be found in the discussion of I. xii. 89–92 (p. 31). Mr. Tozer informs me that there are instances of 'pie' in some MSS. of Strabo ; and Professor Bywater, *Textual Criticism of the Ethics* (pp. 11, 17, 18, &c.), shows how this confusion may have sometimes arisen from an accidentally omitted word or words having been inserted in the wrong place.

several instances of this in my own MS. of the *Convivio*. This confusion of transposition is sometimes found in regard to single letters, as e.g. *cierco* for *cireco*, i.e. *ci recò* (II. vi. 16), and still more in reference to unfamiliar names, as those of the seven sages in III. xi., or unfamiliar words, as *d' un torchio* (III. v. 150), where B and H have *d' intorno*, M omits the word, and R boldly substitutes *strettoio*.

3. There are several sources of confusion which are by no means peculiar to prose writings, but which are naturally found more commonly in any work in proportion to the obscurity of the subject-matter and the difficulty of following readily the sense of a passage.

Such for instance are (*a*) mistakes arising from the fusion of two or more words in MSS., and the ambiguous resolution of such fusion either by copyists or editors. Thus *delloro* may represent ' dell' oro ' or ' de (i.e. di) loro '—the omission or insertion of double consonants being a pure matter of accident in many MSS. In II. i. 84 both of these readings occur in different editions [1]. (*β*) Or, again, the confusion of words slightly different such as *e, è, e'*, or even *ẽ*. Some MSS. never attempt any distinction between the first three; and in any case the omission of such slight distinguishing marks as those affecting the last three is a common accident. Similarly *che* may stand for *che, chè, ch' è*, or *ch' ei*. So combining (*a*) and (*β*), *nella* may be a confusion for *nè è la*, and this simple change in I. ix. 42 seems to me at once to restore a passage which has been roughly handled by successive editors.

Words of less close resemblance than these are often confused, and sometimes perhaps through a mistaken interpretation of abbreviated forms, e.g. *cagioni* and *cognizioni* are both found at *Conv*. II. xvi. 88. My MS. has some curious blunders of this kind at III. iii. 8, 9. For *come le* it has *colle* ; for *hanno* or *anno* it gives ' *&nõ* [2],' and for *naturato, ĩcurato*.

---

[1] Thus in *Inf.* xxxiii. 97 I found in one MS. *alquanto divenuti* for ' al quarto dì venuti.'

[2] The same MS. frequently writes ' & ' for *è* in error and even for *a* (see *infra*, p. 9, for the confusion of *a* and *e*), as in III. v. 193 (' & questi luoghi '). This scribe is fond of the symbol ' &.' It seems sometimes to stand for *che*. ' Eziandio ' is once written ' &dio.'

Again it reads *si fanno* (*fifanno*) for *diafano* (III. ix. 69) and *innançi vanno* for *imaginiamo* (III. v. 89). As an instance of a blunder probably due to a misread abbreviation we might instance I. xiii. 23, 'essere *sempre* non stesse (or fusse)' in B, H, and M, where *se per me* was perhaps written sepme, and so mistaken for sĕpme or sempre.

The following may be taken as examples of these causes of confusion separately or in combination. In I. xi. 106 M has 'nella sua essenzia dubbio,' which should be 'nella sua. E senza dubbio,' &c. In III. x. 78 'dello datore' evidently represents 'del lodatore.' The MS. marked T abounds with such peculiarities, vide *infra*, p. 133. In II. xiv. 121 'dallettera' has been interpreted as 'dalla terra' or 'dalla lettera.' In I. vii. 48 we find 'e dispone' where 'ed espone' is correct[1]. For the confusion of different forms of 'e' see III. vii. 32 (*infra*, pp. 77, 78. So in IV. xxvii. 75, 'se a grado è dato' appears as '*et* dato,' where the copyist finding e for è improved it into *et*. Similarly in I. xii. 37 H has 'et più' for 'è più.' See further *infra*, p. 132, under description of MS. 'Q.' We are not surprised to find *matterìa* in II. xi. 76 appearing as *materia*. Compare the confusion of *sarria* and *saria* in *Purg*. vii. 51, and see *Textual Criticism*, pp. 382 *seqq*.

All these sources of confusion are intensified by the 'personal equation' (so to speak) of some MSS. or copyists. Thus in the Bodleian MS. *r*, *c*, *i* and even *t* are often scarcely distinguishable, so that words like *pacie* (= *pace*) and *parte* may be easily mistaken for one another. Hence 'ragione' and 'cagione' are constantly interchanged in the text of MSS.[2], and it is often difficult to say which is intended.

---

[1] Dr. Rendel Harris gives instances of similar blunders in the Latin version of the Greek text in Codex Bezae, from which he argues its French origin. Thus 'de usque' would sometimes be 'jusque' dialectically, and so it might be inferred that the Latin form of such words as 'Judaei,' 'juventus,' would be 'diudaei' and 'diuventus.' This would account for τῶν Ἰουδαίων being represented by 'ad Judaeis,' i.e. a blundering interpretation of an original 'a diudaeis.' Similarly we find 'ad juventute' for 'a diuventute.' In Acts ii. 6 'quiaudiebant' (='quia audiebant') was wrongly taken to be 'qui audiebant' and the Greek text tampered with to bring it into correspondence.

[2] e.g. at I. ii. 20: v. 7; vide *infra* on I. ii. 20. An important instance of a

So in III. xi. 163 for *la luce* my MS. has *ſalute*, and the forms of *r* and *t* are so similar that such words as *rarezza* and *ratezza* (interchanged at II. iv. 59), *fornire* and *fornite*, are scarcely distinguishable.

There can be little doubt that *persona* reported in most MSS. at I. xi. 45 is an error for *perforza* or *perforça*, which resembles *perſona*, if the cedilla be by chance omitted.

As the vowels *a*, *e*, and *o* are constantly confused or interchanged, one might at first sight feel inclined to apply to MSS. the cynical epigram which was long ago levelled at the rising science of Comparative Philology, that 'vowels seem to be of no consequence and consonants very little.'

Thus we find *col* (or *chol*) *corpo* where *che 'l cor, o* is meant ; *alle forme* for *e le forme* ; *perciò* for *par ciò* ; *come parla* for *come per la* ; *è ferma* for *affirma* ; *e la* for *alla*[1]. It seems most likely that *a sei* is a blunder for '*e* sue' at I. v. 12 (p. 25). The prefixes *pro* and *pre* are so frequently interchanged that MS. evidence on this point is almost worthless. The conjunctions *e* and *o* are also interchanged *passim* ; and the same confusion attaches even to the final vowels of adjectives and pronouns causing startling false concords. Hence we might feel justified in changing such genders[2] or in substituting a subjunctive for an indicative verb if the sense requires it, when it merely involves the question of the final letter being *e* or *a*. The following is a curious instance of such blunders crowded together from my MS., in III. v. 114, 115, where ' e Delle proprietà degli Elementi' appears as ' ed alle propriatà degli alimenti.' In fact 'elementi' and 'alimenti' are often confused, e.g. IV. xxi. 36, and 'effetti' and 'affetti' constantly so in MSS. of the *Divina Commedia*. It is evident that in editing a text depending on MSS. not one of which is found on trial to be free from serious and frequent corruption, conjecture of some kind must occasionally be allowed. But, as

---

lect.fals. in *Ep.* VI. vi. 169, '*Punica* barbaries,' has been recently corrected to *punita* ; *c* and *t* being often scarcely distinguishable.

[1] Thus H, at least twice, has 'exenza' for 'assenza.' In the same MS. at II. xiii. 60 *portare* is probably a mistake for *parlare.* At II. xi. 30 *a sè* or *asse* in several MSS. seems certainly meant for *e sì*.

[2] See an example at I. viii. 110 (*infra*, p. 28).

I have already said, this necessary but dangerous tool must be employed under very strict conditions and limitations. The most important of these I will endeavour to point out. Or, at least, whether they are accepted or not, I will state them as the conditions under which I have in fact placed myself in such contributions as I venture here to offer for the improvement of the text.

First as to the weight to be allowed to the MSS. I am far from having a superstitious reverence for the *ipsissima verba* of MSS., especially in such a case as that before us. We have seen that they are beyond doubt very corrupt, and for the most part very carelessly transcribed. Further (as I have said elsewhere) the copyists often constitute themselves anonymous and irresponsible editors, a task for which they are wholly unfitted, being often very ignorant and incapable persons. Thus we may have to contend with the sinister influence of ill-regulated conjecture even at the fountain-head. Still, for all that, if a reading is not in any MS., nor can be shown to have any likely connexion with anything found in any MS. upon recognized principles of criticism, on what possible ground can it rest? It only represents what the author might, could, or should have written, in the opinion of some *other* person, and to this sort of conjecture there is no assignable limit. Such conjectural emendation as this often degenerates (as I have already said) into a sort of missing word competition. My fundamental principle has been (except in the rarest and most desperate cases, to be explained presently) to admit nothing into the text which is wholly out of connexion with any MS. authority, either directly or inferentially. If I might take leave to borrow a familiar phrase, I would admit nothing which is not either ' found in MSS., or can be proved thereby ' ; interpreting the latter clause liberally so as to mean that which cannot be derived from, or brought into connexion with, some MS. authority on some recognized principles of ' transcriptional probability.' If a sentence is manifestly imperfect and MSS. give no clue at all to the missing words, I prefer to leave a lacuna rather than to supply (as has been

commonly done) something thought to be suitable[1]. Thus
at II. i. 21 I left a lacuna in the text, which now one of the
latest MSS. examined has enabled me to fill satisfactorily[2].
At IV. xiv. 3 the words 'è da riprovarsi,' inserted after 's'
appoggiava' by Edd. Mil. and in all subsequent editions, have,
as far as I know, no MS. authority whatever. They have been
adopted by successive editors as suitable to the sense, and so
they are, but many other words might be supplied which
would do that equally well. Whatever words Dante may
have written here were probably omitted through pure accident by some very early copyist in a MS. no longer extant.
We have lost them, and so it is better to acknowledge the
fact, by marking a lacuna as in the Oxford text.

I alluded above to some few extreme and desperate cases,
where the sense is either hopeless or quite unsuitable to the
context, and the MSS. afford no clue to a remedy. One
cannot but suspect that either by a sheer blunder, or by some
misunderstanding of the sense, some word or words may have
been wrongly inserted or wrongly omitted in some very early
or archetypal MS. no longer extant. The relative antiquity
of a MS. offers no corresponding immunity from such error as
this, and in that case we cannot but fear that the actual words
of the author's autograph have been irretrievably lost. To
mark a lacuna will often not meet the case. It will not do to
print actual nonsense. It then becomes necessary to hazard
a conjecture, but in the few cases when I have done so by
proposing to insert or to omit a word without any MS.
authority, it has been *distinctly indicated in the text*[3]. The

---

[1] Vide *infra*, p. 13 *n*., for an illustration. Also in the discussion of II. i. 21 (*infra*,
pp. 35, 36) it will be seen how utterly futile it is to attempt to fill an obvious
lacuna by mere conjecture from the variety of ways in which it has been done
in that passage. Another example may be found in *Epist.* v., l. 3. Between
splendescit and *demonstrans* there is a gap in the Vatican MS. which editors have
supplied by 'albam,' 'alborem,' and other words, which suit the sense well
enough, but the discovery of the Cod. S. Pantaleo in the Bibl. Vitt. Em. at
Rome enables us now to supply the actual words omitted, viz. 'ab ortu Auro-
ram.' (See Dr. Toynbee's article in *Mod. Lang. Rev.*, vol. vii, No. 1.)

[2] See the discussion of this passage, *infra*, pp. 35, 36.

[3] See *Oxford Dante*, p. 237. This has not been done where a word has been

reader, being thus forewarned, may use his own discretion in accepting or rejecting the suggestion offered. The extremest case is the proposal to omit or insert a *negative* without any authority from MSS. But it may be noted, (*a*) even such a word may be lost or inserted by a copyist through accident, or by design, like any other[1]; (*b*) in *some* cases it is not difficult to suggest the motive of such a design; (*c*) in one or two cases I have had the satisfaction, through a more complete examination of MSS., of finding such a conjecture justified[2], so that the warning mark may now be removed from the text. There remain, I think, two passages where we must have recourse to the drastic remedy of inserting a negative,—thus [non]— without MS. authority, viz. II, xiii. 62, III. ix. 119 and xv. 64. See notes on these passages. In IV. vi. 128, 'nè da Socrate non presono vocabolo,' both the words *nè* and *non*, one at least of which is clearly quite necessary to the sense, are omitted in M. This shows how it may be legitimate sometimes even to insert a negative, since if this MS. had been an archetype the negative might have disappeared without a trace.

Speaking quite generally, the textual critic should when employing conjecture aim at undoing the processes of corruption by moving along the recognized lines of its operations in a reverse direction. Just then as a legitimate hypothesis must assume nothing but a *vera causa*, so a conjecture should be able to justify its claim to represent the original reading by suggesting *how* the error is likely to have arisen out of it by some admitted *vera causa* of depravation[3]. Hence if some

merely conjecturally substituted for another found in MSS., where the two forms might reasonably be thought to have been confused : as for instance in the almost desperate passage, IV. xviii. 41, where I have ventured to substitute *dice* for *di sì* ; since neither of the signs in *Oxford Dante*, p. 237, would meet the case.

[1] Thus both B and H omit ' se non ' in I. ix. 54, destroying the sense altogether. Here, however, there is no need for conjecture, as other MSS. have preserved the words. See further, note on II. xiii. 62.

[2] e. g. II. i. 31, where the important word *non* was inserted, with the usual warning, in the first edition. Also I. vii. 59, where [quando] appeared *e conj.* : but now has been found to have some MS. authority. See also notes on II. vi. 25 and III. viii. 181, where *non* was wrongly obelized in the first edition.

[3] Thus in I. v. 102 I have printed ' nel quale più debitamente rispondono ; [e più debitamente rispondono] in Latino, che in Volgare,' inserting conjecturally the words in brackets. It is quite obvious from ὁμοιοτέλευτα how these words

expression has been arbitrarily introduced into the text merely for improvement of the style or expression (after the fashion of Bentley)[1], or even for correction of erroneous statements of fact (unless under some rare and special circumstances), it should be forthwith repudiated. This work alone will keep the reviser's hands full for some time!

But the distinction between legitimate and illegitimate conjecture will be illustrated better perhaps by a few concrete examples than by attempting to enunciate abstract principles. Moreover these examples will serve to prove the need which I allege to exist for a drastic revision of existing texts.

First of all, as stated above, wholly inadmissible conjectures are those which merely aim at improvement of style, elegance of expression[2], greater clearness of meaning or exposition, more suitable illustrations, *et hoc genus omne.* There is scarcely a page in the whole of Giuliani's edition which does not afford startling examples of this actual rewriting of the author's words, at least as they have come down to us in MSS. Thus at II. i. 55, after the words *senso litterale*, he introduces a parenthesis: '(o narrativa di vicende terrene).' This merely embodies in the text an editor's private gloss, and rather a superfluous one too. It is needless to say that the well-known lacuna at l. 21 of the same chapter is arbitrarily filled up by about twenty words, wholly independent of any authority. I have noticed elsewhere (*infra*, p. 74 n.) the deplorable changes introduced by Giuliani at III. v. 176, where Dante writes 'non a modo di *mola*' (vide *supra*, l. 147) 'ma di *rota*.' Giuliani happens not to have understood this admirably clear and graphic illustration, and has perverted

are likely to have been lost. So I have felt justified in inserting them in the text. Other editors have inserted 'e ciò fanno più,' which gives equally good sense, but there is no ground for assuming these words to have been written. Another example will be found at II. vi. 137 (p. 50), where this principle would apparently justify the conjecture of '*per* lo,' but not ' *entro* lo' for the inappropriate *verso* of the MSS.

[1] See *Textual Criticism*, Prol., p. ix.

[2] Thus at I. v. 9 the awkward combination 'disconvenevole disordinazione' has been improved by some editors to 'disconvenevole ordinazione.' They seem to have overlooked the fact that the expression recurs later three times over—vi. 6, viii. 2, and x. 25.

the text thus—'non a modo di vite ma di mola,' which makes sheer nonsense [1]. However, I need not pursue such illustrations any further, since no one now would suppose such treatment of an author's text to be justified by any amount of obscurity and corruption. Besides it would be an ungrateful task to dwell needlessly upon the weakest aspect of Giuliani's work, when one remembers the debt which we owe to his unrivalled knowledge of all the works of Dante in the way of illuminating illustrations from one to the other, in fact, 'Dante spiegato con Dante.'

But besides arbitrary insertions of this kind, both Giuliani and the 'Edd. Milanesi' frequently strike out words or clauses on the ground that they are tautologous or superfluous. Thus at IV. xvii. 4, in the words 'e dice e comincia' Giuliani strikes out 'e dice' as being 'del tutto inutile[2].' So in I. i. 84-6 the whole sentence from 'di quello pane' to 'essere ministrata' is simply omitted on the ground that it is 'superfluous' after what has been said in the previous sentence! Again in IV. vii. 134, 'Colui è morto, che [non si fe' discepolo, e che] non segue il Maestro,' the words in brackets are omitted, because 'Qui . . . si ridice in due modi la stessa cosa!' Similarly in the expression 'che pur da natura nudamente viene'

---

[1] But there is another correction (?) introduced by Giuliani in this chapter which is really so comically absurd that I cannot help noticing it. At ll. 81 *seqq.* we read 'se una pietra potesse cadere da questo nostro Polo, ella cadrebbe là [oltre nel mare Oceano, appunto in su quel dosso del mare] dove se fosse un uomo,' &c. Giuliani expresses the greatest astonishment ('Par incredibile') that the Edd. Milanesi and others should have admitted the words between square brackets, because Dante believed the sea to occupy the whole of the S. *hemisphere*, in regard to which the words are appropriately applied a few lines below (ll. 94 *seqq.*)! As if this excluded the possibility of a northern arctic sea also, which moreover was certainly a necessity on the belief—common to Dante and every one else then—in the circumambient 'Oceanus' on whose bosom the whole earth lay. (See 'Essay on Geography,' *Studies*, iii. pp. 114 *seqq.*) Other instances of short-sighted and arbitrary alterations due to a pure misunderstanding of Dante's meaning will be found in the notes on IV. xxiv. 34 and 47.

[2] *Inf.* v. 115, 116 :—

> Poi mi rivolsi a loro, *e parla' io,*
> E *cominciai*

is clearly open to the same objection, but here Dante is fortunately protected by the metre from such uncalled for 'improvement' of his language.

(IV. xxii. 43), Giuliani strikes out *pur*, 'perchè è rinchiuso in *nudamente.*' I might multiply such instances by scores. I will, however, take leave of them by quoting Professor Jebb's stricture of similar criticism applied to Sophocles : ' It is to be regretted when a habit of mind such as might be fostered by the habitual composition of telegrams is applied to textual criticism.'

Another class of wholly inadmissible conjectures is found in changes that are frequently made by editors merely to improve the run of a sentence, or to express the same meaning with greater clearness or elegance[1]. This practice, which would be entirely uncritical treatment of any author (imagine its being applied to Thucydides !), is so for a special reason in the case of Dante. We must not forget that Dante was but a pioneer in the development of Italian prose. He was, as it were, feeling his way with a new instrument. This was so in a special and peculiar sense in the *Convivio*, since he was writing on subjects for which Latin was the accepted medium, and on which no one had thought of employing the ' Volgare ' before[2]. Dante himself draws attention to this in *Conv.* I. v. 84 *seqq.*: ' Onde conciossiacosachè lo Latino molte cose manifesta concepute nella mente, che il Volgare fare non può (siccome sanno quelli che hanno l' uno e l' altro sermone), più è la virtù sua, che quella del Volgare[3].' If any one is ' offended ' at ruggedness

---

[1] Not only editors, but also, I think, copyists sometimes. For it is curious to note the frequency of small changes in the order of words in different MSS., which are quite immaterial to the sense. I suppose it is due to the same idea of improving the run of the sentence. A good example occurs at II. v. 124 *seqq.*

[2] In fact, as far as the Volgare is concerned,

'Things unattempted yet in prose or rhyme.'

The same idea is expressed, ' sotto figura d' altre cose,' when Dante says, 'della donna, di cui io m' innamorava [i. e. Philosophy], non era degna rima di Volgare alcuno palesemente parlare ' (II. xiii. 58-60).

[3] And as to the greater clearness of Latin see I. vii. 48 *seqq.*, where Dante says that a Latin Commentary upon anything written in the Volgare would be unsuitable, because it would express so much more than would be possible for the original Volgare :—' lo Latino... avrebbe sposte molte parti della sua sentenza [i.e. dell' autore]—ed espone, chi cerca bene le scritture latinamente scritte—che nol fa il Volgare in parte alcuna.' Erasmus felt the same, and described himself as unable to use any language but Latin on serious and difficult subjects. On this Froude remarks that ' the vernacular idioms were only beginning to shape

of style or awkwardness of expression not unfrequently in the *Convivio*, let him turn (as I have suggested *supra*, p. 1) to a page of Ristoro d'Arezzo (*c.* 1280), or even perhaps of Dante's friend and contemporary, Giov. Villani (*c.* 1300), and he will see what contemporary, or nearly contemporary Italian prose was like. Struck as he must be at the immense advance made by Dante, he will also cease to be surprised if his prose style   ' tiene ancor del monte e del macigno[1].'

It may be worth while to note briefly some of the more obvious characteristics in detail by which Dante's prose style falls short of the finish of later Italian. If the *fact* of such comparative ruggedness, or indeed of personal peculiarities of any kind in Dante, be admitted, it will at once appear how uncritical and illegitimate it is to endeavour by deliberate conjectural alteration to bring his text 'up to date.' Such ' touching up' tends to obliterate the distinctive features of an author's style, just as injudicious architectural restoration destroys the historic character of a building. It means deliberately substituting something which he himself is not likely to have written. A few representative peculiarities of this kind may perhaps be suggested, such as demonstrative pronouns, *questo*, *quello*, &c., referring to very distant antecedents, sometimes with new subjects intervening to increase the awkwardness ; the same pronouns or relatives repeated in reference to different antecedents [2]; the confused use of ' suo ' and 'loro'[3]; the inelegant repetition of single words suggesting a. poverty of diction, which editors have been assiduous in offering to remedy[4]: the word *che* is *repeated* redun-

themselves into intellectual instruments, and Latin was the universal tongue in which men of intelligence exchanged their thoughts.' Much more was this true when Dante was writing. Petrarch also set greater store upon his own compositions in Latin ; and Milton too preferred at first to write in Latin rather than in English.

[1] *Inf.* xv. 63.

[2] See some examples given *infra* under II. xv. 157.

[3] See note on I. v. 12 ; II. xiv. 15 ; and add II. viii. 86, 87.

[4] e.g. ' dico che dice' (II. x. 17, 30), ' dico che *dirò di quello valore*' (IV. ii. 94), is altered by Giuliani into ' intendo dicere di quello valore,' as he admits, 'contra all' autorità dei testi.' Again, in IV. ii. 39, ' dico, siccome detto è,' Giuliani substitutes *dichiaro* for *dico* on the express ground that ' il diligente Maestro '

dantly[1](especially in long sentences) or *omitted* when later usage would require it; or *used loosely* as a connecting particle in a variety of meanings[2]. Dante also, I think, freely uses participles and adjectives, or equivalent expressions, to denote temporal, causal, and other logical relations, where a later writer would probably have supplied some definite particle to indicate this more precisely, as sometimes modern editors have superfluously done for him. See note *infra* on III. ix. 79, and passages from the *Divina Commedia* collected in *Textual Criticism*, p. 387. This leads frequently to a sort of nominative absolute or an awkward *mutatio subiecti*, in the prose of the *Convivio*, where an 'ablative absolute' would be found in Latin, e.g. IV. i. 38 (*corrotta*); iv. 43 (*preso*); v. 162 (*presa*); vi. 4 (*ragionato*); vii. 21 (*agguardando*); &c.

Dante's use of the infinitive as a substantive, even when an obvious substantive was ready to hand, is so frequent as to suggest its being a sort of 'personal equation' of his style. This being so, I think the MS. reading at IV. xxiii. 70, 'più a durare,' probably represents 'più ha durare,' and we need not, as Giuliani suggests, read 'più ha da durare.' So in l. 99 of the same chapter, 'stare in *discrescere*' (as in some MSS.) is probably what Dante wrote. Some MSS. have *discrescione*, which looks like a *facilior lectio*, and Giuliani (*more suo*) boldly alters it to *discensione*. Again at III. vii. 153, in the words 'nel quale mirando possono fare parere gentile,' *parere* seems to be equivalent to *apparenza*. If I am right that this substantival infinitive is exceptionally common in Dante's style, there is no need here to read 'possono farsi parere' with Giuliani, or 'fare sè' as suggested by Edd. Milanesi. Again, III. ix. 101, *il nostro vedere* = our power or process of vision. We may add IV. xxvi. 64, 'E quanto *raffrenare* fu quello.'

could not possibly repeat 'dico' thus in two lines, 'quando dico . . . dico, siccome detto è.' (Similarly in the *De Mon.* III. xi. 14 we find ' Dico quod nihil dicunt.') He also 'improves' *questo* into *quello* in l. 40. Another of these ' inelegant repetitions' is found in I. v. 13–15, ' ragioni . . . ragione . . . ragionare.' Compare I. xi. 34, 35. There are many such cases to be found in the *Divina Commedia*. A case in which a similar improvement even *in MSS.* may be suspected occurs in I. vii. 13 (see *infra*, p. 26).

[1] e.g. I. i. 135 and 137. Comp. *Inf.* xxvi. 23, 24.
[2] See latter part of note on *Conv.* III. v. 154 (*infra*, p. 75).

In *Conv.* IV. xxiv. 34, 'lo *tenere* dell' Arco is equivalent to the Greek λαβή, the place where the bow is held, ' nel quale poco di flessione si discerne.' Giuliani alters this to *tendere*, which is quite unmeaning, and altogether inappropriate to the explanatory words just quoted! So also at *Par.* xvii. 119 :—

' Temo di perder *viver* tra coloro,'

where a number of MSS. substitute the easier *vita*. Comp. *Par.* xv. 131. Again, *Par.* xxx. 108, ' che prende quindi vivere e potenza'; *Par.* vii. 54, ' Del qual . . . solver s' aspetta'; *Par.* xviii. 57, ' Vinceva gli altri e l'ultimo solere.' Compare *esser* for *essenza, Canz.* xix. 73, 74 ; ii. 27 ; ix. 31 : and similarly *esse* in *Ep.* viii. 154, ' principium ipsius quoque esse.' Also *Ep.* x., l. 537, ' propter transcendisse humanum modum ' ; and *Quaestio* xxii. 4, ' pro posse.'

A curious result of this usage of the infinitive is that it sometimes receives a plural inflexion after the manner of a noun. Thus Dante has *soffriri* and *saliri* in *Purg.* xix. 76, 78, and again we have *i lor diri* in *Canz.* iii. 75. Mr. Vernon (on *Purg., loc. cit.*) remarks that this plural inflexion of the infinitive is found in Boccaccio.

One of the most surprising liberties[1] ever taken with an author's text, by way (as I have said above) of suggesting for him ' a more suitable illustration,' occurs at IV. v. 122. In his enumeration of the long roll of heroes of Roman history, Dante pauses—like the author of the Epistle to the Hebrews in xi. 32, ' Et quid adhuc dicam ' &c.—and adds, ' Chi dirà de' Decii e delli Drusi che posero la loro vita per la patria ?' Dr. Witte, thinking that the *Drusi* were scarcely sufficiently distinguished for such a eulogium, calmly proposes to substitute *Curzii*, ' o qualche altra famiglia celebre ' ! Giuliani, highly approving of the principle of ' così assennata conghiettura,' prefers to read ' Fabj ' ! Apart from the monstrosity of thus mangling the text, both the distinguished critics appear to have forgotten the lines of Virgil :—

' Quin *Decios Drusosque* procul saevumque securi
Aspice Torquatum et referentem signa Camillum[2].'

---

[1] The audacious manipulation, also by Witte (who is again followed by Giuliani), of I. vii. 59 (vide *infra*, p. 27) is perhaps equally flagrant.

[2] *Aen.* vi. 825, 826.

Torquatus and Camillus are also mentioned here by Dante within a few lines, as well as others occurring in the same context in Virgil.

Two further questions of some importance suggest themselves. (1) How far is it legitimate to rectify errors of fact? (2) How far may inaccuracies in the subject-matter of quotations, or in their attribution, be corrected? or more generally, within what limits may quotations be employed for modification of the text? It is easier to answer such questions by examples than by attempting to form any code of rules. Indeed we feel almost tempted to give as a reply ἐν τῇ αἰσθήσει ἡ κρίσις, 'each case must be judged on its merits.' One obvious precaution, however, is this. The point corrected should be one on which the author could in no way be supposed to have been ignorant, and also, if possible, the origin of the inaccuracy, whether by accident or design, should be accountable.

There are two cases in which the numbers 600 and 700 are confused in MSS., where I think we are quite justified, in accordance with the above principles, in inserting 700. The first (III. v. 88) presents no special difficulty, because both readings, 2600 and 2700, are found, but even if all MSS. had 2600 here, we might, I think, still make the correction, because it is absolutely necessary to suit the addition made a few lines below, where we find the total of 10200 arising from this sum added to 7500. Hence it *must* have been 2700 and not 2600. In the other passage (III. xi. 24)[1], the date of the foundation of Rome is given in *all* the MSS. here examined (nearly thirty) as about 650 years instead of 750. Still I think we may introduce the correction, for (1) Dante could not have been ignorant of such a well-known chronological fact; (2) in this case he definitely quotes Orosius as his authority, and we find on referring to the passage (VII. iii. 1) the number 752, which also accounts for Dante adding to the round number 750 the words 'poco dal più al meno.' (3) The two numbers would be easily confused, especially if written in numerals, but even 'setecento' and 'seicento' are not far apart. But in some

---

[1] See further *infra*, p. 83.

MSS. I find *vil* = 650, between which and *viil* = 750 there is not much difference. Further, the former passage (III. v. 88) affords an actual instance of the very same figures 6 and 7 being interchanged.

Next, in regard to the use of quotations in rectification of the text. In III. xv. 171 we may confidently, I think, insert 'etera' in a long quotation from Prov. viii. 27–30, since (1) so conspicuous a word in a passage pretty closely quoted is not likely to have been omitted; (2) the sentence is incomplete without an object to *fermava*; (3) It is a well-known habit of copyists to omit a word they did not understand, or could not read[1]; (4) This very word *etera* has similarly disappeared from a long quotation from Ovid in IV. xv. 76 *seqq.* In the place where the word appears in Ovid, the passage, as quoted by Dante, reads in MSS. 'corpo sottile e diafano,' which is obviously a marginal gloss which has supplanted the word 'etera.' Another case of an almost certain correction due to a passage, which, though not directly quoted, was pretty obviously in Dante's mind, occurs at IV. v. 91. Here we feel justified in reading *re* instead of *tre* in the teeth of MS. authority, since the whole context clearly shows Dante to have had in his mind a passage from Virgil (*Aen.* vi. 777–819), where we find 'Tarquinios *reges*'[2].

It is a necessary precaution that, before using any quotation for such a purpose as this, we should take account of possible differences between the text used by Dante and that of modern editions. Thus in *Conv.* IV. xxvii. 173 *seqq.* it seems as if the *modern* text of Ovid[3] had been applied by editors to manipulate a quotation of Dante, which is shown from several points of detail to have been derived from a different text. Thus (to take one instance) where the present text of Ovid reads

'superat mihi miles et hosti.
Gratia Dis';

---

[1] There are many instances of this in MSS. of the *Divina Commedia* as well as in those of the *Convivio*, and Dr. Rendel Harris mentions the same practice in MSS. of the Vulgate. See further on the above passages, *Studies*, i. pp. 36, 53.

[2] See further, *Studies*, i. p. 195.

[3] *Metam.*, vii. 508–511. See this discussed in *Studies*, i. pp. 219, 220.

the MSS. of the *Convivio* have 'e lo avversario è grande.'
Dante's text therefore must surely have read—

'et hostis

Est grandis.'

This, therefore, is clearly no case of an accidental error either
of author or copyist, and we have no grounds for interfering
with the MS. reading[1]. Another instance, in which a correction has been (in my opinion) erroneously made in the text on
the strength of rectifying the misquotation of a name, by substituting 'Ettore' for 'Enea,' will be found in III. xi. 159.
(See again *Studies*, i. p. 194.) Also, I think, Edd. Mil.
and Giuliani are scarcely justified in altering *vive* into *vige*
without MS. authority in I. iii. 76, merely because the passage
quoted in *Aen.* iv. 175 has 'Mobilitate *viget.*'

There is a curious blunder, said to be in all the MSS., in
IV. xv. 120, where the first of three terrible infirmities,
associated with an evil disposition of soul, is described as
'naturale *sustanzia.*' This evidently gives no sense, and has
no connexion with the description of the vice following, which
is evidently an extreme type of boastfulness. Further, it is
(adds Dante) specially reprobated by Cicero in the first book
of the *De Officiis*. This appears to refer to c. xxvi. *init.*, 'etiam
in rebus prosperis, . . . superbiam, fastidium, arrogantiamque
magno opere fugiamus.' This seems fully to justify the conjectural substitution of *jattanzia* for *sustanzia*. On this see
further, *Studies*, i. p. 269. See also *Studies*, i. p. 271, for a case
in which a correction in the text at *Conv.* IV. xxviii. 45 *seqq.*
seems to be justified by a quotation.

It is perhaps hardly necessary to multiply examples.
Further instances will be found in abundance in the notes on
special passages which follow. Enough has probably been
said already to show the very serious need which exists for
a careful and critical revision of the published texts. I hope
the MS. evidence here collected will be of service in this

---

[1] Compare with this the reading 'Naiade' in *Purg.* xxxiii. 49, where modern
texts of Ovid, as well as considerations of suitableness, would suggest the alteration 'Laiade.' See this discussed in *Studies*, i. p. 218. I have there in error
described 'Laiades' as found in some MSS. It is a purely editorial conjecture.

respect in some of the more difficult passages. There is, however, a very large number of places where the notes of the over-assiduous editors themselves render the aid of any further 'apparatus criticus' superfluous, for 'habemus confitentem reum.'

(ii) LIST OF *CONVIVIO* PASSAGES DISCUSSED.

Tratt. I.	*Tratt.* II. (*continued*).	*Tratt.* III. (*continued*).
ii. 20.	vii. 106.	xii. 46 *seqq.*
108–110.	ix. 43–48.	xiii. 93–95.
iii. 2.	xiii. 14.	101.
64.	62.	xiv. 99.
iv. 50–53.	xiv. 15.	xv. 64.
v. 12.	120–122.	98 and 105 *seqq.*
101–103.	145.	171.
vii. 11–14.	234.	*Tratt.* IV.
59.	xv. 42.	
viii. 50.	129.	iv. 24.
110–112.	135.	v. 91.
ix. 41–43.	157.	122, 123.
xii. 71–74.	xvi. 28–30.	vi. 48 *seqq.*
89–92.		79.
xiii. 22, 23.	*Tratt.* III.	vii. 114, 115.
25.		viii. 103–112.
Tratt. II.	i. 72.	137.
	ii. 59–61.	xi. 81.
i. 19 *seqq.*	124, 125.	xii. 123–125.
26–34.	155–157.	xiii. 69–71.
75.		xiv. 62.
83–86.	iii. 118 *seqq.*	xvii. 126.
ii. 20.	v. 101 *seqq.*	xviii. 37 *seqq.*
32–38.	154.	xix. 32.
42.	vi. 47.	xx. 80.
iii. 60.	vii. 23 *seqq.*	xxi. 24.
iv. 28.	30.	34 *seqq.*
v. 27.	117 *seqq.*	xxii. 11, 12.
89–96.	viii. 36.	24–26.
124–128.	178–183.	xxiii. 73 *seqq.*
vi. 24.	ix. 79.	xxiv. 34.
25.	119.	47.
95–99.	xi. 24.	xxvii. 75.
137.	47.	xxviii. 37–39.
158.	159.	45.

I. ii. 20.

The text usually printed here (e.g. Edd. Mil., Frat., and Giul.) reads thus :—

    ' Le quali due cagioni rusticamente stanno a fare parlare di sè.'

This seems to require two corrections, (1) the substitution of ' ragioni ' for ' cagioni,' and (2) the omission of *parlare*.

ragione and *cagione* are so constantly interchanged in MSS. both of the *Convivio* and the *Divina Commedia* that it seemed hardly worth while to collect MS. evidence on this point[1]. But *ragioni* seems absolutely required here, and that in the very common, though often misunderstood, sense of ' discourse ' or ' conversation [2]' (*modo di parlare*). The two kinds of discourse (i.e. of praise or of blame) are awkward to employ (*fare*) about oneself in any one's mouth. Thus *parlare* is simply superfluous, and was probably added because either *cagioni* was read or *ragioni* was misunderstood. With *rusticamente stanno* compare *sta male* and other such adverbial expressions. The MS. evidence is very decisive. Out of twenty-nine MSS. examined I found ' parlare ' in one only (γ), and there in the altered order, *fare di sè parlare*. B has ' duo cagioni rusticamente stanno a fare dire di sè.'

I. ii. 108–110.

    Ne diede esemplo *e* dottrina, la quale per *sì* vero testimonio ricevere non si poteva.

This is not a point of much importance, but it affords an instructive instance of the arbitrary way in which the text has been tampered with. It is admitted that there is no variation in the text of the MSS., but Giuliani (after recognizing this) adds ' ma io mi son consigliato con Dante (!) ponendo nel testo esemplo *di* dottrina.' This is to match ' per via di

---

[1] Vide *supra*, p. 8; and e.g. *Purg.* xiii. 20; xviii. 65; xxii. 30; *Par.* vii. 101, &c.

[2] This sense is, as I say, very common, and especially in the case of the verb *ragionare*. See examples in *Purg.* xiv. 126; xxii. 130; xxiv. 2; xvi. 120; *Par.* iii. 35; ll. 91 and 102 of this chapter; *Canz.* i., l. 54; and probably in I. vii. 31. See several other passages in *Textual Criticism*, p. 390. In *Conv.* I. v. 14, 15 the different senses of *ragione* and *ragionare* seem to come awkwardly near together.

dottrina,' *supra*, 1. 103, and ' desiderio di dottrina dare,' *infra*, 1. 115, though *di* there goes with *dare*. Utterly unnecessary, it need hardly be said.

Again *più* has been arbitrarily substituted for *sì* confessedly in the teeth of all authority by Edd. Mil., Frat., Giul. Though the sense of *sì* is perfectly obvious, it is described as *sciocca lezione* (Edd. Mil.), as one which ' grida la croce addosso ' to all copyists and editors who allow it to pass (Monti). The latter even suggests as an alternative emendation to substitute *ricusare* for *ricevere*, and so avoid a palpable contradiction !

I. iii. 2.

The slight improvement in the order of the words in my text—'tôrre alcuno difetto, e per sè medesima quello induce ' —instead of ' torre alcuno difetto per sè medesima, e quello induce '—is not conjectural, but made on the authority of M.

I. iii. 64.

The words 'siccome qui suo effetto' are admitted by editors to be found in all the MSS. consulted, but they all, I believe (following Edd. Mil.), either delete *qui* or propose to read *quasi*, or, as Giuliani, introduce the slight change *chi*. I do not see why *qui* should not stand. The words mean ' as being at this point (lit. "here") his own work,' i.e. the exaggerated form which he has given to the story has now made it something original. The sense of *qui* might perhaps have more usually been given by 'già.' For the sentiment we may compare *Nic. Eth.* IV. ii. 20 ; IX. vii. 3, especially in view of the affection produced ('carità in lei generata,' 1. 64) towards this creation of his mind.

I. iv. 50–53

> Incontanente sono invidi, perocchè veggiono a sue pari membra e pari potenza ; e temono, per la eccellenza di quello cotale, meno essere pregiati.

As far as I know, though I have not had the opportunity of collating this passage, the MSS. generally (as reported) appear to read *assai* before *pari*. That word appears to me very weak and almost superfluous. It will be remembered that

Dante emphatically declares elsewhere that Envy implies a
parity of condition between the envier and the envied. Thus
Purg. xvii. 118–120 closely resembles the concluding words
of the above quotation; and in *Conv.* I. xi. 113 the present
passage is referred to and the parity of condition in the case
of Envy again insisted on.

I cannot help thinking that the word 'assai' in the MSS. is
a blunder for *a sue*, which would very probably have been
written *assue* and thus have passed very easily into *assai*.
It seems to me to give much more point to the passage,
i.e. 'limbs and powers like their own.' Giuliani confidently
substitutes *essi*, which seems to me even poorer than *assai*.
He appears to claim some MS. authority in the suspiciously
vague words, 'si può raccogliere dai codici la sovrallegata
lezione.'

I. v. 12.

All the MSS. I have examined here (D M P Q Tr ω)
read 'E queste *cose a sei* ragioni.' B has 'per sue ragioni'
(signs of alteration in 'sue'). Giuliani says that this is the
reading of 'tutti quanti i testi a penna,' i.e., I suppose, in all
those examined by him, besides the above. If so, it would
give strong evidence for *cose*, since it might easily have been
altered to *cause* (which would thus be *facilior lectio*) from the
influence of the words *cagione* and *ragione* in the context.
But *a sei* must surely be wrong, as there is no possibility of
finding that number by any combination of 'reasons.' I think
the conjecture which most editors have adopted, *e sue*, is quite
reasonable. *Sue* for *loro* need cause no difficulty (vide *supra*,
p. 16), and for interchange of *a* and *e* see *supra*, p. 9.

I. v. 101–103.

All MSS. appear to have lost some words here, since they
read 'nel quale più debitamente rispondono in Latino che in
Volgare.' All modern editors, I believe (e. g. Edd. Mil., Frat.,
Giul., Witte), insert *e ciò fanno più* after *rispondono* and *le
parole* before it, maintaining that otherwise there is no subject
for *rispondono*. No doubt this would be a distinct improvement if one were revising one's own proof-sheets. But it is

possible, even if awkward, to go back to *le voci* as the subject, though somewhat harsh, since *voci* would have to be thus supplied in a different sense, viz. as equivalent to *vocaboli* (for which see IV. vi. 15, &c.) or *parole*. This kind of zeugma is not an unknown figure. But though the two insertions thus suggested by editors would make good sense, there is nothing which would account for their having been dropped out. I therefore inserted (*vide* Oxford Text) after *rispondono* the words *e più debitamente rispondono*, the loss of which words is explicable at a glance from ὁμοιοτέλευτα. As I have since had the satisfaction of finding these words in the MS. marked π (*Bibl. Ricc.* 1044), the square brackets, indicating a conjectural emendation, may now be deleted.

I. vii. 11–14.

E però era impossibile essere obbediente. Che allo Latino fosse stato impossibile essere obbediente, si manifesta per cotal ragione.

(*a*) Here is obviously a fine field for ὁμοιοτέλευτα. Thus the Holkham MS. reads: ' e però era impossibile essere stato obbediente si manifesta per cotal ragione,' the copyist's eye evidently having travelled back to the second ' obbediente.'

(*b*) But the passage has also apparently been tampered with intentionally (as we often find) to improve the diction. Thus in l. 13 some MSS. read ' impossibile essere obbediente,' and others ' impossibile, come detto è.' Others insert both expressions. The explanation I take to be this: ' Come detto è ' was originally an alternative to avoid the repeated ' essere obbediente,' which seemed clumsy. The appearance of both expressions in some MSS. is, I suspect, an instance of ' conflation.'

I. vii. 59.

E l' uomo è obbediente alla giustizia [quando] comanda al peccatore.

I felt bound in this passage to insert ' quando ' *e conj.*, indicating by square brackets that I had no MS. authority in support of it. It seemed to be absolutely necessary to the sense (*vide* previous context also), and its accidental omission might have arisen from the similarity of the words ' quando ' and ' ꝯmanda ' (=comanda). I have since had the satisfaction of finding it in a MS. in the Vatican Library, ' σ ' [Ottob. Lat. 3332], so that the marks of conjecture may be removed from the text. The variations in MSS. here are curious, but they may all, I think, be explained by supposing the omission due to this quasi-ὁμοιοτέλευτον blunder, i.e. ' quando 9manda ' to have occurred in a very early copy, so that these many variations represent different attempts of copyists to remedy an obviously defective sentence.

The following are the *varr. lectt.* which I have noted :—

(1) After the accidental omission of ' quando ' in the manner supposed the text would read—

' e l' uomo è obbediente alla giustizia comanda al peccatore.'

This was found in eleven MSS., viz. B H T δ ε ζ η ι μ ν ω.

(2) ' e l' uomo obbediente alla giustizia comanda al peccatore' in ten MSS., Q α β κ λ ο τ φ χ ψ.

(3) ' e l' uomo chubidiente (= che è ubid:) alla giustizia comanda ' in two MSS., ξ π.

(4) ' e l' uomo è ubbidiente alla gustixia (*sic*) che comanda,' in one MS., γ.

(2), (3), and (4) represent different attempts to give sense to the passage : (2) by omitting *è* before *obbidiente* ; (3) by inserting *che* before *è*; and (4) by inserting *che* before *comanda*.

(5) P is singular in the confused reading : ' e l' uomo è ubidiente alla natura (*sic*) giustizia comanda al peccatore.'

(6) The omission of *comanda* in three MSS.—M θ ν—makes the sentence still more fragmentary, and was probably accidental. (It is interesting to note here and elsewhere the agreement of these three MSS.)

σ alone preserves what I believe to have been the original reading, as explained above, ' quando comanda,' &c. As to the accidental omission of *quando*, I might note that my MS. (M) omits the word apparently without reason in II. i. 53, where it is absolutely necessary to the sense. Further, *quando* was sometimes severely abbreviated. See Chassant, *Dict. Abrév.*, p. 79, and Cappelli, *Diz. Abbrev.*, p. 279.

It is amusing to see how this passage has been simply rewritten by Witte and Giuliani, thus : ' e l' uomo è obbediente alla giustizia *quando fa quello che comanda la legge, e non più nè meno* (!).'

I. viii. 50.

> Non è in esso perfetta virtù nè pronta. Questa letizia non può dare, &c.

Giuliani alters this thus without any allegation of MS. authority : 'non è in esso perfetta virtù, nè pronta questa *liberalità, che* non può dare,' &c. This is hardly worth notice except to call attention to the thoroughly uncritical *reason* given for it, viz. that *pronta* cannot be joined with *letizia*, because it is constantly throughout the chapter applied to *liberalità*. Obviously it is a very natural and tempting collocation, with the expression *pronta liberalità*, as it were, ringing in one's ears throughout the chapter. I have called attention to the erroneous alteration of words by 'association of ideas' in my *Textual Criticism of the Divina Commedia*, p. 404 note. Words are thus affected by a sort of magnetic 'induction' from the neighbouring words.

I. viii. 110–112.

This passage is commonly (e.g. Frat., Edd. Mil., Monti, and Pederzini) printed thus :—

> Conviene, acciocchè sia con atto libero, la virtù essere libera, *e lo* dono *dirizzarsi* alla parte, &c.

It is admitted that the two words in italics have no MS. authority, but it is claimed that they are demanded by the context. Giuliani in a very long note contends for other and larger changes. I believe that nothing is needed except a revision of the punctuation (which has no authority) and the very trifling alteration *libero* for *libera* after *essere*. The text will then run :—

> Conviene, acciocchè sia con atto libero la virtù, essere libero lo dono alla parte, &c.

As to *libera* and *libero* I have already pointed out (*supra*, p. 9) how carelessly these terminal vowels are interchanged in some MSS. But in this case it is easy to see how *libera* would seem to be required by the proximity of 'virtù.' There is a precisely similar false reading in *Purg.* xix. 132, viz. *dritta* for *dritto* in supposed agreement with 'coscienza,' and again in *Purg.* xxi. 45 *altra* for *altro* because of 'cagione.' See *Text. Crit.*, p. 394.

I. ix. 41–43.

The MSS. are reported as reading 'nulla cosa è utile se non è in quanto è usata nella sua bontà in potenza che non è essere perfettamente.' This is at any rate the reading in M. The editions punctuate differently, and some insert (without claiming any MS. authority) *sanz' uso* between *è* and *essere*. But if we merely resolve (with one or two editions) *nella sua* into *nè è la sua* and punctuate as follows, the meaning comes out clearly :—

Nulla cosa è utile, se non in quanto è usata ; nè è la sua bontà in potenza, che non è essere perfettamente.

I. xii. 71–74.

Questa è la giustizia, la quale è solamente nella parte razionale ovvero intellettuale, cioè nella volontà.

This passage has been needlessly tampered with by some editors on the trivial ground that the Will is not identical with the whole of the rational or intellectual part of man. Monti, in his *Saggio* (p. 56), proposes to alter it thus : ' la quale è *non* solamente nella parte razionale, ovvero intellettuale, *ma anche nella parte operativa,* cioè nella volontà.' Giuliani declares that the text of the MSS. ' contradice al vero, giacchè la volontà non costituisce *di per sè sola* la parte razionale ovvero intellettuale dell' animo, ma sì essa insieme coll' intelletto.' So on the strength of the more precise language of Dante in *Conv.* IV. xxii. 96, ' la parte razionale, cioè la Volontà e lo Intelletto,' he alters the text here thus : ' parte razionale, cioè nell' intelletto e nella volontà.'

But all this is quite unnecessary, for *cioè* in the text above is not to be taken as implying equivalence, but rather as introducing not an equivalent, but only a more explicit, statement; indicating the particular department of ' razionale ovvero intellettuale' referred to—as we might say, ' *in point of fact,* the Will.'

And now a few words on the more general question of Dante's Theory of the Will. He often treats it as if it were

a purely intellectual faculty.   Whatever view may be held
as to its precise nature, or its relation to our other faculties or
operations, it would be generally admitted to have affinities
with Reason on the one hand and Impulse on the other.   As
Aristotle says of προαίρεσις, it involves an element of judgement
and an element of Desire (see *Nic. Eth.* III. ii.[1], and also *De An.*
iii. 10, δύο φαίνεται τὰ κινοῦντα, ὄρεξις καὶ διάνοια πρακτική).   In
the Will of the lower animals, the impulsive element is pre-
dominant[2]; in that of man, according as in the individual
nature the θεός or θηρίον is more developed, either element
may predominate ; but in the σπουδαῖοι ('negli uomini studiosi,'
as Dante has it in *Conv.* IV. xix. 85) the rational element has
such pre-eminence that the Will may be considered as
entirely rational, the other element being practically all but
suppressed.

The following passages will illustrate this :—

(1) *Purg.* xviii. 62, 63 :—

> 'Innata v' è la virtù che consiglia,
> E dell' assenso de' tener la soglia.'

That the Will is 'la virtù che consiglia' is clear from the
context.   See l. 68, where this 'virtù' is described as 'esta
innata libertate,' and still more explicitly in ll. 73, 74 :—

> 'La nobile virtù Beatrice intende
> Per lo libero arbitrio.'

The language of *Purg.* xviii. 62, 63 may almost have been
suggested by that of Aquinas, *Summa*, I. xxii. 2, r. 4 : ' ut
creaturae rationales [*sc.* agunt] per liberum arbitrium, quo
consiliantur et eligunt.'   He proceeds to quote in illustration
Ecclus. xv. 14, 'Deus ab initio constituit hominem et reliquit
illum in manu *consilii sui*,' where the context will be found to
be asserting the freedom of man's Will.

---

[1] Note also its definition in c. iii. 19 as βουλευτικὴ ὄρεξις τῶν ἐφ' ἡμῖν.   Compare Dante's expression *appetito razionale* in *Conv.* IV. xxii. 100.

[2] Compare again *De An.* iii. 10 *ad fin.*, ὅλως μὲν οὖν, ὥσπερ εἴρηται, ᾗ ὀρεκτικὸν
τὸ ζῷον, ταύτῃ αὑτοῦ κινητικόν· ὀρεκτικὸν δὲ οὐκ ἄνευ φαντασίας· φαντασία δὲ
πᾶσα ἢ λογιστικὴ ἢ αἰσθητική. ταύτης μὲν οὖν καὶ τὰ ἄλλα ζῷα μετέχει.   See also
the quotation presently from *De Mon.* I. xii.

(2) In *Conv.* IV. xxii. 96, as we have seen (p. 29), Dante distinctly describes the Will as belonging to the ' parte razionale ' of Man.

Hence *only rational* beings can have Free Will; see *Par.* v. 23, 24 :—

> ' Di che le creature intelligenti,
> E *tutte* e *sole* furo e son dotate.'

Cf. *Summa*, I. lix. 3 r., ' Solum id quod habet intellectum potest agere iudicio libero . . . Unde ubicunque est intellectus est liberum arbitrium,' and a little before ' [animalia irrationalia] agunt quodam arbitrio sed non libero.' Compare with this *De Mon.* I. xii. 27, quoted *infra*.

(3) A very important passage occurs in *De Mon.* I. xii. 5–10. It is too long to quote, but note especially l. 9. Some affirm ' liberum arbitrium esse liberum de voluntate *iudicium*,' and Dante adds, 'Et verum dicunt.' Again, l. 21, ' Si ergo iudicium moveat omnino appetitum, et nullo modo praeveniatur ab eo, liberum est. . . . (l. 27) Et hinc est, quod bruta iudicium liberum habere non possunt, quia eorum iudicia semper appetitu praeveniuntur.' Thus it is implied that this interposition of appetite or desire in the exercise of Will is (or should be) absent in the case of man, and consequently the intellectual element in Will alone remains, and so it is not unnatural that Will when Free should sometimes be spoken of as belonging wholly to the rational or intellectual part of man's nature [1]. I feel confident, therefore, that the text of this passage need not, and should not, be tampered with.

I. xii. 89–92.

The three MSS. (B H M) here examined, with slight variations, read thus :—

' Provato è adunque la bontà della cosa più propria, è da vedere [B inserts *quella*] che più in essa [*al.* esso] è amata e commendata e quell' è essa.'

This passage needs to be considered carefully in relation to the whole context. That will, I think, show us what Dante is likely to have said in this confused sentence.

[1] Compare Milton, *Areopagitica* : ' When God gave Adam Reason, he gave him freedom to choose, for Reason is but choosing.'

The general purpose of the chapter is to show the claims on one's affection of one's own language, and of the Italian language in particular in Dante's own case. This is argued on two grounds : its *nearness* to one (ll. 30–59) and its *excellence* (ll. 60 *seqq.*). Confining our attention to the latter, it is stated :—

Whatever excellence is most appropriate to anything is most lovable in it (ll. 60–68).

Hence in man, while any virtue is lovable, righteousness (*giustizia*), his most appropriate and peculiar excellence, is most lovable (ll. 69–88).

Now to return to the subject of the chapter (l. 88), i.e. to apply this to the case of language, and our own language ('Volgare') in particular.

Then comes the passage before us which restates what has been already 'proved,' that it may form the major premiss of the argument in its application to language.

What then has been proved ? Apparently that the 'bontà più propria' is always the chief object of affection and admiration for anything. This 'bontà' then is what we have to ascertain in the case of language, and if that excellence is found to exist in the case of our 'Volgare,' its claim on our affection will have been established.

Hence we have in effect the following syllogism :—

Whatever is most admired in anything is its special excellence. In the case of language, clearness in expressing thought is most admired[1]. Therefore in the case of language, clearness in expressing thought is its special excellence.

Then it is maintained that this merit belongs to our own language (Volgare) and therefore is the cause of our love and admiration for it. I believe the sense will come out quite clearly if we simply transpose the words *è da vedere*, and for *quell'* read *qual*, which may not unlikely be found in some MS.,

---

[1] Vide *supra*, c. v., l. 101, though there, when Latin and Volgare are in contrast, Latin is said to have the advantage in this respect.

and is at any rate a very trifling change. Or even both *quella* and *qual* may stand. The sentence will then become :—

'Provato è adunque la bontà della cosa più propria che più in essa è amata e commendata ; ed è da vedere qual è essa.'

'That is proved to be the special excellence of anything which is most beloved and admired in it ; and we have now to see what that is' (in the case before us). Giuliani reads : 'è da vedere *nel Volgare* qual essa è.' The italicized words inserted no doubt make Dante's meaning clearer, but there is no MS. evidence for them. Dante probably trusted to the intelligence of his readers to supply them from the statement that he was now returning to the subject of the chapter, 'torno al proposito.' This is a good instance of what I have described (*supra*, p. 6) as a sentence having fallen into ' pie,' and demanding nothing but a rearrangement of the order of the words. We have only to suppose the words ' è da vedere ' to have been accidentally omitted, and afterwards written in the margin. Then a later copyist inserted them in the wrong place, the word ' che ' seeming to suggest a natural construction for them.

The word *quella*, which I printed in the Oxford text, is not necessary. It was supported by its occurrence in B. A further examination of the MSS. in this passage (which I unfortunately omitted) would probably indicate whether *quella* should be retained or not. It is, however, quite an unimportant point.

I. xiii. 22.

... di essere, se per me non stesse.

B H and M (the only MSS. here examined) read ' di essere sempre non stesse.' This, I suspect, arose from the abbreviation sepme (=' se per me ') having been mistaken for ' sempre.' See on this cause of error *supra*, p. 8.

I. xiii. 25.

Non è secondo a una cosa essere più cagioni efficienti, avvegnachè una sia massima delle altre ?

Very strange liberties have been taken by different editors with the text of this passage. The only variation in the

D

MSS. appears to be the insertion or omission of *a* between *secondo* and *una cosa*.

The MS. evidence gathered since the publication of the *Oxford Dante* is as follows:—

a (or *ad*) is inserted by fifteen MSS., viz. B D H M P Tr U ε θ σ υ φ ψ ω F.

a is omitted by nine, viz. Q a β γ δ ζ η τ χ.

For π see *infra*.

This evidence is strongly in favour of its insertion; and further it seems to me to be certainly right, and almost necessary to the sense; indeed absolutely so, on one, and that probably the best, interpretation of the passage. Its omission probably arose from the notion that *secondo* was a preposition governing *cosa*, and therefore *a* somewhat superfluous. I think it is probably an adjective, *if* the passage stands complete as above, but I strongly suspect that some word has been lost after *secondo*, such as 'ragione' or 'natura' or 'sperienza,' &c., and that it might be better to mark a short lacuna, indicating the probable loss of a word, the exact form of which we have no evidence to supply. Such loss may have been purely accidental, or the word may chance to have been illegible or obliterated in some very early copy. But *if*, as I say, the passage is to stand as it is, then *secondo* would probably mean *conforme* or *connaturale* (as Edd. Mil.), *conforme alla natura di una cosa* (as Giuliani). Some take *a una cosa* after *secondo*; others after *essere*. The latter appears to me probably-right (if there is a word omitted), and hence I regard *a* as necessary to the sense. I ought to have said that the principal objection made to the general sentiment of the passage is easily met by making it interrogative instead of assertive: 'Is it not natural that a thing should have several (contributory) efficient causes, though one of these may be the principal one?' But *secondo* used thus absolutely in the sense of 'suitable' or 'natural' seems to me so harsh and devoid of any authority, that I prefer to suppose the accidental omission of a word.

The following 'rifacimenti' of the passage are veritable 'curiosities of literature':—

'Non è *assurdo in* una cosa essere più cagioni *influenti.*' (Giuliani.)
  'Non è una sola la cagione efficiente dello essere delle cose, ma tra più cagioni efficienti una è la massima delle altre.'

So Fraticelli, who says this is found in Cod. Ricc. (π), but Giuliani points out that the MS. has itself been altered thus by a later hand.

This would give an excellent sense, but it is difficult to see by what error (ὁμοιοτέλευτα or otherwise) this and the *lect. vulg.* could be brought into relation.

II. i. 19 *seqq.*

L' uno si chiama *litterale*, e questo è quello . . .
. . . .
. . che si nasconde sotto il manto di queste favole.

It has long been recognized that a sentence must by some accident have dropped out here. Dante is here describing the difference between the four methods of interpretation—literal, allegorical, moral, and anagogical (or mystical)—and in this passage in particular the first two are dealt with. As the text stands in nearly all the known MSS. the *literal* sense is described as ' Quello che si nasconde sotto il manto di queste favole, ed è una verità nascosa sotto bella menzogna.' Of this the *hidden meaning* of the fable of Orpheus is given as an example.

Now this is clearly quite inappropriate to the *literal* meaning, and as clearly gives an apt description of the *allegorical*. This, it may be observed, is otherwise passed over altogether, though the occurrence of the word 'allegorico' at the end of the clause (l. 40) implies that what has preceded has, in fact, dealt with it. We may note also that in l. 123 *allegoria* is described in these very words as *l' ascosa verità*.

It has been usual, therefore, either to mark a hiatus (as in the first Oxford text and others) or else to supply a sentence from pure conjecture (as by Biscioni and Giuliani). I had the pleasure of finding the following reading in a Paris MS. (Bibl.

Nat., 'Ital. 536'), which seems to make all clear : ' L' uno si chiama litterale, *e questo è quello che* non si stende più oltre che la lettera propria; l' altro si chiama allegorico, *e questo è quello che* si nasconde,' &c., as in the ordinary texts.

The words italicized explain at a glance how naturally the omission arose from the familiar error of ὁμοιοτέλευτα. When preparing the text of the *Oxford Dante* I was aware, from the notes of Giuliani, that the Riccardiana MS. (here marked π) contained those words, but with the addition of an almost certainly spurious expansion which naturally cast suspicion over the whole passage, occurring, as it appeared, in this one MS. only :—

' L' uno si chiama litterale, e questo è quello che non si distende più oltre che la lettera propria, siccome è la narrazione propria di quella cosa che tu tratti : che per certo e appropriato esempio è la terza Canzone che tratta di Nobiltade.'

All that follows after ' siccome ' seems to be clearly a gloss. For (1) the addition is easily accounted for by the supposed need, on grounds of symmetry, that an example should be given of this method of interpretation as of the three later ones. Fraticelli and the Edd. Milanesi express this opinion, though holding that the example given by Dante has been lost. Thus the same opinion appears to have been held by some early copyist also. But in fact no such illustration is required to explain what is meant by the *literal* sense. (2) The example given is not only superfluous, but it does not even correspond with the later ones. It is not a definite ' example ' at all, but a very vague and general reference to a later portion of the treatise itself.

As, therefore, the Paris MS. supplies the missing words in a perfectly natural and satisfactory manner, while the cause of their omission is one that is obvious and generally familiar, I have no hesitation in introducing them into the text.

Fraticelli inserts the whole of the words as they stand in Cod. Ricc. 1044 (π). Giuliani (*more suo*) rewrites the passage quite independently thus : 'questo è quello che risulta dalla Favola o dalla Storia della lettera, nè si stende,' &c.

II. i. 26–34.

 Orfeo . . . fa muovere . . .

       . . . quasi pietre.

In l. 31 it seemed to me that the insertion of *non* was absolutely necessary to the sense, while at the same time plausible reasons for its intentional omission might be given. I felt, therefore, justified in inserting it between brackets in Ed. I, though I could not allege any MS. authority for it. It has now been reported to me in two MSS. (γ ε) and in a third (θ), *secunda manu*. This will now justify the removal of the brackets, though it must be admitted that numerically the MSS. are nearly unanimous for the omission of the negative, in fact thirty against three, viz. γ ε and θ (*secunda manu*). I think (as I say) that plausible reasons might have occurred to a copyist for omitting the negative. (1) There is a sort of *prima facie* attractiveness in establishing an antithesis between *coloro che hanno* and *coloro che non hanno* in the next clause. It is curious that my MS. omits *non* in the second clause also (l. 32), and so does κ. This looks like an attempt to make the two clauses correspond (as they evidently ought to do) by striking out the second *non* after the first had been dropped out in error. But this remedy unfortunately spoils the sense of *both* clauses. (2) It might have been argued that those who were capable of good leading must have some good qualities; must be to some extent προδιειργασμένοι τοῖς ἔθεσιν, and that Dante would not attribute this amenability τοῖς ἀνοήτοις. Compare the quotation from Hesiod in *Nic. Eth.* I. iv. *fin.* Also in the *Convivio* itself Dante would seem to have said as much in IV. vii. 31–42.

II. i. 75.

I inserted in the Oxford text the words ' la sentenza litterale ' (guarding them by square brackets) in deference to what seems to be the unanimous opinion of editors for their necessity, though they are not, I believe, found in any MS., and I have examined as many as thirty-one here. Of course there may have been a very early omission of them by pure inadvertence, but there are no ὁμοιοτέλευτα in the sentence to account for it.

Possibly they may not be *absolutely* necessary. Might it not be possible to translate : ' Wherefore since in all writings there must be an outside, it is impossible to arrive at the other meanings, especially the allegorical, without first arriving at the literal ? ' For it is perfectly clear from the previous context that ' the outside' would mean the ' literal '; and though the word ' other' comes rather prematurely, we have not to wait long for its meaning to become obvious. Moreover it has already been anticipated in ll. 66–71. Dante often makes larger demands than this on the intelligence of his readers.

II. i. 83–86.

> Impossibile è la forma *dell' oro* venire, se la materia, cioè il suo suggetto, non è prima digesta, &c.

Several MSS. and some editions have *di loro*. I have already drawn attention to the frequency of errors of this kind, *supra*, p. 7, and the consequent legitimacy of their correction. For *materia* Giuliani has quite arbitrarily substituted *miniera*. The following passages are amply sufficient to establish the correctness of *materia* rather than *miniera*. In III. iii. 14, though the word 'materia' does not occur, it is clear that it is something more elementary than *miniere*, which are already *corpora composte*. See the similar passage in *De Mon.* I. iii. 45–50. Also *materia* in *Conv.* III. vii. 52 *seqq.*, where *materia* enters in different degrees into man, animals, *minerals*, and elements. See also the Essay on Dante's Theory of Creation, pp. 136 seqq.

II. ii. 19, 20.

The following are the varieties of reading and punctuation here :—

> ' E così fatti dentro lei, poi fêro tale.'
> ' E così fatti dentro me, poi fêro tale.'
> ' E così fatti, dentro me poi fêro tale.'

I find *dentro lei* in three MSS. (B H M) examined here, and Giuliani reports *dentro me* in two (viz. σ and τ). I think 'fatti dentro *lei*' may seem to have been suggested by ' a lei si fêro ' in the previous line. Further, it is in favour of ' dentro *me*' that this seems to be a sort of paraphrase of *V. N.*

xxxviii. and xxxix., to which Dante is here explicitly referring. Compare the expression 'tal dentro mi fei' in *Par.* i. 67.

II. ii. 32–35.

> Perocchè l' uno era soccorso dalla [*al.* della] parte dinanzi continua-
> mente, e l' altro dalla parte della memoria di dietro.

Such is the reading apparently in all MSS., and there is no
need to tamper with it. It is fully explained by the passage
(quoted by Giuliani) from B. Latini, *Tesoro*, i. 15, on the three
cells within the head, which is the 'magione dell' anima':
'una *dinanzi* per *imprendere*; l' altra nel mezzo per conoscere;
la terza *dietro* per *memoria.*' Giuliani says that the Tuscans
still speak of 'memory' as 'the back of the head.' Bearing
this passage in mind, Dante might well attribute 'imprendere,'
i. e. learning more of the present 'gentil donna' continually, to
the 'parte dinanzi'; while, on the other hand, the 'memoria
di dietro' was ever dwelling on the absent Beatrice; the
former naturally strengthening day by day, and the latter
weakening. Hence the words 'della vista,' added by Edd.
Mil.—'dalla parte *della vista* dinanzi'—as they say, '*neces-
sariamente,*' though without any MS. authority, are not
only superfluous but positively misleading[1]. Equally unnecessary is Giuliani's more modest alteration, '*o* di dietro,'
and also the alternative suggested, '*ch*' *è* dietro.'

The passage continues: 'E 'l soccorso dinanzi ciascuno dì
crescea (che far non potea l' altro) *comente* quello che impediva
in alcuno modo a dare indietro il volto.' The three MSS.
I have consulted here read *comento*, and it is said by editors
to be the reading of MSS. generally. This is obviously a
blunder, and it occurred to Perticari to suggest that it may
be a corruption from *comente*, as an archaic form of *come*, like
French *comment*[2]. The very fact of its being archaic and all

---

[1] They are adopted also by Monti, Pederzini, and Fraticelli.

[2] Other similar forms quoted are *quasimente, insiememente,* and *finente* (=*fino*).
Monti, *Saggio*, p. 116, says that *comente* may still be heard in the neighbourhood of Cortona; but I must admit that the form is not recognized in the large
new Della Crusca Vocabolario. Gigli, *Vocab. Cateriniano*, p. 214, also gives
'comente' as a dialectic variety about Cortona. There are certain cases of
rare words in the *Divina Commedia*, where Dante has been supposed by
commentators to be using local or dialectic words (*voci contadinesche*). I will

but obsolete would account for the change in MSS. I have
not found it in any edition consulted. The meaning becomes
perfectly clear, as Giuliani in fact admits, but he prefers to
read *come*, which does not explain the reading *comento*.
Dionisi (who is followed by Edd. Mil.) suggested *contra a*,
putting a comma at *crescea* and removing the parenthesis.
Fraticelli, giving the same sense to the passage, reads *contrario
a*. The objection to all these three readings is that they have
no root in any MS. evidence.

II. ii. 41, 42.

Per iscusare me della *novità*.

The MSS. generally as reported (as well as the two or three
here seen by myself) have *verità*. This seems clearly a
blunder. Edd. Mil., Pederzini, and Fraticelli read *avversità*.
I think Giuliani is certainly right in preferring *novità*, as the
difference in MSS. between *novità* and *uerità* would be extremely slight, both *n* and *r* being constantly confused with
u or *v*[1]. Also (as Giuliani points out) the word is strongly
supported by its occurrence in the related passage in the
Canzone, l. 10 :—

'Io vi dirò del cor la *novitate*.'

To this we may add that in the place in the *V. N.* on
which this chapter is declared to be based (vide *supra*, l. 9)
Dante says : 'Recommi la vista di questa donna in sì *nuova*
condizione, che molte volte ne pensava come di persona che
troppo mi piacesse '[2] (the very point just confessed in the
present passage). Further, the *novità* of the situation is again

---

mention the following, without committing myself in all cases to the explanation
offered :—'erro' (*Inf.* xxxiv. 102), 'sobbarco' (*Purg.* vi. 135), 'rosta' (*Inf.* xiii.
117), 'conca' (*Inf.* ix. 16), 'a pruovo'='appresso' (*Inf.* xii. 93), 'rocco' (*Purg.*
xxiv. 30), 'vigliare' (*Purg.* xviii. 66). See Vernon's *Readings* in most of these
passages.

[1] Thus *sentirà* and *sentiva* are both found *infra*, l. 68 ; and M in one place has
nello cissimo for *velocissimo*.

[2] *Vita Nuova*, § xxxix *init*. Compare further the 'molta battaglia intra
'l pensiero,' &c., of l. 28 *supra*, with the 'battaglia de' pensieri' in *V. N.*
xxxix. 26.

dwelt upon in c. vii., ll. 26, 65 ; and viii. 78. See also the third line of the Canzone itself :—

> 'Ch' io nol so dire altrui, sì mi par *novo*.'

II. iii. 60-63.

> Che vide . . . la Luna, essendo *nuova* (not *mezza*, as in Oxford text, Ed. I), entrare sotto a Marte dalla parte non lucente.

I am now convinced that I was wrong in following Witte's correction of *mezza* for *nuova* in the first edition of the *Oxford Dante*, and that Giuliani is perfectly right in retaining the latter.

It is fair to say that I had then the evidence of only two or three MSS. for *nuova*, and I considered also (1) that *nuova* was *impossible*, since the ' New ' Moon must be invisible, while the Moon is here spoken of as partly light and partly dark ; and (2) that Dante expressly declares that he is quoting a definite passage of Aristotle, where the word is found to be διχότομος, or, as it would probably be presented to him, 'dichothomus.' But the argument becomes even stronger if we consider that Dante is really quoting as 'Aristotle' the reproduction of him by Albertus Magnus, as is frequently the case elsewhere[1]. Now the passage in Albertus, *de Coelo et Mundo* (L. II. Tr. iii. c. 13), reads thus: 'Vidimus lunam quae *media* et accensa, mota sub stella Martis, et occultavit Martem, eclipsando eum per id quod remanserat nigrum lunae, et post . . . exivit et oriebatur Mars ex parte illuminata in luna versus Occidentem.' There is nothing in Aristotle corresponding to these two last words, but Dante (it will be seen) adds ' ch' era verso occidente.' It certainly seemed to me (and it still seems) very hard to resist this evidence for *mezza*. But I think it must yield to the fact that, as I have now discovered, the MSS. (thirty-two in number, one being defective here) are *absolutely unanimous* for *nuova*.

The other argument from the supposed 'impossibility' of *nuova* may be answered by supposing *nuova* to be used in a

---

[1] As Dr. Toynbee has pointed out in an interesting and learned article in his *Dante Studies and Researches*, p. 50. See note on *C*. II. xiv. 145, where Dante quotes as Aristotle a comment upon him of Aquinas.

popular and not strictly astronomical sense. Not only do we commonly speak of a young moon as the 'new' moon, but Dante himself does so in *Inf.* xv. 19:—

> 'Guardar l' un l' altro sotto nuova luna.'

Alfraganus (c. i.) says that each month begins 'a prima Lunae *visione.*' Again we read of a sect among the Jews, the Karaites, who maintained that the New Moon (with a view to fixing the day of the Passover) was to be determined not astronomically, but from its first appearance in the sky[1]. I think, therefore, that Dante might apply the term to a Moon a few days old, or in fact up to about the first quarter, which would be implied by διχότομος. Dante may have intentionally substituted *nuova* for the more obvious *mezza* (as Giuliani suggests) to avoid the possible ambiguity of the latter term, as in *Purg.* xxix. 54, 'luna . . . nel suo mezzo mese,' i.e. the Full Moon.

I have, therefore, replaced *nuova* in the text of the third edition.

II. iv. 28.

> É quieto e pacifico è lo luogo di quella somma Deità, &c.

Witte, Fraticelli, and Giuliani alter thus: 'E questo quieto e pacifico cielo è lo luogo,' &c., partly because these words are 'necessary' (?) to carry on the sense, and partly to make this sentence correspond mechanically with the three following in ll. 30, 35, and 40.

This appears to me a typical instance of a mere 'fancy' improvement of the author's style, and therefore to be rejected, as I have noted *supra*, p. 13.

II. v. 27.

> Tutte le ricchezze.

The *lect. vulg.* here appears to be *larghezze.* I had not noticed the passage for collation, so I cannot speak of the evidence of MSS. My own MS. (M) and also σ (*Auct. Giul.*) have *le ricchezze* (B has *larghezze*). Evidently *lerichezze* and *larghezze* might easily be confused, or one substituted in error for the other. Dante has given as examples of 'spezie di cose'

---

[1] *Vide* Tholuck on Gospel of St. John, p. 308, Clarke's Translation.

or Platonic Ἰδέαι, one for 'man' generally, another for 'gold,' and another for 'riches' generally, including not only gold, but precious stones or any other form in which wealth may consist. Riches would evidently be more suitable than *larghezze*. Fraticelli adopts the astonishing suggestion of reading *argento*, which is wholly devoid of MS. support; has no relation in form to any MS. reading; and is quite otiose as another illustration added to *oro*.

II. v. 89-96.

'E non è contro a quello che pare dire Aristotile nel decimo dell' *Etica*, che alle sustanze separate convegna la speculativa vita, come pure la speculativa convegna loro. Pure alla speculazione di certe segue la circolazione del cielo, che è del mondo governo.'

The above is the form of this difficult passage adopted in the last edition of the *Oxford Dante*, differing considerably from that which found place in the first edition[1].

The following is some of the evidence of MSS. :—

'convegna pure la spec. vita,' $\alpha\,\beta\,\gamma\,\delta\,\zeta\,\kappa\,\lambda\,\mu\,o\,\xi\,\pi\,\rho\,\tau\,\chi\,\psi$ P.

Ditto, omitting *pure*, $\epsilon\,\eta\,\iota\,\nu\,\phi$ M Q.

v has the following curious punctuation &c.: 'come parla speculativa. Convegna loro pure alla speculazione di certe segue la circulazione,' &c. This seems a mere jumble of blunders.

M has 'come parla speculativa convegna loro pure all' attiva vita alla speculazione di certe.'

B has (with no stops anywhere) 'come pure la speculativa vita convegna loro pure alla speculazione,' &c.

ζ adds a third 'pure' before 'loro.'

θ has 'come parla speculativa convegna loro pure all' attiva vita alla speculazione di certe,' &c.

In spite of a certain amount of confusion in the MSS. owing to the frequent repetition of certain words, leading, as usual, to blunders of ὁμοιοτέλευτα, there seems little need for emendation here beyond the revision of punctuation. Let us note the context leading up to this passage. Dante has spoken of the

---

[1] I am inclined, however, to insert another 'pure' after 'convegna' in l. 92, in accordance with the strong MS. evidence (vide *supra*). Also it seems to give further emphasis to the argument here, as explained below.

familiar distinction between the Happiness of the Active Life and that of the Contemplative. He has, however, attributed to some of the Angels or Higher Intelligences the regulation of the celestial motions and the Government of the Universe. This implies for them some share in the Active type of Life ('vita attiva, cioè civile,' l. 72), and the participation, therefore, in that lower kind of Happiness which belongs to it. . . . But to attribute this to such Higher Beings is not really (as it might seem) inconsistent with what Aristotle says in *Ethics*, Book X, viz. that only speculative or contemplative life can be attributed to Divine Beings. But activity is not to be limited to outward action. There is an activity in Contemplation (ἐνέργεια θεωρητική), and this is the Activity which we attribute to those 'Angeli Movitori' (*supra*, ll. 5–8). They are referred to in 'loro' (l. 93), which is emphatic. Then he proceeds: It is solely on the 'speculation' of certain of them (i.e. those out of the whole body of Angels who are selected to be 'Angeli Movitori') that the circling movement of the heavens depends, and that constitutes the government of the world[1]. Thus there is no *external* activity implied in the functions assigned to them. This idea is most explicitly set forth at the end of the next chapter (ll. 151 *seqq.*): 'Questi movitori muovono, *solo intendendo*[2], la circolazione in quello suggetto proprio che ciascuno muove. La forma nobilissima del cielo, . . . gira toccata da virtù motrice che questo intende : e dico toccata, non corporalmente, per tatto di virtù, la quale si dirizza in quello.' (See also c. vii., l. 9.) That seems to give the key to the present passage, just as it is found in most of the MSS., viz. as follows :—

'A quello che pare dire Aristotile nel decimo dell' *Etica* che alle sustanze separate convegna la speculativa vita come pure la speculativa convegna loro pure[3] alla speculazione di certe segue la circolazione,' &c.

[1] See *Purg.* xx. 13 ; xxx. 109–111; *Par.* viii. 97–99, 127, 128; *Conv.* II. v. 6; III. vi. 65 ; *De Mon.* II. ii. 15, 25 ; and many other passages.

[2] Compare *intesa* as used in *Conv.* IV. i. 65, and *intenzione* in III. vi. 50. Also for the idea of κινεῖ οὐ κινούμενον comp. Arist. *Metaph.* Λ, c. 7.

[3] After this 'pure' some editors insert 'l' attiva,' e. g. Edd. Mil., Fraticelli. I only remember noticing it in two MSS., and it seems entirely to distort Dante's argument.

The MSS. in some cases have no stops, and when they have, these are very haphazard, and the same applies to the divisions of sentences. The above illustrates well how an apparently hopelessly confused passage may sometimes be cleared up by mere punctuation without any conjectural emendations.

Dante here holds that the Angels exercising these functions were but a small proportion of the whole body ; see ll. 87–89, and 94. But he maintains elsewhere that all the Angels were created simultaneously (see *Par.* xxix. 28–30 and *Conv.* II. vi. 49) ; and that that moment was identical with the Creation of the material Universe, and not (as St. Jerome supposed) long anterior to it (*Par.* xxix. 37–39). This he argues on the ground that on the latter supposition the Angels would have existed for many ages without any functions and therefore in a condition of imperfection (*Par.* xxix. 43–45).

II. v. 124–128.

> Siccome afferma chi ha gli occhi chiusi l' aere essere luminosa per un poco di splendore, ovvero raggio che passa per le pupille del vipistrello.

There are no variations of any importance here in the MSS. Some substitute the collateral form *pipistrello* for *vipistrello* ; and several have unintelligent blunders, such as ' palpestrello,' 'polpastrello,' &c.[1] But at the point where editors have indulged in conjectural alterations there are no variations[2], viz. in the words ' ovvero raggio che passa '[3]. The construction is harsh and awkward, but it is no part of an editor's business to try to improve upon that when the meaning is intelligible enough. ' As one affirms who has his eyes closed that the air is luminous through a little brightness, or indeed a ray that (*or* such as) passes through the pupils of a bat.' We might, however, perhaps translate, ' or indeed as a ray,' by

---

[1] The Paris MS. (P) has a change of the prepositions thus : ' *alle* pupille *pel* palpestrello.' This might be significant, if 'palpestrello' could bear any appropriate meaning. But even so it would be an objection that the obvious quotation from Aristotle would be excluded.

[2] At least not in $\alpha \beta \gamma \delta \zeta \eta \theta \mu \nu \xi \pi \rho \sigma \tau \nu$ B M P Q.

[3] The Edd. Mil. conjecturally altered *ovvero* to *o come*. Frat. adopts this, and suggests more considerable changes in a note. Giul. boldly rewrites thus: ' ovvero raggio che *vi* passa *come* per,' &c.

understanding 'siccome' again from above, though the form of construction introduced by it would be changed. In that case perhaps a semicolon might be better than a comma at 'splendore.'

The illustration from the bat is borrowed from Arist. *Metaph.* A (min.) c. i. (993 b 9), the passage definitely cited by Dante a few lines above. It is applied by Aristotle also exactly as by Dante here. It runs thus in the *Antiqua Translatio*:—

'Sicut enim nycticoracum oculi ad lucem diei se habent, sic et animae nostrae intellectus ad ea quae sunt omnium naturae manifestissima.'

The word 'vipistrello' occurs again in *Inf.* xxxiv. 49.

II. vi. 24.

Maria, giovinetta donzella di xiij [*al.* xiiij] anni.

The MSS. here vary between thirteen and fourteen years. My records are :—

xiij. B D H P Q Tr $a \beta \gamma \delta \zeta \lambda \mu \xi o \pi \rho \omega$ F.

xiiij. M T $\epsilon \eta \theta \nu$.

I am not quite sure that I have *always* distinguished whether the number is given by a word or by figures, but the difference was certainly noted in the following cases :—

xiij. $\beta \gamma \delta \zeta$.

xiiij. M T $\eta \theta \nu$.

tredici a F B P.

quattordici ϵ.

In the case of the numerals the distinction is very slight and confusion might easily arise[1], and the MS. evidence leaves us free to adopt either figure, the mere numerical preponderance being of little account. The question must then be decided on other grounds, viz. the evidence of early tradition, which Dante would naturally follow. The references and quotations following seem to leave no doubt that fourteen is the correct reading here. The tradition appears commonly in the Apocryphal Gospels[2]. Thus in the Gospel of the Pseudo-Matthew

---

[1] Compare the date in III. xi. 24 (*supra*, p. 19 *fin.*).

[2] The page references are to the edition of B. H. Cowper.

we read that the Virgin was betrothed to Joseph at the age of fourteen (p. 40). The same appears in the Gospel of the Nativity of Mary, c. vii. (p. 91). Again in the History of Joseph the Carpenter, c. xiv., the birth of Christ was in the fifteenth year of her age (p. 111). [In the *Protevangelium* of St. James, c. xii. (p. 14), there is a great variety of readings, fourteen, fifteen, sixteen, seventeen, and eighteen being all found.]

Later ecclesiastical writers seem likewise all agreed as to the age of fourteen at the Annunciation. Thus Ribadaneira, *Flos Sanctorum*, 'de Vita B.M.V,' '*Desponsata* fuit trede-cennis et trimestris.'

Euodius, quoted by Nicephorus Callistus, *Eccl. Hist.* II., c. 3:—

'Trimula quum esset in templo erat presentata, et ibi . . . traduxit annos xi. Deinde vero sacerdotum manibus Iosepho ad custodiam est tradita, apud quem quum menses peregisset iv, ab angelo Gabriele coeli illum accepit nuntium. Peperit autem Mundi ipsius Lumen *annum agens quindecimum*[1].'

A note on the same work, L. I., c. 8, says: 'Mariam Virginem ante Christum Iesum filium eius natum anno 15mo genitam esse Chronici scriptores memorant'[2].

Dr. Toynbee has kindly sent me the following references :—

St. Bonaventura says in chaps. iv and v of his *Meditazioni della Vita di Gesù Cristo* (translation of Cent. XIII):—

'Essendo la Vergine Maria piccola di tre anni, si fu offerta dal padre e dalla madre nel tempio, e quivi stette infino alli quattordici anni . . . E poi ch' ebbe quattordici anni fue disponsata a Joseph per rivelazione di Dio, e tornò a Nazaret . . . Et essendo la vergine Maria già disponsata a Joseph e tornata a Nazaret, Dio onnipotente chiamò l' angelo Gabrielo e sì li disse: Vanne a Maria,' &c. (pp. 4-5, ed. 1851).

In the *Legenda Aurea* it is said (in Legenda L. *De Annunciatione dominica*) :—

'Cum virgo beata a tercio anno etatis sue usque ad quartum decimum in templo cum aliis virginibus exstitisset, et votum de servanda castitate

---

[1] So Landor, *Pentameron* (p. 165), writes, 'Imagine her, in her fifteenth year, fondling the lovely babe, whom she was destined to outlive.'

[2] I am sure I ought to acknowledge indebtedness to some one for these last three references, but I have no note whence I obtained them.

emisisset, nisi deus aliter disponeret, eam Ioseph desponsavit, domino
revelante . . . Ipsa in Nazaret in domum parentum rediit . . . ubi
angelus ei apparuit et ipsam salutavit dicens : Ave gratia plena,' etc.

And again (in Legenda CXXVI., *De Nativitate gloriose
virginis Marie*):—

'Quartodecimo etatis sue anno pontifex publice denunciavit ut virgines
que in templo instruebantur et etatis tempus implessent domum reverte-
rent et viris legittime iungerentur,' &c.

The legend goes on to say, as in the other, that Mary was
espoused, and went to Nazareth, where the Annunciation
took place.

With such practically unanimous evidence it appears to me
that the reading 'xiiij' in the passage before us is conclusively
established.

II. vi. 25.

Da parte del Santo Re celestiale.

This was a conjectural reading on which I ventured long
ago on the strength of the statement that the reading found
in most MSS. was *Sanatore*, as in the text of Edd. Mil. I
felt sure that this rather inappropriate word was a corruption
from *Sanctore*, i.e. *Sancto re*. The other readings found in
editions, e.g. *Senatore* (Pederzini), *Salvatore* (Fraticelli), *Senato*
(Giuliani), seemed on no account to be accepted. That of
Giuliani is the worst. It is a pure conjecture, and the
explanation of it as a description of the Trinity makes it
worse! *Senatore* and *Salvatore* are at any rate found in MSS.,
but the former seems to be merely a blunder or the conjectural substitution of a copyist for *sanatore*—(God could
scarcely be described as a 'Senator'; nor does a Senator send
'Legati')—and the latter is an obvious *facilior lectio*; and
besides it would refer to God the Father in this line, and to
the Son in the very next line. The MS. evidence which I
have gathered is as follows, and as I have the satisfaction of
finding that my conjecture has the support of three MSS.,
I leave it confidently in the text, where this reading appears
for the first time :—

'sanatore,' α β δ η κ μ ξ ο ρ τ χ ψ ω f.
'senatore,' H P QT γ ε ζ λ σ.
'salvatore,' B D T ι π υ φ.
'sanctore,' M θ ν.

Thus the initial *san-* as against *sen-* is very strongly supported, while the difference between *sanatore* and *sanctore* is extremely slight.

It should be added that the reading proposed makes the passage correspond very closely with St. Luke i. 19 : 'Ego sum Gabriel, qui adsto *ante Deum* et *missus sum* loqui ad te.'

II. vi. 95–99.

> Dico che di tutti questi Ordini si perderono alquanti tosto che furono creati, forse in numero della decima parte ; alla quale restaurare fu l' umana natura poi creata.

Though there are no textual difficulties here, it may be worth while to illustrate three quite definite statements, all disputable and disputed, that are here made :—

1. That the Fall of the Angels followed immediately upon their Creation ;
2. that the number of those who fell was possibly (*forse*) one-tenth ;
3. that the Creation of the human race was destined to supply the number thus lost.

1. See this matter discussed in the Essay on Dante's Theory of Creation, *infra*, pp. 152–154.

2. I have not been able to find elsewhere any source for Dante's guess as to *decima parte*. But that the major part remained faithful was a general belief, e. g. Aquinas, *Summa*, I. lxiii. 9 ; among other reasons on the strength of 2 Kings vi. 16. So Hugh of St. Victor, *De Sacramentis*, I., pars v, cap. 31 ; again on the strength of 2 Kings vi. 16 (Migne, vol. 176, p. 261).

3. This also was very commonly held, e. g. Aquinas, *Summa*, I. xxiii. 7. Hugh of St. Victor, relying on Deut. xxxii. 8, which he quotes 'iuxta numerum *angelorum Dei*.' This is a translation of the LXX reading, κατὰ ἀριθμὸν ἀγγέλων Θεοῦ, but this reading is not found in the Vulgate.

P. Lombard boldly says, 'in Scriptura *interdum reperitur* (!) quod factus sit (homo) propter reparationem angelicae ruinae.' *Sentt.* II., Dist. i., § 9, and ix. 7 (*fin.*).

St. Anselm, *Cur Deus Homo*, I. 16–18, where he also refers to the LXX reading in Deut. xxxii. 8. In c. xix., *init.*, he ventures to affirm : ' *Constat* Deum proposuisse, ut de homini-bus angelos qui ceciderant restauraret ' ; and Boso is made to reply, ' Certum est.'

Origen, *de Princ.* I. viii. 4, holds the same view as to a certain portion of the Angels, but in II. ix. 8 thinks that the number of the saved will equal the portion 'non eorum qui ceciderunt, sed eorum qui permanserunt,' following in this Greg. *Hom.* xxxiv. ; but in § 9 he recognizes that the other view is also held, quoting St. Aug. *Enchir.*, c. 29, who there says that not less, and possibly more, than the Angels lost will be thus supplied.

It may be added that Milton refers to this traditional belief in *P. L.* ii. 830–835 and vii. 150 *seqq.*

II. vi. 136, 137.

Uno, secondochè la stella si muove *per lo suo* epiciclo.

The usual reading in editions here is '*verso* lo suo epiciclo' (e.g. Edd. Mil., Ped., Frat.). But *verso* seems cer-tainly wrong, for a planet could not move *towards* its epicycle, since it was attached or 'fixed' to it, as we read *Conv.* II. iv. 88, and with or along this it revolved. Hence we could use *con*, *in*, or *per* (i. e. along or over), but not *verso*. Thus we have *in* at *Par.* viii. 3 and *Conv.* II. iv. 92. Most MSS. are reported as having *verso* here. I suspect that *perlo* was mistaken for *verfo*. I find, in fact, *per* and *ver* interchanged in MSS. at III. v. 157. In the present passage B has not *verfo* but *verlo*.

As to the suitability of *per*, I find the following passage quoted in the new Della Crusca Dictionary : 'le Comete, se. . . per eccentrici o per epicicli si rivolgessero' (Marchetti, *Nat. Comet.* 73). Also I noticed in Golius' Translation of Alfra-ganus, c. xv., ' Luna ex suo *per* epiclum incessu ' ; and so in other passages. I have therefore inserted *per lo*, since it can be derived in a natural way from *verfo*. This cannot be said for *entro*, which Giuliani substitutes. It has no such connexion whatever, nor do I think this preposition is itself very appropriate.

II. vi. 157, 158.

> Toccata, non corporalmente, per *tatto* di virtù.

The MSS. are said to read *tanto*, and so I found it in B and H. M has the blunder *portando*. Giuliani defends *tanto* in the sense of ' per quel più o meno di virtute.' But I think the conjecture of Pederzini and Fraticelli, involving as it does the extremely slight change of *tacto* for *tanto*, or perhaps *tãto*, may well be accepted, as it gives such a very clear and natural antithesis between the bodily touch and the 'touch' of spiritual influence expressed by *solo intendendo*. Still I admit that the change is not absolutely necessary, and if I found the MSS. on further examination nearly unanimous for *tanto*, I should not interfere with it.

II. vii. 106.

> Quanto è *fin* al mezzo della terra.

The MSS. which I have seen read *più*, and so others are reported, and that word is found in several editions. But as *fin* (or *fin* as Giul.) and *più* are almost undistinguishable in MSS., so small a change where the sense obviously demands it scarcely needs an apology.

II. ix. 43–48.

This is one of the most obscure and corrupt passages in the *Convivio*, owing partly to the confused state of the text in the MSS., and partly to the freedom with which conjectural emendation has been applied by editors in order to bring out the divergent views which they have entertained as to the correct meaning of the passage. The only safe method is to look very carefully to the context, and then endeavour with the smallest possible changes (and those only such as can be explained or justified) in the MSS., to elicit, if we can, some intelligible sense. As to the context, the following seems to be a fair paraphrase of it. Dante has explained how the influence of the Intelligences who regulate the orbit of Venus has tended to extinguish the love of the departed and absent Beatrice by substituting for it the love of the present 'Donna gentile.' A difficulty arises, how can the influence of those whose function is to generate love also destroy love? How can a cause which naturally loves its own effect ever destroy that effect? The answer is, that these Intelligences can only operate upon objects that fall within their influence; that are in fact present to them. They are really therefore striving to preserve and perpetuate their natural effect, viz. Love, by transferring it from a departed and absent object (Beatrice), now beyond their influence, to a living and present object (Donna gentile) still within their influence. Love is thus perpetuated unbroken[1], even as human nature preserves its continuity in human form by transmission from father to son; and just because 'the individual withers' the maintenance of the type, in actual realization and objective existence, can only be secured by a change in the object in which it is manifested or resides, from time to time; and thus 'vitai lampada tradunt.' Thus does human nature preserve its *effetto*, or its ἔργον, viz. the production of a living human form existing ἐνεργείᾳ uninterruptedly, though the individuals in which it is embodied change and perish. As says St. Thomas (*Summa*, I. Q. 22, Art. 2), 'corruptio unius est generatio alterius, per quam species conservatur.' Comp. Averroes, *de Anima*, f. 133, 'Sollicitudo divina, quum non potuerit facere ipsum permanere secundum *individuum*, miserta est eius, dando ei virtutem qua potest permanere in *specie*' (from Renan, *Averroès et l'Averroïsme*, p. 153). But this language may be open to misconception, and it might seem to trench upon the doctrine of the immortality of individual souls. It is to be understood, therefore (Dico *effetto*), that the 'effetto' or ἔργον is here used only to express the result of union of soul and body ('effetto di quella,' *sc.* 'umana natura')

---

[1] Compare *Epist.* iv. § 2: '. . . sermo Calliopeus . . . quo sententialiter canitur . . . intentum amorem huius posse torpescere atque denique interire, nec non quod corruptio unius generatio sit alterius in anima reformati.' See also *ibid.*, § 1. A comparison of this with the present passage seems to suggest that this Canzone is probably the 'sermo Calliopeus' which accompanied the Epistle.

by which man exists actually as a man; the realization in fact or actuality (ἐνεργείᾳ) of human nature, by which 'man becomes a living soul' (compare τὸ σύνθετον in *Nic. Eth.* x. 7 and 8). When the soul is separated from the body (*partita*) it exists in *another* state, which is *above* what we describe as 'human nature.' This seems to give a connected and intelligible sense, and it can be obtained from the readings of MSS. with extremely small changes.

I will take the reading of my own MS. as a starting-point and explain the principal variations supplied by other MSS.: 'dico effetto in quanto l' anima col corpo *congiunti* sono effetto di *quelle* che perpetualmente dura che è partita in natura più che *in altra vita* umana.' I have italicized the words which call for special remark.

(1) Having then very slight MS. evidence available I read *congiunta* in the first Oxford text. I now find *congiunti* in as many as thirty MSS., and *congiunta* in two only. *Congiunte* also appears in one, but this too points to *congiunti*, so that the reading *congiunti* seems fully established. It also somewhat lessens the harshness of the construction with *sono*. A comma, or rather a slight pause, before and after *congiunti* might help it still further.

(2) The word *quelle* I take to be a mere slip for *quella*, as I have met with other similar cases in my MS. and I have only found it here in two other MSS., viz. θ and ν, which, as often, agree with M.

(3) *in altra vita* seems quite clearly a marginal gloss to explain 'in natura più che umana.' This has come to be inserted unintelligently in the text, where it might have stood without difficulty, though somewhat superfluous, either after *partita* or *umana*. Had it been original it would not have been likely to have got thus out of place. I felt therefore so sure that it was intrusive that I omitted it. I have since had the satisfaction of finding that it had no place in twenty-two out of thirty-one MSS. examined. I found it with slight variations in eight.

I would now propose to read the whole passage thus: 'Dico *effetto*, in quanto l' anima col corpo congiunti sono effetto di quella ; chè perpetualmente dura, che è partita, in natura più che umana : così è soluta la quistione' (as in fact it stands in the revised Oxford text, where *congiunti* is now substituted for *congiunta* on MS. evidence). None of the MSS. examined have, I believe, any stop after 'quella,' nor do I remember noting any after 'dura.' The text (as is common) runs on, like a legal document, without any stops, and we may therefore fairly use our own judgement as to where they should come, since some are practically necessary.

It might also be possible to read the passage thus :—

'Sono effetto di quella che perpetualmente dura ; chè è, partita, in natura più che umana.'

I have supposed that *quella* in l. 45 is 'umana natura,' from the way in which 'il suo effetto' is used in l. 43. But sometimes *anima* is in preference understood, so that it may be the nominative to 'dura' and to 'è,' because, it is argued, it would seem awkward to say that 'umana natura' exists 'in natura più che umana' : also that 'partita,' as applied to 'anima,' quite naturally repeats the idea of 'partita d' esta vita' in l. 38.

I think the above explanation gives a connected and satisfactory sense to the whole passage. But with the many elements of uncertainty, such as punctuation and the ambiguity of *che* (which may just as well be *chè* or *ch' è*), I should not like to speak too positively as to the result.

I now add some details of the MS. evidence :—

(*a*) *congiunta* is found in two MSS. only—P τ.
    congiunte   „   „   one MS.—ξ.
    congiunti in all the other thirty.

(*b*) 'che partita che perpetualmente'—D M ϵ η ι ν υ ϕ (eight).
    'che partita perpetualmente'—B H P Q T α β γ δ ζ θ κ λ μ ξ o π ρ σ τ ψ ω χ [with . at 'perpetualmente'] (twenty-three).

    [M θ ν have *quelle* for 'quella,' in error apparently.]

(*c*) 'in natura più che in altra vita umana'—D M ϵ η θ ι ν υ (*om.* in) ϕ.

    'in altra vita' is omitted in B H P Q Tr α β γ δ ζ κ (*altura* for *natura*) λ (ditto) μ o ξ π ρ σ τ χ ψ ω.

I have not thought it worth while to distinguish those MSS.

that read distinctly *che è*, because the simple *che* is often intended for this (vide *supra*, p. 7).

II. xiii. 14, 15.

Quello da molti non conosciuto libro di Boezio.

I have slightly altered the order of the words, as I find them in the editions which I have consulted, from 'non conosciuto da molti' to 'da molti non conosciuto.' I have done so on the strength of the reading found in my own and some other MSS. among those consulted in this passage, because in this order they seem to me to suggest a slightly different, and a more appropriate sense. I take the former words to imply that the *De Consolatione* of Boethius was a book but little known, whereas it was very much the reverse. I know they have been so understood, and a difficulty felt in consequence as to the statement. The latter order of words appears rather to suggest that many persons have neglected to make themselves really acquainted with the contents of the book ; they have omitted, to their loss, to study so valuable and easily accessible a work. It was by many not known as it ought to be. This could be said even of many Books in the Bible itself. Thus one might describe it as a book

'Paucis ignotum, paucioribus notum,'

to borrow the language of the graceful epitaph on the author of the 'Anatomy of Melancholy' in Christ Church Cathedral, Oxford.

II. xiii. 62.

Che avessero sì leggiero le [non] fittizie parole apprese.

This seems to be one of the very few cases in which the desperate remedy of inserting a negative (with due acknowledgement) must be resorted to, though no MS. evidence can be quoted for it.

Dante is excusing himself for not expressing in plain and direct terms his devotion to Philosophy, and for doing so rather 'sotto figure d'altre cose.' In other words he employs 'fittizie parole,' describing his devotion to a 'Donna gentile,' by whose tender sympathy for him in his affliction he represents himself as having been deeply touched. In all this, to use words of his own, 'altro intende' (*Par.* iv. 46). Let us set out the context clearly thus :—

(1) To the expression of his devotion to Philosophy these terms are applied : 'sentenza allegorica e vera' (xiii., ll. 1–3) ; 'palesemente parlare' would be inappropriate in Volgare (xiii., l. 60) ; and in the same sense would be 'parole non fittizie' (*h. l.*).

(2) To that of his devotion to the 'Donna gentile': 'sposizione fittizia e litterale' (xvi., l. 15); 'parola fittizia' (xiii. l. 78); 'sotto figura d' altre cose' (*ibid.*, l. 57); with which may be compared the expression 'bella menzogna' (II. i. 24).

Dante says that he substituted (2) for (1) for three reasons :—

(a) The Volgare would not be suitable for (1), l. 60 (see *supra*, p. 15).

(b) His audience or readers were not so well disposed to him as to have received the more direct treatment. They would prefer to consider him to be fickle and inconstant in his affections.

(c) They would not be so likely to put faith in (1) as in (2); in the plain statement as in the disguised ; 'alla sentenza vera come alla fittizia' (l. 64).

As to the three reasons (a, b, c) a note may be added :—

(a) This corresponds with the feeling (vide *supra*, p. 15) that Latin and not the Volgare was the fitting medium for discoursing of Philosophy.

(b) Dante has before complained with some bitterness (in B. I., c. 3) that he was surrounded by malevolent persons, by whom all that concerned him was taken in evil part. He felt, like Milton, that he was

'fallen on evil days,
On evil days now fallen.'

(c) The reason for this is added by Dante himself, viz. that it was *generally believed* that he was devoted to this fictitious person and not to the 'lady of his mind,' divine Philosophy. As then the actual truth stated barely would not have gained credence, he acted on the principle of *Inf.* xvi. 124, 125 :—

> 'Sempre a quel ver ch' ha faccia di menzogna
> De' l' uom chiuder le labbra finch' ei puote.'

From all this it seems, I think, quite clear that '*non* fittizie' is absolutely necessary in l. 62. One can only suppose that the 'non' was early lost by pure accident, or else by some primitive misunderstanding of the passage. Possibly some confusion may have arisen from the somewhat inverted use (according to our notions) of the terms 'literal' and 'allegorical' as applied here. We might perhaps rather have described (1) as literal (and true) and (2) as allegorical (and feigned).

II. xiv. 15.

> Il quale [*sc.* centro] per suo movimento non si muove.

This is the reading of the three MSS. which have been consulted (B H M), and I do not find any other recorded. The sense seems quite clear and satisfactory, but the text has been altered by Giuliani to 'per quanto sia quello movimento.' In Frat., Ped., and Edd. Mil. we find 'quanto per lo suo.' As there is no note on the subject they may perhaps be following some other MS. reading. The use of *suo* for 'illius' is perhaps awkward, but we find similar cases in viii. 86, 87, and x. 53, &c., and the unclassical mediaeval use of the Latin *suus* is parallel to this. [V. *supra*, p. 16.]

II. xiv. 120–122.

> Appare da sera, cioè retro, quando della lettera per la parte remota si parla per lo Rettorico.

The above is my reading in the Oxford text, and this is, I think, confirmed by the fuller evidence of MSS. which I have gathered since its publication.

The passage appears as follows in other editions ; at least it does so in those which I have consulted, viz. Ped., Edd. Mil., Frat., and Giul. :—

'Appare da sera, cioè retro, quando la lettera per la parte remota si parla per lo Rettorico' (Giul. has *sì* for *si*, and *dalla* for *per la*).

The MS. evidence is as follows :—

'dalla lettera per la parte,' $\sigma \tau F$ (*marg.*)

'dallectera in parte,' v[1].

'dalla'
'della' } terra per la parte,' $BHMTr\alpha\beta\gamma\epsilon\zeta\eta\theta\pi\chi\psi F$ (fifteen)

' „   „ e in parte,' ϕD ['e' is omitted in D and seems added later in ϕ].

' „   „ e alla parte,' P.

'la lettera per la parte,' $\delta \omega$.

I suspect that some copyist thought there was a sort of suitableness of association in the words 'per la parte remota della terra.'

Now (1) *dalla* or *della* seems thus well established, as against either *lettera* or *terra* in the nominative case, since it is found in twenty-one out of twenty-three MSS. (The difference between *della* and *dalla* is not worth registering as they are constantly interchanged in MSS.)

(2) It might be said that *terra* appears in eighteen as against *lettera* in five, but whereas the difference between $\genfrac{}{}{0pt}{}{della}{dalla}$} and *la* is well marked, that between *delaterra* and *dellalettera* is very slight, since single and double letters are frequently and most capriciously interchanged. It is clear that *dallectera* can only stand for *dalla lettera*, and so *dallettera* or *dalletterra* may do the same. In some cases where I have registered $\genfrac{}{}{0pt}{}{dalla}{della}$} *terra* the two words were probably run together in the MSS. We have a very similar case in *Par.* i. 141—

'Come a terra quiete in foco vivo'

—where the first three words often appear as *Comatera* or *Comatēra*, and this has been mistaken for *Con matera*, or *Con materia*[2]. The meaning of the passage I take to be this :— I think 'la lettera' is something like 'the letter' in the New

---

[1] In the previous line v has *agli orecchi* instead of *dinanzi al viso*.

[2] Again, a few lines below (l. 191), for 'anima intera' some MSS. and editions have 'in terra'! See further the discussion of this passage (*Par.* i. 141) in *Textual Criticism*, pp. 439–442.

Testament, i.e. the literal or plain meaning. Its use in this
sense is by no means uncommon in Dante. Thus at the
beginning of c. xii, 'secondochè di sopra disse la *lettera* di
questo Comento,' i.e. the text of this Commentary. So in III.
xii. 9, 'volgendo il senso della lettera.' And 'litera' is found
in this sense in the Commentary of Benvenuto *passim.* Again,
Conv. II. i. 61, 'essere vero *secondo la lettera,*' i.e. 'in its literal
meaning.' In IV. i. 92 Allegory stands in contrast with
'*secondo la lettera* ragionare.' And II. i. 20, 21, the passage
lately recovered in the Paris MS., describes the literal sense as
that which 'non si stende più oltre che *la lettera propria.*' We
might add another illustration from the title of St. Augustine's
Commentary, *De Genesi ad Literam.*

Hence I take Dante to mean that, instead of speaking as it
were face to face with his hearer, the Rhetorician's treatment
of the text or plain subject before him is obscure, allusive, and
far-fetched, or, as we say, in the way of *distant* allusion. We
have had examples of the process in the last two chapters,
e.g. xii. 39, 'suole lo rettorico *indirettamente* parlare altrui,
dirizzando le sue parole non a quello per cui dice, ma verso
un altro,' not, in fact, 'dinanzi al viso dell' uditore,' as we read
here. Compare xiii. 56–67 ; and also IV. viii. 89, where Dante
refers to a Rhetorician speaking 'dinanzi all' avversario.'

The explanation given of the ordinary text is that Dante is
drawing a distinction between the Rhetorician addressing
others '*viva voce*' in their presence, and doing so ' on paper,'
' per iscritto,' in a book, which he can do from a distance.
La lettera = ' writing ' or ' litera scripta ' is personified as
taking the place of the voice of the Rhetorician. But this
contrast between speech and writing is not a distinctive
peculiarity of Rhetoric, whereas that between direct and
allusive presentation of a subject is so. Also this would surely
be conveyed more naturally by '*per* la lettera *dalla* parte,' if
there were MS. authority for this. I cannot feel at all confident
that my interpretation of the passage is the right one. But it
has at least the merit of attempting to explain the reading
indicated by the MSS., and it also points to well-known
distinctions in the practice of Rhetoric itself, such as are

referred to by Dante himself in the previous chapters, e. g. xii. 39. [See further in 'Supplementary Notes', pp. 285 *seqq.*]

II. xiv. 145.

Here we must certainly read *Fisica* with all the MSS. examined, and not [*Meta*]*fisica* as in the several editions of the *Oxford Dante*. The square brackets enclosing the first part of the word indicate that that part of the word was inserted *e conj.* to correct what appeared to be a mistaken reference. The grounds for this were explained in *Studies in Dante*, i. p. 120. But Professor Proto, in *Atene e Roma*, July–August 1913, has shown conclusively that *Fisica* is right, but that Dante has not verified his reference here, but has quoted the language of the Commentary of Aquinas in the *Antiqua Translatio*[1] on a passage in the *Physics*, as though they were the words of Aristotle himself.

Note these three points in which this is clearly the case :—

(1) On *Phys.* I. i. Aquinas comments, ' Ens mobile est subiectum Naturalis Philosophiae.' Compare ll. 133, 134 of this chapter of the *Convivio*: 'Siccome nella Scienza naturale è suggetto il corpo mobile.' This is not found *totidem verbis* in the *Translatio* itself.

(2) Next compare ll. 136–140 with the following from the *Summa Libri* given by St. Thomas : 'Naturalia principia . . . tria esse statuit, *materiam* scilicet, ac *formam* per se, *privationem* vero per accidens.'

(3) There is no reference in this part of the *Physics* to the Pythagorean doctrine about numbers, though there are many such in the *Metaphysics* (by which I was misled in adopting the conjectural correction in the *Oxford Dante*). But observe the comment of St. Thomas on the words of the *Ant. Translatio* of the *Physics, h. l.*: '*alii* autem imparem et parem' (corresponding with the vague Greek ἕτεροι) ' quorum aliqui posuerunt principia parem et imparem, *scilicet Pythagorici* existimantes substantiam omnium esse numerum.' These words correspond exactly with ll. 144–147 in Dante.

[1] For the proof of Dante's use of this Translation see *Studies in Dante*, i. pp. 305 *seqq.*, and especially pp. 316–318.

Hence beyond all doubt the reading of the MSS., *Fisica*, should be retained.

Mr. Wicksteed has lately called my attention to another case in *Quaestio* xxi. 56 *seqq.*, and especially l. 59. In *De Coelo* II. 5 (287 *b* 31) the *Antiqua Translatio* has ' magnae *promptitudinis*' for προθυμίας, on which St. Thomas comments 'magnae promptitudinis idest magnae *praesumptionis*,' and this is the word given by Dante in his quotation (l. 60).

Professor Sandys, in a Paper read before the British Academy on Roger Bacon, casts a similar suspicion upon a vague reference of his to Plato for the statement that ' that State is the best ordered in which every one is in the dark about his own kindred.' The Professor says that it seems far less probable that Bacon had a first-hand knowledge of the *Republic* than that he found this saying in Avicenna, whom he quotes immediately before and immediately after this passage.

There is another curious instance in which Dante, when apparently quoting Aristotle, is evidently indebted to the commentary of Aquinas. See note *infra* on IV. xiii. 71, and also *Studies*, i. p. 105.

II. xiv. 234.

I have ventured to adopt Giuliani's emendation of *vuole* for *volge* or *volve*. For (1) the change is very slight ; (2) it seems extremely natural from its use in the statement parallel to this five lines above; (3) as Giuliani observes, it is not a question of what Astrology *does*, but of what it *demands* from those who study it ; (4) *volve* or *volge* may have been suggested by 'association of ideas' with 'tempo' (on this influence in changes of text *vide Textual Criticism*, p. 404 *fin.*).

II. xv. 41-43.

. . . mostra la Fisica, siccome nel quinto del primo suo libro è provato.

Though there is no question of ' reading' in this passage, I may take the opportunity of correcting the suggestion, tentatively made, in *Studies*, i. p. 153, as to a possible explanation of the peculiar form of this quotation reference. I owe now the true explanation (as I do not doubt it to be) to

Mr. Wicksteed. It appears that Albertus Magnus uses
'Physica' (*scil.* philosophia) as a feminine singular to include
the whole study of 'corpus mobile.' Compare *Conv.* II. xiv.
133, 'nella Scienza naturale è suggetto il corpo mobile¹,' and
ibid., l. 60, 'la Scienza naturale, che *Fisica* si chiama.' Albertus
includes under this wide sense of 'Physica' the Psychology,
Natural History, Astronomy, and Meteorology of Aristotle,
and he goes on to enumerate them and much more as divisions
of 'Physica'². In Albertus Magnus we find the 'Physics' in
the narrower sense (as a neuter plural) described as 'Primus
Liber' of the 'Scientia quae est de mobili simpliciter accepto,
non contracto ad materiam,' i.e. 'Primus Liber Scientiae
Naturalis.' See *Conv.* II. xiv. 59, 'All' ottava spera . . .
risponde la Scienza naturale, che *Fisica* si chiama.' Also
Aquinas, at the beginning of his Commentary on the Physics,
says 'Quia liber Physicorum, cuius expositioni intendimus, est
primus liber scientiae naturalis, in eius principio oportet,' &c.,
and in the Prooemium to his Commentary on the *De Generatione et Corruptione* he describes that treatise as 'tertia pars
Scientiae Naturalis.' Mr. Wicksteed also informs me that
in the printed Avicenna, throughout the *Physics,* we find
'sufficientie *libri primi*³; and for the *De Coelo et Mundo,*
'sufficientie Libri *secundi.*' Observe that in *Conv.* II. iii. 30
Dante himself describes the *De Coelo et Mundo* as '*secondo de'
Libri naturali.*'

Hence the general Science of Physics sets forth the doctrine
here described by Dante in the fifth (Book) of the first of the

---

¹ Comp. Arist. *Metaph.* V. i : φυσικὴ . . . θεωρητικὴ περὶ τοιοῦτον ὃν ὃ ἐστι
δυνατὸν κινεῖσθαι.

² Mr. Wicksteed also points out that Albertus (Tract. I, cap. i) says :—'Ultima
autem (the notice of Metaphysica and Mathematica having preceded) est Physica,
quae tota secundum esse et rationem concipitur cum motu et materia sensibili.'

Mr. Wicksteed also points out to me that in Avicenna's introduction to the
De Anima he describes as the successive 'libri' that he has already dealt with :—
(1) The *Physics* ; (2) The *De Coelo* ; (3) *De Generatione et Corruptione* ; (4) The
Meteorica ; (5) *De Mineralibus.*

³ It seems probable that 'sufficientie' represents a genitive singular ; since
Professor Margoliouth has kindly explained to me that 'Avicenna's reproduction
of Aristotle is called the "Book of Shifa" of which "Sufficientia" is a fair
translation '.

divisions of that whole Science: viz. in the fifth Book of the *Physics* (in the more restricted sense) of Aristotle. The passage quoted thus occurs in Arist. *Phys.*, Bk. V, c. i. But Dante's references never include the chapter, and there is no evidence that the division of chapters then existed.

II. xv. 129.

> La giustizia legale ordina le scienze [1] ad apprendere.

This seems to be admitted by editors to be the reading of MSS. generally, though π and σ are stated on the authority of Fraticelli and Giuliani respectively to read ' ordina gli uomini ad apprendere le scienze.' This has the appearance of a *facilior lectio*; and further, *if* I am right in supposing this quotation, which purports to come from *Nic. Eth.*, Bk. V, to be really from I. ii. 6 [2], 'quas enim esse debitum est disciplinarum in civitatibus et quales unumquemque addiscere, et usquequo, haec [politica] praeordinat' (*Antiqua Translatio, h. l.*), the reading above will more nearly, and indeed very closely, correspond with the original of the quotation. It is true that the words *giustizia legale* do not occur in Aristotle, but they would not unfairly represent πολιτική in its function of authoritative legislation (as νομοθετούσης is applied to it by Arist. *loc. cit.*, immediately afterwards), and in the same context he is arguing that πολιτική is the highest form of ἠθική or moral philosophy, of which Dante is here speaking.

II. xv. 135.

> Tutti quelli ricevono quaggiù la virtù, &c.

Pederzini professes to have found this unintelligible, and to have appealed to the Edd. Mil. for help. They suggested in reply the insertion of 'e mandano' after *ricevono*, which has been adopted by Giuliani without comment. Pederzini's ecstasy at this 'improvement' is quite comic. In this 'emenda-

---

[1] The comma after *scienze* in the first edition of the Oxford text should be removed.

[2] See *Studies*, i. p. 103, where I have pointed out that both *h. l.* and in I. xii. 75 it looks as if Dante, when quoting Aristotle on the subject of *Giustizia*, assumed that the passage would naturally be in Bk. V. without 'verifying his references.'

zione bella e sodisfacentissima' all students of the *Convivio* are
laid under an obligation of gratitude to the editors in question,
and he himself is deeply impressed with the 'singolare cortesia,
colla quale si degnarono ascoltare le sue parole'! The strange
thing is that the change seems so entirely unnecessary. All
the other heavens may surely be described as *quaggiù* in reference to the *Primum Mobile,* speaking of which in *Par.* ii. 112–
114 Dante says :—

> 'Dentro dal ciel della divina pace
> Si gira un corpo, nella cui virtute
> L' esser di *tutto suo contento* giace.'

But the question of their further *transmission (i. e. mandano)*
of the influence thus received by them from above is reserved
for the next sentence, 'poco di *loro* virtù quaggiù verrebbe.'
This, again, is recognized in *Paradiso* ii. 123 :—

> 'Che di su prendono, e di sotto fanno.'

II. xv. 157.

> E 'l movimento degli altri sarebbe indarno.

Every modern edition that I have seen substitutes *astri*
for *altri* here, and some of the editors who do so state
that all the MSS. have *altri.* Now there would be no
objection to such a change—*aſtri* and *altri* being in some
MSS. almost undistinguishable—*if* the sense required it. But
(1) I have no doubt that 'altri' means 'altri *cieli,*' these being
in contrast to 'questo' [cielo], l. 137, the actual word 'cielo'
to which this 'questo' refers occurring in l. 132. The sense
seems quite plain. If this heaven ceased to move the motion
of the others would be in vain. Further (2) I can hardly
imagine (though I may be wrong) *astri* being used in ordinary
prose for the stars. The word occurs only once in the *Divina
Commedia,* and there in rhyme (*Par.* xv. 20), and I believe
nowhere else in any of Dante's works.

No doubt the word required to explain *altri* is inconveniently
far off; but Dante often expects his readers to have 'long
memories.' I have noticed many places in the *Convivio* where
demonstrative pronouns, *questo, quello,* &c., are used where we
should have expected the writer, for the sake of clearness, to
have repeated their nouns. In fact, Giuliani often thinks it

necessary to insert them in brackets; as in II. iv. 1 '*dei cieli*' is supplied after *sito*; and *traslazione* after *Nuova* in l. 64 of this chapter, and *Beatrice* after *anima* in II. xiii. 6. In III. vii. 69–88 will be found a sentence of portentous length, in which Edd. Mil., Giul., &c., have inserted *siccome* in l. 80, since the word *perocchè* on which the clause depends is so very distant (l. 69). Even in the next sentence to the present passage the reference of *scritte* (l. 162) to *scienze* (l. 159) is somewhat awkward owing to the new subjects of the intervening clause.

II. xvi. 28–30.

Le quali . . . innamorano l' anima, libera nelle condizioni.

The expression 'libera nelle condizioni' is at first sight a little obscure. Giuliani has, therefore, forthwith substituted ' nelle sue azioni.' But is not '*azioni* dell' anima' a strange expression? If that idea had been intended, we should surely have had *operazioni*. But on the admirable principle (so often and so worthily expounded by Giuliani), 'Dante spiegare con Dante,' the meaning of the words given in the MSS. is not very difficult. They appear to mean—when the soul (*anima*) is free, i.e. unhampered in its conditions or circumstances or surroundings. So the mind (*intelletto*) is described just below in l. 45 as 'libero' and full of certitude when the clouds of doubt (like the morning mists on the face of the sun) have been cleared away. Then a few lines further on (l. 66) Dante speaks of ' *anime libere* dalle misere e vili dilettazioni, e dalli volgari costumi.' When this is so, then the soul is 'libera nelle condizioni.' So again in the important description of the conditions of Free Will in *De Mon.* I. xii. 21 *seqq.*: ' Si ergo iudicium moveat omnino appetitum, et nullo modo praeveniatur ab eo, *liberum est*; si vero ab appetitu, quocunque modo praeveniente, iudicium moveatur, *liberum esse non potest.*' Hence we see clearly that ' anima libera nelle condizioni ' is one that is not hampered or fettered by disturbing passions. Then it is ' salva dalla morte della ignoranza e delli vizi ' (l. 36) : then it is able to receive the demonstrations of Philosophy ' eye to eye ' (l. 28). This last expression again is illustrated

by l. 62 *infra*; and the further idea then introduced, that love
is kindled by that direct and uninterrupted gaze, is amplified
in c. x. ll. 32–48. Finally, for *condizioni* in the sense of
'circumstances' or 'state of things,' compare *Purg.* xx. 13,
14:—

> 'O ciel, nel cui girar par che si creda
> Le condizion di quaggiù trasmutarsi.'

The following are the variants noticed here :—

'libera   } nelle condizioni.'   B α γ δ ε ζ η κ λ μ ξ π ψ.
'liberata'

   „   dalle   „   ' β ρ τ χ.

   „   delle   „   ' σ.

ι ν υ have 'libẽta' which explains 'liberta' in M θ φ.

π has 'deliberata.'

M has 'l' anima mia.' So also ε η θ ι ν υ φ.

III. i. 72.

All editors agree in reporting the absence in the MSS.
of any verb to account for the infinitive *commendare*. It has
been suggested to supply *mi sforzò di lei* (Edd. Mil.); *bramo*
(Giul.); and Monti prefers *impresi* (as in l. 95) or perhaps
proposi. It would be easy to suggest a dozen words that
would equally well fill the gap, but as there appears to be not
the slightest evidence of what Dante wrote, this kind of
'missing word competition' is no part of legitimate criticism.
I should be disposed to insert *di lei*, or at any rate *lei*, since
(1) this word must have been the object of 'commendare'; and
(2) the ὁμοιοτέλευτον of the repeated *lei* would at once explain
the cause of the original blunder of omission. Besides, I may
add that the MSS. B and H have 'da lei di lei commendare.'
I regret not to have gathered further MS. evidence here. The
only course open seems to be to mark a lacuna.

III. ii. 59–61. [See further 'Supplementary Notes', pp. 285 *seqq.*]

> E perocchè nelle bontadi della natura [umana] la ragione si mostra
> della divina, viene, &c.

Thus I would now read (following Edd. Mil.) in this passage,
which I failed to examine in the MSS. These, as reported here,
are in much confusion. The general result is something like
this : 'E perocchè nelle bontadi della natura della ragione si

mostra (*al.* dimostra) la divina vena (*al.* verità B).' It seems to
be agreed that for *vena* we should read *viene*, since 'la divina
vena' in the sense of the divine character, or in some such
figurative sense, seems quite impossible. [See Dr. Jackson's
excellent note upon this, and other points, in his *Convivio* translation, pp. 302, 303.] The misunderstanding of *ragione* may
have contributed to the confusion. It has nothing to do with
'Reason', but seems to signify 'special meaning, character, or
aspect,' in short almost any of the meanings of the Aristotelian
λόγος. A valuable note on this subject, contributed to
Dr. Jackson by Mr. W. H. V. Reade of Keble College, will
be found in the Translation just referred to, pp. 308, 309.
On this interpretation of the passage we recognize the important truth that the standards of moral excellence for man
must correspond with those which we believe to exist in the
Divine nature. It was reliance on this fundamental principle
which prompted Wesley's indignant outburst upon Whitefield,
who had been enouncing some of the extremist Calvinistic
teaching on the subjects of Predestination and Reprobation,
with the declaration that he had no hesitation in believing
all this to be attributable to God. 'If so,' replied Wesley,
'I can only say that your God would be my Devil.'

III. ii. 124, 125.

Siccome dice il Filosofo massimamente nel terzo *dell' Anima.*

'All MSS.' are declared by editors to read 'nel sesto *del-
l' Anima.*' So at any rate do B, H, and M, which alone
I happen to have examined on this point; and Dr. Toynbee
informs me that this is the reading of the first five editions.
As I observed in *Studies*, i. pp. 37, 144, Dante was so
thoroughly well acquainted with the *De Anima* that he
cannot possibly have been ignorant that it contained only
three books, and therefore the blunder can scarcely be supposed
to have originated with himself. Also if the number were
given in Roman figures, VI might, if carelessly written, be
confused with III. Further, I observed (p. 144) that, though
the several powers of the Soul here mentioned can perhaps
be found 'up and down the *De Anima*, B. III,' yet that there
is a much closer resemblance to the passage in Dante in

Nic. Eth. VI. i. 6—and elsewhere in that book. Since that
volume of *Studies* was published, the late Professor Ritchie
of St. Andrews kindly sent me a suggestion which is ingenious
and attractive, viz. that the *sesto* in the MSS. is correct, and
that *dell'Anima* is a blunder for *dell'Etica*. The word *Anima*
occurs so very frequently throughout this chapter, and the
De Anima itself has been the subject of a considerable part
of it, that it is easy to imagine a copyist assuming that
a reference to it was much more likely than one to the *Ethics*.
Now in *Nic. Eth.* VI. i. 6, we have the division of intellectual
'virtues,' τὸ μὲν ἐπιστημονικόν, τὸ δὲ λογιστικόν κτλ., or as Dante
would read it in the *Antiqua Translatio*: 'hoc quidem
scientificum hoc autem ratiocinativum. Et consiliari enim
et ratiocinari idem.' This seems to be almost directly reproduced by Dante in ll. 126–128. As to the other 'virtues'
'in quello medesimo luogo,' Professor Ritchie suggests that
in these 'certe virtù' Dante is thinking of σύνεσις and εὐβουλία
in VI. ix. and x. If this be so, I think Dante is perhaps
quoting rather from the language of Aquinas' Commentary
h.l. than directly from Aristotle[1]: 'in speculativis in quibus
non est actio est solum duplex opus rationis : scilicet *invenire*
inquirendo et de *inventis iudicare*. Et haec quidem duo opera
sunt rationis practicae, cuius *inquisitio* est consilium, quod
pertinet ad eubuliam, *iudicium* autem de consiliatis, pertinet ad
synesim.' This would appear to justify the MS. reading
inventiva (as in B and M) in l. 130, and the deletion of the
suggested *imaginativa* in the Oxford text. [I believe it was
suggested by Dr. Witte.] Professor Ritchie also notes the
parallel passage in *Summa*, 2². li. 4 r² : 'Ideo eubulia, ad
quam pertinet *inquisitio* consilii, est una de omnibus; non
autem synesis, quae est *iudicativa*.' Cf. *Eth.* VI. x. 2. Compare also *Summa*, *l.c.*, art. 2. *fin.*

I am now inclined to suppose the blunder to have occurred
in the word *Anima* and not in *sesto*, and to read *nel sesto del-
l'* [*Etica*]. The difference too is not so very great between
dellãia and *delletica*.

---

[1] This has been clearly proved to be the case in *Conv.* II. xiv. 145 (v. *supra*,
pp. 60, 61), and probably also in some other passages, by Professor Proto.

III. ii. 155–157.

> *Mente*, che è quel fine, e preziosissima parte dell' Anima.

A quite small point is here involved, but one in which a reading stated to be found in all MSS. (so B H M) and in the first five editions has been confidently altered by the Edd. Mil., followed, I believe, by all subsequent editors. They have altered *quel fine* into *quella fine*, making an adjective of the latter word. But (*a*) is this at all a likely epithet in such a context, and can any parallel usage be produced from Dante? (*b*) Also *fine* seems to be fully explained by *ultima potenza* in l. 115; and in l. 137 *ultima e nobilissima parte* closely resembles *fine e preziosissima parte* in this passage. Thus *fine* would be the perfection or culmination of the Soul. The proposed change seems to give an obviously *facilior lectio*.

III. iii. 118 *seqq.*

> E dico che li miei pensieri (che sono *parlar d' Amore*) su nan dolce, sì che la mia anima, cioè 'l mio affetto, arde di potere ci con la lingua narrare.

The ordinary reading here is 'li miei pensieri, che so *parlar d' Amore*, **sono di lei**, sì che,' &c.

Observe Dante is here analysing the first ten or twelve lines of the *Canzone*. He points out that it describes two *ineffabilità*, two kinds of things or thoughts that he is unable to reproduce in language in regard to the converse of Love within his mind (*Amor, che nella mente mi ragiona*, &c., l. 1). This converse he has already explained to be his own thoughts dwelling in Love upon Beatrice ('i miei pensieri, di costei ragionando,' l. 104), and this is again stated in the present passage. Now (1) some of these thoughts surpass the understanding itself, which is baffled even as the sight is, when objects are too far removed from the eye (ll. 105–114), and these obviously, therefore, cannot be expressed in language (*Canz.* ll. 1–4), as has been fully explained in the previous paragraph of the text. But (2) other thoughts, even if within the understanding, are so ineffably sweet that they transcend the power of expression in words. This at least is what we should expect Dante to say here in the Com-

mentary, following quite naturally the sequence of the lines
in the *Canzone* commented on, viz. ll. 5–8. So clearly are
these two distinct ideas (defect of *understanding* and defect
of *language*) fixed in his mind that he proceeds to emphasize
them by repetition in the *Canzone*, in ll. 9–13, and indeed
by a further or double repetition, in ll. 16–18. Moreover,
we have the same two 'ineffabilità' clearly distinguished in
Par. i. 5, 6 :—

> Vidi cose che ridire
> Nè *sa*, nè *può* chi di lassù discende,

and the distinction is insisted on in the comment on this in the
Epistle to Can Grande, § 29, 'Diligenter quippe notandum est
quod dicit *nescit et nequit.* *Nescit*, quia oblitus; *nequit*,
quia, si recordatur et contentum tenet, sermo tamen deficit [1].'
Many other passages in the *Paradiso* will occur to every one
in which sometimes one and sometimes the other of these
'ineffabilità' are pleaded by Dante in excuse for the insuffi-
ciency of his language (e.g. xiv. 79–81 ; xviii. 8–12 ; x. 70–73,
&c.). Once more, see the next chapter here, ll. 37 *seqq.*,
where the distinction is repeated between 'la debilità dell' intelletto e la cortezza del nostro parlare.' Also *Conv.* III.
i. 11, 12.

It is perfectly clear then that the passage before us is
a comment or paraphrase of ll. 5 *seqq.* of the *Canzone*, and
it seems necessarily to follow that some corruption lurks in
the words *sono di lei.* For (1) in the *Canz.*, l. 5, there is
nothing said as to the *object* of his thoughts, nothing, that
is, to correspond to *di lei*; and (2) on the other hand in the
text here there is nothing to correspond to *sì dolcemente*, which
is the prominent thought of l. 5 in the *Canzone*. I cannot but
believe, therefore, that the text should read '*suonan dolce*,
sì che,' &c., especially as it is easy to trace the causes of the
corruption. My MS. reads *sono ĩ lei*, which is very significant,
since the word *in* (not *di*) at once suggests that *sono in* is

---

[1] Compare also the curious passage in § 29 of the same Epistle: 'Multa
namque per intellectum videmus quibus signa vocalia desunt; quod satis Plato
insinuat in suis libris per assumptionem metaphorismorum : multa enim per
lumen intellectuale vidit quae sermone proprio nequivit exprimere.'

probably a corruption of *sonŏ* or *suonŏ*. It may be noted
that in MSS. of the *Divina Commedia sono* and *suono* are
very often interchanged, and it need hardly be added that
the superposed mark (~) is frequently overlooked. Note
further how easily *dolce* or *dolci* (as it was very likely to be
written to agree with *pensieri*) could be mistaken for *dilei*.[1]
It amounts to little more than the confusion of 'o' and 'i' for
the second letter, and 'i's' were often not dotted. Suppose
then that the original was *suonŏ dolce*. This could easily
be misread either *suono* (or *sono*) *di lei* or *sono in di lei*. The
omission of the superfluous preposition *di* would naturally
follow, so that we should at once arrive at the readings found
at present in MSS.—*sono di lei* (as most have, in fact sixteen
out of twenty-five examined) or *sono in lei* (as my MS. reads
with six others).

Dr. Witte strangely proposes to read ' ai miei pensieri lo
suo parlare d' Amore sona sì dolce.' Not only does this deal
rather freely with the text, but it seems to involve a misunderstanding of the sense required. *Love* is himself the speaker,
la Donna is the subject spoken of. What, therefore, can be
the sense of ' lo *suo* parlare *d' Amor*'? And again, as appears
from l. 104 of the text, '*ai* miei pensieri' would be wrong,
since the *ragionamenti di costei* attributed to Love are
identified with the *pensieri* of Dante, not *addressed* to them.

III. v. 101 *seqq.*

In this passage the MS. readings have been pronounced
unintelligible, and have given rise to several conjectural
emendations.

The reading of my MS., which differs very little from the
lect. vulg. as given by Fraticelli, is as follows:—

'e di spazio, da qualunque parte si tira la corda, dieci mila dugento
miglia, cioè X^m CC, *e lì*, tra l' una e l' altra, mezzo lo cerchio di tutta
questa palla.'

(The punctuation is of course not in the MS.)

For *e lì* other MSS. have *egli*, and for *parte*, *lato*.

---

[1] I noted, in fact, in one MS. that ' dilei' might easily have been mistaken for
' dolce', if not carefully looked at.

Fraticelli inserts *sia di* before *dieci mila*, alters *di spazio* to *lo spazio*, omits *egli* or *e lì* altogether, and inserts *cioè* before *mezzo*.

Giuliani adopts *lo spazio* as above, inserts *di* before *dieci mila*, alters *e lì tra* into *infra*, and finally inserts *cioè* before *mezzo*.

Witte reads *e spazio* (omitting *di*) and also inserts *cioè* before *mezzo*. Further, he reads *evvi* for *egli* or *e lì*, following the reading of his own MS.

It seems to me that absolutely no change is necessary except reading *e sì* for *e lì*, the difference between *e lì* and *e sì* being almost infinitesimal.

Then the translation will be:—'Let us imagine another city, to be called Lucia; and of space, in whatever direction the line is drawn, 10,200 miles, and so, between one city and the other, half the circumference of the whole globe.'

I omitted, unfortunately, to collate this passage further: but the change proposed is so extremely slight that it is hardly necessary to produce MS. evidence for it.

III. v. 154.

I reprint here a note on this passage from *Studies*, iii. pp. 107, 108.

This passage involves a difficult piece of textual criticism, since the text in all the MSS. is so corrupt as to be quite unintelligible. Before therefore attempting to explain it, we must endeavour to recover, if possible, the true reading. I have discussed this point in the *Bullettino della Società Dantesca Italiana*, N. S. vol. ix, fasc. 5–6, p. 131.

The following is an abbreviation of the note in question.

Dante is describing the maximum altitude of the Sun at the North Pole at the Summer Solstice. Now as the sun is then at the Tropic of Cancer, his altitude must obviously be $23\frac{1}{2}°$, since the Equator is the horizon of the Pole. The difficulty lies in the fact that Dante does not directly mention this figure (which he knew quite well, see l. 139), but, instead of doing so, gives merely a rough illustration of the Sun's height, saying that it is about as much ('quasi tanto quanto') as it is under the conditions presented to us in such confusion in the MSS.

Now the text in about thirty MSS. which I have examined is as follows :—

'Io suo montare è a Maria quasi tanto quanto esso monta a noi
{ nella mezza terra,
alla mezza terra,   } che è del giorno e della†mezza†notte eguale.'
nel mezzo della terra,

It was long ago suggested by Dionisi (*Anedd.* iv. p. 76) that we should read 'mezza *terza*' for 'mezza *terra*'. This is an expression found in Dante (*Inf.* xxxiv. 96, and *Conv.* IV. xxiii. 153), meaning 7.30 a.m., since *Terza* is 9 a.m. It is not found here, as far as I know, in any MS.; but any one familiar with MSS. will be aware (1) that *terza* (i.e. *terça* or even *terca*) and *terra* are very easily confused ; and (2) that the phrase *mezza terza*, being comparatively rare, would be sure to be mistaken by many copyists for *mezza terra*. But unfortunately the conjecture of Dionisi gives no sense to the passage. For the Sun 'with us' (wherever that might be) never rises to the height required at 7.30 a.m., *except at the Equator*, as to which, after Dionisi's alteration, nothing is said in the text. I am convinced therefore that *both* the expressions *mezza terra* and *mezza terza* are required. I propose, therefore, to read the passage thus :—

'Io suo montare è a Maria quasi tanto quanto esso monta a noi nella mezza terra [*or* nel mezzo della terra] alla mezza terza, ch' è del giorno e della notte eguale,' i.e. 'the sun's altitude at the North Pole [at the summer solstice] is roughly that which we should find at the Equator at 7.30 a.m. at the time of the Equinox.'

Certainly, if we read the text thus, the meaning is perfectly clear. Three conditions are implied, (1) the spectator is at the Equator ; (2) the hour is 7.30 a.m.; (3) the season is the Equinox.

Now Dante describes a few lines below very graphically the appearance of the Sun's revolution at the Equator on the day of the Equinox. It is a vertical revolution like that of a wheel (not, as when seen from the Pole, a horizontal revolution like that of a millstone[1]), of which only one half is visible to the spectator, i. e. 180°. Consequently, at noon, the sun's altitude is 90°, and at 7.30 a.m. it is $\frac{90}{4}$°, i.e. 22$\frac{1}{2}$°. Thus we have a very good rough illustration of the sun's altitude at the North Pole at the summer solstice, that being exactly 23$\frac{1}{2}$°. The narrow limit of error, being only 1°, is far less than could possibly be detected by the eye. Observe, finally, how natural are the steps by which the proposed text, if original, would become corrupted into its present form. These are the stages :—

    1. quanto esso monta a noi nel mezzo della terra [*or* nella mezza terra] alla mezza terza ch' è, &c.

    2. quanto esso monta a noi nel mezzo della terra [*or* nella mezza terra] alla mezza terra ch' è, &c.

Next would follow the omission of one of these superfluous descriptions of the same thing, which were naturally suspected of having arisen from a ' conflate' reading ; and we should then have

    3. quanto esso monta a noi nel mezzo della terra [*or* nella mezza terra] ch' è, &c.

as in the MSS. at present [2].

I ought to say a word as to the superfluous word *mezza* before ' notte.' I have found it, so far, in all MSS., but it makes no sense, and I suspect that it represents the second *mezza* of the original text gone astray.

There are two difficulties to be noticed, though neither perhaps very serious. (1) The expression ' noi ' is strange as applied to the uninhabitable Equator; for so Dante generally considers it, though the Garamantes are spoken of in this passage as living there, and at any rate ' we ' may be thought to have more possible relations with the Equator than with the wholly inaccessible Pole, nowhere near which was any life

---

[1] See ll. 176 (*rota*) and 147 (*mola*). But in the first of these passages (l. 176) Giuliani has most deplorably altered the text—' non a modo di vite ma di mola '— thus entirely obliterating Dante's admirably clear illustration.

[2] The MSS. vary between ' nel mezzo della terra,' ' nella mezza terra,' and ' alla mezza terra.'

conceivable ; (2) the last clause, ' che è del giorno,' &c., is a
very harsh expression to describe when there is equality of
day and night. But in archaic Italian, and in the writings of
Dante frequently, ' che' is a connecting particle of extreme
flexibility of meaning, e.g. see Sonnet I, l. 6 :—

> ' Del tempo che (= when) ogni stella è più lucente.'

Inf. ii. 102 :—

> ' al loco dov' io era,
> Che (= where) mi sedea con l' antica Rachele.'

Add *Inf.* i. 3, 12; xxvi. 22; *Purg.* xxi. 53; *Par.* i. 27; x. 142;
xxvii. 79, &c.; *Conv.* III. i. 17, 18; III. xiii. 64; II. ix. 46.

Without saying that many of these are precisely similar
to the case in the text, they seem to show that *che* may stand
for almost any connecting particle. See also *Diz. Tomm. e
Bell.*, s.v. *che*, No. 10 (p. 1368).

III. vi. 47, 48.

> Conoscendo Lui, tutte le cose conoscono secondo il modo della
> intelligenza.

The nominative to ' conoscono' is surely ' Intelligenze' as
far back as l. 35, but practically repeated in ' ciascuno Intelletto' in l. 39. But its inconvenient distance has caused
trouble both to copyists and editors. Thus B has *conoscono si*;
H has *conoscendosi* ; M has *che conoscono*. Several editions
have *conosconsi*. Clearly, I think, as *Intelligenze* is the subject,
so *tutte le cose* is the object of *conoscono*. This not only suits
the context, but surely *tutte le cose* would be strangely used
as the subject since *intelligenza* could scarcely be attributed
to this wide term.

For other examples of a somewhat distant subject word,
see note on II. xv. 157 ; and again see in this chapter l. 116,
where *l' anima* has been inserted by some editors to help short
memories, since the word itself occurs as far back as l. 112.

III. vii. 23 *seqq.* (esp. ll. 31, 32).

Dante is here showing that Divine influence, though itself
one and indivisible, is very varied in its effects in consequence
of the different receptive qualities of the beings or objects on
which it falls. He illustrates this by the different effects of

the light of the Sun upon different objects (l. 22): for, as he says in III. xii. 52, ' Nullo sensibile in tutto 'l mondo è più degno di farsi esemplo di Dio, che 'l sole.' The same truth is enforced by the same illustration in III. xiv. 21–28. It seems to me that Dante here distinguishes four classes of objects.

(1) (ll. 28–34.) Some have a sort of ' latent diaphaneity' [1] of their own ('per molta chiarità di diafano avere in sè mista'), which, combining with the kindred light of the Sun—(this exactly corresponds to *sup.*, l. 21, ' riceve . . . secondo il modo della sua virtù e del suo essere')—renders them intensely bright. Hence the Sun's light + their own produces a ' multiplication' of light. Gold and precious stones are given as examples.

(2) (ll. 34–38.) Some are so entirely transparent that they allow to pass through the whole of the Sun's light and also transmit with it some of their own colour, which is thus transferred to other objects. Coloured glass (comp. c. ix. 95–99) would be an obvious example, though it is not specifically mentioned.

(3) (ll. 38–43.) Objects entirely reflecting, e. g. mirrors.

(4) (ll. 43–45.) Objects entirely opaque, e. g. earth.

This is all borrowed from the passage to which Dante himself refers in Albertus Magnus. It is as follows, and it will be seen at a glance how many of its expressions are reproduced by Dante:—

(1) ' Propter multam victoriam et per mixtionem perspicui clari in corporibus terminatis [2], videmus quosdam colores in luminis adventu scintillantes et spargentes lumen ad illuminationem aliorum: (2) et aliquando, si vere in toto sit perspicuum corpus coloratum si lumen superveniat, illi colores colorant alia corpora sibi apposita, sicut videmus in vitro colorato, per quod lumen veniens secum trahit colorem vitri, et ponit eum super corpus cui per vitrum incidit lumen. (3) Quaedam autem sunt ita vincentia [3] (' overpowering') in puritate diaphani, quod adeo radiantia efficiuntur quod vincunt harmoniam oculi, et videri sine magna difficultate non possunt. (4) Quaedam autem sunt spargentia tantum

---

[1] I use this phrase on the analogy of the old theory of 'latent' heat.

[2] Comp. *Conv.* III. iv. 12, where Dante says of his mind that it receives light or truth, and that his mind, ' come corpo *diafano*, riceve quello non *terminando*,' i. e. it retains it, and does not reflect it back.

[3] Cf. ' vincente' similarly used III. ix. 119.

luminis et diaphani, quod vix discerni possunt visu propter parvitatem suae compositionis ex perspicuo, cuius proprius actus est lumen.' [Alb. Mag., *De Intellectu et Intelligibili*, Lib. I. Tract. iii. Cap. 2, vol. v. p. 250, Ed. Lugduni, 1651.]

I have inserted the figures to exhibit more clearly the four classes indicated by Dante. It is curious that Dante gives examples of Classes 1, 3, and 4, but not of Class 2, while Albertus gives an example of Class 2 only.

Returning to the first class, in reference to which the difficulty of reading occurs, in ll. 31, 32, we note that (1) ' per mixtionem perspicui clari ' corresponds with ' per molta chiarità di diafano avere in sè mista '; (2) ' in luminis adventu ' corresponds with ' tosto che 'l sole gli vede '; (3) ' spargentes lumen ad illuminationem aliorum ' corresponds with ' rendono agli altri di sè grande splendore.' The intermediate words, in which the difficulty arises, seem to have been added by Dante. I think the ' multiplicamento di luce '[1] refers to the combination of the Sun's light from without with their own inherent or ' latent ' light, the latter being perhaps referred to as the ' luce in quelli,' and the former as the ' luce in lo loro aspetto.' I would propose therefore to read thus :—

' per multiplicamento di luce in quelli e 'n lo loro aspetto, e' rendono agli altri,' &c.

This seems to me to give a clear sense to the passage, having regard to its quotation from Albertus, and there is practically no difference of reading, but only the interpretation to be given to the highly ambiguous word ' e,' which occurs twice in l. 32. When the *Oxford Dante* was first published I had only the evidence of two MSS., both of which read ' è ' in the first of these instances, which I therefore felt bound to follow in the

---

[1] The sense seems indeed almost determined by a closely parallel passage in *Conv.* IV. xxi. 71 *seqq.* :

' E s' egli avviene che, per la purità dell' anima ricevente, la intellettuale Virtù sia bene astratta e assoluta da ogni ombra corporea, la divina bontà in lei *multiplica*, siccome in cosa sufficiente a ricevere quella : e quindi si *multiplica* nell' anima di questa intelligenza, secondochè ricever può.'

We may also compare *De Mon.* I. xv. 50–53: '. . . forma . . . una in se multiplicatur, secundum multiplicationem materiae recipientis.'

absence of further information. I have now examined several other MSS. with the following result :—

'e (*or* et) lo loro' . . . in 18
'è'. . . . . „ 2
'ee' (ambiguous) . . . „ 7
'e i loro aspetto' . . . „ 1 (γ) [probably = e ĩ, *i.e.* e 'n]

in the second case—

'e (*or* et) rendono' . . „ 19
ambiguous 'errendono' . „ 4

But as I have pointed out before (*supra*, p. 7), very little reliance can be placed on MSS. when such alternatives as *e, et, è, ẽ,* and *e'* are in question, the distinguishing marks being very commonly omitted. If therefore we read, as I now propose, 'e 'n lo loro aspetto, e' rendono,' we do not go beyond what is justified by the MSS. Some of those editors who read 'è lo loro aspetto, e rendono,' feeling the need of a predicate for *è,* boldly insert before it *e conj.* 'appena discernibile,' e. g. Edd. Mil., Pederzini, Fraticelli. But though we find in Albertus the words 'vix discerni possunt,' they occur in a different context and relate to a different class of the objects discriminated, viz. the *fourth,* and not the *first.*

How easily 'è' and 'en' (*or* 'e 'n') are interchanged may be seen from the occurrence of both readings in *Purg.* xvi. 121, *Par.* xv. 77, and the well-known line *Par.* iii. 85, 'E (*or* E 'n) la sua volontate è nostra pace,' and elsewhere.

III. vii. 117.

The text is set down by editors as being very corrupt, but, as I think, unnecessarily. There is very little variation in the twenty-four MSS. which I have examined here except one or two blunders (see *infra*) easily accounted for. It may be taken that the passage stands practically thus :—

'... si rappresentano. Onde siccome la immagine delle corpora in alcuno corpo lucido si rappresenta, siccome nello specchio: così la immagine corporale che lo specchio dimostra non è vera: così la immagine della ragione . . . non è vera.'

Now it has usually, I believe, been accepted that the passage must be rearranged thus :—

'. . . si rappresentano, siccome la immagine delle corpora in alcuno corpo lucido si rappresenta. Onde siccome nello specchio la immagine corporale che lo specchio dimostra non è vera ; così, &c.

The changes involved are (1) the transposition of 'Onde' to a later clause and (2) the omission of the first 'così.' The changes of punctuation are a matter of editing only.

It will be noticed that in the Oxford text the MS. reading is followed with exception of substituting 'e' for the first 'così.' I have since seen that Dr. Witte (*Giorn. Accad.* 1825) suggested the substitution of 'ma' for 'così.' But 'e' seems a slighter change, and therefore preferable.

I had then the evidence of only two MSS. Since that, I have examined about a score of others, with the result that seventeen of these read *così*, as in the two MSS. previously consulted. Two, however, read *e così*. With this evidence I should perhaps have retained *così* while inserting *e*, and I have done so in the third edition. For though it is rather awkward and superfluous, it gives an intelligible sense.

The evidence seems to me to point to something like this. Dante may perhaps have written *e* or *e così*. In the former case a copyist may have changed *e* into *così*, being in too great a hurry to supply *siccome* with its complementary clause. In the latter case, one who thought (short-sightedly, but copyists are often very short-sighted) that this *così* was intended to introduce the complementary cause, may have omitted *e*, which in that case would be clearly superfluous.

In any case the reading which I have proposed involves an extremely slight change, one not without some MS. support, and one from which, if original, the variations in other MSS. are easily accountable.

Two MSS. omit the words '*e così . . . non è vera*,' occurring after *specchio*. This is probably due to ὁμοιοτέλευτα, *così* coming at the beginning of two clauses in juxtaposition.

It is hardly perhaps necessary to remark that *lucido* has its regular signification of a bright *reflecting*, not *refracting*,

surface, i.e. it is not (as sometimes mistranslated, e.g. at *Purg.*
xv. 69) transparent, or translucent. Besides that passage the
following may be referred to in illustration : *Purg.* vii. 74, and
especially *Conv.* III. ix. 80, where *trasparente* and *lucida* stand
in contrast. So also *traluce* of the reflecting surface of bur-
nished gold in *Par.* xxi. 28. This is the regular meaning
of *lucido* in Ristoro d'Arezzo. Also in *Legenda Aurea*
(ed. Graesse), p. 43, we find three classes of bodies distinguished : (1) *opaca* ; (2) *transparens, sive pervia* ; (3) *lucida*.

III. viii. 36.

I believe the reading I adopted in the *Oxford Dante* in this
passage is correct. The only change which I introduced into
the MS. reading (with the slight evidence then before me) was
to omit *e* between *piaceri* and *intra*, and to enclose the words
intra gli altri di quelli in a parenthesis. Giuliani (*more suo*),
finding no reference to any *other* pleasures in the passage of
the *Canzone* commented on, simply omits the words in question and reads *piaceri di Paradiso*, bringing the words into
the exact form of the line in the *Canzone*. But the 'other
pleasures' intended by Dante are actually set forth in III. xv.
111–115, 'Poi quando dico : *Sua beltà piove fiammelle di fuoco*,
discendo a un *altro piacere di Paradiso*, cioè della felicità
secondaria a questa prima, la quale dalla sua *beltate* procede.'
This shows the words here to be genuine, and explains clearly
what was in Dante's mind in speaking of 'other pleasures.'
Also the partitive gen. '*dei* piaceri' is consistent with this.

The reading (with slight variations) was found in twenty
MSS. out of twenty-four examined, the other four substituting
an unmeaning *quali* for *altri*. It is to be observed that the
omission of *e* before *intra*, as in my text, is now supported by
three MSS. (B M *ι*).

III. viii. 178–183.

I wish to make a 'retractation' of a note which I wrote
upon this passage in my first series of *Studies* (pp. 145, 146)
and to correct the text in accordance with a suggestion which
I then made, though then only to reject it. It will of course be
remembered that in most MSS. of the *Convivio* the punctua-

tion is not in the least to be depended upon. It is often very scanty and sometimes quite haphazard, and in this respect conjecture may claim a fairly free hand. I would now read the passage thus :—

'del tutto non se ne vanno quanto al primo movimento (ma vannosene bene del tutto, quanto a durazione), perocchè la consuetudine non è equabile alla natura, nella quale è il principio di quelle.'[1]

Bad passions acquired by habit can be wholly eradicated by contrary habit; those which are innate, depending on the peculiar nature or constitution of the individual, can be completely conquered by habit in respect of their *continuance* or '*duration*,' though not in respect of their first motions. The 'motions of sins... working in our members' (to use St. Paul's phrase) will be aroused on occasions by a sort of physical necessity, but being immediately checked by the control of a moral habit, they will have no 'duration,' as Dante puts it, and so a man may be 'tempted yet without sin.' The effective control of habit is thus limited, because the strength of habit is not equivalent to that of nature :—

'Naturam expelles furca, tamen usque recurret.'

I am glad to be relieved of the rash and almost desperate course of recommending the omission of a 'non' supported by MS. authority. When I ventured on this I was aware that 'non' was 'found in all the MSS. hitherto examined,' but that number was comparatively small. I was not aware, as I am now, that all the known MSS. are unanimous in supporting it.

III. ix. 79 *seqq.*

This is not a passage of much importance in itself, but as it illustrates something of a principle, it may be worth a brief notice. The general meaning is clear enough. Dante is explaining the phenomenon of vision. The object, or rather its 'form,' passing though the medium of the colourless fluid of the pupil, is 'stopped' (*terminata*) by the retina (as the ray of light is stopped by the lead at the back of a looking-glass), and then first, and on the same principles, becomes visible, and

---

[1] The emendation of this passage is primarily due to Dr. Jackson—see his translation of the *Convivio*, pp. 156, 303-4.

'so (he concludes) the "form" which does not show in the transparent medium, becomes bright when it is stopped.' Some editions, e. g. Edd. Mil. and Frat. (the latter, however, suggesting alteration in his note), put the comma after, instead of before, *lucida*. This seems quite to destroy the meaning of the passage. Giuliani, arbitrarily and quite unnecessarily, changes *lucida è terminata* into *luce dov' è terminata*. I say 'quite unnecessarily,' because it does not alter the meaning, and I think no attentive reader can fail to notice that it is characteristic of Dante's prose style [1] to use past participles and even adjectives sometimes to express various temporal, causal, and other logical relations, when later writers would generally add particles expressive of such relations. This is no doubt one of the many traces of the strong influence of Latin impressed upon Dante's *Volgare*. If this be so, an emendation intended to 'remedy' such peculiarities is not only unnecessary, but has something of a presumption against it. I feel sure (MS. evidence apart) that Dante would have been more likely to have expressed the required idea by the words *lucida è terminata*, than by the smoother phrase *luce dov' è terminata*. In any case one must again enter the protest which the treatment in some editions of the text of the *Convivio* renders necessary, that it is no part of an editor's business to 'touch up' his author's style, or to improve the elegance of his diction.

III. ix. 119.

E però [non] pare più lucente.

In this case it seems really necessary to adopt the suggestion of Witte to insert 'non,' since the whole context requires that *stella* should be the subject of the verb, though superficially it might seem to be *lo mezzo*, i.e. the atmosphere. I think it is possible that the unnoticed *mutatio subiecti* may have caused the mistake of omitting *non* in some very early copy. I find no trace of *non* in any of the MSS. (29) which I have examined in this passage, and I observe that neither

---

[1] V. *supra*, p. 17. And not of his prose style only, as there are several striking instances in the *Divina Commedia*, where also they have in some cases provoked alteration of the text, e. g. *Purg.* i. 48, x. 30, xix. 132 ; or an adjectival expression as *di pietra*, *Inf.* xvii. 24.

Witte nor editors who have followed him in the insertion of
'non' plead any MS. authority for it. (V. *supra*, p. 12.)

III. xi. 24.

Though *seicento* is clearly an error for *settecento*, there is
no variation in the date in any of the MSS. examined, except
that one has 'seicento cinquant' anni cinque.'   But two MSS.
(Tr and μ) have vi^{c}l, from which it can be seen at once how
easily another 'i' might have been dropped.   So again M
reads 'secento cinquanta anni, cioè cccccc$^{ol^a}$ poco dal più,' &c.
Here the superscript 'o' (which seems out of place as
implying an *ordinal* number) might easily have arisen from
a seventh 'c'. (See further *supra*, p. 19.)

Errors in numerals, especially with the cumbrous system
of Roman notation, were frequently made by scribes.   It is
curious to find Bede complaining of this: 'Numeri ... negli-
genter describuntur et negligentius emendantur' (from Plummer's note, i. p. lvi).

Another error of the same kind occurs in II. vi. 24, where
the MSS. have xiii and xiiii.   See note *supra* on that
passage.

I have examined nearly thirty MSS. here, and they all
agree in presenting *seicento* in one form or another.

III. xi. 46 *seqq.*

The variations of the text here are as abundant as the
ample opportunity for blundering offered by ὁμοιοτέλευτα might
lead us to expect.

> 'Amatore di sapienza chiamato, cioè *fidosofo*;'

My MS. has :—

> 'Filosofo, che tanto vale come in Greco philos quasi amore e sofia che
> vale a dire amatore di sapientia.'

The Bodleian MS. :—

> '... cioè filosofo ... che tanto vale come [*in Greco* is omitted] filos che
> è a dire amore in latino, e quindi dicemo noi filos quasi amore e sofia quasi
> sapienza per che vedere si può.'

These may be taken as general specimens of the state
of the text in this passage.   Some further MS. evidence

which I have collected is (speaking numerically) as follows :—

'tanto vale in Greco filos che (*or* come) a dire amore'
3 MSS.

' „   „   „   „   „ che viene   „   „' 3 MSS.

'tanto vale come (*or* quanto) in Greco filos {che a dire amore'
che è a dire amore'}
14 MSS.

' „   „   „   „   „   „   „   „ quasi amore' 4 MSS.

There are other minor variations too numerous to mention. The main results might perhaps be summarized thus :—

(1) *Amore* as explaining *filos* before *in Latino* was (I believe) in all the MSS. examined, but as *amatore* occurs correctly just before (at least I have no note to the contrary), this seems to be an obvious blunder which may be legitimately corrected.

(2) Both *come* before *in Greco* and *che* or *ch' è* after *filos* seem fairly well supported.

We might then, I think, read somewhat as follows :—

'Chè tanto vale come in Greco *filos*, ch' è a dire *amatore* in Latino.'

III. xi. 159.

Che chiama *Enea*, &c.

Here all MSS. are said by editors to read *Enea*, though the context in Virgil clearly shows Hector to be addressed, and Aeneas to be the speaker. But it is, I think, very doubtful if we have any right to make the correction, for such a slip of memory is quite conceivable (as Calypso for Circe in *Nic. Eth.* II. ix. 3) on Dante's part ; or even a copyist with the word *Eneida* just before might have written *Enea* in error, and there is nothing in the present context inconsistent with either name. This passage will be found further discussed in *Studies*, i. p. 194, to which reference may be made.

III. xii. 46 *seqq.*

This is a difficult chapter not only, or chiefly, in respect of the text, but rather in respect of its interpretation. I would

paraphrase the passage beginning here somewhat as follows:—
In treating of matters which appertain to the Senses as well
as those which appertain to the Intellect, it is sometimes
advantageous to approach them *indirectly*; so that the things
of Sense may best be treated through things that are not
apprehended by Sense (*insensibili*), and the things of Intellect through things that are not apprehended by Intellect
(*inintelligibili*). In the former case the means employed will
naturally be *above* Sense, but in the latter they will as naturally
be *below* Intellect. Obviously we must not translate the words
by 'intelligible' and 'unintelligible.' Dr. Jackson's translation
slightly modified gives the meaning very clearly: 'As it is
proper to treat of objects of sense, by means of things which
sense cannot perceive, so it is proper to treat of objects of
intellect by means of things which are not grasped by intellect': in effect, by *sensibili*. Indeed one would not be far
wrong if one paraphrased Dante by saying that *Sensibili* are
sometimes best approached through *Intelligibili*, and con-
versely *Intelligibili* are sometimes best approached through
Sensibili. At least this would fairly describe the two actual
processes to which the present passage refers. The former
process might be illustrated by II. xiii. 47–65, where we find
that some persons must be led to the *literal* meaning of things
(like *sensibili* here) through *allegorical* (like *intelligibili* here).
The latter process is that which is explained in the following
context, viz. in which God and His purposes (*intelligibili*) are
approached through a description of the Sun and his functions
in the visible world, i. e. through *sensibili* or *inintelligibili*.
The point which has misled most editors is that they have
failed to see that the *inintelligibili* here are *below* the *intelligibili*, being apprehended by a lower faculty. They have
assumed that they must be *above* them. Thus Giuliani in his
note, p. 372, strangely advocates the (correct) reading *ininteli-
gibili* on the (wrong) ground that '*s' adatta meglio* a significare
le cose che *soverchiano* il nostro intelletto, l' abbagliano sì
che non le può guardare.' Pederzini, followed by Fraticelli,
observes oracularly that what Dante says in this sentence suits
his present purpose, but is entirely contrary to reason, since the

natural course is always to proceed from the more known to the less known ; referring no doubt to the familiar principle ἀρκτέον ἀπὸ τῶν γνωρίμων. Also Monti, *Saggio*, p. 66, protests against 'questa eretica lezione' of a 'Dio intelligibile,' not apparently noticing that He is described only four lines below as 'lo Sole spirituale e *intelligibile*, ch' è Iddio,' and forgetting also that in *Conv.* IV. xxii. 142 Dante says that God is 'sommo intelligibile.' So the sense of the whole passage is that the Divine nature and operations may be 'clearly seen, being understood by the things that are made,' viz. in the present case by the analogy of the Sun in the visible world. See *Ep.* v. 120–125. And thus the *intelligibile* is best approached through the *inintelligibile*.

Another passage very similar to this is found in *Conv.* III. viii. 139 *seqq*.

The MSS. read as follows (in l. 47) :—

(*a*) 'per cosa intelligibile.' (ten), H M P Tr γ δ ζ η λ ω.

(*b*) '   „   non intelligibile' (eight), B Q β θ κ ο ρ F.

(*c*) '   „   inintelligibile' (two), σ *auct.* Giuliani (I seem to have no record). But I think *v* should be added, which has 'intelligibile' (*sic*).

Of course there is no difference of meaning in the two last, but I should prefer 'inintelligibile,' since (1) it forms the most natural antithesis to 'insensibile,' while at the same time (2) the cumbrous form of the word would make the substitution of the supposed more elegant *non intelligibile* very probable ; (3) the duplicated initial 'in-' would be likely to lead to the reading *intelligibile* by a natural blunder. In any case the omission of *in-* would be much more likely than that of *non*, so that, as between (*b*) and (*c*) above, the MSS. under (*a*) might fairly be thought to support (*c*) rather than (*b*). Similarly in IV. viii. 105 we find in some MSS. (e. g. M) 'la reverenza' for 'la irreverenza,' which gives no sense at all. It may be noted that in I. x. 66 we have three variants like those discussed above : 'non litterato' in σ (*auct.* Giul.); 'litterato' in γ (*auct.* Frat.); 'illitterato' in δ and ω (*auct.* Frat.), and 'allitterato' in M.

It may be added that Edd. Mil., Monti, Pederzini, and Fraticelli have *inintelligibile* again in l. 52, where it is obviously entirely out of place. They admit that the change is made against 'tutti i MSS. e le stampe'! But Bisc. and Giul. have *intelligibile* correctly.

III. xiii. 93–95.

> Che sempre attrae la capacità della nostra natura, la quale fa bella e virtuosa.

I cannot imagine why all editors have followed Witte in altering *attrae* into *superata ne è*, for which no claim of any MS. authority is made. It seems to suit neither the preceding nor following context. For *piace* is conformable to *attrae*, but not to *superata ne è*; and also *la quale fa bella e virtuosa* follows naturally from the *attractiveness* of philosophy, but not from its *overpoweringness*. Also *Canz.*, l. 29, ' Oltre il dimando di nostra natura' implies that she gives more to us than we can ' desire or deserve.' ' Beyond our nature's utmost claim or plea ' (Plumptre). This seems more in harmony with the former than the latter attribute. To justify so bold an alteration of the text, the reverse should surely be strongly the case.

III. xiii. 101.

> E qui si vede l' ultima sua lode.

Ultima has been generally accepted here as a conjectural emendation for *umile*, which is supposed to be the reading of all MSS. I have, however, found it in *one* MS. (ι) out of thirty collated in this passage [1]. In any case it is difficult to imagine any intelligible meaning for *umile* in this context. *Ultima* is quite suitable, either in its simple sense of ' last,' since several kinds of praise have been mentioned in succession. *Ultima* would fall in with ' nel *principio* delle lode' in l. 1 of this chapter, and with ' le seguenti commendazioni' in l. 88. Compare also c. xiv, l. 2 and c. xv, l. 155. Or again *ultima* might perhaps better be taken to mean its supreme and highest praise. See *Par.* xxii. 124 and xxxiii. 27. Also *Conv.* I. i. 8 ; xiii. 39; II. viii. 17, and other places. Thus either

[1] ι itself has *umile* in margin.

prima or *ultima* might be used to convey the same meaning as in English we may speak of a *primary* or *ultimate* principle in the same sense. Compare ' la prima sua bontà ' in I. xii. 95. Similarly sometimes ἀρχή and τέλος may become interchangeable, as perhaps in *Nic. Eth.* I. xii. 8.

III. xiv. 99.

    Ch' è per sua cagione, e non per altrui.

In the first place, in the previous line all the MSS. are said to read *secondo*, which has been altered by some editors to *primo*, since the passage, which is very closely followed, is found in Book I, c. 2. But I doubt whether we have a right to correct in the teeth of all MSS. (as it is asserted) a slip of memory such as this might be on the author's part. See further notes on I. xii. 75 (in *Studies*, i. p. 103) ; III. xi. 159 (*supra*, p. 84).

I have not, unfortunately, gathered MS. evidence on this point. But the MSS. are said to read (at any rate B H and M do so) ' che per sua cagione dice.' I think it is very likely that *dice* stands for *di sè* (as possibly *di sì* for *dice* in IV. xviii. 41), and this has been suggested here by Witte, who therefore omits *sua* before *cagione*. In the first edition of the *Oxford Dante* I thought it better to omit *dice*, because it looks as if it were intended to supply a verb to the sentence, the verb ' è ' having been lost in *che* (as it is in B H and M). If ' dice ' be retained with ' ch' è,' it should, I suppose, be printed (dice), the word being thus repeated parenthetically from l. 97. If *di sè* be read, might it be just possible still to retain both it and *sua*, like the Latin construction *sua ipsius causa* ?

III. xv. 64.

    Certissimamente [non] si veggono.

I have examined twenty-eight MSS. in this passage and ' non ' is not found in any of them, but this seems to be a case where we can hardly help inserting ' non,' acknowledging it to be *e conj*. Thus only can these two statements (ll. 64–66) be consistent with the two preceding ones, viz. ' certe cose *affermano essere* ' and ' l' intelletto nostro *guardar non può*.' The only possible escape would seem to be to give the forced interpretation suggested by Pederzini, that *veggono* relates to the mere *fact* of their existence, while *guardar non può* relates to their nature, or the manner of their being. But in that case there is no need for *fede*. The only edition I have seen in which the 'non' is not inserted is that of Biscioni. We might also refer to III. viii. 140, 141, where of the same incomprehensible ideas he says that 'lo intelletto nostro vincono sì che *non può vedere* quello che sono.' When Dante observes that these 'Summa Genera' can only be 'defined' (or rather described) by negatives, i.e. by denying of them qualities belonging to lower genera, we might illustrate this recognized process of Logic by the 'definitions' of the *Quicunque Vult*.

III. xv. 98, and 105 *seqq*.

> Terminato *in quanto* in quella sapienza che la natura di ciascuno può apprendere.

A number of MSS. are quoted here by editors as reading *in quanto*, but apparently all except Biscioni have omitted 'in' or made some other change. I have printed *in quanto* in italics to indicate that I take it to be Latin, i.e. 'in respect of amount.' The general sense of the passage from l. 76 is this :—The object of all desire is knowledge, but the natural desire is in all cases limited or measured by that amount of knowledge which in each case is attainable; else had Nature done something in vain, which is impossible (πρόεισι γὰρ οὕτω γ' εἰς ἄπειρον, *Nic. Eth*. I. ii. 1). This applies to Angels as well as to Man (see *Par*. III. 70 *seqq*.). Even Angels do not 'stretch themselves beyond their measure' in this respect. Thus *in quanto* here means 'in respect of amount.' And in exactly this sense 'nel quanto' is used in *Par*. II. 103. Also 'il quanto e il quale' occurs three or four times for quantity and quality. Edd. Mil., Frat., and Ped. substitute *è* for *in*, and Giul. reads *in quanto ha quella*.

In ll. 105–7 M reads : 'conoscere di iddio e dire altre cose quello esso non sia possibile.' So H, except that 'et' is inserted after 'esso,' in mistake probably (as often) for 'è.'

B reads : 'conoscere iddio e di certe cose quello esso è non sia possibile.'

π (*auct.* Fraticelli, who adopts this reading) quite differently : ' conoscere Dio e certe altre cose, come l' eternità e la prima materia, non sia possibile.' (These words, occurring apparently in this MS. only, seem to me suspiciously like a gloss from *supra*, ll. 63, 64.)

The chief other editors read as follows :—

Edd. Mil. : ' conoscere Dio e altre cose, e dire, " quello esso è," non sia possibile,' &c. (the chief change being the transposition of ' dire').

Giuliani (with his usual freedom of conjecture) : ' conoscere Dio e certe altre cose, cioè, intender quello ch' ei sono, non sia possibile.'

There are few passages as to which I felt more difficulty in coming to a decision, or more doubt as to the form of the passage at last and provisionally adopted in the *Oxford Dante*, since it was necessary to print something intelligible in the text. Since that, however, I have examined a good many MSS. with the following result :—

' di certe altre cose ' (eight MSS.), α δ ζ μ ξ π σ ψ.

' dicere ⎫
' dire   ⎭ altre cose ' (fourteen MSS.), M β γ η θ ι κ λ ν ο ρ τ φ χ.

' di certe cose ' (two MSS.), B υ (' *da* ').

It seems to result that

(1) There is no evidence for the repetition of the syllable *di* in *dire di*, as in some texts.

(2) *altre* is strongly supported. Of the two MSS. at first available to me, one had the word and the other omitted it.

(3) *di certe* and *dicere* are alternative readings ; *dire* being no doubt a later ' improvement' of the latinized and archaic form *dicere*, or, as it would sometimes be written, *diciere* (as ' conosciere' is found just before). Now it is evident that these forms *diciere* and *dicerte* might be easily confused. I noted in fact in one MS. (η) that I was not quite sure which was meant.

The reading that would appear to be thus pointed out would be ' conoscere di Dio, e di certe altre cose,' &c., which I should now be disposed to recommend.

Next as to the following words, printed *quello e' sono* in the *Oxford Dante*. This I felt to be extremely harsh, but as I had only the evidence of two MSS., reading (1) *quello esso non*, &c., and (2) *quello esso e non*, &c., I thought this might represent *quello essoñ*, and this possibly might be resolved into *quello ei sono*. But I now find that twenty-three MSS. here examined read as follows:—

'quello esso e non,'	sixteen MSS.
'quello esso et non,'	three „
'quello esso non,'	three „
'(cose) che sia esso non,'	one „

Hence I am inclined to think that, as far as these words go, the Edd. Mil. are perhaps right, and we should read the whole passage:—'conoscere di Dio, e di certe altre cose, "quello esso è," non sia possibile,' i.e. it is not possible to know about God and certain other things, 'that is this,' or 'that is what it is,' or 'that is so and so.' The same effect might be given in Greek by prefixing the article, thus:—γιγνώσκειν περὶ Θεοῦ, καὶ περί τινων ἄλλων τὸ ὅτι τοῦτό ἐστιν. We might perhaps compare I. xii. 91, 92, 'è da vedere quella, qual è essa.'

The words here form a sort of quotation, or undigested fragment of Oratio Recta, like εἶπεν αὐτῷ τὸ εἰ δύνασαι πιστεῦσαι (St. Mark ix. 23), or again the still stranger expression in Rev. i. 4, ἀπὸ τοῦ ὁ ὢν καὶ ὁ ἦν καὶ ὁ ἐρχόμενος (cf. xvi. 5). There seems to be a fairly close parallel in Arist. *Poet.*, c. iv, § 5, συμβαίνει θεωροῦντας μανθάνειν καὶ συλλογίζεσθαι τί ἕκαστον, οἷον ὅτι οὗτος ἐκεῖνος.

Again in IV. xiii. 28, 29 and 37–39 the same idea is expressed less harshly: 'Ma conoscere che sieno li principii delle cose naturali, e conoscere *quello che sia* ciascheduno.' So the copyist of the MS. who in the present passage wrote 'che sia esso' (vide *supra*) apparently felt that a subjunctive would be more correct, and he thus betrays himself very much as does the scribe who introduced the somewhat similar 'improvement' of an optative (which St. John never uses) in St. John xiii. 24, εἰπὲ τίς ἂν εἴη [*ver. lect.* τίς ἐστι] περὶ οὗ λέγει.

With the phrase ' conoscere *di* Dio,' &c., we might compare St. John vii. 17, ' cognoscet de doctrina utrum,' &c.

III. xv. 170.

Quando suso fermava [l' etera].

On the conjectural insertion of 'l' etera' here on the strength of its occurrence in the passage quoted, see note in *Studies*, i. p. 53, and *supra*, p. 20.

IV. iv. 24.

Ma sempre desideri *terra* acquistare.

Most editions read *gloria* here (e.g. the first four Edd. Bisc., Edd. Mil., Ped., Frat.). Giul. reads *terra*, which he says is found in τ. I have not collated the passage, except in B H M, all of which have *gloria*, and this, I expect, in the absence of any authority but τ being quoted, and in the general consensus of editions, is probably the reading more commonly found in MSS. But having at any rate some MS. authority for *terra*, I think we should be right to adopt it. (1) The change of *terra* to *gloria* seems more probable than *vice versa*, as being *prima facie* more ' elegant' than the repetition of *terra*, especially if the corrector overlooked the strongly emphatic word *terminata* just before. (2) Dante is describing the growth of communities of men from the earliest gatherings of society, and in that primitive condition it is *terra* rather than *gloria* that stimulates warlike aggression ; the latter is the product of more advanced civilization (compare *Nic. Eth.* I. v. 4, οἱ δὲ χαρίεντες καὶ πρακτικοὶ τιμήν· τοῦ γὰρ πολιτικοῦ βίου σχεδὸν τοῦτο τέλος). Again the passage (with 'terra') may be compared with IV. xii. 166, where the continued desire of the *same* object on an ever increasing scale is applied to riches.

IV. v. 91.

The MSS., almost without exception[1], read ' *tre* Tarquinii,' but I have shown in *Studies*, i. p. 195, and *supra*, p. 20, that the passage in *Aen.* vi. 777–819 having been apparently in Dante's mind, he is most likely to have written ' re Tarquinii,'

---

[1] At any rate I have found it in twenty-eight MSS., and one other (*F*) has the singular reading *e 'l re Tarquinio*, with *li tre* in margin. M has the blundering enumeration ' Romulo Numa Tullio et anche li tre Tarquini.'

as = 'Tarquinios reges.' The significant omission of Servius both in Dante and Virgil shows the connexion of the two passages ; and the desire to make up the correct list of seven kings betrays the motive for the alteration of *re* to *tre* ; to say nothing of the apparent superfluity of *re* with Tarquinii, since all the others were equally kings. Witte proposed boldly to insert *Tullio* after *Anco* and to read *li re Tarquinii*. Giuliani after *Tullo* boldly inserts *Anco Marcio, Servio Tullio* (!).

Then again, in the same line these kings are described as 'bali (*al.* baili) e tutori della puerizia' (di Roma): i.e. 'the nurses and tutors of its childhood.' Witte proposes to read 'bajuli,' claiming the support, it is true, of one MS.[1], but chiefly on the strength of the expression 'bajulo seguente' in reference to the Emperor Augustus: to which might be added the description of the Emperor Henry VII, 'Romanae rei baiulus,' in *Epist.* vi, § 6. But although this metaphor of the bearer of the burden of the Roman State may very well suit the emperors, the metaphor of a nurse is far more appropriate to the present context, and indeed seems almost required by the other words in the clause. The fem. form of the word ('balia') occurs in *Par.* xxx. 141, but the masc. is said by Giuliani to be still in use in Tuscany, and indeed the Dictionaries supply examples of its use in literature. One instance occurs in the *Ottimo Comento* at *Inf.* xii. 71, 'Questo Chiron fu balio d' Achille.'

IV. v. 122, 123.

On the astonishing proposed substitution *h. l.* of *Fabii* (Giul.) or *Curzii* (Witte) instead of *Drusi*, as being better known for their services to Rome, see *Studies*, i. p. 196, and *supra*, p. 18.

IV. vi. 48 *seqq*.

The MSS. are said to read here (at any rate B H and M do so) :—

'*Autoritade* vale tanto quanto atto degno di fede e d' obbedienza. Manifesto è [che le sue parole sono somma e altissima autorità] [che Aristotile sia degno di fede e d' obbedienza et] così provare si può.'

---

[1] As a matter of fact *bajuli* has numerically somewhat more support than *baili* or *balii*. I found *bajuli* in fourteen and *baili* or *balii* in twelve.

Most editors have assumed a lacuna before ' Manifesto ' as there is no antecedent to explain ' *sue* ': e. g. Edd. Mil., Monti (*Saggio*, p. 67), Ped., Frat., and various suggestions have been made for supplying the gap or otherwise altering the text. It appears to me that nothing is needed but the transposition of the words enclosed in the two square brackets above, each of which occupies just a line in M, without altering a word found in the MS.

This change has been máde in the Oxford text.

IV. vi. 79.

Avvegnachè universalmente siano uno.

No MS. authority is quoted for the word *uno*[1], though the sense clearly requires it, but it might easily have been lost in the termination of *siano*. Or again we might read (as Giul. suggests) *sia uno* or *si è uno*, the word *uno* having attracted the verb into the singular, in spite of its subject being *appetiti*. Dionisi suggested *non siano* (*scil.* ' diversi ') ; Witte, *sieno pari* from the following *pure*, &c.

IV. vii. 114, 115.

On the insertion of *muovere* in the case of men and its omission as a necessary property of animals, and the consequent tampering with the text by editors, see *Studies*, i. p. 149. The statement there made as to ' all the MSS.' is too sweeping. I cannot remember on what authority it was made. In any case one MS. (that here designated by ψ) is said to insert *muovere* also after *vegetare* in the case of animals.

IV. viii. 103–112.

Dante is here distinguishing the two kinds of opposite terms recognized in Logic as *privative* and *negative*, the former denying of anything a quality which it was capable of possessing, the latter denying a quality which it was incapable of possessing. These in Dante's example would correspond to irreverent and non-reverent respectively. You are not irreverent in refusing to the Empire some quality to which it has no claim, but only non-reverent, because there is in that case no call for

---

[1] I have however met with *siano uno* in γ.

the feeling of reverence. Thus you could say of Euclid that he is a non-Christian or non-religious writer, but not that he is unchristian or irreligious. But as the text has come down to us it seems necessary to adopt the very drastic remedy of both inserting and also of omitting a negative against all MS. evidence. In l. 107 *non* must be inserted and in l. 110 *non* must be omitted. As I have examined nearly thirty MSS. here, the evidence is fairly complete. In l. 107 it is surely quite clear that non-reverence is refusing a quality that is *not* due, and in l. 110 it is equally clear that irreverence is offending against the truth (omitting *non*) by refusing a quality that *is* due.

IV. viii. 137.

In più vera irreverenza si caderebbe.

Though I have not collated this passage, it is stated that the majority of MSS. read *men* and not *più*. So it is in B H M at any rate, but then let it be noted all these (and probably others) read ' reverenza ' and not ' irreverenza.' The first four Editions and Biscioni read ' in men vera riverenza.' All other editions that I have seen read ' in più vera irreverenza.' It will be remembered that the first syllable of ' *in*intelligibile ' was lost in some MSS. (V. *supra*, p. 86 *med.*)

IV. xi. 81.

Forse più di mille anni l' avevano aspettato.

The majority of MSS. are said to read ' più di due mila d' anni.' This corresponds with my evidence, which shows them to be nearly unanimous :—

' di due mila,' $\beta \gamma \delta \kappa \xi o \pi \rho \sigma \tau \psi$ Q Tr B H P Q (seventeen).

' di due mila persone,' M $\eta \theta \iota \nu \nu \phi$ (seven).

' di due milia l' avevano,' $a \zeta \lambda \omega$ (four).

' di mille anni,' χ (one).

This causes one to hesitate about the omission of *due*, which I made before I had collected this evidence. But at the same time (*a*) one might suppose that *dimila* or *dimilia* may in some very early copy have been mistaken for *dumilia* (as H and Q have), and another *di* prefixed. (*b*) 1000 is more naturally used for a vague large number than 2000, as over

and over again in *Divina Commedia*. Also *mille anni* occurs
thus three times in *Purg.*, viz. xi. 106, xiv. 65, xxvii. 26 ; also
Conv. I. v. 62. (*c*) 2000 would be obviously and palpably too
large a figure. But it must be confessed that (*b*) and (*c*), and
especially the latter, are dangerous arguments. The occasional reading *persone* is curious, and it might possibly have
been substituted by some copyist, who noticed *due mila anni*
as being in fact too much.

IV. xii. 123–125.

> Adunque per la distruzione del conseguente, il crescere desiderio
> non è cagione di viltà alla scienza.

There are two words here which we are compelled to adopt
without being able to plead MS. authority : *distruzione* must
clearly be substituted for *distinzione* in l. 123, and *scienza* for
ricchezze in l. 125, or possibly *scienze* as reported in δ only.
As to *distruzione* and *distinzione*, it was hardly worth while to
collect MS. evidence, as the words are so very similar and so
very easily confused. The expression *distruzione* or ' destruc-
tio' in the logical sense of 'denying the consequent' or
refuting an argument occurs in *De Mon.* and *Quaestio* three or
four times, and *infra*, c. xiv, l. 12. It is argued that if Knowledge, like Riches, increases desire, it is therefore imperfect
and therefore vile. But Knowledge, as the philosopher declares,
is not imperfect but perfect. Thus the consequent is denied
or destroyed, and therefore it follows that Knowledge does
not increase desire in the way that Riches do, but ' per altro
modo' (l. 137). If it did, there would be imperfection, as we
argued, and rightly argued, in the case of Riches (see last
chapter, ll. 31–36 and next chapter, ll. 29 *seqq.*). Knowledge
rises constantly to *higher* levels and ideals, not merely more
of the same kind of thing. Its *quality* rather than *quantity* is
enhanced. The desire ' non *cresce* ma *dilata*' (c. xiii., ll. 9–10).
Also see ll. 152 *seqq.* of this chapter and III. xv. 93–100. In
the words of *Purg.* xxxi. 129 :—

> ' Saziando di sè, di sè asseta.'

As to *ricchezze*, in l. 125, which is stated to be in all MSS.
except δ, there is a sort of *prima facie* plausibility about it.

It may have been thought that Dante's line of defence might be that not even in the case of riches was unsatisfied desire necessarily the cause of their imperfection and vileness. But having regard to the different line of defence adopted (as explained above) in this whole context, and up to the middle of the next chapter, it is clear that his argument is that the unsatisfied desires are *different in kind* in the two cases, and the whole argument distinctly requires us to read *scienza* and not *ricchezze* in this place.

IV. xiii. 69–71.

> Dice Aristotile nel decimo dell' *Etica*, contra Simonide poeta parlando.

There is, in fact, no mention of Simonides in the passage referred to in *Ethics*, X. vii. 8 (1177 b 31). Aristotle merely says οὐ χρὴ κατὰ τοὺς παραινοῦντας, κτλ. Another point to notice is that there is nothing to correspond to Dante's ' si dee *trarre* alle divine cose quanto può.' In Aristotle we find [χρὴ] ἐφ' ὅσον ἐνδέχεται ἀθανατίζειν. The fact is that, as in II. xiv. 145 [see note *supra*], Dante is really not quoting directly from Aristotle, but from the Commentary of Aquinas on this passage, where he says, '*fuit hoc dictum Symonidis poetae.*' Not only this, but ' trarre alle divine cose' is not a very obvious representation of ἀθανατίζειν (the *Antiqua Translatio* has ' immortalem facere'). This expression, however, occurs also in Aquinas, *Summa contra Gentiles*, I. c. 5, ' homo debet se ad immortalia et *divina trahere* quantum potest[1].' References in *Conv.* IV. xv. 125 and xxx. 29, and *De Mon.* II. iv, show Dante's acquaintance with this work of St. Thomas. It may be observed that the passage cited in *Conv.* IV. xv. 125 comes from the same chapter in the *Summa* (I. c. 5) and within a very few lines of the other passage just quoted.

Var. lect.: B and M have :—

' Contro a' sermoni dei poeti.'

---

[1] It is very remarkable that this quotation occurs again in the *Quaestio*, § 22, l. 3, in this precise form. Surely a striking evidence of the Dantesque authorship of that work.

H

IV. xiv. 62.

There is much corruption of the text in the MSS. here, and the conjectures of editors are numerous and differing much *inter se*.

The *lect. vulg.* is given by Fraticelli and Giuliani and Edd. Mil. as 'conciossia commemorata la cosa che quanto è migliore tanto è più cagione di bene.' So first four Edd. So also B. (*al.*: 'chomonorato' or 'comonorata ').

The principal conjectural emendations are :—

'com' è narrato, la cosa quanto,' &c., Edd. Mil.

'com' è onorata la cosa quanto,' &c., Frat.

'com' è mostrato, l' uomo quanto,' &c. (!), Giul.

I find the following reading in my MS. :—

'Conciosiacosa chome meno onorata la cosa quanto è più migliore tanto è più cagione di bene.'

I suppose *chome meno onorata* in this text is meant for *com' è meno onorata*, into which possibly *commemorata* or *chomemorata* was changed to help out the defective construction. But it is a corruption apparently not found in other MSS., except the related θ and *v*. We need, therefore, take no further account of it, nor of the redundant *più* before *migliore* (also in *ι* and *v*), which was probably introduced to make the antithesis with 'tanto è *più* cagione' more mechanically complete.

It appears to me that the only change required in the *lect. vulg.* is the very simple one of resolving *commemorata* of the MSS. into 'ch' è memorata,' the difference in most MSS. being simply that between *chomemorata* and *chememorata*. Then the passage will run :—

'Conciossiacosachè è memorata la cosa che quanto è migliore tanto è più cagione di bene.'

i. e. seeing that anything is remembered in that in proportion as it is better it is productive of more good. With *memorata* thus used compare the twice repeated *smemorati uomini* a little lower down. This at any rate perfectly well suits the context, and it makes the line of argument quite clear. Or perhaps even this change of the *lect. vulg.* is not necessary if we take 'conciossia (V. *infra*) commemorata' as supplying the verb *sia* to complete the construction.

The argument in either case may be represented as follows :—

The position of the adversary (l. 48) is that ' Nobiltà ' may come to a family of base origin, provided, and as soon as, that origin should be forgotten. Dante replies that among other unsuitable results of such a theory, the first would be that in proportion to the merits or goodness of nature of such ancestors, if in low station, the more difficult and tardy would oblivion of them be, and, by consequence, the more difficult the attainment of Nobility by the family. For, as he says in the passage now before us, it is clearly the case that anything is remembered longer in proportion as it is a better thing, and is in so far more the cause of good. Now Nobility is certainly commemorated among things good, so that we may lay it down that anything will be more remembered in proportion to its tendency to produce Nobility. Consequently the possession by any one of qualities tending towards Nobility would be an obstacle to that oblivion, which, according to the absurd contention of our opponents, is the necessary antecedent of Nobility under the circumstances supposed.

The following are the principal variations noticed in my collations :—

'conciosia commemorata la cosa che quanto,' B P $\eta \iota$ ('più migliore') v (do.) $\mu \xi \phi$.

'conciosia comonorata,' &c., Tr $\alpha \delta \zeta \psi \omega$ H ('pigliore').

'conciosia cosa comonorata la cosa che,' Q $\beta o \pi \rho \chi$.

'   ,,   ,,   meno onorata la cosa quanto,' M θv.

'   ,,   ,,   che commemorata la cosa quanto,' τ.

'   ,,   ,,   commemorata la cosa che quanto,' σ.

ω has 'comonorata' with 'memorata' in *marg*.

IV. xvii. 125.

   E *unite* nell' aspetto di fuori.

Most editors have *vedute* here (e.g. Edd. Mil., Ped., Frat.). The MSS. have ' unita,' ' unitade,' ' unitadi,' &c. I have had

no hesitation in inserting *unite* here, since, as I have observed
in the Introductory Note, many MSS. are very careless and
casual in respect of vowels, and especially in the final vowels
of words, so this merely involves the change of *a* to *e*.   The
sense is clearly explained in the next chapter ; there being no
such unity in the case of διανοητικαὶ ἀρεταί.   Or perhaps it
may be (see l. 45) that *Nobiltà* is the *aspetto di fuori* in which
all are united.   Biscioni reads *unità*, but the MSS. are not of
course responsible for the accent on the final *à*.   Giuliani
boldly substitutes *Nobiltade*!

IV. xviii. 37 *seqq.*

I find this perhaps the most difficult passage in the whole
Treatise, on which to arrive at a satisfactory conclusion.

The general reading of all the MSS. is evidently confused
and corrupt.   It is mainly as follows :—

> ‘ Ove è da sapere che qui non si procede per necessaria dimostrazione
> sì come sarebbe a dire se il freddo è generativo dell’ acqua e noi vedemo
> i nuvoli di sì bella e convenevole induzione.’

In thirty MSS. which I examined here there was no
variation of any consequence, except that some have a comma
and some a full stop at *acqua* with ‘ Et ’ following, which
clearly makes nonsense.   Moreover, variations of punctuation
are generally of no account in MSS. and are often quite
haphazard.

Editors have generally altered *di sì* into *ma bensì per*,
which has no MS. authority ; besides making various conjectural transpositions.   Giuliani's *rifacimento* of the passage
is startling : ‘ siccome sarebbe a dire *che pioverà* (!) se il freddo
è generativo dell’ acqua, e noi vedemo i nuvoli.’

The first point to determine is whether the words following
siccome sarebbe a dire to *nuvoli* (the next words clearly
involving some corruption) are intended as an example of
a *dimostrazione* or an *induzione*.   The connecting words
siccome sarebbe a dire seem clearly to imply the former, the
word *vedemo* being emphatic.

If it is certain that cold generates rain, and we actually
see the clouds [‘ discharging,’ as Dr. Jackson inserts], we

may be said to be demonstratively certain (by the evidence
of our own eyes) of the operation of this natural law. The
text would thus exhibit technically an Enthymeme of the
third Order, i.e. with the conclusion left unexpressed, viz.
that cold is now prevailing. But after all, such a conclusion
would clearly seem to involve the fallacy of affirming the
Consequent of a Hypothetical Syllogism, or of a Syllogism
with Undistributed Middle.

It seems better to consider the Argument to be Inductive.
In this case, we must, I suppose, understand *si procede* again
before *siccome*. If so, though Dante calls it 'bella e convenevole
induzione[1],' it is rather obscurely stated, though if it means,
as Dr. Jackson suggests, 'we refer the discharge of moisture
from the clouds to cold because there are other instances
of moisture which are also referable to cold,' the principle
of such an argument is certainly inductive. Its application
here would be somewhat as follows :—Dante has been arguing
that as Nobility and (Moral) Virtue produce similar effects
(ll. 22–28, and *Canzone* III, ll. 89 *seqq.*), one is either the cause of
the other, or if they appear to be on an equal footing, both may
be the effects of some third thing, which would be their joint
cause. Now as we have found Nobility to include every Moral
Virtue (ll. 7 *seqq., supra*, and 51 *seqq., infra*) after the manner of
a cause and its effects, we may surely argue that when several
phenomena are included under, accompany, or follow one
circumstance or condition, this latter is the cause of those
phenomena. This would not indeed be a 'necessary demon-
stration,' but it would be a 'right good induction' (ll. 37–42).
In this case 'Nobiltà': virtue :: production of water by cold
generally : production of rain by clouds in particular. If
Induction means referring a particular to something more
general, in this sense of Induction we refer 'Virtù' to 'Nobiltà,'
as we refer rain from clouds to the more general case of
moisture being an effect of cold.

Next as to the words after *nuvoli*, where a colon or even
a full stop seems required, for the words *nuvoli di sì bella*

---

[1] This combination of epithets occurs similarly again in the next chapter,
ll. 35 and 69.

... *induzione* make nonsense.' I rather think that *di sè* may be a blunder for *dice* (V. *supra*, p. 38 *med.*). I suspect the possibility of an almost converse mistake in III. xiv. 99 [1], where *dice* after *cagione*, as in my MS., is clearly superfluous (though not therefore necessarily to be rejected), but I think it may possibly represent *di sè*, adding emphasis to *sua*. 'Dico' or 'Dice' is, it must be remembered, Dante's regular way of referring to the language quoted from the *Canzoni*, e.g. in this chapter *passim*, and he is here commenting on ll. 98–102, as the rest of this paragraph shows. But I feel sure that there is some corruption in the whole passage, though we have no MS. evidence that will avail for its correction. I think it is extremely probable that it is due to a marginal note that very early came to be incorporated in the text, and possibly in the wrong place. The words (as Dr. Jackson suggests) from *siccome sarebbe* to *nuvoli* may have been such a marginal illustration, intended either for *dimostrazione* or for *induzione*. I should propose, therefore, to *obelize* these words in future reprints of the *Oxford Dante*, which would mean that they may be *conjectured* to be a marginal note, and not originally an integral part of the text itself, though found in all MSS. examined so far.

IV. xix. 32.

> Non è questo vero *e converso*, cioè rivolto, che dovunque, &c.

I am afraid I must admit having made a mistake in the Oxford text (following Giuliani, Fraticelli, and Edd. Mil.) in omitting the words 'cioè rivolto.' Having only the evidence of two MSS., and not observing that *e converso* should be treated as Latin words (both here and in the *Canzone* itself), I thought the words seemed to be an obvious marginal gloss that had been wrongly inserted in the text. As I find them in all the nine MSS. here examined, and as they are quite natural as explanatory of a Latin phrase, I think they should certainly be retained, and the correction is already made in the last edition.

---

[1] Frat. and Giul. read : '... ch' è per cagione di sè.' Biscioni, following MSS. as usual, '... dice.' Edd. Mil. and Ped. omit *dice* as 'lezione manifestamente scorretta.' B and M have 'per sua cagione dice e non per altrui.'

IV. xx. 80 *seqq.*

The text here is evidently in much confusion, but not so much from MS. readings as from editorial punctuation. It reads thus:—

'Ultimamente conchiude e dice che per quello che dinanzi è detto, cioè che le Virtù sono frutto di Nobiltà, e che Iddio questa mette nell' anima che ben siede, che *ad alquanti*, cioè a quelli che hanno intelletto, che son pochi, è manifesto che Nobiltà umana non sia altro che *seme di felicità Messo da Dio nell' anima ben posta.*'

I have purposely omitted stops in the latter part, as it is variously punctuated in editions.

Now I observe first that the *Canzone* has been regularly explained line by line as far as 'perfettamente star,' (l. 118 *med.*), so that the words introduced by 'Ultimamente conchiude' must be intended to explain the last $2\frac{1}{2}$ lines of this division, viz. :—

> 'sicchè ad alquanti
> Lo seme di felicità s' accosta,
> Messo da Dio nell' anima ben posta.'

The following points seem to me then perfectly clear:—

(1) The words *ad alquanti* (l. 84) are certainly part of a quotation from the *Canzone* (l. 118 *fin.*); though they are not so printed in any edition that I have seen (I have eight before me).

(2) So also are the words *seme di felicità*, three lines below, though also not generally so printed.

(3) It is wrong to punctuate or interpret in such a way as to take *è manifesto* with *ad alquanti* as in some editions (e.g. Bisc., Ped., Edd. Mil., Frat.). This is so (*a*) because the *Canzone* states that *alquanti* are recipients of God's special favour, not that Nobility being the source of Happiness (or anything else) 'is manifest to them;' (*b*) because we find the words *manifesto è* repeated a few lines below (l. 92), with an object clause which is also a repetition of that which follows here (l. 87), having no limited reference to *alquanti*. The words added (l. 93), *come detto è*, draw attention to there being such a repetition.

(4) It is equally wrong to punctuate, or put in parenthesis, 'che son pochi è manifesto.'

The drift of the passage is evidently to justify the limitation of this favour of God to ⸢alquanti. It follows from the two statements that Virtue arises from Nobility, and that Nobility is the gift of God to souls that are well-fitted by nature to receive it (ll. 81–84)—it follows, that to *some* only is the seed from which Happiness springs conveyed, since the required qualifications are rare. And Dante proceeds that it is evident that we may thus describe Nobility as the seed of Happiness.

All that is wanted to make the text perfectly clear is to suppose that some of the words to be quoted from the *Canzone* after *ad alquanti* have accidentally dropped out ; viz. *lo seme di felicità s' accosta.* (*a*) They are needed to complete the construction of *ad alquanti* (since *è manifesto*, &c., cannot be held to complete it, for the reasons already given) ; and (*b*) if not absolutely required by the way in which the words *seme di felicità* are introduced in the next sentence (l. 87), they naturally lead up to them.

As to the loss of this part of the quotation, I would suggest (1) that though it is not exactly a case of ὁμοιοτέλευτον, yet some confusion might have arisen from the repetition almost immediately of the same words. (2) In some MSS. quoted passages are rubricated, and occasionally also (as in the Bodleian MS.) written in a separate line. Now to save trouble and the interruption caused by using a separate material, initial letters, rubricated introductions, and so on, were often temporarily omitted, and were occasionally afterwards forgotten, so that we find such spaces still left blank. An accident of this kind in some early MS. might account for the omission of such a quotation as this, and the gap left might be neglected by some one copying the MS. (3) The two words *ad alquanti* were perhaps not treated by the scribe as part of the quotation (as is the case with most editors).

I have, therefore (with the usual warning of square brackets), reconstructed the text by supplying these words in the Oxford text. It should be added that twenty-six MSS. examined in this passage exhibit no variation of any consequence.

IV. xxi. 24.

When editing the text of the *Oxford Dante* I had only the readings offered by the two MSS. B and M (for which see *infra*), and the conjectural alterations of Witte, Fraticelli, and Giuliani, viz. :—

‘ tutta la differenza delle corpora era forma,’ W.

‘ „ „ „ è forma,’ F.

‘ „ „ sia de’ corpi non delle forme,’ G. !

all of which entirely fail to give the meaning required by the context. What Dante says is that as far as nobility goes, the Pythagoreans held that the souls of men and plants and brutes and the forms of minerals were on an equality [1], and that the only difference resided in the bodies and forms and not in the souls (*anime*). From l. 12 onwards Dante is speaking of the differences of *anime*, not of *corpora*, though the Pythagoreans reduced the differences to those of *corpora* and *forme* only. I have now examined twenty-six MSS. with the following results :—

‘ le differenze delle corpora e forme,’ M Q $a \beta \eta$ (‘tutti li differentii’) $\iota o \rho \tau \upsilon \phi \chi$ ($\beta \rho \chi$ with *delle* before *forme*).

‘ la differenza delle corpora e forme,’ H Tr $\gamma \delta \zeta \kappa \lambda$ (‘forma’) ξ (do.) $\sigma \psi F$.

‘ le differenze delle corporali forme,’ θ.

‘ la differenza delle corporali forme,’ B P.

κ has ‘ la differenza delle corpora era forma.’

υ has ‘ le differenze delle corpora forme ’ (*sic*).

Hence it appears that as between *la differenza* and *le differenze* the evidence is evenly balanced ; but that as between *corporali* and *corpora* the latter occurs in twenty-three MSS. and the former in only three. I think with this evidence that we should read :—

‘ Tutta la differenza è delle corpora e forme.’

I suspect that the verb *è* was run into *differenza* and the word was then mistaken for the plural *differenze*, and that *la* was altered to *le* accordingly.

[1] For this compare IV. xiv. 91 *seqq.*

This seems to me to account in a reasonable way for the loss of the verb in the sentence and to be a simple and justifiable process for restoring it.

In regard to the expression 'soul' as applied to plants, compare *Purg.* xxv. 52, 53, where the first stage in the development of the human soul is said to be identical with that of a plant ; the only difference being that in the latter case the first stage is also the final stage. Also *Conv.* III. iii. 21, where plants, as distinguished from minerals mentioned just before, are 'prima animate' in the ascending scale of being from minerals to man.

IV. xxi. 34 *seqq.*

The chief points to determine here are :—

1. *elementi* or *alimenti.*
2. *legati* or *legata.*
3. The punctuation and reading after *complessione.*

(1) The MSS. which I have examined are almost unanimous for *elementi*, which I find in twenty-seven MSS. against only three which have *alimenti.* *Alimenti* seems to have been proposed *e conj.*, and without any alleged MS. authority, by Witte, and is adopted by Fraticelli. The alteration was suggested by the tempting, though misleading, analogy of *Purg.* xxv. 37–39, and the parallel in Arist. *De Gen. Anim.*, which doubtless Dante had in his mind at *Purg. l. c.* But I think the reference to *alimenti* is entirely out of place here, while the significance of *elementi legati* is distinctly explained presently in c. xxiii, ll. 65–75 and 113–117. It is there stated that the duration of life depends on the 'materia della nostra seminale complessione' (*complessione* being the word employed here also, l. 36), and that is further stated to be the result of the degrees of admixture of warmth, cold, moisture, and dryness in it. These are qualities of the elements, and there are 'quattro combinatori delle contrarie qualitadi' possible (l. 113), and the four elements are constituted in fact by these four combinations :—

Cold + Moist = Water.   Warm + Dry = Fire.

Cold + Dry = Earth.   Warm + Moist = Air.

(See further B. Latini, *Li Tresors*, I. part iii. ch. 100, also ch. 102.)

Hence *complessione* is defined in the passage before us as ' la virtù degli elementi legati.'

After *complessione* Witte and Fraticelli insert, without, I believe, any authority whatever, *del seme*.

(2) As to *legati* the MSS. are practically unanimous. I do not know on what authority *legata* has been suggested. I have found it in one only of twenty-nine MSS. examined, viz. *f*.

(3) I confess I have not found any distinct authority for *e* after *complessione* (as in the Oxford text): but this *e* may easily have become absorbed in the final letter of *complessione*, most MSS. having no punctuation. About one-third of the MSS. examined, however, retaining *matura*, begin a new sentence with *Et dispone*. It is evident that they at any rate regard *matura* as 'an adjective agreeing with *complessione*. Another third read *complessione innata e naturale e dispone*. It is very difficult with such conflicting evidence to feel confident as to the determination of the text.

IV. xxii. 9 *seqq.*

> E perocchè in questa parte occorre a me di potere alquanto ragionare [della dolcezza dell' umana felicità], intendo, &c.

I propose to insert the square brackets as above in the next edition of the *Oxford Dante*, because I have found that no MS. authority is claimed for these words. They were inserted by the Edd. Mil., and have been accepted in subsequent editions. They seem necessary, for (1) there is not otherwise any subject for the vague *ragionare*; nor (2) is there any antecedent to explain *la* in l. 14; and (3) the actual words seem to be supplied at once by the conclusion of the previous chapter, and they explain *questa dolcezza* in l. 18 just below. The omission was probably a pure accident on the part of some early copyist.

IV. xxii. 24–26.

> E massimamente è da gradire quegli che a coloro che nol veggono
> l' addita.

The corrupt state of the text in this passage was unfortunately not noticed by me in time to include it in my list for
collation.

Giuliani says that all MSS. have 'è da gridare quelli che
a coloro che non vogliono la dica.' This is quite inaccurate,
for Witte registers *gradire* for *gridare* in three MSS.[1]: and
I have found it also in H. I may add also that M has
lo dita.

B has 'è di gridare quelli che a coloro che non vogliono
la dica.'

M has 'è da gudicare [i. e. *giudicare*, since this MS. constantly omits *i* after *g*, e. g. *maggo, peggo, veggo*, &c.] a quelli
che non voglono lo dita'.

Witte ingeniously conjectured *l' addita*, though not pleading
any MS. authority for it. But it seems justified by the readings in B and M. For an original *l' addita* would be sure
sometimes to appear as *la dita* or *la dica* (*c* and *t* being often
undistinguishable in MSS.), and the alteration of *la* into *lo*
would naturally follow, in the absence of any antecedent for
the supposed feminine *la*. It may be observed that the verb
additare occurs five times in the *Purgatorio*.

The Edd. Mil. make the preposterous alteration *l'Etica*
without any MS. authority, being content to say '*noi teniamo
per fermo* che *la dica* sia correzione di *l' Etica*' (!). This is
adopted by Giuliani, who, after first paraphrasing *voglono* or
volgono by *studiano*, substitutes for it the word *leggono* in his
text!

Next as to *voglono* or *volgono*, I observe that M constantly
writes *velgono* for *veggono*, and I suspect that this latter may
be the word thus disguised, for it seems almost required by
the emphasis on the repeated word *vedere* in ll. 17 and 23.

---

[1] *Gradire* and *gridare* are both found as variants for *guardar* in *Purg.* xxiv. 61.

IV. xxii. 46.

E non pur *nelle biade*, ma negli uomini e nelle bestie ha similitudine.

For *nelle biade* we should certainly read *negli uomini*, and this correction will, I hope, be made in the next edition of the *Oxford Dante*. *uomini* is said to be in *all* MSS. It is so, at any rate, in B H and M, which are at hand. The so-called ' correction' *biade* was introduced by Edd. Mil.

Dante argues that appetite (*hormen*), i.e. any appetite innate in man (l. 36), shows no distinction at first, whether it comes from bare nature or from God's influence: just as different kinds of grain (*biade*, ll. 37, 45) are at first undistinguishable. But he adds not only in men is this the case, but also in men and brutes when compared *inter se*. We might illustrate this by the early stages in the development of the embryo in *Purg.* xxv. 52–63.

The insistence on *biade* again would seem to be out of place. The point is that the nascent desires in different kinds of men look the same, and not only so, but also in men and brutes, when compared with one another they do so.

IV. xxiii. 73 *seqq.*

The MSS. read (as reported), since I have myself only examined two here (B and M), as follows :—

' L'arco della vita d' un uomo è di minore e di maggiore tesa che quello dell' altro. Alcuna morte violenta ovvero per accidentale infermità affrettata, ma solamente,' &c.

This has been variously altered by editors. It has been usual to omit the full stop after *altro* and insert *per* before *alcuna*. So Edd. Mil., Ped., Frat., Giul. But Giuliani more boldly (as usual) alters thus :—' Benchè per alcuna morte ovvero per accidentale, il termine affrettato ne sia, solamente quello,' &c. (!). This is a mere reckless rewriting of the whole passage. It seems to me perfectly evident that no change is needed in the MS. reading except the infinitesimal one of inserting ' è ' after *morte*, in the final letter of which latter word it would be very likely to be merged. This is an accident of which examples may be found in almost any page of a MS. The sense then at once becomes clear and suitable.

IV. xxiv. 34.

Lo tenere dell' Arco.

This clearly means the place where the bow is held (= Greek λαβή), where, as Dante explains, there is less visible flexure than at any other part of the bow. The *Vocab. Tramater*, p. 80 *med.*, gives two or three instances of ' tenere ' in sense of ' handle.' Giuliani absurdly alters *tenere* into *tendere*, which gives no sense to the words immediately following.

IV. xxiv. 47.

'mesi,' B H P Q *a β γ δ ζ η κ λ μ ξ o π ρ σ τ φ χ ψ* (twenty-two).

anni
μ has ' mesi ' (*sic*).

'anni' M ι θ ν ν (five).

ν has ' per lo modo che detto è a viij anni.'

ε is defective.

This is an interesting difference of reading, the change, whichever may be thought to be the original word, being evidently made deliberately, in order to give effect to a particular interpretation of the passage which was supposed to embody Dante's meaning. μ (vide *supra*) affords an example of the process.

I have now no doubt whatever that *mesi* is what Dante wrote, and that some misunderstanding of the words ' pigliandola per lo modo che detto è ' probably gave rise to the alteration[1]. The expression, however, is a very common one in reference to something which Dante has said shortly before. In this case it means in effect ; ' taking " adolescenza " in the sense just mentioned ' (viz. in l. 38) : i.e. as including the first twenty-five years of life. This is the sense in which it is generally, and we might even say universally (*supra*, ll. 10-12), understood. But if ' adolescenza ' means the period of the *growth* of life (see ll. 3, 4, ' Adolescenza, cioè *accrescimento* di vita'), the popular use of the word, dating it from birth, makes

---

[1] Unfortunately, being misled like others, I adopted *anni* in the first edition of the *Oxford Dante*.

it begin about eight months after the beginning (' principio ') of life, during which period life must of course have been growing. This theory, though in a sense philosophical and scientific, was not by any means generally unfamiliar, as will be seen from the references which follow.

The exact moment of the commencement of life was a matter of lively controversy. It was very commonly thought to begin either immediately, or very soon, after conception. This was the reason why March 25, as the day of the Annunciation, was often held to be the true beginning of the year, this being the day of the very commencement of our Lord's life or incarnation. This was the usage in Florence and Pisa and in some provinces of France, and generally in Spain, Germany, and England[1]. The Roman usage beginning the year on Dec. 25 embodied the other view referred to above, which dated the beginning of life from the moment of birth. These two extreme limits represent the ordinary popular opinions, which were not likely to entangle themselves with the ' doubtful disputations ' of scientific or theological theories. There was, however, a very considerable literature on this subject ; both scientific, in medical treatises ; and theological, in reference to injunctions as to intra-uterine baptism. This would no doubt be familiar to Dante, and, as we shall see, it appears fully to explain the *otto mesi* of the passage before us.

The subject is treated first of all by Aristotle, *Hist. Anim.* VII. iii. (583 b). Movement (κίνησις)—an indication of vitality—occurs generally in the case of male embryos about the fortieth day after conception ; in the case of females about the ninetieth day, though we must not in either case regard these limits as very precise. But approximately at those periods the embryo acquires some articulate form. Before that ἄναρθρον συνέστηκε κρεῶδες, which corresponds with the stage described as ' coagulando prima ' in *Purg.* xxv.

---

[1] See further, *Studies*, iii. p. 148. Also compare *Par.* xvi. 34, where Cacciaguida dates the commencement of Anno Domini from March 25 : ' Da quel dì che fu detto *Ave*.'

50. We might compare *Purg.* xxv. 68 *seqq.*, where Dante dates the creation and infusion of a living soul—

> ' sì tosto come al feto
> L' articular del cerebro è perfetto,'

though he gives no indication of the time when this usually occurs.

Albertus Magnus, *de Animalibus*, L. IX. Tr. ii. c. 5, states that ' formatio completur in xxx diebus.' He adds that the *minimum* time is thirty, or sometimes even twenty-five, days, and the *maximum* forty days. I do not see any reference here to the Aristotelian distinction between male and female embryos, but it is cited in the previous chapter. These computations would evidently place the time of birth at ' presso a otto mesi ' after the first commencement of life, i.e. at about one month after conception.

This question was familiar to at least three of the early commentators on Dante : (1) Pietro, commentary on *Purg.* xxv. 71, says : ' hoc (i.e. the infusion of the soul) per spatium xl dierum a conceptu ; licet quidam dicant hoc in mare ; in femina autem lxxx dierum a conceptione dicti embryonis.' (2) Benvenuto on *Purg.* xxv. 49, 50 gives several periods in detail, which, added together, make forty-two days as the time when ' membra figurantur.' (3) Buti on *Purg.* xxv. 60 gives similar details to those of Benvenuto (which are attributed to ' li autori de la medicina '), but with variation in the length of one of the periods, so that his total comes to forty-five days. Neither Benvenuto nor Buti refers to the Aristotelian distinction between the male and female embryo.

Another treatise in which these theories are noticed is the *Tractatus de formatione humani corporis in utero*, by Cardinal Egidio Colonna, a contemporary of Dante. It was discovered and edited for the first time by Moncetti in 1515[1], who dedicated it to Henry VIII. It was this Moncetti who similarly discovered and edited (or, as some would say, forged), in 1508, the *Quaestio de Aqua et Terra* of Dante. But there appears to be no doubt as to the genuineness of the treatise of

---

[1] See Biagi on *Quaestio de Aqua et Terra*, pp. 30, 179.

Colonna, and the trend of opinion is now setting more and more strongly in favour of that of the *Quaestio*.

The author quotes Aristotle, Averroes, Avicenna, and St. Augustine, with the general result that in forty (*al.* forty-five) days the formation of the male embryo is complete, and in eighty (*al.* ninety) days that of the female. Different stages of development in the case of the male are given at intervals of six, nine, twelve, and eighteen days, which together make forty-five. (These are the same as in the Commentary of Buti, quoted *supra.*) He says that some 'medici' say thirty for male and forty for female, and that Avicenna says for male, *min.* thirty, *max.* forty days, average thirty-three or thirty-five ; and for female, *min.* forty, *max.* fifty (ch. 15). In c. 12 he says: 'in utero femina tardius formatur quam mas, sed extra uterum citius perficitur et completur'; and in c. 14, the principal members are formed first, 'cor, epar, cerebrum ; omnino primum formatur cor.'

I have no doubt that such speculations as these were in Dante's mind, and the purposely vague words 'presso a otto mesi' denote the deduction from nine months of the forty days, 'more or less,' of Aristotle ; and would also be consistent with the limits of thirty to forty-five days in the different authorities above quoted. Like some of these he ignores the different periods in the case of male and female, and would no doubt consider the former to represent the normal and most perfect condition.

It should be noticed here that St. Thomas Aquinas argues at some length that in the exceptional case of our Lord, life began instantaneously upon conception. See *Summa*, III. Q. 33, Artt. 1, 2, and 3.

So also Peter Lombard maintains that the flesh of Christ 'non ante fuisse conceptam quam assumptam' (*Sentt.* IV, Lib. iii, Dist. 3, §§ 4, 5). He protests that St. Augustine should not be quoted against this assertion by reason of his language in *Comm. in Ioannem*, Tract. X. ii. 12, and in *De Trinitate*, Lib. IV. v. 9. St. Augustine, it will be seen, is there endeavouring to elicit 'aliquod sacramentum' from the forty-six years in which the Temple was building, 'quia, ut dicunt

physici, *tot diebus forma humani corporis perficitur.*' Hence
the days of completion of the formation of [the temple of]
Christ's body would correspond with the number of years of
the completion of the temple itself[1]. Peter Lombard offers
this astonishing suggestion to ' save the face ' of St. Augustine :
viz. 'membrorum illius dominici corporis distinctio in ipso
momento conceptionis unionis Dei et hominis adeo tenuis erat
et parva ut humano visui vix posset subiici, diebus autem illis
quos Augustinus memorat perfecta est et notabilis facta !'

The meaning of the whole passage before us may thus, I
think, be summarized.

Dante divides human life after birth into four periods :—

' Adolescenza ' . . . 1 to 25 = 25 years.
' Gioventute ' . . . 25 to 45 = 20 years.
' Senettute ' . . . . 45 to 70 = 25 years.
' Senio ' . . . . . 70 to 81 = c. 10 years, more or less.

But his love of symmetry requires something *before* ' Adolescenza ' to balance the period *after* ' Senettute,' and he finds
this in the pre-natal existence of ' about eight months.' He
then in a curious manner justifies the *prima facie* anomaly of
treating ' about eight months ' in one case as an equivalent to
' about ten years' in the other (see ll. 48 *seqq.*). It is seen that
in rising upwards our nature is eager and keen, in descend-
ing (the vale of years) it lingers and holds back. (Hence we
may say of the early period, ' τελειωθεὶς ἐν ὀλίγῳ ἐπλήρωσε πολ-
λοὺς χρόνους.') And we are reminded how Aristotle (*Nic. Eth.*
I. xiii. 12) says that the life of nutriment and growth (' accrescimento ') ' ἐνεργεῖ μάλιστα ἐν τοῖς ὕπνοις,' this being the same
function, as he says three lines above, as exists in embryos.
Indeed it is obvious that the activity of growth and change in
the few months of embryonic existence far surpasses that of
the lingering process of ' calm decay ' in the last stage of life.

We must not omit to notice in passing Dante's curious

---

[1] See *Studies in Dante*, iii. p. 276, for other fanciful exercises of this kind.
Mr. Wicksteed has kindly called my attention to the following passage in
Honorius of Autun, in evident recollection of St. Augustine's treatment of the
name Adam as being equivalent to the number 46 : ' Per hunc numerum
descendit caro Christi de Adam : quadraginta enim et sex diebus formatur infans
in matre ' (ed. Migne, *Patrol. Latina*, vol. clxxii, col. 741).

reason for adding *Senio* to the generally accepted Psalmist's limit of seventy years. Dante recognized a peculiar perfection about the number 81 as being 9 × 9; 9 itself being 3 × 3. (For this see *V. N.*, §§ 29 and 30.) Hence it was natural that Plato ('ottimamente naturato,' &c.) should live to the age of eighty-one, as Cicero tells us that he did; and Dante adds that if our Lord had died 'a natural death' it is probable that His 'mortal would have put on immortality' at that age (see ll. 65–68).

The reading *anni* was upheld on these grounds :—

(1) '*c*. eight years' was supposed to offer a better equivalent to '*c*. ten years' than '*c*. eight months' would do.

(2) Dante elsewhere recognizes a distinction between *puerizia* and *adolescenza*, treating the latter as beginning at about the ninth year. See *V. N.* xii. 58 (with which compare *Purg.* xxx. 42) and *Conv.* IV. v. 92 and 98. Hence his first meeting with Beatrice is noted as taking place just about this period of transition in both their lives. *V. N.* ii. 13–15.

It does not seem to have been observed that, as these eight years would have to be *taken out* of the twenty-five assigned to *adolescenza*, the balance between that period and *senettute* would be entirely upset. There would be only seventeen years of *adolescenza* to set against twenty-five of *senettute*.

Giuliani, *more suo*, calmly alters '*otto* anni' into '*dieci* anni' to suit l. 55! It need hardly be said this is wholly without MS. authority. Besides, it renders superfluous the elaborate defence of the inequality of the two balanced periods in ll. 47–56.

There can, I think, be no doubt whatever as to the right reading being *mesi*. It may be added in conclusion that *anni* is very obviously *facilior lectio*, since all the other time calculations in the chapter are in terms of *years* and not of *months*.

Through the kindness of Professor Osler, of Oxford, I have been able to see a very curious and rare book entitled 'Embryologia Sacra[1].' The author is Cangiamila, a priest

[1] The very title is curiously unscientific, like that of the geographical treatise of Cosmas Indicopleustes, 'Topographia Christiana, sive Christianorum opinio de Mundo.' I have since obtained for myself a compendium of this curious work, entitled *Sacra Embryologia, sive de Officio Sacerdotum, Medicorum, et Aliorum*

at Palermo, and the first edition was published in 1758. He repeats the theory of Aristotle given above, as the 'common opinion' (I. v. 1), but he says that the 'best physicians' put the beginning of life much earlier than the fortieth day, and further that another popular opinion is that it begins either immediately after conception, or at least 'primis diebus.' In c. 7 he states that four stages may be traced in the growth of the embryo : (1) beginning of some sort of form soon after conception ; (2) heart and brain developed (cf. Dante, *Purg.* xxv. 69) ; (3) all limbs formed rudimentarily ; (4) ready for birth. He says that the beginning of life has been variously assigned to every one of these four stages. But the last he peremptorily rejects as being refuted by St. Luke i. 44, compared with *v.* 36. He states that the theory of Aristotle was accepted by P. Lombard, Aquinas, and the 'scholastici' generally.

There is a curious discussion in St. Augustine, *Enchiridion*, Capp. 84 *seqq.*, of various difficulties in detail that might be raised concerning the Resurrection of the Body, and first of all in respect of embryonic abortions, and in various degrees of imperfect formation ('in cui formazion falla[1]'). This suggests the question of the actual beginning of life in the embryo[2]. As to this, St. Augustine says (c. 86 *init.*), in spite of the minutest investigations and discussions of the learned, 'utrum ab homine inveniri possit ignoro, quando incipiat homo in utero vivere; utrum sit quaedam vita et occulta, quae nondum motibus viventis adpareat.' Thus even the usual test of the occurrence of motion may not be conclusive. He adds that even in respect of dead embryos, that have to be removed limb by limb to save the mother's life, we cannot presume

---

circa aeternam Parvulorum in utero existentium salutem, Libri Quattuor . . . in Compendium redacti. This was published at Ypres, dedicated to the Bishop, and approved by him in 1775. There is bound up with this a further 'Kortbegryp' in Dutch, published at Antwerp 1780.

[1] *Purg.* x. 129.

[2] The question of 'monsters' of various kinds is discussed in reference to the same question in cap. 87. In particular, the problem of Siamese twins, 'illum bimembrem qui nuper natus est in Oriente' (and in fact at 'Lydda nigh to Joppa'), in the resurrection is dealt with. This phenomenon is again referred to in *C. D.* xvi. 8.

to say that there never has been any life. And if there ever has been life, there must have been death, and if so, 'the resurrection of the dead' must take place even in such cases as these.

IV. xxvii. 75.

> Siccome dice nostro Signore : 'A grado ricevo, se a grado è dato.'

There is a curious dislocation here of the passage to which the direct reference is given. This is doubtless St. Matt. x. 8, 'gratis accepistis, gratis date.' Dante seems to have combined with this the sense of another passage, 2 Cor. ix. 7, 'hilarem datorem diligit Deus.' They are obviously quite in accord, and either might be inferred from the other. There was no variation affecting the form of the quotation in nearly thirty MSS. examined. I observe that (as usual) M θ ν agree in the slight variation, '*Di grado* ricevo se *a grado* è dato.' This perhaps may have been in some other MSS., as my attention was chiefly directed to the possibility of some variation in the loose form in which a professedly direct quotation is given.

IV. xxviii. 37–39.

> Così alla nobile Anima si fanno incontro[1] †e deono fare† quelli cittadini della eterna vita.

The words which I obelized as above in the *Oxford Dante*, having then very little evidence from MSS., and finding a general consensus for their rejection among editors (e.g. Edd. Mil., Ped., Frat., Giul.), I have now found to have the practically unanimous support of thirty MSS. That is to say, there is no evidence whatever for their omission, though four have the evidently blundering substitution of *dicono* (M θ ν ξ). I think, therefore, the obeli should now be removed. Giuliani substitutes *ad osannare* for *e deono fare*, supporting the conjecture by a reference to *Par.* xxviii. 94. If we retain the words (which might quite possibly be a marginal note) in the text, we might parallel such a parenthetical comment by *Inf.* xxvii. 8 ('e ciò fu dritto'); or *Par.* viii. 55, 'Assai m' amasti, ed avesti

---

[1] Compare Bunyan :—'Here they were within sight of the city they were going to ; also *here met them some of the inhabitants thereof*, for in this land the shining ones commonly walked, because it was on the borders of heaven.'

bene onde.' It has also been suggested that the words, if originating in a marginal note, might possibly have been intended to come after 'contemplazioni' in l. 41, where they would seem more in place.

IV. xxviii. 45.

See *Studies*, i. p. 271, for a probable correction of the text *h. l.* by the help of the direct quotation from Cicero.

LIST OF THE MSS. OF THE CONVIVIO.

Here designated	Place.		Press mark.
α	Bibl. Laurenziana, Florence		Laur. Ashburnhamiano, No. 843.
β	„	„	134 Gadd. Plut. xc. sup.
γ	„	„	135 primo Gadd. Plut. xc. sup.
δ	„	„	135 secondo „ „
ε	„	„	Codd. 3 Gadd. Plut. xc. inf.
ζ	„	.,	Plut. xl. Cod. 39.
η	„	„	Plut. xl. Cod. 40.
θ	„	„	Plut. xl. Cod. 41.
ι	Bibl. Nazionale	„	II. ix. 95.
κ	„	„	II. iii. 210.
λ	„	„	II. iii. 47.
μ	„	„	Class VI. vii. Cod. 186.
ν	Bibl. Riccardiana	„	1041.
ξ	„	„	1043.
ο	„	„	1042.
π	„	„	1044.
ρ	Bibl. Nazionale	„	Palat. 654.
σ	Vatican,	Rome	Ottob. Lat. 3332.
τ	„	„	Cappon. 190.
υ	„	„	4778 Lat.
φ	„	„	4779 Lat.
χ	„	„	Cod. Vat. Urb. 686 Lat.
ψ	Barberini Palace	„	xlvi. 28.
ω	Bibl. Marc.,	Venice	Class XI, Cod. xxxiv.
F	„	„	Class X, Cod. xxvi.
B	Bodleian,	Oxford	Canon. Ital. 114.
D	British Museum (a fragment),	London	Additional MSS. 28840.
H	Earl of Leicester,	Holkham	
M	Rev. Dr. Moore,	Canterbury	
P	Bibl. Nat.,	Paris	Ital. 536.
Q	„	„	Ital. 1014.
Tr	March. Trivulzio,	Milan	1090.
U	„	„	1089.

Description of MSS. of the Convivio.

I proceed now to give a very brief description of the MSS. examined, and the designations adopted for them. The Greek alphabet has been adopted as far as it will go for the MSS. in foreign Libraries, chiefly, as might be expected, in Italy. In some cases the information about the MSS. is rather meagre, since I at first intended to give only the *number* of MSS. in which a reading was found without further speci- fication. The indication of the MSS. themselves will assist in establishing relationships and founding 'families' of MSS.

α.

A MS. now in the Laurentian Library, and formerly in that of Lord Ashburnham [Cod. Laur. Ashburnhamiano, No. 843]. It contains a book-plate of Baron Ricasoli, and a still earlier entry, 'Di franchescho di Sandro Battiloro e delli amici.' The writing is very upright, with long loops and tails to the letters, and it is on rather thick paper. Probably (if I may trust my notes) early fifteenth or even late fourteenth century? There is no title or colophon.

β.

In the Laurentian Library [134 Gadd. Plut. xc. sup.]. A beautiful MS. on vellum in two columns. There is a finely illuminated initial ' S,' and alternately red and blue illuminated initial letters to the chapters. There is no title or colophon, and the writing which is very clear and fairly upright at first becomes sloping and inferior towards the end. I noted the following peculiarity in punctuation which under certain circum- stances might have to be taken account of in citing the evidence of this MS. A sentence often begins with a capital letter after a full stop, where a colon at most would be expected. Also a sentence without a capital follows a full stop, where a comma or at most a semicolon would be more natural.

γ.

In the Laurentian Library [135 primo Gadd. Plut. xc. sup.]. A fifteenth-century MS. on paper, in a flowing hand, rounded but quite clear. Fol. 1 begins with a colophon to a translation of the *De Monarchia* (which has apparently disappeared) :—

'Tradotta di latino in lingua toscana da Marsilio ficino fiorentino . . . xxi di Marzo 1467.'

Then follows :—

'Qui a piè una frotola di Guido Cavalcante, filosofo sommo.

> Guarda ben ti dich' io
> Guardate guarda
> Non avere vista tarda
> Che a pietra lombarda
> Arme val pocho,' &c.

On fol. 7 begins the *Convivio* with this title :—

'Qui a piè seguirà el convivio delle tre canzoni di dante aldighieri, citadino fiorentino, comentate per lui proprio, che fu principio delle quattordici canzoni, chome scrive nel convivio . chella morte ne tolse el fine di questa dignissima opera.'

On fol. 114 there is the following colophon :—

'Convivio delle tre canzoni di dante finito primo dì x pom. de dicembre 1477 per matteo cierretano.'

The scribe is careless about double letters : and such forms as 'giustixia,' 'filoxofia,' &c., point to a Venetian or N. Italian origin for the MS.

From fol. 114 to the end (fol. 169) there are several compositions in prose and verse which I had not time to investigate. From 119 to 155 there is a long treatise in a different and much smaller and neater hand, beginning :—

'. . olone [capital letter omitted, but no doubt "Solone" was intended] il cui petto uno umano tempio di divina sapienza era riputato, e le cui sacratissime leggi sono anchora alli presenti uomini testimonianza dell' anticha giustizia,' &c.[1]

This MS. and also ε have alone preserved the essential 'non' in II. i. 31. I felt obliged to insert it conjecturally in the first edition of the Oxford text as being quite necessary to the sense, though then without MS. evidence. This is happily now forthcoming. This MS. is also found to lend some support to a conjectural emendation which I had made in III. vii. 32 since publishing the first edition of the *Oxford Dante*, v. *supra*, p. 78.

---

[1] This is the beginning of Boccaccio's *Vita di Dante*.

δ.

Also in the Laurentian Library [135 secondo Gadd. Plut. xc. sup.]. It is on paper, which looks like fourteenth-century, and the writing also seems to me to point to such a date. It has no title or colophon. The initials to chapters are (as often) coloured red and blue alternately, and there is a fine initial S on a blue ground.

ε.

In the Laurentian Library [Cod. 3 Gadd. Plut. xc. inf.]. A most beautifully written MS. of fifteenth century, on very white vellum, with print-like hand, and exquisitely illuminated initial letters. It is unfortunately imperfect, ending abruptly on fol. 135 vº in the middle of the fifth line of the page with the words ' che esser non può' (this is at III. vii. 88 of the Oxford text), and there is added below the word 'Finis.' Foll. 1–35 are occupied with the *Trionfi* of Petrarch.

ζ.

Again in the Laurentian Library [Plut. xl. Cod. 39]. (This and the next two MSS., η and θ, are all three bound alike in old red morocco with bronze corners and old clasps. They all have heavy chains attached.)

This MS. is on paper (watermark apparently a crossbow), without title or colophon to indicate date. The writing is rather ' tondo,' but very clear and upright, with very long tails to letters like *d, l, s,* &c. The second and third Canzoni are in red letters throughout, with blue initials to the stanzas.

η.

In the Laurentian Library [Plut. xl. Cod. 40]. The paper and the writing, which is very sloping, much rounded, and cursive, are much later than in the last. Forms like ' esendo,' ' medeximo,' ' virtuoxo,' &c., seem to imply a N. Italian scribe.

θ.

Again in the Laurentian Library [Plut. xl. Cod. 41]. This is a very interesting MS., having several independent and peculiar variants,[1] and, moreover, exhibiting so many well-

---

[1] It appeared to me to be perhaps as much worth further collation as any that I examined.

marked resemblances with M and *v* as to indicate a distinct
'family' relationship between these three MSS. It is on
paper (watermark a spread eagle), the writing is very thin
and scratchy, sloping and cursive, but very neat and clear.
The initial page is gracefully illuminated in blue and gold.
The date is given in a colophon (fol. 90 v°) as follows :—

'Die xxiiij mensis Septembris æ. indict. xii M°cccc°lxiij scripsi[1].'

On fol. 91 r° we have 'Vita di Dante' by Leonardo d'Aretino, followed on fol. 97 r° by 'Vita di messer Franceso
Petrarcha' by the same author.

On fol. 100 v° 'Oratio facta per uno studiante in laude di
Dante.'

'Se il più splendido et lampengiante dei nostri animi spectabili et nobi-
lissimi citadini dal corporeo instrumento impedito non fusse, certo giamai
sarebbe d' alchuna tenebra d' ignoranza offuscato,' &c.

This ends on fol. 102 r° with the words :—

'debolezza del mio povero ingegnio over doctrina. Laus Deo. Finis.'

In the following passages will be found some of the unmis-
takable resemblances with M and *v* above referred to, and in
several cases the readings seem most likely to be correct
ones :—

I. vii. 59.
II. vi. 24, 25 ; ix. 45.
III. viii. 36, 104.
IV. xiv. 62 ; xxi. 36; xxiv. 47 ; xxvii. 75 ; xxviii. 37.

ι.

In the National (Magliabecchian) Library at Florence
[II. ix. 95; formerly Palch. ix. Cod. 95]. A fifteenth-century
MS. on vellum of a very unusual size, $7\frac{3}{4} \times 5\frac{1}{4}$ inches. It is in
a very minute flowing hand, with the ink much faded, and so
often very difficult to read. It has eighty-nine folios and the
capitals are illuminated in blue. I noted a few peculiarities of
orthography such as 'miglore,' 'ragone' (='ragione'), 'stolti-
ximo', 'complexione,' &c. See note *infra* under *v*.

---

[1] On this date see *infra* under M.

κ

In the National Library at Florence [II. iii. 110; formerly Palch. vi. Cod. 7]. It is on paper and contains both the *Convivio* and the *De Monarchia.* The *Convivio* ends on fol. 92 v° with the colophon ' Finito questo xx di Settembre 1456.' The name of the scribe is carefully erased, but it is found at the end of the *De Monarchia*, which is written by the same hand. This begins on fol. 93 r°, and ends on fol. 128 v° with this colophon : —

' Scritta da mano di me bernardo del nero di filippo, et finito questo dì xxvii di Ottobre mcccclvi . iddio gratias. Amen.'

Thus the transcription of the *De Mon.* occupied a little over two months. (v. *infra*, under ξ.)

The initial letters of the chapters are left blank for illuminations, which were never executed.

λ.

Also in the National Library [II. iii. 47; formerly Palch. iii. Cod. 47]. It is on thick and woolly paper, which seems to me to be certainly of fourteenth century.[1] The writing might well, I think, be the same. Though it is rather coarse and rounded, it is perfectly upright and with extremely long tails and flourishes to the letters. The scribe often inserts the vulgar initial 'h,' as in 'horgani,' 'hubidiente,' &c. I have noted *grolioso* for *glorioso*, which would point to a Tuscan origin for the MS.

Its contents are rather miscellaneous. Foll. 1–94 contain Ovid, *Metamorph.*, 'parafrasto in Volgare da Arrigo Simintendi' : foll. 89–94 containing the preparation for an index of names, &c., to which the references have not yet been supplied. On fol. 95 we read : ' Mo passiamo al tesoro delle cose trovate, e di tutte le parti della Rettorica custodevole memoria.' This goes on to fol. 100 r. Then, after some blank pages on fol. 104 r, we find ' Tractato di abstrologia d' Alfonso,' beginning ' Come è scripto nella tavola d' Alfonso abstrologo,' &c. This lasts till fol. 111 r°, and then, after some more blank pages, the *Convivio* begins on fol. 118 r°.

[1] Fraticelli registers it as fifteenth-century.

μ.

Again in the National Library [Class VI. vii. Cod. 186]. This is on paper of an unusual form, nearly square, $7\frac{3}{4} \times 7\frac{1}{8}$ in. The writing is very ugly, sloping, and straggling, and seems to be late fifteenth-century, and is often very hard to read. The scribe seems to have been an ignorant one (writing such forms as *hordinata, partitta,* &c.). The text, however, presents occasionally some independent variants.

It has ninety-five leaves, the *Convivio* ending on fol. 86 r°.

ν.

In the Bibl. Riccardiana at Florence [1041]. It is on paper, and is dated 1447. The writing is very bad, sloping, and cursive. The scribe seems to have been extremely ignorant, and hopelessly mangles proper names and unusual words; e.g. the third, fourth, fifth, and seventh of the Sages in III. xi. appear as Parmenides, Dedalo, Lodo, and Perioneo[1]. In orthography we have the frequent substitution of *x* for *s* or *ss,* as *dolciximo,* &c. (a Venetian or Lombardo-Venetian peculiarity). I also noted *miglore*[2] and *fregdo* (=*freddo*). The MS., however, has a special interest from its marked relationship to θ and M, as has been already noted under θ.

ξ.

Again in the Bibl. Riccardiana [1043], and also, like the last two MSS., dated. It was written by 'Pierozzo di Domenico di Jacopo di Rosso,' and 'finito xxj di Maggio 1461.' The writing is rounded, cursive, and abounding in flourishes, but very clear and regular. The ignorance of 'messer Pierozzo' is shown in such frequent forms as *hogni, honde, horgani, horrigine,* &c., and in the strange distortions of proper names.

The *Convivio* occupies foll. 1–84 r°. It is then followed by *De Monarchia* on foll. 85 r°–119 r°. As this was finished on June 18 in the same year, it took just four weeks in the copying (v. *supra* under κ).

---

[1] λ, ξ, π and ρ have very similar blunders, except that the fifth name appears as Lido in λ, and as Lidio in the other three.

[2] Vide *supra* under ι, and *infra* under π and M.

o.

Also in the Bibl. Riccardiana [1042]. This is much better written than *v*, but it bears a later date (1468), as appears in the colophon:—

'Explicit per Andrea de' Medici nelle Stinche a dì xviij di gungno (*sic*) MCCCCLXVIII.'

It exhibits in a still more marked degree the fondness for the letter *x*, as in *oppoxito, scuxa, paradixo, philoxophia*, &c. The writer also frequently writes *y* for *i*, as *yn, inphyma*, &c.

π.

A fifteenth-century MS. on paper in the Bibl. Riccardiana [1044]. The *Convivio* ends on fol. 109 v°, and there is added the Sonnet of Dante [No. 43] beginning:—

'Parole mie, che per lo mondo siete.'

This is followed by genealogies of the Catos and Scipios.

On p. 13 r a curious list is given of the *Canzoni* which Dante is supposed to have destined to be the subjects of the fourteen Trattati of the *Convivio*. It is as follows:—

1. 'Voi ch' intendendo'   [Canz. vi. in *Conv*. II.][1]
2. 'Amor che nella '   [Canz. vii. in *Conv*. III.]
3. 'Le dolci rime'   [Canz. viii. in *Conv*. IV.]
4. 'Amor che muovi'   [Canz. ix, quoted *V. E.* II. v. and xi.]
5. 'Io sento sì d' Amor'   [Canz. xiv.]
6. 'Al poco giorno'   [Sest. i, quoted *V. E.* II. 10 and 13.]
7. 'Amor tu vedi '   [Sest. iii, quoted *V. E.* II. 13.]
8. 'Io son venuto'   [Canz. xv.]
9. 'E' m' incresce di me'   [Canz. xiii.]
10. 'Poscia ch' amor'   [Canz. xix, quoted *V. E.* II. 12.]
11. 'La dispietata mente'   [Canz. xvi.]
12. 'Tre donne'   [Canz. xx.]
13. 'Doglia mi reca'   [Canz. x, quoted *V. E.* II. 2.]
14. 'Amor dacchè convien'   [Canz. xi.]

There seems to be no authority for such a selection, or any special propriety in it[2].

---

[1] See *Oxford Dante*, p. 156.

[2] The following are the references made by Dante himself to the unfinished Trattati. In I. i. 103 he states that fourteen *Canzoni* are to be commented on, which would imply fifteen 'Trattati,' as Tratt. I is introductory. The seventh Treatise is referred to in IV. xxvi. 66. The fourteenth ('penultimo') in II. i. 35.

The scribe often treats *g* as soft before *o* and *u*, omitting the usual *i*, e.g. 'disgunto,' 'ragonato' (*vide* under ι φ and M). We find also the vulgarisms of 'hogni,' 'haltri,' 'huniversale,' &c., and the ignorant distortion of proper names.

ρ.

In the National Library at Florence [Palat. 654], on paper, and having 193 folios, writing very clear and like printing, hence probably *c.* 1460 or 1470, as in the case of some beautiful MSS. of the *Divina Commedia* formerly in the Ashburnham Collection.

There is a note on the fly-leaf : 'Questo codice è fidelissima copia del Cod. 134 Gaddiano in Laurenziana.' This is the MS. above described as β. This statement is borne out by the collations I have made, as far as they go. For though ρ has not been so fully examined as β, yet I think it will be found that they agree perfectly in every passage here registered[1], with a single exception. That exception (III. vii. 117 *seqq.*) is instructive, because it is evident that ρ has fallen into error from the common snare of ὁμοιοτέλευτα (v. *supra* p. 79).

The following are a few peculiarities of orthography noted : —'subgiaccia,' 'subgiugne,' 'receptaculo,' 'complexione,' 'oppinione,' 'dyaffano,' 'socto,' 'dolceza,' 'Numma' (='Numa '), 'biltade,' 'phylos,' &c.

σ.

In the Vatican Library [Ottob. Lat. 3332]. The paper and writing clearly of fifteenth century. The date '1489' occurs on the first page, but it is not made with authority, and indeed may only refer to the date of acquisition of the MS. It belonged to ' Jo. Car. de Salviatis.'

This is the only MS. in which I have found the undoubtedly correct insertion of *quando* in I. vii. 59. It appeared to be so essential to the sense, and the accidental omission so easily to

And in I. xii. 86 and IV. xxvii. 100 ' Justice' is stated to be the subject of it. The fifteenth ('ultimo') in I. viii. 131 and III. xv. 144, the subject apparently being about conferring and receiving benefits, or perhaps ' Liberality.'

[1] Even in places where their reading is rather an uncommon one, as e.g. III. xiv. 129, thus :—'per ragione. E per conseguente vedere per ragione,' &c. (This punctuation cannot be right.)   IV. xxi. 24 (v. *infra*, p. 105).

be accounted for, that I inserted it *e conj.* in the Oxford text between square brackets, which are now removed.

τ.

Also in the Vatican [Cappon. 190], beautifully written on vellum, and probably fairly early fifteenth-century.

v.

In the Vatican [Vat. 4778 Lat.]. A fifteenth-century MS., on paper, very neatly written, the letters rather ' tondo' and fairly upright at first, but changing on fol. 21 to a much more flowing and sloping hand. It has *x* for *s* and *ss, passim.*

φ.

Also in the Vatican [Vat. 4779 Lat.]. A fifteenth-century MS., on paper. It has lost the first leaf, and begins at I. i. 120 'ad altra.' It has the same peculiarity in the use of *g* noticed under ι π and M (e. g. ' gustizia,' ' gudicare,' &c.).

χ.

Again in the Vatican [Cod. Vat. Urb. 686 Lat.]. This is a very beautiful MS. on vellum, probably in first half or towards middle of fifteenth century. It has a fine illumination on the first page. The last twenty-four leaves contain the *Canzoni* of Dante. As the press-mark indicates, it came from the Library of the Duke of Urbino. I noticed *sprendore* for *splendore*, which, as far as it goes, would be a Florentine peculiarity.

ψ.

In the Barberini Library at Rome [xlvi. 28]. It is on paper (watermark a hatchet, 1¾ in. long). The handwriting is small, sometimes very small, with long tails and large loops to the letters. It seems to be probably late fourteenth-century or possibly early fifteenth. The MS. contains also a variety of other matters[1].

---

[1] There is another MS. in the Barberini Library [xlvi. 60], of which, though not containing the *Convivio*, a brief notice may have some interest. It consists of 155 folios, and includes a very miscellaneous collection. There are a great many epistles, including some to, or from, Frederic II, e. g. *to* Frederic from Gregory IX, Innocent IV, Louis of France, and *from* Frederic to Louis of France, to princes of Italy, &c. These are translated into Italian, and it is stated that some are published and some unpublished.

The MS. ends with a fragment of Dante's epistle to Henry VII (Epist. vii)

ω.

A MS. in the Library of St. Mark at Venice [Class XI, Cod. xxxiv.]. It is on paper (watermark a small crossbow); the writing is beautifully regular and in very black ink. Both the paper and the writing are, I think, undoubtedly of fourteenth century. There is no title or colophon. The *Canzoni* are written in much larger letters and of quite a different type, and their lines run on like prose.

F.

Also in the Library of St. Mark [Class X, Cod. xxvi.]. This is the only MS. which I have not personally examined. It was most unfortunately away on loan when I was at Venice. But the Librarian, Dr. Coggiola, has most kindly sent me the collation of the most important passages in my list, and also a full description of the MS., on which the following account is based. It is a fifteenth-century MS. on paper, containing both the *Vita Nuova* and the *Convivio*. It contains eightyfour leaves, of which fol. 24 is blank between the two works. These are written by different hands. On an initial parchment fly-leaf we read, ' Questo libro è di Lucha di Simone della Robbia . . . ,' the rest of the sentence being erased or rather cut out. See Barbi's edition of the *Vita Nuova*, Introd., p. L, where it is stated that Farsetti (who formerly owned this MS.) has made a note that it was the foundation of Biscioni's text, ed. 1723.

B.

This MS. is in the Bodleian [Canon. Ital. 114]. It is a fifteenth-century MS. on paper, of 190 leaves. The scribe is frequently guilty of the vulgarism of the initial *h*, as in ' hordinato,' ' Tullio negli Hufizi,' &c. There is scarcely any punctuation in this MS.

translated into Italian. A torn leaf has lost about the first ten lines, and it ends at ll. 58, 59 of the Epistle with these words :—' l'onda del mare anphierico (*sic*) a pena dingnata d'essere citta (i. e. cincta) cholla non utile onda del mare occioano (*sic*).' There the MS. stops.

It contains also (1) the *Vita Nuova.*

(2) A considerable number (28) of Canzoni, Ballate, Sonetti, &c., of Dante.

(3) The *Convivio.*

See further, Mortara, *Catalogo dei Codici Canoniciani Italici,* pp. 128, 129.

D.

In the British Museum [Add. MS. 28840]. This is a mere fragment, since all between III. ii. 15 and IV. xxiv. 71—i. e. rather more than half of the whole work—is missing. It was acquired by the Museum in 1871. It is of the fifteenth century, on paper, the writing rounded, sloping, and with many contractions and flourishes. It has no title, colophon, or date. In foll. 27 v and 28 r there are two insertions by the copyist (as appears by a marginal note in pencil to that effect) of about twenty-seven and seven lines respectively. These occur at II. xiv. 155 and II. xiv. 195.

H.

This very fine MS. belongs to the Library of the Earl of Leicester at Holkham [1]. Both the handwriting and the exceptionally white vellum are extremely beautiful. It is probably late fourteenth, or possibly (as estimated by Roscoe) early fifteenth century. One might safely say *c.* 1400. The initial letters of the chapters are illuminated. There is practically no punctuation ; seldom even any full stops. It abounds with Latinized and also unassimilated forms of words such as *cipta* (*città*), *scripto, lectera, licterato, sententia, scriptura, tractato,* and the like. For *e* we generally find 'Et' at the beginning of a sentence, and a symbol something like ' & ' in the middle; *è* is generally written ' *e* ' (*sic*), but not always [2].

It has the colophon :—' Explicit. Deo gratias. Amen. Per me Antonium Marii Francesci Nini.'

---

[1] I am grateful to the late Earl for kindly allowing it to be deposited at the Bodleian for my inspection.

[2] These points, though small, are worth noticing, as it will be seen later that many readings are uncertain through the confusion of *e, c,* and *e'*. See *infra* under P and Q, and *supra,* p. 7.

K

Errors from ὁμοιοτέλευτα are specially frequent. This is evidently the cause of the omission of the words bracketed in the following passages:—

I. i. 39, 'cioè la prima dalla parte [di dentro e la prima dalla parte] di fuori non sono,' &c.

I. vii. 11 *seqq.*, 'e però era impossibile essere obediente [Che allo Latino fosse stato essere impossibile essere obediente] si manifesta,' &c.

I have noted a good many resemblances between B and H, but allowance must perhaps be made for the fact that only these two MSS. were examined side by side.

M.

This is a MS. which I had the good fortune to purchase from Fratelli Bocca of Rome in 1880. It is interesting from the record which it contains of its previous ownership and also for the clear relation of its text to two other MSS., θ and ν[1]. It bears its date in the colophon, 'Fine alla terza canzona di maggo[2] a dì 18, 1463,' or 1493, the last figure but one having been altered from 6 to 9, or 9 to 6. More probably the latter, since the earlier date would be more acceptable to an owner. It is curious that the related MS. θ (*vide supra*) bears the actual date 1463 (ν is dated 1447). There is a title (in a later hand) as follows:—

'Convivio de dante alighieri fiorentino
di pierantonio de benedetto
buonaparte
e delli amici parenti e di tutti quelli
che si volessino servire.'

On the fly-sheet opposite a modern owner has entered the following interesting note:—

'Pier Antonio di Benedetto di Piero Buonaparte, e non Bonaparte come scrivesi generalmente, appartengono (*sic*) a quel ramo di detta famiglia che da Firenze si trasferì a Sarzana. Benedetto padre di Pierantonio, già possessore di questo codice, e autore delle cinque linee che ci stanno in fronte,

---

[1] See some illustrations of this collected *supra* under θ.

[2] This peculiarity of orthography is common throughout the MS., e.g. 'maggormente,' 'cagone' (= 'cagione'), 'gusto' ('giusto'). Other peculiarities of 'g' are 'fregdo,' 'nugoli,' &c.

fu fratello di quel prete Giacomo che si trovò al sacco di Roma del 1527. (V. Genealogia della famiglia Bonaparte, in fine al Ninci, Storia dell' Isola d' Elba).'

I have extracted the following from Foissy, 'La famille Bonaparte depuis 1264,' Paris, 1830 :—

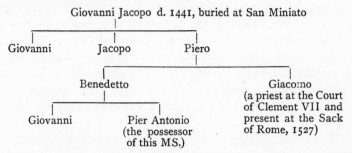

```
                  Giovanni Jacopo d. 1441, buried at San Miniato
                  |
  |               |               |
Giovanni       Jacopo          Piero
                                  |
            |                              |
        Benedetto                      Giacomo
            |                          (a priest at the Court
  |                    |               of Clement VII and
Giovanni          Pier Antonio         present at the Sack
                  (the possessor       of Rome, 1527)
                  of this MS.)
```

There is a finely illuminated initial letter (S), and at the bottom of the page a coat of arms surrounded with a richly illuminated framework ; the arms belonging, I believe, to the Bonaparte family.

The writing of the MS. is very clear, regular, and print-like, but the text, though I think (as remarked under θ) of a good character, is disfigured by an exceptionally large number of blunders due to ὁμοιοτέλευτα ; also grotesque distortions of unfamiliar words, such as proper names, e.g. *Scargieri* for *Stagirita* (IV. vi. 131), and *accidentiani* for *Accademia*, (*ib.*, l. 128). I have noticed one or two variants which look like 'improvements' of the text, e. g. in III. v. 140, where for 'e uno punto più' M has 'e trenta minuti,' which is very nearly the exact amount, viz. 28′. In II. iii. 46, after *ore* M reads 'e xv minuti d' un' ora,' but this is far less accurate than the *lect. vulg.*, viz. $\frac{14}{15}$ of an hour, the true amount being 56′.

P.

This and the next MS. are in the Bibliothèque Nationale at Paris. I am greatly indebted to the courtesy of the Librarian for allowing them to be sent over to the British Museum for my inspection. [The press-mark is ' Ital. 536.'] This MS. belonged to Jacopo Corbinelli, who has inserted short notes. It is on vellum, of fifteenth century, and in a clear and print-like hand. The first thirty-two leaves contain an Italian translation of the *De Monarchia*. The *Convivio* begins on fol. 33. On the first page of each Trattato, or each Book, of both these works are finely illuminated initials. The copyist habitually ignores any distinction between *e* and *è*[1]. We find (as in the case of H) unassimilated forms of words *passim* as *scripto*, *subjecto*, *Pyctagora*, &c., and also the vulgar initial *h*, as *homai*, *ha* (= the prep. *a*), &c. A most important passage is found at II. i. 21, where this MS. alone[2] has preserved the undoubtedly true reading, and enables us to fill the lacuna which in other MSS. has arisen obviously from ὁμοιοτέλευτα.

A peculiar (though obviously incorrect) reading is found at III. xi. 24, where 'cinquanta' is omitted. Also I. vii. 58 may be noted: 'e l' uomo è ubidiente alla natura (*sic*) giustitia comanda,' &c.

There is no date or colophon.

Q.

In the Bibliothèque Nationale at Paris [Ital. 1014]. Sumptuously bound in red morocco, ornamented with fleurs-de-lys on the back and the royal arms on the front cover, with a finely illuminated title-page, and the initial letters to chapters (as commonly) alternately red and blue. It is on vellum and consists of 138 leaves. It has the brief colophon, ' Finito il Convivio di Dante.' The hand is print-like, the letters quite distinct, but much rounded and rather sloping. As in the last MS., unassimilated words occur *passim*, as *decto*, *tucto*, *scripto*, *socto*, *subgecto*, *mecto*, *quactro*, &c.

The copyist does not accent *e* when it obviously = *è*. When *e* = 'and,' it is very generally (if not always) written '*et*' or ' &.' So that it may be taken that *e* regularly means *è*.

There is no colophon.

---

[1] See Introduction, *supra*, p. 7.

[2] The MS. π also has these words, but in combination with a good many besides, which seemed to me like a spurious addition infecting the whole insertion with suspicion. See Fraticelli's text and note *h. l.*

Tr.

In the Library of the Marchese Trivulzio at Milan [No. 1090]. Both the writing and paper seemed to me to be of late fourteenth century, but if we said *c.* 1400 we should not probably be far wrong. The letters have long tails and flourishes and are perfectly upright.

The title is curious—'Hic incipit *Monarchia* solennissimi Danti Aldigerii.' The *Convivio*, however, follows. The same unassimilated forms abound as in the last two MSS. (generally an archaic sign). Also *x* is often found for *s* and *ss*, as noted in several cases previously. A more singular feature is the great frequency of strange and unintelligible divisions of words, as *de luditore* for *dell' uditore*; *della legorica* for *dell' allegorica*, and the like[1].

As usual, the text has suffered from ὁμοιοτέλευτα, e. g. at III. xiv. 128 it reads thus: 'Siccome *per lei* si crede,' where more than two lines, ' molto di quello . . . così *per lei*,' have been dropped, evidently owing to the recurrence of the words ' per lei.'

U.

This is a second Trivulzian MS. [No. 1089]. It is extremely difficult to read, being written in a very flowing and apparently almost modern hand. I did not attempt to collate more than a very few passages, in which nothing peculiar was noted.

The MSS. above described include *all* that I have been able to trace. Possibly a few others may exist in other Libraries. I should add that Dr. Witte, in his *Centuria di Correzioni*, frequently refers to a MS. in his own possession, and also to one belonging to Baron Kirkup, but in the absence of any description I have not been able to trace or identify these. I have not made use of such references, partly because many of my selected passages are not included in them; and still more because both MSS. probably, and the latter almost certainly, may have found their way into public libraries, and may possibly be identical with some of those already collated.

---

[1] On this, *vide* Introduction, pp. 7, 8.

DANTE'S THEORY OF CREATION

SYNOPSIS

PRINCIPAL passages bearing on this, pp. 134–136:—(i) *Par.* vii. 121
seqq.; (ii) *Par.* xxix. 16–36; (iii) *De Mon.* I. iii. 45–62 ; (iv) *Quaestio,* § 18.

Explanation of technical terms in connexion with this subject: (1)
Prima materia (pp. 136–140) ; (2) *intendere* (pp. 140–142).

Distinction of Immediate (pp. 136–156) and Mediate Creation (pp.
156–163).

'Immediate' applies to *prima materia* (pp. 136–140); the Angels
(pp. 146–156); the Heavens (pp. 142, 143) ; the Soul of Man (pp. 143–146);
also his body in its original state of innocence (pp. 145, 146). Creation of
Angels (*a*) in its metaphysical aspect (pp. 146–152) ; (*β*) in regard to
moral or theological questions (pp. 152–154) ; (*γ*) psychological conditions
(pp. 154–156).

Processes of 'Mediate' Creation (pp. 156–163).

The four 'Elements' (pp. 157–159) ; *corpora composte* or higher forms
of corporeal existence (*ibid.*). The technical term *complessione* (pp. 159–
161). The 'medium' of all such Mediate Creation was angelic agency
operating through the Heavens and the heavenly bodies in them (pp.
161–163). Bearing of this upon Astrology as it was regarded by Dante
(pp. 163, 164). Dante's teaching on Anthropomorphism (pp. 164, 165)
and in its possible relation to Evolution (p. 165).

The passages which embody Dante's Theory of Creation
are *prima facie* very difficult on account of the number of
highly technical terms occurring in them. But when the
precise meaning attached to those terms by himself and
other mediaeval writers is clearly recognized, his teaching on
this matter is no longer, I venture to think, obscure.

It would be well to take note at the outset of the principal
passages bearing on this subject. They are mainly these:—

(i) *Par.* vii. 121 *seqq.*

This Canto deals with three difficulties by which Dante's
mind is beset, in the endeavour to 'justify the ways of God
to men' in respect of the sacrifice of Christ.

(1) As the Jews only carried out God's purpose, why were they afterwards punished, as the Emperor Justinian has declared in vi. 92, 93?

(2) Why was it needful that Man's redemption should be carried out in the way it was? With these two points we are not now concerned, but a third difficulty is raised out of a passing statement of Beatrice in ll. 67–69 as follows :—

'That which from It (Divine Goodness) immediately proceeds [i.e. without any intermediate or secondary agency of creation or causation] hath thenceforth no ending, because Its impress is never removed when It sets its seal '—i.e. anything created *directly or immediately* by God can never perish. It is endowed with an eternity *a parte post*. Hence the difficulty now stated, ll. 124 *seqq.* :—

'Thou sayest, I see Water, I see Fire, Air, and Earth, and all their combinations come to corruption and endure but a little while, and these things were still created things [meaning, as the context shows, *created by God Himself*], so that if what I have said has been true, they ought to be secure from corruption.'

Now follows Beatrice's 'explanation,' ll. 130–148 :—

'The Angels, brother, and the pure region in which thou now art [i.e. Heaven] can be said to have been created even as they are in their entire being. But the elements which thou hast named[1], and those things which are made up of them have been informed by an influence itself created. Created was the matter which they possess ; created was the informing influence in those stars which revolve around them. The rays and movement of the sacred lights [i.e. the Stars] draw forth from composite matter, endued with capacity therefor, the soul of every animal and of plants. But your life supreme beneficence breathes into you immediately, and It makes it to be enamoured of Itself, so that thenceforth it ever longeth for It. And hence thou canst further argue for your resurrection, if thou again considerest how the human flesh was then made when our first parents both were made.'

Here we have at once the vitally important distinction in Dante's system between Mediate and Immediate Creation clearly set forth.

Next (ii) *Par.* xxix. 16–36.

As I shall have occasion to speak in detail of this passage

---

[1] In the language of St. Augustine, *C. D.* XI. x., they are 'non simplicia, et ob hoc mutabilia.'

later, I will not quote it at length now. It bears specially on the question of the Creation of the Angels.

(iii) Another passage to be noticed is *De Mon.* I. iii. 45–62. This deals with the several grades of Being, from the lowest form of existence to the highest; and in particular it introduces us to the technical expression 'complexionatum,' which together with the Italian 'complessione' enters largely into the discussions of the subject before us. See further especially *Conv.* III. iii. 23; IV. xxi., xxiii., xxiv.

(iv) Another such passage to which we shall have to refer is found in *Quaestio*, § 18.

There are two technical terms recurring frequently in passages bearing on the subject before us in Dante and other writers, which specially call for explanation :—

(1) 'Prima materia,' and (2) 'intendere.'

First as to *Prima materia.*

This is the formless *substratum* of all material existence. It is not as yet any particular thing or object—it is 'without form and void'—but it is *capable* of becoming anything whatever. It is no definite thing, not even any so-called 'element' *in actu,* but any and everything *in posse, in potentia,* 'ἐν δυνάμει.' It is 'the potentiality of everything, the actuality of nothing'—the 'pura potenza' of *Par.* xxix. 34. It is itself entirely imperceptible, until impressed with 'Form.' To all or any existing things, even the 'elements,' it bears the same relation as the lump of clay to the finished work of the potter; or the block of marble to the sculptor's statue. In order that it may become anything *in actu,* even one of the so-called 'elements,' it must become 'complexionata,' 'conditioned,' or 'qualified.'

St. Augustine, commenting on Gen. i. 1, 'In the beginning God created the heaven and the earth,' says: 'Nihil aliud his verbis quam materiae corporalis informitatem insinuare [Scriptura voluit], eligens eam usitatius appellare quam obscurius[1].' This 'formlessness of corporeal matter' is the 'prima materia,' though here described in more intelligible

---

[1] *De Genesi ad Literam,* II. c. xi. § 24.

and less obscure terms (or, as we might say, more 'popularly')
as 'heaven and earth.' This was created 'in the beginning.'
St. Augustine says of it elsewhere: 'Ipsa vero materies
coelum et terra, *velut semen coeli et terrae*, appellata.' The
Coelum, or Heaven, *as we see it*—i.e. 'firmamentum'—was
the work of the second day; and the 'elements' (or 'species
propriae') of water and earth were the work of the third day,
and this is indicated by the *fiat*—'Congregentur aquae et
appareat arida[1].'

So, again, in *Conf.* xii. 8, he contrasts 'coelum coeli' of
v. 1 with 'firmamentum' of *vv.* 6–8, which was 'coelum terrae
huius et maris, quae fecisti tertio die, *dando sꞥciem* visibilem
informi materiae quam fecisti ante omnem diem.' Also the
'terra' of *v.* 1, 'non erat talis qualem nunc cernimus et
tangimus. Invisibilis enim erat et incomposita, et abyssus
erat, super quem non erat lux[2].'

Here is Milton's account of this 'prima materia[3]':—

'Before their eyes in sudden view appear
The secrets of the hoary deep—a dark
Illimitable ocean, without bound,
Without dimension; where length, breadth, and height,
And time, and place, are lost; where eldest Night
And Chaos, ancestors of Nature, hold
Eternal anarchy, amidst the noise
Of endless wars, and by confusion stand.
    *   *   *   *   *
                . . . this wild abyss,
The womb of Nature and perhaps her grave,
Of neither sea, nor shore, nor air, nor fire,
But all these in their pregnant causes mixed
Confusedly, and which thus must ever fight,
Unless the Almighty Maker them ordain
His dark materials to create more worlds.'

[1] *Lib. Imperf.* § 10. See further, § 11. In § 32 the mention of 'aquae' above
and below the firmament on the second Day, St. Augustine supposes probably to
refer to 'ipsam mundi materiam,' or 'confusionem materialem,' the 'congregatio'
of which on the third day was 'ipsa formatio ut talis esset species.' And that
the same would apply to the 'earth' as spoken of in v. 1, he argues from the
language of v. 2, 'Terra erat invisibilis et incomposita,' *Gen. ad Lit.* I. i. § 3.
Thus when the terms 'aqua' or 'terra' occur before the third Day, they are to
be referred, as it were proleptically, to the *prima materia* itself, which was
destined shortly to be developed into these distinct 'species.'

[2] Compare a similar passage in *Civ. Dei*, XI. ix.

[3] *Par. Lost*, II. ll. 890 *seqq.*

Among other sources likely to have been accessible to Dante we may add these:—

Albertus Magnus similarly defines 'prima materia' as 'substantia in potentia existens et nullam omnino formam habens in actu[1].' Here again we recognize Dante's expression 'pura potenza' in *Par.* xxix. 34.

Aquinas also follows Augustine and comments thus: 'Ideo per congregationem aquarum et apparentiam aridae impressio talium formarum designatur[2],' i.e. these 'forms' were impressed or stamped (a very common metaphor with Dante) upon the *prima materia*, causing it to become *complexionata*, 'conditioned' or qualified, and thus the so-called 'elements' of Water and Earth were created or brought into actuality.

Peter Lombard also [*Sentt.* II. Dist. 12, § 5], with some variations in detail, holds similar views. He further explains that the 'prima materia' was described as 'terra,' or as 'terra et aqua,' 'ut res ignota notis vocabulis insinuaretur imperitioribus. . . . Sub his nominibus significata est materies illa *confusa et informis* quae nulla specie cerni et tractari poterat.'

Once more, Brunetto Latini says that God made at the beginning 'grosse matière sans forme et sans figure,' but of such a nature that *from it* he could form all things, and this is called 'ilem,' i.e. ὕλην. Such is the teaching on the subject of the *prima materia* of authors, with all or any of whom Dante may be supposed to have been familiar.

Dante does not go into the details of the creative acts of the first three days, and indeed (as we shall see later) he would probably not assign them to the direct or immediate operation of God. But the 'prima materia' he would hold to have been created, or as he would say 'intesa' or 'thought out' by God, 'ante omnem diem,' or in his own words, 'in sua eternità di tempo fuore' (*Par.* xxix. 16).

These are some of the passages in which he speaks for himself on the subject:—

In *Conv.* IV. i. 64 he declares that in youth, i.e. shortly

---

[1] *C. et M.* I. Tr. iii. c. 4.   [2] *Summa,* I. xliv. 2; lxvi. 1; lxix. 1.

after the death of Beatrice—when he became devoted to the
pursuit of philosophy personified in the Donna Gentile—
he was specially interested in the problem of the '*prima
materia* degli elementi,' whether it was 'da Dio intesa.'
(This difficult expression will be considered later.) One is
reminded of the confession of Socrates in the *Phaedo* (96 A)
that '*νέος ὢν*' he keenly desired '*τὴν περὶ φύσεως ἱστορίαν* . . .
*εἰδέναι τὰς αἰτίας ἑκάστου, διὰ τί γίγνεται ἕκαστον καὶ διὰ τί
ἀπόλλυται καὶ διὰ τί ἔστι*.'

Further, in *Conv.* III. viii. 125 *seqq.* he declares that 'prima
materia' is absolutely unknowable save in its effects. He
is pointing out that any things which transcend our intellect—
so that we cannot contemplate them in themselves, any
more than the human eye can gaze directly at the sun
—that such things are most suitably treated by means of
their effects. It is only thus (he adds) that we can obtain
some cognizance of God, of His Angels, and of the *prima
materia* (ll. 143-145).

It is much in the same way that he declares that we assume
the existence of the Ninth or Crystalline Heaven or *Primum
Mobile*, 'quello che non è sensibile.' It is not only in itself
invisible, but it is not (like the other heavens) distinguished
even by any visible object whatever. Its existence is simply
proved '*by its effects*,' i.e. by the uniform motion· imparted by
it to all the other heavens.

Again in *Conv.* III. xv. 59 *seqq.* Dante speaks of certain
things which dazzle, in some sense, our intellect, inasmuch as
we affirm their existence, though our intellect cannot behold
them, as for example, God, Eternity, and *prima materia* (l. 63).
These we cannot see, but with firm faith we believe in their
existence. Yet we cannot understand what they are except
by denying things of them ('se non cose negando,' l. 67). In
this way one can approach to a knowledge of them, and not
otherwise. (We might illustrate this by the numerous negative definitions of the *Quicunque vult*.)

It was generally agreed then by all the writers on this subject whose teaching would be familiar to Dante, that this *prima
materia* or 'primal Matter' was in some sense 'created' by

God Himself, and that it was His first step towards the creation of the material universe.

(2) Next as to the word *intendere* as used by Dante.

We ask next what was Dante's conception of the *process* or processes of this so-called 'creation,' as applied both to this primordial 'matter' and also to subsequent developments of being. This brings us to the consideration of the difficult word *intendere* in the above passage (*Conv.* IV. i. 64) and several times elsewhere in Dante. Though I cannot satisfy myself as to a good English equivalent, I do not think its meaning is difficult to explain. It has, however, been much disputed in the particular passage just quoted. Fortunately Dante has himself, in another passage of the *Convivio*, explained his use of the word quite clearly. This occurs in reference to its occurrence in the first line of the first Canzone, which poem forms the subject of the second Treatise of the *Convivio*—

'Voi che *intendendo* (by Thought) il terzo ciel movete.'

The beings here addressed are the Angels by whom the movements of the third Heaven are governed—the *Angeli Movitori* who preside, each according to his allotted function, over the revolution of the several Heavens and 'all that is therein.' The manner in which that control is exercised is described as 'intendendo,' and this process is carefully explained in II. c. vi. (last ten lines). 'These movers do set in motion by thought only—*solo intendendo*—the revolution in that particular object which each one moves. The most noble form (or essence) of the heaven, which hath in itself the principle of this passive nature, i.e. which is so constituted as to receive such angelic influence and guidance passively.'—[I interpose a short parenthesis to explain this word 'passively.' It seems to mean that the heaven receives that angelic influence without in any way resisting or impeding it, and thereby losing some portion of it. This is always the case with the *sorda materia* of lower grades of being, so that much of such influence from above is lost as it were in transmission. See *Par.* i. 129, 'Perch' a risponder la materia è sorda.' Illustrate also by the contrast of such phrases as 'inobedientia materiae' in

Quaestio, § 18, and 'la mala disposizione della materia' in *Conv.* III. iv. 66, and several similar passages.] To resume— 'This most noble "form" of the Heavens . . . revolves *touched* by the moving virtue "*che questo intende*" (perhaps) "which embodies or envisages this (motion) in thought": and when I say "*touched*," I mean not by bodily touch, but by the touch of virtue (or power) which is directed thereto.'

Again, in *Conv.* II. vii. 9, where this line of the Canzone is again cited, we have a similar gloss: 'Voi che *intendendo*, cioè collo intelletto solo.' Another curious gloss occurs in III. xii. 82, in connexion with the words 'Non vede il sol che tutto 'l mondo gira.' It is explained that the Sun is here the symbol of the spiritual Sun, i. e. God, and that thus the words 'il sol che tutto 'l mondo gira' mean—'Iddio, che tutto *intende*; chè suo *girare* è suo *intendere*.'

A consideration of these several passages together seems to show that 'intendere' means to make to be an object of thought, and that when this takes place in the mind of God that object of thought thereby acquires existence, comes into being, or, in other words, is created. Thus we may not only say, 'He spake and it was done,' but 'He thought and it was done[1];' or, in the language of Browning, 'From thy will stream the worlds' ['Saul,' § 18]. The primordial substance, then, or *prima materia*, may and must become subject to further developments or embodiments later. Yet its initial existence or its 'creation' is brought about in this manner. And if this be the frequent meaning of the word *intendere* in such connexion, I cannot doubt that it has the same sense in that passage, evidently a highly technical one (*Conv.* IV. i. 64), in which Dante refers to his early speculations as to whether 'la prima materia degli elementi era da Dio *intesa*,' i.e. was

[1] We may perhaps illustrate this by the pantheistic theory of Plotinus (to which, however, Dante would by no means subscribe) that the material universe was one of the forms or hypostases of the Divine Being—λόγος προφορικός—the Thought of God coming forth or projected beyond Himself—as distinguished from that Thought immanent in the depths of His Being, 'λόγος ἐνδιάθετος'; itself another hypostasis or aspect or qualification of His Absolute Essence. One might almost venture to apply to these two *hypostases* of God Dante's term 'esse complexionatum,' i. e. 'Being' qualified or conditioned, in contrast with 'Esse' pure and simple.

(in popular language) *created* by God in the manner just described. The actual question 'Utrum materia prima sit creata a Deo' forms the text of Aquinas, *S. T.* I. xliv. 2 ; and the following ' Quaestio ' begins :—' Deinde quaeritur de modo *emanationis* rerum a primo principio, qùi dicitur *creatio.*' It is declared to be ' sine motu ' and ' sine mutatione.' The synonym ' emanation ' recalls such phrases of Dante as these : '*raggiò* insieme tutto ' in *Par.* xxix. 29 ; ' L' ardor santo, ch' ogni cosa *raggia,*' in *Par.* vii. 74; and 'quum omnis *vis causandi* sit *radius* quidam profluens a prima causa, quae Deus est' in *Ep.* x. c. 25 *seqq.*

Again, when Aquinas describes Creation as being effected ' per intellectum et voluntatem Dei ' (I. xix. 4 r), and further insists that in God ' voluntas et intellectus sunt idem ' (I. xxii. 1 *fin.*), he seems to be describing a creative process exactly similar to that which Dante denotes by ' *intendere.*'

Another illustration may be found in Aq. *S. T.* I. lxi. 3 (quoting Damascenus) : ' ut theologus dicit Gregorius : " Et primum quidem Deus *excogitavit* angelicas virtutes et coelestes ; et excogitatio opus eius fuit."' Add *Summa*, I. xv. 2 r, ' Ordo universi est proprie a Deo *intentus,*' and I. xv. 2 r, xviii. 4 r.

It results then that the *prima materia* was created by God Himself *immediately*, without the employment or intervention of any secondary agencies, and by that process of His own Thought which has been now expounded.

But further this process of *immediate Creation* by God is not limited to the *prima materia*. It applies also to the *Angels*, or *sustanze separate* (as they are often called), and to the *Heavens*, and to the *Soul* of Man.

For the two first of these see *Par.* vii. 130–2 : ' The Angels, Brother, and the pure region in which thou now art [i.e. Heaven] can be said to have been created even as they are, in their entire being.'

(1) As regards the *paese sincero*, or Heaven, I think this must certainly refer to the whole system of the Heavens, not (as has been thought) to the Tenth Heaven only, or the immediate abode of God, for of this it could not be said to Dante, ' in which thou now art,' since he is in the Heaven

of Mercury. Here I think the passages already quoted from St. Augustine help us, by the distinction which he draws between the 'coelum coeli' and the 'coelum terrae huius et maris,' called in Genesis 'firmamentum,' which was the work of the second day. In reference to the primordial Creation of Gen. i. 1, St. Augustine in *Conf.* xii. 7 says, addressing God— 'Tu eras, et aliud nihil ; unde [i.e. ex nihilo] fecisti coelum et terram ; duo quaedam, unum prope te, alterum prope nihil '— 'one almost Thyself,' i. e. Heaven ; 'the other almost nothing,' i. e. the *prima materia*[1], here designated by 'terram,' as St. Augustine expressly says in one of the passages already quoted (*supra*, pp. 136, 137). And observe that this distinction would certainly be accepted by Dante. For the heaven of which he is now speaking (*Par.* vii. 130–132) being created immediately by God under the conditions described in ll. 67–72, 'non ha poi fine.' But he was fully aware that the 'heavens and the earth which are now (*firmamentum*) . . . are kept in store, reserved unto fire against the day of judgement.' They would correspond with 'the elements' of the next line (133), which were undoubtedly to pass away, not being created immediately by God : and these 'elements shall melt with fervent heat' (2 Pet. iii. 7, 10). The distinction between 'coelum,' in this sense, and 'the elements' is very clearly expressed in *Epist.* X. xxiii. 435–437, 'ut patet de coelo et elementis, quorum quidem illud incorruptibile, illa vero corruptibilia sunt.' It is most important, therefore, to note carefully from the context the precise sense in which the highly ambiguous word 'heaven' is being used from time to time.

(2) Reserving for the present the larger question, or indeed the many such questions, relating to the Creation of the Angels, we will speak next of the other subject of God's immediate Creation, viz. the Human Soul. See later in this same Canto (*Par.* vii), ll. 142–144 :—

> 'Ma vostra vita senza mezzo spira
> La somma beninanza, e la innamora
> Di sè, sì che poi sempre la disira.'

---

[1] Aquinas, quoting this passage in *S. T.*, I. xliv. 2, comments : '*unum prope te*, scilicet Angelum ; *unum prope nihil*, scilicet materiam primam.' 'Angelum' is surely wrong, having regard to the context in St. Augustine.

In contrast with this, the previous *terzina* declares that the life or soul of every other animal, and also that of plants, is brought forth not by God directly, but mediately by the light and the movements of the heavenly bodies, or by stellar influences. But as regards the Soul of Man, Dante frequently and emphatically maintains the theory of Creationism as opposed to Traducianism, i.e. that every individual Soul comes into being by a distinct and immediate act of Creation by God. Besides the passage above quoted we need only refer to the explicit and dogmatic declaration which Dante puts into the mouth of Statius as a solemn refutation of the false teaching of Averroes, in *Purg.* xxv. 68 *seqq.* :—

' And know that so soon as in the embryo the organization of the brain is complete, the Prime Mover to it turns, rejoicing over such skill of Nature, and breathes into it a new spirit, full of power, which draws to its own essence that which it finds active there, and forms a single soul, which lives and feels and is centred in itself.'

We cannot fail to recognize here the echo of the simple declaration of Genesis: 'God breathed into his nostrils the breath of life, and man became a living soul' (Gen. ii. 7). See also *Conv.* IV. xxi., which closely resembles in its details the account of the generation and development of the embryo given in *Purg.* xxv. See once more another emphatic declaration in the same sense in *Purg.* xvi. 85–90.

It is almost needless to say that Dante follows St. Thomas Aquinas in this as in so much else. To quote only two passages : *Summa*, I. lxxv. 6 r, ' anima brutorum producitur ex virtute aliqua corporea, anima vero humana a Deo.' He here quotes Eccles. xii. 7, 'the spirit shall return to God who gave it.' Add I. xc. 3 r *fin.*, 'Anima rationalis non potest produci nisi a Deo immediate.' We observe that in *Par.* vii. 139–143 Dante is little more than (as he has been termed) 'a poetic Aquinas' in respect of these two passages.

But if we turn once more to the concluding lines of *Par.* vii. we shall see that from this doctrine of the immediate, as opposed to mediate, Creation, Dante feels justified in arguing for not only the Immortality of the Soul, but also the Resurrection of the Body.

> ' E quinci puoi argomentare ancora
> Vostra resurrezion, se tu ripensi
> Come l' umana carne fessi *allora*
> *Che li primi parenti intrambo fensi.*'

Here Dante evidently refers to the description in Genesis, chapters i. and ii., of the creation both of Adam and Eve by a direct and immediate act of God Himself. So that here ' resurrezion' includes the resurrection of the body (in a restored condition) as well as the immortality of the soul. Human nature

> ' Qual fu creata, fu sincera e buona '

and in that condition it was assumed by Christ, and will be resumed by us (see ll. 35, 36); and so to it the declaration (ll. 67–69) applies:—

' Whatever proceeds from It (" la divina bontà ") *immediately* ("senza mezzo") thenceforth has no ending, because Its impress cannot be removed when It sets Its seal.'

Further, the teaching of Dante as to all these objects of immediate creation (p. 142) is evidently derived from Aquinas, *S. T.* I. xcvii. 1 r, who similarly enumerates ' Angelus, Corpus caeleste, Anima,' and he adds further: 'man in his primal nature of innocence in Eden [1].' He then shows how each of these in a different manner or on different grounds is, or was, incorruptible. And his explanation in detail of this primal nature of man (in a passage which was almost certainly in Dante's mind) throws much light on the above compressed argument in *Par.* vii. *fin.*, especially in its bearing on the resurrection of the body. St. Thomas, *l. c.*, quotes St. Augustine as follows: ' Tam potenti natura Deus fecit animam ut ex eius beatitudine *redundet in corpus* plenitudo sanitatis et incorruptionis vigor.' Aquinas then proceeds to state his own view thus: 'Non enim corpus eius erat indissolubile per aliquem immortalitatis vigorem in eo existentem; sed inerat animae

---

[1] This last is stated quite explicitly in *S. T.* I. xci. 2 r: 'Prima formatio humani corporis non potuit esse per aliquam virtutem creatam, *sed immediate a Deo.*'

vis quaedam supernaturaliter divinitus data per quam poterat corpus ab omni corruptione praeservare quamdiu ipsa Deo subiecta mansisset' (see also I. cii. 2 r). He adds, however (r 4), that this form of immortality of the body was different from that to which we now look forward, which has been gained for us by Christ—'differt immortalitas gloriae quae promittitur in praemium, ab immortalitate quae fuit homini collata in statu innocentiae.' Obviously the 'spiritual body' of St. Paul is something different from the material body of 'li primi parenti,' whatever may have originally been its special privileges or immunities as contemplated by Dante and Aquinas.

There is another passage that may have been present to Dante's mind in St. Anselm, *Cur Deus Homo*, II. ii. and iii. He argues on *a priori* grounds that man, as created, would not have died, had he not sinned, because he would have done nothing to deserve death; and then he proceeds to argue almost in the words of *Par.* vii. 145, ' Unde aperte quandoque futura mortuorum resurrectio probatur,' viz. because restitution to the state from which man fell would be incomplete otherwise. So the body when itself 'delivered from the bondage of corruption' recovers once more the condition—

> 'Come l' umana carne fessi allora
> Che li primi parenti intrambo fensi.'

Thus the imperishability of an immediate work of God, declared in vii. 67-69, is still realized, for

> 'Solo il peccato è quel che la disfranca,
> E falla dissimile al Sommo Bene,'

and 'he that is dead is freed from sin,' so that the sole disqualifying condition is again removed through the complete redemptive work of Christ.

(3) We now pass on to the remaining subject of the immediate creation by God, viz. the Creation of the Angels. It is the most difficult of all both from the technicalities of the philosophical language in which the doctrine is expressed, and also from the theological questions and problems to which it gives rise.

The principal passage or *locus classicus* (as we might call it) in Dante occurs in Par. xxix. 13 *seqq.* 'Not to secure for himself any acquisition of good, which cannot be [1], but in order that His splendour [i.e. as always in Dante, '*reflected* glory'] might be able by shining forth [i.e. beyond Himself] to say, 'I *exist*'; in His Eternity beyond all time, beyond any other limitation [i.e. of space, as well as of time] according to His own pleasure, the Eternal Love expanded itself in new [2] Loves [3]

[1] Comp. P. Lomb. *Sentt.* II. Dist. i. 3: 'Cuius (Dei) tanta est bonitas ut summe bonus beatitudinis suae qua aeternaliter beatus est alios velit esse participes.' Also, in nearly the same words, Hugh of St. Victor, *Summ. Sentt.* Tract. II. i. 1. Also Aquinas, *Summa contra Gentiles,* II. 46 : 'Ad productionem creaturarum nihil aliud movet Deum nisi sua bonitas quam rebus aliis communicare voluit secundum assimilationem ad ipsum.' Add Aquinas, *S. T.* I. xix. 2 r.

[2] In l. 18 there is a variant *nove* for *nuove*, which would refer to the Nine Orders of Angels, who are often elsewhere described as *Amori.* Both readings are well supported in MSS., but the difference is so slight, and even possibly only a matter of orthography, that we could not quote such evidence with any confidence. But in any case 'Amore', though often applied to an Angel, could scarcely be so to an *Order* of Angels.

[3] A word of explanation should be added as to two of the words just translated, which are often misunderstood.

(*a*) *Subsisto* is not to be confused with *sum*, and the word has no reference whatever to the name of God in Exod. iii. The use of *subsisto* in the Vulgate would prove this, as may be seen at once from any Concordance. Further, the nominative to 'subsisto' here is not 'God', but 'suo splendore.'

(*b*) Note that *splendor* in Dante is regularly *reflected* light, not the actual source of light. See ll. 136-138 of this canto. Compare also *Par.* xiii. 53 :—

'Ciò che non more, e ciò che può morire,
    Non è se non *splendor* di quella idea
    Che partorisce, amando, il nostro Sire.'

Purg. xxxi. 139:—

'O isplendor di viva luce eterna.'

See also *Conv.* III. vii. 32-44 ; also xiv. 38, and especially ll. 43 *seqq.* where *lume, raggio*, and *splendore* are distinguished ; and *splendore* is used 'in quanto esso (*sc.* lume) è *in altra parte alluminata ripercosso.* Dico adunque che la divina virtù senza mezzo questo amore [he is speaking of an Angel] tragge a sua similitudine.' Hence in the passage above translated the meaning will be that God's motive in Creation was not to display or to enhance His own glory,* but (as Mr. Tozer puts it in his notes) 'out of pure beneficence God endowed certain beings or creatures with the glad consciousness of their separate

---

* Comp. St. Augustine, *Enarr. in Psalmos* on Ps. cxxxiv. 6 : 'Deus bonitate fecit ; nullo quod fecit eguit.' Add *Summa*, I. xix. 2 r, and Pet. Lomb. *Sentt.* II. Dist. i. § 3, 'quo beatus erat, sola bonitate, non necessitate, aliis communicari voluit.'

Nor before that did He lie as though inert; because neither
before nor after did go forth the moving of God upon the face
of these waters.' [In other words, the movement of the Spirit
of God described in Gen. i. 2, 'Spiritus Dei *ferebatur* super
aquas' (*Vulg.*), was '*In principio*' (*v.* 1): it had no relation to time or its sequences. In Eternity there are none
of these distinctions of Time. On this see St. Aug. *Conf.*
xi. 13.] Form and Matter, in combinati⊙ and unmingled,
issued forth into Being which was without flaw, like three
arrows from a three-stringed bow. And as in glass, in amber,
or in crystal a ray is resplendent in such wise that from its
first coming to its completeness, there is no interval, so did
the threefold result beam forth from its Lord simultaneously
in its completeness, without any distinction in its beginning [1].

existence,' or, as we might say, He lovingly imparted to them the 'joie de
vivre.' Thus this *splendor*, or ἀπαύγασμα τῆς δόξης, might joyously feel and say,
Subsisto, 'I exist.' The special sense of *splendor* as above explained is admirably illustrated by this quotation from the Cambridge Platonist John Smith :—
   'God made the universe and all the creatures contained therein as so many
glasses wherein He might reflect His own glory. He hath copied forth Himself
in the Creation.' (From J. S. Johnston, *Philosophy of the Fourth Gospel*, p. 153.)
   May I venture to quote in contrast with this the following nonsense from
a Scotch Theological Treatise of the eighteenth century on the Creation of
Angels ?—' God from all eternity enjoyed perfect bliss in contemplation of His
own perfection. But the Divine Mind *presently found* [what an expression !]
that He could get an additional revenue of glory by creating rational creatures
who should sing eternal Hallelujahs.' !! (From Graham's *Social Life in Scotland,*
&c., p. 130.)
   [1] Observe that *tutto*, occurring in l. 27, is again emphatically repeated in l. 29.
The simultaneous character of the whole of creation was a very general belief.
Dante may have met with it in Hugo of St. Victor, Peter Lombard, Anselm,
Aquinas, B. Latini, &c., &c., to say nothing of St. Augustine. This was
generally thought to be established by Ecclus. xviii. 1 : ' Qui vivit in aeternum
creavit omnia *simul.*' This is lost in the English Version, ' all things *in general,*'
and in the Revised Version, ' all things *in common.*' See further Studies,
I. p. 79. This, of course, refers to the Creation *in principio*, and is not
inconsistent with the gradual processes of Creation *in time.*
   See Aquinas, *S. T.* I. lxxiv. 2 r₂. All things were created ' in the beginning,'
and simultaneously ' non in actu sed potentialiter.' Add *S. T.* I. lxi. 3 r₃: 'Creata
materia corporalis creaturae, omnia quodammodo sunt creata.' St. Augustine
more boldly, and almost with the freedom of a modern controversialist, explains
away *dies* as standing for *cognitio mentis angelicae*, and so the story of Creation
records a series of successive pictorial revelations to the Angelic intelligences.
This curious notion is developed in *C. D.* XI. c. 7. See also *De Gen.* IV. xxxv. § 56.

This threefold result, viz. that already indicated in l. 22, is now more definitely expounded in ll. 31–36. 'Forma (puretta)' in l. 22 = 'puro atto' in l. 33; 'materia (puretta)' in l. 22 = 'pura potenza' in l. 34; 'forma e materia congiunte' in l. 22 = 'potenza con atto' in l. 35.

To resume the translation. The next few lines are full of highly technical terms, and their interpretation is very much disputed throughout. But as I am not writing a commentary on this Canto, I will content myself with giving the interpretation which I believe to be the correct one.

'Simultaneously was order created and established[1] for the Existences [i. e. the Angels or the *nuovi amor* of l. 18], and these were the summit[2] of the world in which Pure Act was brought forth[3] [*puro atto*, i.e. mere actuality of conscious Existence, the capacity of feeling "Subsisto" (l. 15)]. Pure Potentiality held the lowest place; in the midst such a bond united Potentiality and Act as never can be unbound.'

I believe that we have here the same three subjects of God's immediate creation with which we are now familiar (see *supra*, pp. 142 *seqq.*), viz. (1) The Angels; *Sustanze*, or *Sustanze separate* as they are called *passim* in the *Convivio*, or 'i primi effetti di lassù' in *Purg.* xi. 3: (2) *Prima materia*, which is denominated as *Pura potenza*, for this, as we saw *supra*, p. 136, was described as the potentiality of everything, and the actuality of nothing. (3) Heaven, or the Heavens, i. e. the system of the

---

[1] *al.* 'were order and structure created,' i. e. taking 'costrutto' as a substantive.

[2] Compare Tennyson, 'the top and crown of things.'

[3] This probably means that the Angels were created in the Empyrean or tenth Heaven, the abode of God Himself. Dante would have found this firmly maintained by Aquinas, *S. T.* I. lxi. 4. He says of the Angels: 'Toti creaturae corporali praesident. Unde conveniens fuit quod Angeli in supremo corpore crearentur tanquam toti naturae corporeae praesidentes.' We seem almost to have an echo of these words in 'quelle furon cima nel mondo in che puro atto fu produtto.' Aquinas also quotes Isidore: 'Supremum caelum est caelum Angelorum.' Again Aquinas, *S. T.* I. cii. 2 r and r₁, and civ. 4 r says: 'Caelum empyreum est locus congruus Angelis quantum ad eorum naturam, et ideo ibi sunt creati.' Similarly Pet. Lomb. II. Dist. ii. 6: 'Simul creati sunt Angeli cum caelo empyreo, et cum informi materia omnium corporalium (i. e. prima materia).'

Nine physical or material Heavens[1] in the sense of the 'pure region,' *paese sincero* of *Par*. vii. 130–132, a passage in which its creation immediately by God is distinctly coupled with that of the Angels, and consequently, according to the declaration of *Par*. vii. 68, *Non ha poi fine*, or, as we read here, the bond in which Act and Potentiality were in this case united shall never be unbound[2]. This again clearly, I think, corresponds with the *altro mondo* of l. 39, i.e. the rest of the Universe[3]. The argument there formulated against Jerome's theory that the Angels were created long before the rest of the world or universe (viz. the Heavens as above explained) would lose all its point, since the main function of the Angels, or at least many of them, was the guidance and regulation of these Heavens, which must have therefore been created together with them.

Hence the often recurring phrase in the *Convivio*, 'Angeli movitori,' or 'i Motori' (*h. l.*, l. 44). Reason itself then (proceeds Dante) forbids us to accept the theory of St. Jerome[4] that the

---

[1] That these nine Heavens were material appears from several places in Dante. In *Par*. xxviii. 64 the Heavens are described as 'Li cerchi corporai.' See also Aquinas, *S. T.* I. lxv. 3, where, after again quoting Gen. i. 1, he adds: 'per quae creatura corporalis intelligitur. Ergo creatura corporalis est immediate a Deo producta.' But it may be noted in passing that Dante's language as to the ninth or Crystalline Heaven, or *Primum Mobile*, is a little inconsistent; for, while in *Par*. xxvii. 109 he says it has no other place (*non ha altro dove*) than the Divine Mind, he describes it as a revolving *body—si gira un corpo*—in *Par*. ii. 113, and speaks of it as *il maggior corpo* in xxx. 39. This confusion of language seems to have arisen from the consideration that no visible or material body is associated with the ninth Heaven, as he says in *Conv*. II. iv. 10, ' Lo nono è quello che non è sensibile, se non per questo movimento che è detto di sopra,' i.e. the common diurnal revolution of all the eight lower Heavens, to account for which visible effect the assumption of its existence appeared to be necessary. See also *Conv*. II. iii. 36 *seqq.* and *Par*. xxviii. 70.

[2] The explanation given by several commentators that the combination of 'Potentiality' and 'Act,' or of 'Form' and 'Matter' represents the human race in its state of innocence appears to me very surprising. (α) This creation was not 'In principio,' but 'in Time.' (β) The threefold enumeration here would not correspond with that found, as already shown, in many other places and authors. (γ) No place would be left here for the 'Caelum Caeli,' as distinguished from the 'Caelum huius aquae et terrae' (cf. St. Augustine and others), which, whatever we may think of it now, was a prevailing distinction in all systems of mediaeval cosmogony. See *supra*, pp. 136–138.

[3] The explanation in the text is that given also by Scartazzini and Casini.

[4] This will be found in his Commentary on Titus i. 2. See Liddon, *Essays and Addresses*, p. 147.

Angels were created long ages before the rest of the Universe (*altro mondo*), since these angels at any rate would have remained for all those ages in imperfection, having no proper function to exercise. Dante is bold to claim Holy Scripture as refuting 'in sundry places' the teaching of St. Jerome in this particular[1] (l. 40).

In ll. 46-48 Dante sums up this part of the subject thus:— 'Now knowest thou *where* and *when* these Loves were created and *how*; so that quenched now are three of the burnings in thy desire'—*where*—probably in the Empyrean (see note, *supra*, p. 149); *when*—'in the beginning'; *how*—by God's immediate act[2].

Further, we must not fail to notice the close resemblance of the phraseology adopted by Dante to express these three kinds of primordial existence with a passage in Aristotle which he surely must have had in view. It occurs in *De Anima*, II. ii. *ad fin.* (414 *a*. 14–18), τριχῶς γὰρ λεγομένης τῆς οὐσίας κ.τ.λ. These three degrees in orders of existence are in Aristotle—

1.	2.	3.
εἶδος	ὕλη	ἐξ ἀμφοῖν
or	*or*	
ἐντελέχεια	δύναμις	

---

[1] It may be noted that Aquinas himself discusses this question in *S. T.* I. lxi. 3. He admits that 'invenitur duplex sanctorum sententia. Illa tamen *probabilior* videtur quod Angeli simul cum creatura corporea sunt creati.' A little lower down he admits that Jerome expresses the unanimous opinion of the Greek Doctors, 'qui omnes hoc concorditer sentiunt quod Angeli sunt *ante mundum corporeum* creati.' *Mundus corporeus* would be the *altro mondo* of *Par.* xxix. 39, or the 'creatura corporalis' of *Summa*, I. lxv. 3, already quoted *supra*. Thus Dante maintains strongly the opinion which Aquinas adopts with some hesitation. Peter Lombard similarly rejects the theory of Jerome, and with a sort of apology like that of Aquinas : 'nihil temere asserendum est, et illud Hieronymum dixisse non ita sentiendo sed aliorum opinionem referendo asseramus.' Hugh of St. Victor agrees with this, and further says that Jerome is quoting Origen— 'ex dictis Origenis fuit, nec asserendo dictum est sed dubitando dixit' (*Summa Sentt.* Tract. II. i. 1).

[2] These three points resemble Hugo of St. Victor's plan of discussion about the Creation of Angels, *Summa Sentt.* II. i. 1. He begins at once : 'De quibus considerandum est *quando* creati fuerint, *ubi* facti fuerint, *quales* etiam facti fuerint.'

These appear in the *Antiqua Translatio*[1] as

1.	2.	3.
species	materia	ex utrisque
or	*or*	
actus	potentia	

Compare Dante—

forma (l. 22)	materia (l. 22)	f. e m. congiunte (l. 22)
puro atto (l. 33)	pura potenza (l. 34)	potenza con atto (l. 35)

(with the result)

Angels	prima materia	The Heavens.

The passage from the *De Anima* is quoted in full in *Studies*, i. p. 109, and a table something like the above constructed. But I have there fallen into the *serious error* of putting the vague term ' Created things ' in the third column instead of the more definite ' Heaven,' i. e. the primaeval nine Heavens.

This concludes what we might call the metaphysical aspect of the Theory of the Creation of Angels. But there are seen to arise out of it several further questions involving moral or theological difficulties, to some of which Dante now addresses himself. They relate chiefly to the existence of bad or fallen Angels. That they were not created bad may be assumed at the outset. It is also clear that the inquiry as to *how* or *why* or *when* they fell after their creation, is nothing else than the insoluble problem of the Origin of Evil. But that does not prevent the authors with whom Dante was familiar and many others from pronouncing dogmatically on certain views which seemed to avert the inference that they were actually created with any inherent imperfection. Hence the generally recognized necessity of interposing an interval, however brief, between the Creation and the Fall[2]. Dante expresses this

---

[1] See Essay on Early Translations of Aristotle with the identification of that used by Dante in *Studies in Dante*, i. pp. 305-318.

[2] It is quaintly expressed in an early English Song [published by the E. E. Text Society, 1865] that Angels, and the Devil among them, were created on the First Day (called proleptically Sunday), being included in the Creation of Light. They fell on the Second Day (Monday) through Pride.

' He was made on a Sunedai,
He fel out on the Munedai.'

very quaintly and bluntly in ll. 49–51 by saying that you could not have counted twenty in that interval. Again, in *Conv.* II. vi. 97, that some were lost from all the Angelic Orders[1], as soon as they were created (*tosto che furono creati*). The supposition of an extremely short interval between the Creation of the Angels and their fall is found also in *Aquinas* in I. lxiii. 6, the subject of which is 'Utrum aliqua mora fuerit inter creationem et lapsum Angelorum.' He allows that there is room for difference of opinion, but considers the most probable view to be 'quod statim post primum instans creationis suae diabolus peccaverit.' Among other arguments he cites St. John viii. 44; in *Vulg.*: 'in veritate non stetit[2].' This apparently follows the reading οὐκ ἕστηκεν (i. e. imperf. of στήκω). The other reading is οὐχ ἕστηκεν, which E.V. follows, 'He abideth not in the truth.' R.V. follows the Vulgate and translates 'stood not in the truth'. P. Lomb. (*Sentt.* II. Dist. iii. §§ 5–8) discusses this point, also quoting St. John viii. 44. He does so especially in reference to the inference that if the Angels fell *immediately*, they must have been created evil. He comes to the conclusion that as they must certainly have been created good, so before their Fall 'fuit ibi aliqua morula, licet brevissima.'

In the passage lately quoted from *Conv.* II. 6, Dante adds a curious speculation that perhaps one-tenth of the Angels fell, and that possibly to supply that deficit in the Angelic ranks the human race was created. This notion found much favour with mediaeval writers. Among others may be mentioned Hugh St. Victor[3], Aquinas[4], Anselm[5], and Peter Lombard[6]. The last-named writer is rash enough to claim that '*in Scriptura interdum reperitur* quod factus sit [homo] propter reparationem angelicae ruinae'! He evidently was sufficiently prudent not to 'verify his references.' We have

---

[1] This was also a disputed point. Aquinas hesitates whether Seraphim and Thrones may perhaps have escaped. See *S. T.* I. lxiii. 9 r₃.

[2] St. Augustine discusses St. John viii. 44 at some length in *C. D.* XI. 13–15, but I do not find that he touches on the *duration* between the Creation and the Fall.

[3] *De Sacr.* I. pars 5, cap. 31. [4] *S. T.* I. xxiii. 7 r; lxiii. 9 r₃.

[5] *Cur Deus Homo*, I. c. 16–18. [6] *Sentt.* II. Dist. i. § 9.

just noted a similar rash appeal to 'molti lati' of Scripture by Dante himself in *Par.* xxix. 40, in reference to the time of the Creation of the Angels. (This theory of the cause of the Creation of Man is alluded to by Milton in *P. L.* vii. 150 *seqq.*)

The serious difficulty involved in admitting this flaw in God's *immediate Creation* is dealt with by Dante in *Conv.* III. xii. 66 in this way:—

'If God made the good and the bad Angels, He did not make both intentionally, but only the good: the wickedness of the bad then followed beyond his intention; but not in such sense "beyond his *intention*" that he did not *know* beforehand of their wickedness. But so great was his desire to produce this spiritual creation (comp. again *Par.* xxix. 13–18), that the foreknowledge of some who must needs come to a bad end, ought not, nor could not, debar God from producing it.'

One further question alone remains. With what faculties were Angels endowed at their Creation? This is a subject which Dante desires to clear up in order to correct what he considered to be a serious error in the current teaching of the schools. The general statement that those faculties are Intelligence, Memory, and Will [1] is not open to objection in itself. But this truth, he says (*Par.* xxix. 73–75), is confused by ambiguity—*equivocando* — i. e. by 'equivocation' in the technical sense of Logic, but the confusion or ambiguity in question occurs only in relation to one of these three faculties, viz. Memory. This may mean simply (a) the *retaining* of the knowledge of what is past, or (β) the *recalling* of it when forgotten: in fact, either μνήμη or ἀνάμνησις—'memory' or 'recollection'—memorare or rimemorare (1. 81). In the *former* sense, Angels have it, but not in the *latter*, for they are wholly exempt from forgetfulness. See ll. 79–81. The point at issue is explained in the two *terzine* 76–81:—

---

[1] Observe it is just these three faculties which alone survive, and in greatly increased vigour, in the disembodied human spirit. See *Purg.* xxv. 82–84. Compare St. Augustine, *De Trin.* X. c. xi. § 18: 'Haec igitur tria, memoria, intelligentia, voluntas, quoniam non sunt tres vitae, sed una vita; nec tres mentes, sed una mens; consequenter utique nec tres substantiae sunt, sed una substantia.'

'These Existences ever since they were "made glad with God's countenance," have never turned away their sight from It[1] wherefrom nothing is hidden. Wherefore they never have their vision intercepted by any new object, and therefore there is no need for them to recollect by means of a separate impression': i. e. by means of an impression separated from that of the original object. This (as I have pointed out in *Studies*, i. p. 112) seems to refer to Aristotle's theory of Memory in περὶ μνήμης καὶ ἀναμνήσεως, c. 1[2]. He says that memory is possible owing to the continuance in the mind of a φάντασμα, or τύπος τοῦ αἰσθήματος, which remains when the object itself which excited it is no longer present. This seems to be precisely what Dante means here by 'concetto diviso,' an impression separate and distinct from the object which caused it[3].

Now it is surely surprising to find it stated by some commentators that Dante here attacks with extraordinary boldness (not to say vehemence) a view maintained by Aquinas, that Angels have memory. It appears to me that those who say this themselves fall into just such an error of *equivocando* as Dante is here contending against.

Let us, therefore, see what is precisely the teaching of Aquinas on this subject. He insists much upon the possession by Angels of *Intelligentia* and *Voluntas*, but as regards *Memoria*, he is careful to make the very distinction noted above between μνήμη and ἀνάμνησις, though in phraseology, it is mainly derived from St. Augustine. See *S. T.* I. liv. 5 r: 'Sed tamen memoria in Angelis potest poni secundum quod ab Augustino ponitur in mente; licet non possit iis competere

---

[1] This refers to the 'Vision of all things in God,' as the source of the knowledge of Angels and the glorified spirits. See (among numerous other passages) *Purg.* xxx. 103–105; *Par.* xi. 19–21; xvii. 16–18; xxiv. 41, 42; xxvi. 106; xxix. 10–12, &c., &c.; and as regards the knowledge of Angels in particular see *V. E.* I. ii. 18–20.

[2] See especially 450, a. 25–32; b. 10 and 14–29. We may notice also the curious generalization at the beginning of the chapter that it is generally the dull and slow-witted who have the best memories: 'οὐ γὰρ οἱ αὐτοί εἰσι μνημονικοὶ καὶ ἀναμνηστικοί, ἀλλ' ὡς ἐπὶ τὸ πολὺ μνημονικώτεροι μὲν οἱ βραδεῖς, ἀναμνηστικώτεροι δὲ οἱ ταχεῖς καὶ εὐμαθεῖς' (449, b. 6–8).

[3] Comp. Aq. *S. T.* I. lxxviii. 4 r (*med.*); cxi. 3 r₁.

secundum quod ponitur pars animae sensitivae.' Aquinas very carefully distinguishes 'memoria *intellectiva*' and 'memoria *sensitiva*.' The former is simply 'vis conservativa specierum,' the latter has for its object 'praeteritum ut praeteritum,' and in this sense 'memoria in parte *intellectiva* non erit sed *sensitiva* tantum' (I. lxxix. 6 r fin.). He describes the former as 'thesaurus, vel locus conservativus specierum' I. lxxix. 7, or again, 'habitualis animae retentio' (*ibid*., and similarly, attributing this description to St. Augustine, in I. xciii. 7 r₃). See also I. lxxviii. 4 r : 'Ad harum formarum retentionem aut conservationem ordinatur *phantasia* sive *imaginatio*, quae idem sunt; est enim . . . quasi thesaurus quidam formarum per sensum acceptarum[1].'

Nothing, it appears to me, can be plainer than that Aquinas recognizes clearly the distinction for which Dante is contending, and that they are entirely in accord in respect of the limitation under which the faculty of 'Memory' can be attributed to Angels.

Dante, however, denounces the error with such energy that one cannot but think that he has someone definitely in his mind, though I cannot myself offer any suggestion as to the special object of his attack, but in any case it was surely not Aquinas.

So much as to the limits and process of Creation, so far as it is to be attributed to God *immediately*. We proceed now to speak of the later stages or developments of the creative process. The distinction between *immediate* and *mediate* Creation is, as we see already, a cardinal feature in Dante's Theory of Creation.

The following are the principal points now to be explained :—

---

[1] This metaphor of 'thesaurus' in St. Augustine and Aquinas is repeated by Fuller : ' Memory is the treasury of the mind wherein the monuments thereof are kept and preserved.' He proceeds to point out that in *this* (i. e. μνήμη) the 'brutes equal, if not exceed, men . . . but they cannot play an after-game, and recover what they have forgotten, which is done by the mediation of discourse.' In other words they have μνήμη, but not ἀνάμνησις, as Dante says of the Angels, though for a very different reason. Sir Thomas Browne with characteristic quaintness describes ἀνάμνησις as 'the art of reminiscential evocation.'

(1) The production of the four Elements.

(2) The production of the four 'corpora composte,' or the higher forms of corporeal existence.

(3) What was the mediate agency employed by God in these processes?

(1) As to the first point. There were held to be four primary or fundamental qualities by which the primal matter or *prima materia* could be affected or modified—Warm, Cold, Dry, Moist[1]. These were called 'complessioni' or sometimes 'qualitadi.' Both expressions occur in B. Latini, (*Trésor* I. pt. 3, c. 100 and 102), where he explains that by the combinations of these, two and two together, operating on the *Hyle* (ὕλη) or *Prima materia*, the four Elements came into being : *Fire*, being warm and dry; *Air*, warm and moist; *Earth*, cold and dry; *Water*, cold and moist. It is clearly implied by *Par.* vii. 133–135 (to be referred to presently), that these operations, or combinations, and the consequent evolution of the four ' Elements,' were brought about by some created agency ' da creata virtù,' l. 135, i.e., no doubt, by Angels.

The source of this speculation is to be found in Arist. *de Gen. et Corr.* II. c. 2 and 3. He is speaking of ' αἰσθητοῦ σώματος ἀρχάς.' He says that in all corporeal or material existences there are four ' πρῶται διαφοραὶ καὶ ἐναντιώσεις ' (i.e. different and opposite qualities), and that (for various reasons given) *only* these four are strictly 'πρῶται,' viz. Warm, Cold, Dry, Moist. These διαφοραὶ καὶ ἐναντιώσεις are here called στοιχεῖα. He then proceeds to explain how taken two and two together they would produce six συζεύξεις or combinations, yet that the combinations of opposites, as hot and cold, moist and dry, are out of consideration, so that there are practically only four possible combinations, and that these ' τέτταρες στοιχείων συζεύξεις ' produce the four 'Elements' or ἁπλᾶ σώματα. These ' στοιχεῖα ' are represented by the *com-plexions* or *qualities* of B. Latini; and the whole passage

---

[1] Compare Milton's description of Chaos :—
    ' For hot, cold, moist, and dry, four champions fierce
    Strive here for mastery.'—*P. L.* II. ll. 898, 899.

explains the phraseology of Dante in *Conv.* IV. xxiii. 114, when he speaks of 'li quattro combinatori delle contrarie qualitadi che sono nella nostra composizione.' The 'contrarie qualitadi' correspond with Aristotle's διαφοραὶ καὶ ἐναντιώσεις, 'differentiae et contrarietates' (*Ant. Trans.*), or στοιχεῖα, for we find them just below explained by Dante to be warm, cold, dry, and moist; and the 'quattro combinatori delle contrarie qualitadi' answer to the τέτταρες στοιχείων συζεύξεις, or 'quatuor elementorum coniugationes,' which produce what are commonly called the four Elements, or ἁπλᾶ σώματα or 'simplicia corpora' (Dante's 'corpora semplici'). The particular purpose of Dante in this passage is to show that each of the four ages of human life seems to be appropriated to one of these four *combinatori*. *Adolescence* to warm and moist, i.e. Air; *Youth* to warm and dry, i.e. Fire; *Age* to cold and dry, i.e. Earth; *Senility* to cold and moist, i.e. Water. B. Latini, in the passage referred to, works out an elaborate correspondence of these four combinations, or the resulting elements, with Spring, Summer, Autumn, and Winter respectively. Dante, in the chapter just quoted, also briefly draws attention to a similar comparison of the Elements with the four Seasons, and applies it also, at greater length, to the four divisions of the day. We must be careful not to overlook the ambiguous use of the terms στοιχεῖα and 'elementa,' which may well give rise to apparent inconsistencies of statement in the matter of creation. The term is commonly applied to the so-called four 'Elements' themselves, but it is reserved by Aristotle in the passage cited to the *fundamental qualities*, by the combinations of which the four 'Elements', commonly so called, are formed, and *these*, as we have seen, he terms ἁπλᾶ σώματα, and elsewhere, for distinction, σωματικὰ στοιχεῖα. To the στοιχεῖα, in the primary Aristotelian sense, such a term as 'creation', or coming into being, could scarcely be applied, for they are merely 'qualities' or 'conditions' of matter; not themselves any substances, or existences.

We have thus arrived at a second stage in the production or evolution or 'creation' of the Universe, viz. the four Elements. As to these, Dante distinctly asserts that they do not proceed immediately from any Divine operation, but that they are produced by an energy or agency which is itself created, viz., as we shall presently see, the Angels, presiding over the several Heavens and Stars, and dispensing their influences. Note especially *Par.* vii. 133-138 :—

' But the elements which thou hast named [see ll. 124, 125] and those things which are made up of them [i.e. all more highly developed forms of corporeal existence] are formed by a power which is itself created. Created was the matter which they possess [i. e. the "prima materia"]. Created was the informing power in these stars which revolvr around them ' [i.e. the Angelic natures].

The following are the principal passages in Dante which throw light upon Dante's use of the term ' complessione,' i.e. the *condition* or *quality* which when superimposed on the simple or bare existence of the elements produces the higher forms of material or corporeal objects.

(*a*) In *De Mon.* I. iii. 45 we have (1) ' *esse* simpliciter sumptum,' which belongs to the ' elements ' [i.e. the four commonly recognized ' elements ']; (2) ' *esse* complexionatum,' i.e. existence qualified or conditioned, which is found even in minerals. Then with the further additions of Life, Sensation, and Intellect, we rise respectively to the higher grades of vegetable, animal, and human existence.

(*b*) Next with this should be compared *Conv.* III. 3, where that which is called in *De Mon., l. c.,* ' esse complexionatum ' (though the term itself is not introduced here) is divided into ' corpora semplici ' (' elements,' i.e. ἁπλᾶ σώματα of Aristotle) and ' corpora composte,' rising through the same four grades of mineral, vegetable, animal, and human.

(*c*) Next we should notice the curious argument for the necessary emergence of earth above the water in *Quaestio,* § 18. This throws much light on the successive stages of ' creation' of which we have been speaking.

(l. 28.) ' It is the purpose of Universal Nature [this expression in this context is in effect equivalent to God. So it is also in *Conv.* III. iv. 98, where we read ' fece ciò la Natura Universale, cioè Iddio.' See *Studies,* ii. p. 356] that all the forms [of course in the philosophical sense of this term] which exist potentially in the *prima materia* should be brought to actuality, and according to the distinction of their species should exist in actuality . . .'

Then (omitting a few lines) at l. 36:—

' For since all forms which are in the potentiality of matter ideally exist in actuality in the Mover of the Heavens . . . if all those forms were not always in actuality, the Mover of the Heavens would fail in the completeness of the diffusion of His Goodness—which must never be said. [Compare with this the argument in *Par.* xxix. 43–45 already cited *supra*, pp. 150, 151.] And since all the material forms of things that can come into being and can come to corruption, *except the forms of the elements*, require a matter and substratum, both mixed and conditioned ("mixtum et *complexionatum*"), to which, as to their end and purpose, the elements are ordained so far as they are elements ; and this mixture cannot ensue where the things to be mixed cannot come together,' &c., &c. The inference from all this is that somewhere in the universe there must be a possibility of all the elements thus coming into contact with one another, and therefore earth must rise above water somewhere, else it could not possibly combine, at any rate, with the elements of air and fire. Hence we see that, as a commixture of the four fundamental qualities was necessary for the production of the ' Elements,' the ' corpora semplici ' of the *Convivio* passage last quoted; so a similar mixture of all the *elements themselves* is necessary for the production of ' corpora composte' in their various grades. The elements presuppose a mixture of qualities (*complessioni*) acting upon the *prima materia*; but any more complex form of corporeal existence requires further ' materiam et sub-stratum *mixtum*' as well as *complexionatum*, and that mixture is supplied by a combination or mixture of the elements. Thus *corpora semplici* arise from the simple *prima materia* becoming *complexionata*; *corpora composte* from a further intermixture of the *corpora semplici* or Elements themselves.

(*d*) Finally, in illustration of the words ' complessioni ' and ' complexionatum,' we must recur once more to the passage in

Par. vii. l. 139, 'The rays and the movement of the sacred lights (i. e. the stars) draw forth from composite matter, endued with capacity therefor, the soul of every animal and of plants.'

I have had, in view of the context, to paraphrase rather than translate the word *complession* here. It seems to me to resemble the *esse complexionatum* of *De Mon.* I. iii. Out of the various forms of 'germinal material'—all of which forms are evolved from the *prima materia* by some combination, first of qualities, and afterwards of elements (see pp. 157, 160)— out of these the influence of the sun, moon, planets, and stars draws forth the seeds of life hitherto dormant, latent, or potential in them, so that actually living plants and animals are brought into being, each 'after its kind.'

Once more Aquinas affords an illuminating comment on Dante: 'Sufficit virtus coelestium corporum ad generandum quaedam animalia imperfectiora ex materia disposita' (I. xci. 2 r$_2$). Here *materia disposita* seems to me to be the exact equivalent of *complession potenziata*, i. e. composite matter disposed thereto, and as to the function or virtue here attributed to the heavenly bodies, it is hardly necessary to point out how often this appears in the teaching of Dante. Take two or three passages out of very many.

(a) 'Not only through the working of the mighty spheres that guide every seed to a certain end, according as the stars are in company with it.' *Purg.* xxx. 109-111.

(β) See in full *Par.* ii. 112-144 (too long to quote).

(γ) *Conv.* II. xiv. 28-30, 'della generazione sustanziale tutti i filosofi concordano che i cieli sono cagione.'

(δ) *Conv.* IV. xxi. 39-42, 'la virtù formativa prepara gli organi alla *virtù celestiale,* che produce della potenza del seme l'anima in vita.' (This is then followed by the *direct* gift from the *Motore del Cielo* Himself of the *Intelletto Possibile.*) Compare with this *Purg.* xxv. 61-75.

Finally, and perhaps most explicitly of all, in *Conv.* IV. xxiii. 50-52: 'Conciossiacosachè la nostra vita, . . . e ancora d'ogni vivente quaggiù, sia causata dal cielo.' Also *De Mon.* II. ii. 11–38 should be read in this connexion.

This being, as it appears to me, so obviously the meaning of the sentence in *Par.* vii. 139 (see p. 161 *init.*), in strict accordance with the view of Dante so often elsewhere expressed, I cannot understand how some translators have so entirely missed the point as to make *L'anima d'ogni bruto*, &c., the subject of *tira* and *lo raggio e il moto* its object. This would be surely in Dante's view putting the cart before the horse with a vengeance.

We now see how Dante accounted for the 'creation' or 'evolution' of every kind of material existence by successive stages from the *prima materia* which was created *immediately* by God. It only remains to inquire into the agencies or means by which these successive stages of creation (if we may use the word [1]) were brought about according to the teaching of Dante. We have already seen that they fall outside the the sphere of creation by the immediate operation of God.

Some of the passages lately quoted will have anticipated the answer to this question. The Heavens and their influence, through the virtue or power infused into them by God, are the *organi* or instruments by which His creative purpose has been carried out. Further, Dante warns us that when he speaks of the 'Heavens' in this sense he means, not the material stars or planets which those Heavens bear, but the *Angeli Motori*, or *Intelligenze*, on whom their motions depend, and by whom they are regulated. So, from *Par.* iv. 58–63, we learn that the ancients, and by name Plato, were so far right in attributing such influence to the Planets, but 'Questo principio male inteso' led them into the error of idolatrous worship of those heavenly bodies under the names of Jupiter, Mercury, Mars, &c.

As to the Heavens or Stars being God's chosen means

---

[1] P. Lomb. *Sentt.* II. Dist. i protests against the term 'creation' being used except in relation to the action of God : 'Homo et angelus dicitur aliqua *facere*, sed non *creare*, vocaturque factor sive artifex, sed non creator. Hoc enim nomen soli Deo proprie congruit . . . creationis nomen sibi proprie retinuit, alia enim etiam creaturis communicavit.' Notice the contrast implied by Dante in *Par.* iii. 87: 'Ciò ch' ella (la divina voluntate) *crea*, e che natura *face*.'

through which to exercise His creative or providential activity in the world, see (among many other passages) *Par.* viii. 97–99.

(1) 'That Good which causes the whole realm through which thou art ascending [i. e. all the nine Heavens] to revolve and to be satisfied makes His providence to be an active power in these mighty bodies' [i. e. Stars and Planets].

(2) But the most striking and explicit passage of all is *De Mon.* II. ii. 11–38. It is perhaps too long to quote, but it should certainly be referred to in this connexion.

(3) This firm belief in the Stars (i. e. really their Angels), being the regularly ordained agency for all the mundane operations of God's Providence, is exhibited in a very remarkable expression in *Ep.* V. viii. l. 134. Here, as elsewhere[1], Dante recognizes the finger of God in many of the great events of Roman history, and argues that they transcend the heights of any mere human effort. He argues, therefore, that we see in them the finger of God, who has thus chosen to carry out His purposes by human agency, 'per homines, tanquam *per coelos novos*;' substituting, as it were, *men* for the usual celestial agencies; so that men become 'utensilia Dei,' just as in the passage above referred to in *De Mon.* the heavens are the 'organum' and the 'instrumentum' Dei.

I must in passing note how this throws light on the nature of Dante's firm belief in Astrology. It is really ' God whose never failing providence ordereth all things both in heaven and earth,' but the Angels are the 'ministering spirits' through whom that providential guidance is dispensed[2]; and the stars are the instruments by which their allotted operations are exercised. This sheds an entirely new light upon a belief which is generally associated with credulity and superstition.

In this distinction between immediate and mediate Creation we cannot fail to observe how closely the teaching of Dante resembles that of Plato in the *Timaeus*. I am not saying it was derived from that source, though in fact this one dialogue of Plato was known by Dante to some extent through the

---

[1] e.g. especially *Conv.* IV. v and *De Mon.* II. v.

[2] Cf. Aq. *S. T.* I. lxiii. 7 r : ' tota creatura corporalis administratur a Deo per Angelos ' [citing St. Aug. *de Trin.* III. 4, 5].

translation of Chalcidius. Thus we read (p. 41 A) how the supreme God deputed to the subordinate deities, 'gods and sons of the gods,' the carrying out of the details of creation; and again (p. 42 D) ' τοῖς νέοις παρέδωκε θεοῖς σώματα πλάττειν θνητά.' In the following sentence from Archer Butler we might simply substitute the name 'Dante' for 'Plato': 'The psychology of Plato led him to recognize mind wherever there was motion, and hence not only to require a Deity as the first mover of the Universe but also to conceive the propriety of separate and subordinate agents attached to each of its parts as principles of motion no less than intelligent directors.' The chief motive of all such speculations, whether in Plato, Dante, or others, is the same. The problem of the existence of evil and imperfection overshadows them all. Their purpose is evidently to find some device—like the modern policy of a ' buffer state '—by which evil might be shut off from a too close contact with the immediate work of the Creator. Another example of this ' buffer ' policy we have seen in the insistence by P. Lombard of ' aliqua morula licet brevissima ' between the Creation of the Angels and their Fall (p. 153).

One further remark in conclusion. There is no trace in Dante of that crude anthropomorphism which even in our own day cried out against the recognition of Evolution as an agency in the creative or providential energy of God, as being a doctrine which could ' not be taught without arrogancy and impiety.' Dante would not think God dishonoured by the discovery or by the belief that He had chosen some *modus operandi* other than that of an actual δημιουργός for the execution of His purposes. We have seen that even in the operations of creative power attributed immediately and directly to Him no outward act is assumed, it was ' solo intendendo,' merely by an act of thought. Might not Dante have accepted, at least in principle, the *dictum* of Tennyson—' If He thunder by law, the thunder is yet His voice '—though for 'law' he would himself have preferred to substitute some more concrete or more personal deputed agency ? I am not one of those who seem to think that Dante was infallible, or that he was in the technical and theological sense ' inspired ' ; or that he antici-

pated (as some have in fact imagined) the discoveries of
Copernicus, Newton, or Harvey, still less those of Darwin.
But I do say there is nothing in his theory of Creation which
would constitute such a barrier to his acceptance of some form
of evolutionary teaching such as we have seen operating in
our own day. As to the grosser forms of anthropomorphic
conception we must not forget his protest in *Par.* iv. 43,
'Therefore doth Scripture condescend to your faculties, and
attributes feet and hands to God, but means otherwise.'

And as to the misgiving sometimes felt that in thus restrict-
ing the sphere of the direct personal intervention of God we
are, so to speak, gradually thrusting Him out of His own
Universe, we may cite the language of Dante in *Epist.* X,
§§ 20 and 21. He is commenting on the first words of the
Paradiso, where he declares that the glory of God, who
moves all things, is resplendent through the Universe, though
in different degrees in one place and another. In proof of
this he asserts (§ 20, l. 374) that 'mediately or immediately
everything that exists derives its existence from God because
it is from that which the secondary cause has received from the
first, that it exercises influence upon the thing which it causes,
after the manner of something which receives and throws back
a ray of light.' And so again in the following section, l. 400,
'Wherefore it is clear that every existence and every virtue
proceeds from the First; and lower Intelligences receive as it
were from a radiating source, and reflect, the rays of their
superior to their inferior after the fashion of mirrors.' But it
is needless to multiply quotations any further to prove that
Dante's belief in the employment of intermediate causes and
agencies for even *most* of the operations of God in the world
did not weaken in the least degree his belief that all these
operations, whether of creation or of providence, whether in
heaven or in earth, were none the less His own work. He
enforces this conviction in the following section by several
quotations from Scripture, and finally by an appeal even to the
'scriptura paganorum' in the Ninth Book of Lucan :—

'Iuppiter est quodcunque vides, quocunque moveris.'

THE TOMB OF DANTE [1]

THE death of Dante, as is well known, occurred on Sept. 14, 1321, when he was fifty-six years old. It is thus recorded in the simple and touching language of Boccaccio: 'On the day on which we celebrate the Exaltation of the Holy Cross, he passed away from this present life. His soul, we may well believe, was received into the arms of his noble Beatrice, and presented before the presence of God, so that there in perpetual repose he may be recompensed for the troubles of the past.'

The precise cause of his death seems to be a little uncertain. It occurred just after his return to Ravenna from an unsuccessful embassy to Venice, which he had undertaken on behalf of his friend and patron, Guido Novello da Polenta. It is distinctly stated by Filippo Villani (who died 1404), in his Life of Dante, that the poet died of a fever aggravated by the land journey homewards through marshy districts, the Venetians having refused to allow him to return by sea, though he specially requested this favour, because he was already suffering from fever (*laborans febribus*). Manetti in his 'Vita Dantis' (written probably about half a century later than that of Villani) attributes his death rather to disappointment and vexation at the failure of his efforts, and the contemptuous treatment which he had received at Venice [2]. The same account is given by some other writers [3].

One may be allowed to say just a few words as to his precise age, since it can be very accurately fixed by an interesting

---

[1] Reprinted, with omissions and corrections, from the *English Historical Review* for October, 1888.

[2] Manetti declares that he went by land of his own choice to avoid the danger of falling in with the Venetian fleet (Ricci, *Ultimo Rifugio*, p. 151).

[3] e.g. Rossi (*Hist. Rav.*) and Maffei (*Scritt. Veronesi*), cited by Fraticelli, *Storia della Vita*, &c., p. 258.

story concerning a death-bed utterance of the poet preserved
by Boccaccio, if we believe it—and I know no reason whatever why we should not, except that it is now the fashion to
disbelieve as much as possible of any ancient record, especially
if it be of the nature of an anecdote, or have some touch of
human interest and feeling about it. As Bishop Creighton
complains:—'We have now been taught by a long series of
sceptical inquiries to take almost for granted that if according
to an ancient tradition a famous event happened in some
particular spot, it must really have happened somewhere else ;
unless, indeed, it never happened at all !' It should be first
explained that as to the *month* of Dante's birth, that it was
May, there is little, if any, doubt [1] ; as to the *year*, that it was
1265, there is now practically none, in spite of the learned but
perverse ingenuity with which Grion and others have en-
deavoured to establish another date. As to the actual *day* of
the month which was his birthday, that remains, and probably
must ever remain, a matter of uncertainty, though a great
deal of ingenuity has been spent in the attempt to determine
it. May 8, 14, 18, and 30 have all been fixed upon on various
grounds, which it would be beside our present purpose to
discuss. Dr. Witte [2] has argued with much ingenuity for the
30th. But all I wish now to say is that this anecdote of
Boccaccio seems to make it clear that it must have been
within a day or two of the end of May. Boccaccio [3] states
that Dante, 'while lying ill of that sickness whereof he died,
told Ser Piero di Giardino da Ravenna [4], who himself reported
the words to Boccaccio, that he had passed his fifty-sixth

---

[1] At any rate, he was born when the Sun was in Gemini, i.e. (popularly
speaking) May–June. See *Par.* xxii. 112–117.

[2] *Dante-Forsch.* II, No. iii.　　　　　　　[3] Comm. on *Inf.* I. *Lez.* 2.

[4] It may be noted in passing, that recent researches have discovered abundant
contemporary traces of this Ser Piero di Giardino and his family at Ravenna (see
Guerrini e Ricci *Studi, &c.*, pp. 23, 38, 53, 59), as well as of some family connexions of Boccaccio himself having been at Ravenna at the same time. It may
further be interesting to mention that this same Messer Piero (whom Boccaccio
describes as ' lungamente stato discepolo di Dante, grave di costumi, e degno di
fede ' (*Vita*, p. xxviii, ed. Paris 1844) is also given as his authority for the well-
known story of the loss of the last thirteen Cantos of the *Paradiso*, and of their
discovery by means of a dream that appeared to Jacopo di Dante, eight months
after his father's death. (*Vita*, § 14.)

year, by such a period as had gone by since the last May up to that time,' 'that time' being early in September. This language is very precise, and, in the mouth of one accustomed to such minute accuracy in his words and thoughts as Dante, can hardly mean anything but that his birthday was at the *very end* of May, and probably therefore the 30th, if (as Witte argues) there are other independent reasons (though merely conjectural) which point to that day in particular.

But it must not be forgotten that our main subject is not the death, but the Tomb of Dante. I pass on, therefore, to consider this under these three heads :—

I. The circumstances of his burial so far as they are known.

II. The later fortunes of his tomb.

III. The very remarkable discovery and identification of his bones in May 1865.

I. Boccaccio relates that Guido Novello da Polenta, being grievously afflicted at the poet's death, caused the body to be adorned with the adornments of a poet ('ornare d' ornamenti poetici,' p. xiii), referring no doubt to that laurel crown which Dante so earnestly desired, but on *one* condition, viz. that he might assume it 'nel mio bel San Giovanni,' and 'in sul fonte del mio battesmo ;' that crown which he was urged to accept at Bologna by his friend Giovanni del Virgilio, and which in his Eclogue written in reply he positively refuses to receive except at Florence :—

> ' Nonne triumphales melius pexare capillos,
> Et patrio, redeam si quando, abscondere canos
> Fronde sub inserta solitum flavescere, Sarno ? '

Another 'adornment' may perhaps have been a copy of his divine poem, for though this is not mentioned by Boccaccio, there is a tradition to this effect, recorded by the anonymous author of a long unpublished *terza rima* Canzone 'laudante el famosissimo poeta Dante Alleghieri' which I have found among the Canonici MSS. in the Bodleian. The *writing* of this MS. is apparently about 1430, but I think there are several indications that the *author* was a contemporary or nearly so, since such expressions as 'per quel ch' io sento '; 'che non ai intesi '; 'a quel tempo s' io ben comprendo,' &c., are not infrequent, and seem such as one having access to oral information might naturally use.

This writer gives rather a minute account of the poet's burial, which he says was magnificent, and states (*inter alia*) that

'Come vero poeta fu vestito
Con la corona in testa dell' alloro ;
In sul pecto un libro ben fornito ;
A la chiesa major, per quel ch' io sento,
Fu seppellito in ricca sepoltura, &c.'[1]

To return, however, to Boccaccio. The poet was buried in the church of the Frati Minori at Ravenna, and, as some Franciscan writers have added, clothed in the vestments of the order in which he is said to have expressed a wish to die, he having in earlier life, according to another tradition, joined or contemplated joining that order[2]. I may add that on the strength of this vague and slenderly supported tradition at least one enthusiastic Franciscan has been so bold as to enumerate Dante in the list of the eminent writers belonging to the Franciscan order![3] After the funeral Guido returned to the house where Dante died, and pronounced a panegyric in his memory ('fece uno esquisito e lungo sermone,' says Boccaccio). The poet's remains were deposited in a stone sarcophagus, which Guido intended to have been temporary only, until he should be able to build him a magnificent sepulchre. This purpose was frustrated by his own deposition and expulsion just two years afterwards, viz. on Sept. 20, 1323 (according to a 'Spicilegium Ravennatis Historiae,' given by Muratori, 'Rer. Ital. Scriptores,' I, part ii, p. 579). His death occurred only three years later, viz. in 1326. Already, however, the vicissitudes of Dante's tomb begin, since even his temporary resting-place very narrowly escaped violation within the first year after his death, and while his friend Guido da Polenta still ruled at Ravenna. In 1322 the Cardinal Bertrand de Poyet[4], governor of Romagna and papal legate, threatened

---

[1] This is really from the *Centiloquio* (Canto 55) of Antonio Pucci, who wrote *c.* 1333–73 and was a friend of Boccaccio, Sacchetti, &c.

[2] See *Inf.* xvi. 106, as sometimes explained.

[3] See Cardoni, *Dante in Ravenna*, p. 34.

[4] Dr. Toynbee points out that 'du Pouget' is the more correct French form of 'del Poggetto.' See his *Dante Alighieri*, p. 232.

to break open his tomb and scatter his ashes. The cardinal
was himself a Caorsine, and was doubtless stung by Dante's
bitter language against the ' Caorsini e Guaschi ' in *Par.*
xxvii. 58; also by his association together of Sodom and
Cahors as types of what were in Dante's estimate related vices
in *Inf.* xi. 50; by his violent attacks on the French cardinals
in his letter to the protracted conclave at Carpentras, in which
John XXII was ultimately elected, and by his numerous hostile
allusions to the Avignon papacy. It is related by Boccaccio in
his Life of Dante, that 'Beltrando Cardinale del Poggetto, allora
per la chiesa Romana legato in Lombardia,' formally condemned
the *De Monarchia* and forbade its being read by any of the
faithful, 'siccome contenente cose eretiche.' Boccaccio adds that
it was only the strong personal influence of Pino della Tosa and
Ostasio da Polenta with the legate which prevented his burning
the bones of Dante himself at Bologna, at the same time that
he publicly burnt the condemned book. Boccaccio cautiously
adds, 'se giustamente o no, Iddio il sa !'[1] It was this Ostasio
da Polenta (it may be mentioned) who in the following year
conspired against and expelled his brother Guido from
Ravenna. Meanwhile Guido da Polenta, with a view to his
design of erecting a suitable tomb, invited the contribution of
competitive epitaphs. He invited (as Boccaccio says) 'li quali
in quel tempo erano in poesia sollennissimi in Romagna.'
Many such epitaphs were written and, as we should say,
'sent in,' but, for the reason above mentioned (viz. Guido's
expulsion), none were formally adopted. Boccaccio says that
he saw, *più tempo poi*, several of these rival compositions, and
that he himself selected, as being in his judgement the best, and
he therefore recorded it in his work, the epitaph composed by
Dante's friend, Giovanni del Virgilio. That consists of the
well-known fourteen elegiac lines beginning

　　　' Theologus Dantes, nullius dogmatis expers,
　　　　Quod foveat claro philosophia sinu.'

Just one word in passing about this Giovanni del Virgilio.
Like so many other Italians of note in art and literature, he is

---

[1] This curious expression occurs in the so-called *Compendio* only, and not in
the *Vita Intera*. See note *infra*, p. 189.

better known by his nickname than by his real name. Indeed
this practice seems to be the rule rather than the exception.
He was professor of Literae Humaniores at Bologna 1318–25,
and acquired the title by which he is now known from his
devotion to the study of Virgil, which was no doubt one link
of union between him and his friend Dante. Their fanciful
correspondence in the form and imagery of the Eclogues of
Virgil is preserved among the works of Dante under the title
of *Eclogae*, in which occur numerous interesting allusions of a
personal character.

II. This brings us to the next division of our subject, viz.
the restorations or reconstructions of the Tomb.

There were three chief epochs of such reconstruction, at each
of which a fresh epitaph is supposed to have been added.

The first is in 1483, and was undertaken by Bernardo Bembo,
father of the well-known cardinal, who, being at Ravenna as
representative of the republic of Venice, was moved by the
dilapidated condition of the poet's tomb. It is spoken of as
being then 'oscura tomba,' and is referred to by Bembo
himself in his epitaph with perhaps a little touch of poetic
exaggeration in the words :—

> 'Exigua tumuli, Dantes, hic sorte iacebas,
> Squallenti nulli cognite paene situ.'

Bembo erected a marble mausoleum apparently on the site,
though perhaps not in the precise form, of the present edifice,
employing the architect and sculptor Lombardi, both for the
design of the building and for the sculptured effigy which was
placed within it and which remains there to this day.

The second epoch of restoration is 1692, when Cardinal
Corsi, papal legate, reconstructed the mausoleum after a fierce
conflict with the Frati, who disputed the right of the municipality, or of any one else, to touch the tomb, which they
claimed to be under their sole charge. An amusing account
is preserved of this conflict and its varying fortunes. At last
the Cardinal[1], with the aid of forty policemen (*sbirri*) who

---

[1] Conti, *La Scoperta delle ossa*, &c., p. 16 ; Cardoni, *Dante in Ravenna*,
pp. 81-3.

kept watch by day and by night, guarding his workmen and keeping the angry Frati at bay, completed his work (which was continued without intermission) on May 4, 1692. We shall see presently the probable reason for the Frati being so nervously sensitive about any interference with the tomb. There was something more involved in it than the maintenance of a technical legal right, for the bones had been long ago removed from the tomb, in fact, probably between 1515 and 1519[1].

The third and last epoch of restoration is that at which the mausoleum or chapel was brought to its present form, and this was carried out by Cardinal Valente Gonzaga in 1780, under the auspices of Pius VI, the well-known Angelo Braschi, whose vanity was the subject of so many of Pasquin's brilliant and biting epigrams. In this restoration or reconstruction, as much as possible of the internal work of Lombardi was preserved, and it may be doubted whether even the outward form was much changed, to judge from a description of Cardinal Corsi's work in a contemporary document of 1692[2].

Now a few words as to the various epitaphs extant. There are six altogether, of which, however, four have no special interest for us, and may be dismissed with a brief notice.

1. We have that of fourteen elegiac lines, as follows :—

> 'Theologus Dantes, nullius dogmatis expers
> Quod foveat claro philosophia sinu :
> Gloria Musarum, vulgo clarissimus Auctor,
> Hic iacet, et fama pulsat utrumque polum,
> &c., &c.'

The last four lines are :—

> 'Quem pia Guidonis gremio Ravenna Novelli
> Gaudet honorati continuisse ducis.
> Mille trecentenis ter septem numinis annis
> Ad sua Septembris idibus astra redit.'

This epitaph has been described as the first that was inscribed on the tomb, but it is very doubtful if it was ever placed there, and Ricci op. cit. pp. 251 seqq. affirms confidently that

---

[1] See Toynbee, op. cit. p. 114.   [2] See Conti, op. cit. pp. 12, 13.

it was not. Its *author* was certainly Dante's friend Giovanni del Virgilio, but *by whom* it was placed on the tomb, or *when*, or if indeed it was ever there at all, are matters of much dispute.

2. The most celebrated of all is that which consists of the following six rhyming hexameter lines :—

'S. V. F.

Iura Monarchiae, Superos, Phlegetonta, lacusque
Lustrando cecini voluerunt fata quousque,
Sed quia pars cessit melioribus hospita castris
Actoremque [*sic*] suum petiit felicior astris,
Hic claudor Dantes, patriis extorris[1] ab oris,
Quem genuit parvi Florentia mater amoris.'

This inscription has generally been attributed to Dante himself (on what grounds we shall inquire presently). It still appears in front of the effigy of the poet by Lombardi, where, in fact, it was placed by Bembo in 1483, though it may probably have been carved somewhere in connexion with the monument at some earlier period, for there is distinct evidence of its having been seen there fully a century earlier.[2]

3. That which is the next best known is another of six hexameter lines :—

' Inclita fama cuius universum penetrat orbem,
Dantes Aligherius Florentina natus in urbe,
Conditor eloquii lumenque decusque Latini,
Vulnere saevae necis stratus ad sidera tendens
Dominicis annis ter septem mille trecentis,
Septembris idibus includitur aula superna.'

This is not unfrequently found at the end of MSS. of the *Commedia*, together with one or both of those already mentioned. It is stated to have been there inscribed together with the *Iura Monarchiae*, in a dated MS. of the *Commedia* of 1378. It is also there definitely attributed to Minghino da Mezzano of Ravenna. Again it is assigned in a (probably) fourteenth-century MS. in the Bibliothèque Nationale at Paris to a son of Dante (probably Jacopo is intended), it being there introduced as ' Epitaphium quod filius suus fecit.'

---

[1] On *varr. lectt.* in this line see *infra*, pp. 180, 181.
[2] See Ricci, *op. cit.* pp. 259, 260.

4. We have next the epitaph of Bembo, which is as follows :—

> 'Exigua tumuli Dantes hic sorte iacebas
> Squallenti nulli cognite paene situ.
> At nunc marmoreo subnixus conderis arcu
> Omnibus et cultu splendidiore nites.
> Nimirum Bembus Musis incensus Ethruscis
> Hoc tibi quem in primis hae coluere dedit.

> Ann · Sal · MCCCCLXXXIII · VI Kal · Iun ·
> Bernardus · Bembus · Praet · Aere · suo · posuit · '

This was placed by Bembo on the *right* side of the small chapel, where it is still to be seen.

5. Next comes the epitaph of Cardinal Corsi, added at his restoration in 1692, beginning thus :—

> ' Exulem a Florentia Dantem liberalissime excepit Ravenna
> Vivo fruens, mortuum colens : '

This extends to fourteen lines, in which the previous works of the ' Polentani Principes' and of 'Bembus Praetor' are commemorated, as well as the present restoration by Corsi himself—' Anno Domini MDCXCII.'

This was placed on the *left* side of the mausoleum, but it was removed at the last restoration, in 1780.

6. Finally, we have the epitaph of Cardinal Gonzaga, which replaced that of Corsi, and is still to be seen on the *left* side of the chapel.   It commences thus :—

> ' Danti Alighiero
> Poetae sui Temporis Primo
> Restitutori
> Politioris Humanitatis.'

There are sixteen such lines in all, in which after mentioning ' Guido et Hostasius Polentiani,' and ' Bernardus Bembus ' (but not Corsi), Gonzaga declares that :—

> ' Operibus Ampliatis
> Munificentia Sua Restituendum
> Curavit
> Anno M.DCCLXXX[1].'

Hence Nos. 2, 4, and 6 are still on or beside the tomb.

---

[1] In the Codice Filippino at Naples, and nowhere else that I am aware

But we need further concern ourselves with the *first two*
only, and especially with the second, which has been so
generally attributed to Dante himself.

In regard to the first, the authorship is certain, and the only
matter in dispute is by whom and when (if ever) it was first
placed on the tomb. The evidence is conflicting. On the one
hand we have Boccaccio, who, as we have seen, says that neither
this nor any other inscription was there when he wrote his Life
of Dante. The date of this is generally put at about 1350
or 1360, and Boccaccio about that time is known himself to
have been at Ravenna, when he was commissioned to convey
alms to ' Sister Beatrice,' Dante's daughter, who was then
a nun in a convent at Ravenna[1]. At any rate, Boccaccio states
positively that he himself first selected this epitaph as in his
judgement the best that had been composed, and recorded it
in his Life in default of its appearance on the tomb, hoping
thereby to contribute to the immortality of the poet's memory
and works.

On the other hand we have Giovanni Villani, who died
in 1348, asserting that this epitaph, which he quotes as ' alti e
sottilissimi versi,' adorned the tomb ' poi a certo tempo ' after
Dante's funeral. This implies that the inscription was there
(if Villani's information is correct, for it is to be observed
that he does not say that he is speaking from personal
knowledge), at any rate, some time before 1348. I notice,
however, that these statements occur in a sort of duplicate
or alternative chapter printed by Muratori as 133, apparently
on the authority of *one MS.* only. Chapter 134, which also
gives the account of Dante's death and funeral, at greater
length, and partly in the same words, contains no reference
to the epitaph. This is, I think, worth noticing in reference to
the alleged inconsistency of Villani's statements with those of
Boccaccio.

of, the following two most barbarous lines (by way of an epitaph) are
found:—
　　' Comicus hic Dantes iacet, excelsusque poeta,
　　　　Non solum Comes, Satirus, Liricusque Tragoedus.'
See appendix to *Cod. Cassinense . . . messo a stampa*, p. 587.
　[1] See Del Lungo, *Dell' Esilio di Dante*, pp. 18, 161, 162.

Next, the *nephew* of the last-named chronicler—viz. *Filippo*
Villani, who died 1404, writing, therefore, a good deal later—
makes a similar statement, but with an increase of definiteness,
which is in itself suspicious[1], considering his later date. He
says that *Guido Novello himself* (observe this, and contrast
the statement with that of Boccaccio), after receiving many
competitive verses, 'hos qui fuere magistri Iohannis del
Virgilio iussit in frontispicio solemnis arculae insigniri[2].'
Whatever may be said of the language of *Giovanni* Villani,
this legendary growth found in *Filippo* cannot be set against
the positive and personal details clearly stated by Boccaccio.
Filippo seems to have confused Guido's *intention* with its
accomplishment, and in fact to have 'taken the will for
the deed.'

The next evidence is that of Giannozzo Manetti (1396–1459,
i.e. another half-century later), who, after describing the tomb,
says[3] that it was 'compluribus insuper egregiis carminibus
incisum insignitumque,' and adds: 'Epitaphium ab initio
huiusmodi in quadrato sepulchri lapide incisum fuit "Theologus
Dantes," &c. Quum deinde postea sex dumtaxat carmina,
longe prioribus illis elegantiora, a doctissimo quodam viro
(note especially these words) edita essent, veteribus e tumulo
abolitis, nova haec incisa fuerunt carmina, "Iura Monarchiae," &c.'

We observe here two points—

1. Manetti does not ascribe these lines 'Iura Monarchiae,'
&c. to Dante himself, but to 'doctissimus quidam vir.'

2. He does not say when and by whom the change of
the inscription was made; but, if his statements are to be
believed, the date at which he wrote (at any rate before 1459)
would clearly prove that it was not first carried out, as has
been sometimes thought, by Bembo in 1483. This naturally
leads us on to the second, and far the most interesting, of
the epitaphs, it having been so long and so generally supposed

---

[1] It may be added that the same suspicious multiplication of details charac-
terises Filippo Villani's brief Life of Dante already referred to.

[2] Quoted by Fraticelli, *Vita*, p. 316.

[3] From Mortara, *Catalogo*, p. 111, and Fraticelli, *Vita*, p. 324.

to have been composed by Dante himself, though I fear this pleasing imagination must be unhesitatingly abandoned.

As the epitaph stands at present on the tomb, it is headed by three mysterious letters, which seem certainly to have been prefixed by Bembo—S. V. F. These are a standing puzzle. No one has explained them, though plenty of guesses have been made. They have perhaps most often been thought to stand for 'Sibi Vivens Fecit,' and I believe it is sometimes given as a recognized form of monumental inscription in this sense (see Facciolati Appendix). Other interpretations are 'Suo Vixit Fato'; 'Salve Vive Felix'; 'Senatus Venetus Fecit' (this would not be true, since Bembo's own inscription states that 'aere suo posuit').

Next, when was this epitaph introduced?

Fraticelli boldly says that Bembo first placed it there at his restoration in 1483, and then first removed the epitaph of Del Virgilio (p. 320): 'Solo in quest' anno fu tolto l' antica epigrafe del Del Virgilio.' Against this I would point out—

1. We have the distinct statement of Giannozzo Manetti, who died in 1459, that it stood there in his time.

2. Desiderio Spreti[1], who died in 1474, and who wrote his *Istoria* in 1452 (though it was not published till after his death, in 1489), referring to Dante's tomb, says: 'Cuius epitaphium quod sibi mirum composuit in ipso marmore incisum tale est, "Iura Monarchiae," &c.[2]'

3. This epitaph is often found (*valeat quantum*) written at the end of manuscripts of the *Divina Commedia*, which are in most cases long anterior to 1483, the date of Bembo's work. This would not, of course, prove that the verses were actually on the tomb, at any rate unless it is distinctly so stated, as it is sometimes; and perhaps not even then, since these additions to MSS. are (1) sometimes in a later hand, and (2) even if they are not, are generally anonymous, like the MSS. themselves, and (3) even if they are not anonymous, the writer's signature has no recognized authority. Just to take one or

---

[1] Cardoni, p. 59.

[2] Further Ricci, *op. cit.*, p. 257, shows from a document preserved at Bologna dated 1432 that it was then on the tomb.

N

two samples. In a British Museum MS. (Harl. 3581) dated 1464 the epitaph is introduced by the words, 'Versus qui stant super sepulcrum Dantis.' Very precise and noteworthy however is the evidence of a MS. which I examined at Florence dated 1355 (or rather by an obvious clerical error 1255), where the existence of these verses is very circumstantially described thus: 'Hi versus sunt scripti ravenne in tumulo dantis in introitu ecclesie beati francisci a sinistra parte parve porte ipsius ecclesie pro eius epitaphio.' Mortara accepts this as a proof that the epitaph was set up about the middle of the fourteenth century, i.e., if this be so, soon after Boccaccio wrote. It is true that Batines notes that this addition in the MS. is in a later hand; but, though later than 1355, still I believe it is probably (whatever it is worth) before the time of Bembo. One cannot always venture to lay much stress on these anonymous and irresponsible statements at the end of even dated MSS. It is quite possible that a writer, being familiar with the epitaph, and also with the fact that epitaphs are written to be placed on tombs, took it for granted that it was actually so placed, in the absence of information to the contrary [1].

My conclusion on the whole would be that this epitaph was probably placed on the tomb about the middle of the fourteenth century, and that Bembo, at the time of his restoration

[1] There is a remarkable reference to the burial of Dante and to this epitaph in a fragmentary chronicle called *Spicilegium Ravennatis historiae* in Muratori, *Rer. Ital. Script.* I. part ii. p. 579, as follows:—'Ann. 1321. Hoc tempore [N.B. no more definite date given, as is usual for other events] D. A. moritur Ravennae; qui post mortem suam floruit de multis operibus suis, sicut apparet in Comoedia sua, videlicet Infernum Purgatorium Paradisum et Monarchia [*sic*]. Sepultus est Ravennae ad locum Fratrum Minorum ubi apparet cum istis versibus videlicet "Iura Monarchiae," &c.' This Chronicle ends on Nov. 15, 1346, whence it has been inferred that this inscription was put up before that time. This seems inconsistent with Boccaccio and both the Villani; in fact, with all the other information we possess. But note: (1) the above language about Dante is very vague, and looks as if the chronicler were not personally well informed on the subject. (2) It is not necessary to suppose the chronicle to have been written in 1346 because it breaks off then. It may have been broken off by some accident at that point. It is very fragmentary also, five or six years together being often blank about this period. It may be added that the fifth line of the epitaph as there given reads 'patriis externus ab oris.'

of the tomb of 1483, at any rate prefixed the mysterious
S. V. F. already discussed.

Next as to the question of the authorship of these lines.
Fraticelli says (*Vita*, pp. 315, 318) that Paulus Giovius (1483–
1552) is the first to maintain the Dantesque authorship, misled
probably by a false interpretation of the letters S. V. F., and
partly, it may be, by the employment of the first person
in the verses. This view cannot be maintained, since these
verses are certainly found attributed to Dante in MSS. earlier
than the date of Giovius. Indeed the use of the first person
throughout would be almost sure at any time to have suggested
the tradition of Dantesque authorship, and the conjectural
explanation of the mysterious letters may have confirmed and
perpetuated it[1]. There is no direct evidence of the origin
of the tradition. Two adverse considerations there are, one
negative, and the other positive, and the latter highly important. Negatively, Manetti, who died in 1459, was not aware
of any such reputed authorship, since, as we have seen above,
he attributes these verses, not to Dante, but to 'doctissimus
quidam vir.' There is, however, very important *positive*
evidence to the contrary. I find in one of the Bodleian MSS.
this epitaph quoted, and distinctly assigned to one Bernardus
de Canatro[2]. This is of course noted in Mortara's excellent
catalogue of the Canonici MSS., and it goes far to settle the
question of authorship outright, unless there were any reasons
(of which I am not aware) to suspect the truth of a statement
made so very definitely, though, it is true, anonymously. The
MS. is undated, but may safely be assigned to early in the
fifteenth century. It is introduced thus: 'Epitaffium ad
sepulchrum dantis in Ravenna urbe factum per dominum
Bernardum de Canatro.' Then follows 'Sonettus de laude
dicti domini Bernardi', beginning, 'Vestro sì pio officio offerto

---

[1] E. g., *inter alia*, I have met them in a certainly fourteenth-century MS. in the
Magliabecchian Library at Florence (Batines, No. 98) entitled 'Pathaphium
Dantis quod ipse fecit' and again in a probably fourteenth-century MS. at Paris
(Batines, No. 425) as 'Epitaphium Dantis factum a se ipso.' So that the tradition
seems certainly older than Fraticelli believes.

[2] See Ricci, *op. cit.*, pp. 261, 264, 265.

a Dante,' and then again a sonnet in reply, entitled, ' Responsio dicti domini Bernardi.'

External evidence of any value in favour of the Dantesque authorship there is really none, while such evidence as we have is adverse. As to internal evidence, in spite of the Dantesque touch of tender, yet bitter, pathos, in the last two lines; in spite, too, of Mr. Lowell's enthusiasm for these verses expressed in his noble essay on Dante—' If these be not the words of Dante, what is internal evidence worth ? '— I think we shall probably agree with the majority of critics, who even on this ground have felt compelled to reject the interesting theory.

It may be mentioned that Gabriel Rossetti not only accepts the testimony of Giovius as to the Dantesque authorship of these verses, but also (like Mr. Lowell) appeals to their internal evidence of genuineness, thus : ' più che altro, lo stile di quei pochi versi ne assicura della veracità di Giovio.' It is very curious indeed to find Rossetti then proceeding to apply to this epitaph the same strange principles of interpretation by which he has distorted (if I may venture to say so) the divine poem into a political *brochure*, and professing to discover here a further confirmation of his fanciful theory [1].

One word as to the evidence of MSS. in respect of the reading of line 5. As it stands on the tomb it reads :—

'patriis extorris ab oris.'

Patriis is the usual reading, but I have found *propriis* in three MSS. (including the interesting Bodleian MS. in which the verses are assigned to B. de Canatro) as against *patriis* in eighteen MSS., and *longis* in one MS. As to the word *extorris* there is also a good deal of doubt. I have found *extorris* in three MSS.; *exterus* in seventeen; *externus* in two; *eiectus* in one (that one being the same Bodleian MS.); *expulsus* in one.

Mortara, in his Catalogue, ingeniously suggests that perhaps Bembo intentionally softened *eiectus*, which appears in the

[1] *Com. Anal.* ii. pp. 58, 59.

copy assigned to Canatro, into *extorris*, out of regard to the feelings of the people of Florence. If this were accepted, we might probably imagine a similar consideration having prompted the alteration of *propriis* of the same MS. into *patriis*. The combination *propriis eiectus* of the Bodleian MS. is certainly more uncompromisingly severe than any other. The curious word *exterus*, so generally found, has probably arisen from an early omission to supply the mark of abbreviation indicating an omitted *n*; so that the word would in that case stand simply for *externus*. It might be suggested, too, that it was merely the Latin word *extĕrus*, employed with that disregard of quantity which is common in barbarous mediaeval versification; but its preservation in the familiar and little-changed Italian word *estero* would have been likely to protect it from such a use.

To sum up this long discussion very briefly, I think the most probable conclusion from this tangle of conflicting statements and conjectural inferences is as follows:—

For many years after Dante's burial the tomb bore no inscription.

Boccaccio merely states that he selected the epitaph of Del Virgilio on its intrinsic merits, but he never states that it was adopted for the tomb, and there seems to be no sufficient evidence that it ever found a place there. The epitaph *Iura Monarchiae* was introduced sometime about the middle of the fourteenth century, as there is evidence in the MS. above quoted of its having been seen there in 1378, as well as that of Minghino da Mezzano beginning *Inclita fama*. At the restoration of the tomb by Bembo the epitaph *Iura Monarchiae* was inscribed on the face of the sarcophagus, where it is still to be seen, and probably the letters S. V. F. were then prefixed to it.

III. We pass on now to the most interesting and extraordinary episode connected with the tomb of Dante, viz. the discovery of his actual bones—and that, strange to say, not in his tomb—on May 27, 1865.

On this memorable day, some workmen were engaged in removing a portion of a wall in the chapel of Braccioforte, an outlying chapel of the Franciscan church abutting upon the Strada Dante on one side, and upon a small graveyard on the other, and only a few paces to the west of the mausoleum of Dante. On removing some bricks, by which an ancient doorway had been blocked up, some of which by their projection interfered with the action of a new pump-handle (so trivial and accidental was the cause of all that followed !), the workmen came upon a rude and much-decayed wooden chest. This partially fell to pieces, disclosing some human bones, and also the following words rudely written in ink, on the floor, so to speak, of the chest :—

'Dantis Ossa
Denuper revisa die 3 Iunii
1677.'

On further examination an inscription similarly written was discovered on one of the outer planks of the chest, as follows :—

'Dantis Ossa
A me Fr̄e Antonio Santi
hic posita
Año 1677 Die 18 Octobris.'

The skeleton was found to be complete, with the exception of a few small bones.

It naturally then became a matter of the highest interest to examine the sarcophagus in the chapel, in which the remains were generally supposed to lie. This examination took place on June 7, 1865, and *the tomb was then found to be empty*, with the exception of a little earthy or dusty substance and a few bones corresponding with most of those missing in the chest recently discovered, and these were certified by the surgeon present to belong undoubtedly to the same skeleton. There were found in it also a few withered laurel leaves, which possess a special interest in reference to the description of Dante's burial to which (*supra*, p. 169) I have already referred. I use the conventional term 'laurel,' but they were more probably 'bay'—or perhaps 'Roman laurel,' which seems to be a kind of bay. 'Laurus' in Latin and 'lauro' in Italian

are used indifferently for our ' laurel ' and ' bay.' It contained
further some broken fragments of Greek marble, of the same
material as the sarcophagus itself. These were soon found
to proceed from a rude hole which had been knocked through
the material of the sarcophagus at the back, precisely at a part
accessible only from the inside of the monastery, through
which, beyond all doubt, the removal of the bones had been
effected.[1] This hole had been stopped up with bricks and
cement and then plastered over outside, so as to leave no
mark. Finally the skull found in the chest or box was very
carefully examined and measured by the surgeons, and it was
found exactly to correspond in the most minute particulars
with the mask taken from Dante's face immediately after his
death, which had been brought from Florence for the purpose
of making this comparison. A cast of this mask the Dante
Society at Oxford is fortunate enough to possess, through the
kindness of the late Baron Kirkup.[2]

Three questions naturally occur. 1. When was this pious
theft effected? 2. What was its motive? 3. Did no suspicion
of it previously exist?

1. It will be observed that while the words of an outside
inscription indicate clearly the date at which the chest was
deposited in its final resting-place, the words on the inside,
' denuper revisa' (revisited anew), appear to imply that the
bones had been abstracted from their sepulchre some time before, and they would also seem to indicate a repeated and perhaps periodical official inspection of the precious deposit. It is
of course impossible to say how long the relics may have been
kept hidden somewhere in the monastery, between their first
removal and final immurement. It may have been for many

---

[1] This will be seen clearly from the plan, *infra*, p. 190.

[2] Of course, the authenticity of this mask has been disputed like everything
else. Among other grounds, on the extravagant pretension that the process
of taking such masks was not then known, and is a comparatively modern
invention. The most amusing thing à propos of this precious piece of scepticism
is that the process is to be found fully described in Pliny ! (see *Nat. Hist.* xxxv.
12, a reference which I owe to the President of Magdalen). ' Hominis autem
imaginem gypso e facie ipsa primus omnium expressit, ceraque in eam formam
gypsi infusa emendare instituit Lysistratus Sicyonius, frater Lysippi. Hic et
similitudinem reddere instituit. Ante eum quam pulcherrimas facere studebant.'

years, or even possibly for several generations of Frati, the
perilous secret being rigidly kept by the brethren, and
probably only entrusted to a very few in authority. It is
interesting to note that the documents of the monastery show
this Antonio Santi to have occupied just such an official
position at this time. He is, in fact, recorded as chancellor
of the confraternity first in 1672, and continued to hold that
office till after 1677, the date above mentioned. He afterwards became warden in 1700 and died in 1703.

Till comparatively recent times a significant tradition prevailed among the Frati (how far understood by a few initiated
we cannot say) that ' in the chapel of Braccioforte *lies hid
a great treasure.*' Conti, writing in 1865, mentions that
relatives of the last warden of the monastery still survived
who had frequently heard him repeat these words.

It will be observed that the date we are considering (viz.
1677) preceded by only fifteen years the second restoration,
by Cardinal Corsi in 1692. It seems clear from ample documentary evidence that that restoration extended to the walls
of the chapel only, and that he did not touch the sarcophagus
itself. Had he done so, the removal of the bones would have
been at once found out. It is probable that the extreme
sensitiveness of the monks as to the interference with the
tomb by others, and their violent resistance to it, which has
been already described, were prompted by a fear lest the
terrible discovery might be made. The great secret must
certainly then have been burning in the breasts of some of
them. In fact, Fra Antonio himself, the very man who, as we
have seen, carried out the final removal of the bones, and who
lived till 1703, was still on the spot, and in high authority at
the moment. He could not forget, I am sure, the damaging
evidence of his recent handwriting on the chest, should the
truth come out, and no doubt looked on very nervously as
the good Cardinal Corsi, guarded by his forty policemen,
worked on night and day, little suspecting that he was
adorning a cenotaph.

2. Next as to our second question, which is, of course, very
closely connected with the first, viz. the probable motive for

this strange act. One can suggest two not unlikely motives. One, the fear lest the coveted treasure, the pride of all Italy, should ever be removed to some more distinguished resting-place. Documents still exist which show that at least on four several occasions [1] the people of Florence had the effrontery, if I may so say, to make such a demand : first on Dec. 23, 1396, secondly on Feb. 1, 1430, thirdly in 1476, and fourthly (and this was no doubt a very formidably supported demand) on Oct. 20, 1519, when Leo X was pressed to transfer the poet's remains to Florence, the petition being backed among others by Michelangelo, who appended to his signature these cogent words : ' offerendomi al divin poeta fare la sepoltura sua, condecente, e in loco onorevole in questa Città.' It is interesting also to note among the other signatures to this document,[2] that of Petrus Franciscus Portinarius, one whose family Dante is believed to have immortalized in the person of Beatrice Portinari. Of course that danger had long passed in 1677, which, however, be it remembered, is merely the date of the *final reinterment* or immurement, and not necessarily, or even probably, that of the *original abstraction* of the remains. Whether any similar fresh demands were made or mooted nearer the time in question there is no evidence, and probably, therefore, this was not the case. Another suggestion that might be made is this. The outbreak of jealousy between the Frati and the municipality in 1692 at Cardinal Corsi's restoration above mentioned (p. 171), though there were good reasons then for its special intensity, probably indicates the existence of an earlier and long-standing difference. This is not likely to have been the first time that such disputes had arisen, and the Frati may well have resolved to put their rights beyond the reach of rivalry by thus securing the disputed treasure for themselves, thinking, no doubt, that actual possession was the best form of legal right, or, to borrow Dante's own language, ' fidandosi di sè più che d' un altro.'

However, a very remarkable parallel case occurring in our

---

[1] See Toynbee, *op. cit.*, pp. 112, 113.
[2] Del Lungo, *Dell' Esilio di Dante*, p. 187.

own day and in our own country, in reference to St. Cuthbert, enables and inclines me to believe that the abstraction of the remains from the tomb may have taken place even as long before as the time of the scare (which must have been a most alarming one) caused by the threatened intervention, so powerfully invoked, of Pope Leo X in 1519. It is true this would involve the maintenance of the difficult secret of the concealment of the remains in some hidden spot in the monastery, whether above or below ground, for at least 150 years, before they were finally walled up in the chapel of Braccioforte. But with the experience of the secret relating to St. Cuthbert, I should have no difficulty in believing this to have been the case. But, not to interrupt our present narrative, I will leave the description of this incident till later. [See the note appended to this Essay.]

3. But it is natural now to ask, is there not any trace of a suspicion that something was wrong during the last two centuries, just as after the discovery of a new planet it is often found that observations of it have been recorded before but have passed unnoticed? Yes, there is. A very strange story has been lately unearthed from the archives of Ravenna, which is given by Conti (to whom, as well as to Cardoni, I will here acknowledge, once for all, my indebtedness for many of my facts and details). This is as follows:—In 1694 (just two years, it will be observed, after the restoration by Cardinal Corsi) an escaped prisoner who fled to the chapel in which was the mausoleum of Dante, and claimed the right of asylum, was forcibly removed. A dispute arose between the civil and ecclesiastical authorities, which was ultimately referred to Rome. The archbishop of Ravenna contended that the chapel was an integral part of the sacred enclosure, and partook of the same privileges. The advocates of the municipality met this by the contention that Dante had been declared a heretic after his death [I suppose referring to the action of Cardinal Poggetto already noticed, as I am not aware of any other grounds for such an assertion], and consequently the presence of his remains had deconsecrated the spot and caused it no longer to possess the rights of asylum.

The rejoinder of the monks to this argument was very remarkable, and it is strange that it did not attract more attention. They declared that the bones of Dante were no longer in the chapel, and appealed to an inscription to be seen on the walls to that effect. I am not aware of any other reference whatever to the existence (if it ever existed) of such an inscription. Possibly it was temporarily put up to meet the circumstances. The monks therefore, to preserve their rights, had the audacity to argue that the admittedly once consecrated spot remained so still with its consequent privilege of asylum, because Dante's bones are no longer in a position to interfere with its consecration. In any case, the inscription on the recently discovered chest (1677) shows the statement of the monks to have been strictly true, but it is most strange that it should have been thus publicly made. Witte thinks it characteristic of the age when Chiabrera and Marini were the most admired models, that the monks should have preferred the advantage of securing their immunities to the glory of being the custodians of Dante's remains. I think it is much more probable, as I have said, that the removal of the relics was in the first instance due to extreme anxiety for their security, and that, on this occasion, the cunning monks, knowing that they had the precious treasure in perfectly safe custody, beyond the reach of either friends or foes, were not unwilling to take advantage of the circumstance to secure a legal triumph. It does, however, seem most remarkable, that such a statement should have produced no sensation, and that it should not, apparently, have led to any further investigation.

Then again, after another interval of about seventy years, in 1768, one Lovillet (a feigned name, I believe) once more began 'spargere voces in vulgum ambiguas,' and published a statement that of six illustrious persons whose tombs the people of Ravenna claimed to possess, not one was quite rightly claimed ('nessuno di loro vi ha effettivamente la sepoltura'), and, though he added that he could not deny that Dante was buried in Ravenna, yet it was not in the chapel, as supposed by the citizens of Ravenna, but somewhere in the

church of St. Francesco ' in cui si deve cercare il suo tumulo.'
This statement was, of course, vigorously assailed, promptly
denied, and entirely refuted, to the complete satisfaction of
the *Accademia Arcivescovile di Ravenna,* in April of the same
year.   In short (as Livy says), ' Hoc primum, velut temere
iactum, sperni coeptum est,' and so no action was taken in the
matter.   But in 1780, twelve years later, on the occasion of
Cardinal Gonzaga's restoration, the opportunity of verification
was offered and could scarcely be declined.   What happened
then is very significant.   The tomb was opened, by authority,
in the presence of a few selected witnesses, who were *previously
sworn to absolute secrecy* as to what they might see [or not
see].   An official document was published in the following
significantly obscure and studiously vague terms : ' vi si rin-
venne ciò che era necessario per non dubitarne (!).'   (' There
resulted that which was needful to remove all doubt.')   One
wonders that this curious diplomatic feat could have served
to conceal rather than to reveal the suspected and dreaded
truth.   Probably it was a case in which ' populus vult decipi
et decipitur.'   Conti (p. 42) also mentions a very curious
discovery lately made by some one who was ferreting among
the books of the suppressed Franciscan monastery.   On the
fly-leaf of a mass book the following anonymous entry was
found, which, as will be seen from the date, evidently refers to
the last restoration, by Cardinal Gonzaga: ' 1 Aug. 1780.—The
sepulchre of Dante was taken down and entirely rebuilt . . .'
Then follow details as to the architect and the expenses,
&c., and the note proceeds as follows :—' The coffin (*cassa*)
was opened *and nothing was found within.*   It was sealed up
again with the cardinal's seal, and strict silence was observed
as to everything,' &c.   The writer, though anonymous, invites
a comparison of his handwriting for identification with the
archives of the fraternity, stating that he was then sacristan.
The writing has since been identified in accordance with this
suggestion of the writer.

So ends this strange and most interesting history, for such
it must be admitted to be, however imperfectly it may have
been now narrated.   Thus it came about by a most singular

and almost dramatic coincidence, that on the very eve of the sexcentenary celebration of the poet's birth, probably within a day or two of the anniversary of his actual birthday, and in the midst of the preparations for the great commemorative festival, the chapel of Braccioforte yielded up the 'great treasure' which for wellnigh 200 years it had so effectually guarded.

NOTE.—It should be explained that the quotations throughout from Boccaccio's *Life of Dante* are taken from an edition which happened to be at hand, viz. that of Didot, Paris, 1884. I find that this contains the particular form or recension of the *Vita* known as the *Compendio*, though it is in several places fuller than the so-called *Vita Intera*. The relation between these two (and other) different recensions of the *Vita* that have come down to us is a very curious and still perhaps unsolved literary problem. See however the Article, 'Qual è la seconda redazione del "Trattatello in Laude di Dante"?' in *Studi su Giovanni Boccaccio, per il Sesto Centenario della Nascita di Giovanni Boccaccio*, pp. 104-141, by Michele Barbi, in which he shows that the so-called *Compendio* is a revised version of the *Vita* due to Boccaccio himself.

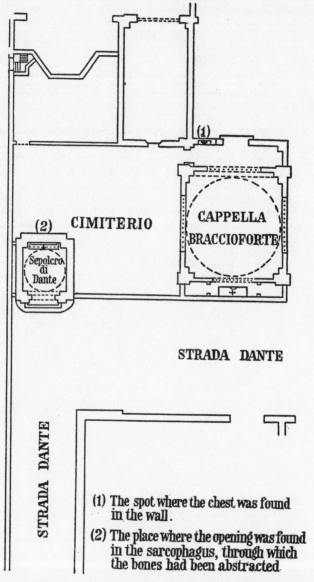

(1) The spot where the chest was found in the wall.

(2) The place where the opening was found in the sarcophagus, through which the bones had been abstracted.

It may be noticed that the approach to the Mausoleum resembles that to the entrance gate of New College, Oxford. It is approached through a narrow street between two blank walls. This street also turns off to the right, just like that which leads to Queen's College Lane.

APPENDIX NOTE ON ST. CUTHBERT.

I now propose to describe two curiously parallel incidents that have occurred in connexion with two of our great English cathedrals, Durham and Canterbury. In neither case is the alleged discovery clearly certain as in that of the bones of Dante. Indeed, in both cases it is still very much disputed, and likely to remain so. But, none the less, there is such a close resemblance between many of the features of the three stories that they seem to throw much light upon one another. The undoubted facts of one tend to add probability to the conjectures by which the missing links of another have been tentatively supplied.

First as to Durham and St. Cuthbert.

The allusion in *Marmion* to St. Cuthbert is well known [Canto ii, Stanza 14] :—

> 'There deep in Durham's Gothic shade
> His relics are in secret laid,
> But none may know the place
> Save of his holiest servants three,
> Deep sworn to solemn secrecy
> Who share that wondrous grace.'

This refers to a tradition that St. Cuthbert's body was removed from its shrine in the reign of Henry VIII and hidden in some secret spot in Durham Cathedral. Also to the fact that among members of the Benedictine Order in England—Durham, it will be remembered, having been a Benedictine Monastery, there are always three who claim to have definite knowledge of some spot in Durham Cathedral in which 'a treasure is hidden.' They do not say St. Cuthbert's body, but it is commonly supposed to refer to this. Another idea is that it may refer to the reliquaries or other like treasures of the ancient monastery. But, whether or no, the similarity of the cases is very remarkable, for no doubt before the discovery of Dante's body, the meaning of the word 'treasure' [*supra*, p. 184] was equally ambiguous.

Whenever one of the three Benedictines dies the survivors elect another to take his place, and they are all, of course, sworn to secrecy. Thus the secret is handed down, and so they declare that it has been continuously handed down for more than 300 years, the brethren hoping for the time when they will 'come by their own again.'

I am indebted for most of the details which follow to the *Victorian History of the County of Durham*, ii. pp. 241 *seqq.*

I need not recount the many removals of the body of the Saint (also described by Scott in the same stanza of *Marmion*), prompted by fear of the Danes and other marauders, during three centuries after his death at Lindisfarne in A. D. 687.

Within about ten years, in fact in 698, the body, still uncorrupted, was transferred from the stone cyst in which it was originally placed, into a new wooden coffin, fragments of which are still preserved in the Cathedral Library at Durham. But (for a reason which will appear later) we must not omit to mention that on the occasion of one of the removals above referred to, viz. that in 875, the head of St. Oswald, some bones of St. Aidan, and other relics of North country Saints, were deposited in the same coffin. Under fear of the Danes this was carried over to the mainland, and after many wanderings, which we need not further refer to, was brought in the year 998 to Durham, or, as it was then called, Dunholme, whence the Latin form, Dunelmum. There the body of the Saint found at last a resting-place, and there it has remained ever since, with the exception of a year or two, 1069–70, when it was removed again to Lindisfarne in fear of the threatened approach of William the Conqueror. It was, however, finally brought back and re-buried in 1104. Details of the process, of the repairs of the coffin, and of its several contents are still extant.

We hear of it next after a long interval in 1537. In that year three Commissioners of Henry VIII arrived in Durham, when the coffin containing the body of the Saint was forced open with such violence that a bone of one of the legs was broken. The coffin with the remains was then deposited in the revestry in the church 'till such time as they did further know the King's pleasure.' There being no great prospect of plunder, 'the King's pleasure' was not so urgently pressing as in the case of the shrine of Becket at Canterbury. Hence there was a considerable period of respite, during which— i. e. some time between 1537 and 1542—it is stated that the body of the Saint was removed from the coffin, no doubt without any disturbance of the wrappings by which it was surrounded, and concealed in some other part of the Cathedral, near the west end. Here is an exact parallel to the action of the monks in the case of Dante, and in both cases it was a most natural precaution in the face of apparently similar dangers. The tradition further states that the bones of some monk taken from the 'Centry Garth,' or Monks' Cemetery, were substituted in the coffin for those of the Saint.[1] This, I believe, is the Benedictine tradition still current. But another tradition asserts that in 1542, the danger being over, the original body was replaced and laid, coffin and all, in an ordinary vault, behind the Neville screen. The bills of cost and a description of this reinterment are still preserved, and it is stated that those who saw it detected no change in the contents of the coffin since it was opened five years before. Above the coffin was placed a large stone slab, to serve as a cover to the vault beneath, on which was engraved 'Ricardus Heswell, Monachus'[2]—but with the inscription *face downwards*. This is expressly stated in an anonymous *Brief Account of Durham Cathedral* published in 1833, containing a record of the opening of the vault in 1827, which will be referred to later. It is naturally suggested that it was purposely turned downwards to show that it was converted to a use not originally intended (p. 58). Above this was another plain slab of marble ' on which may plainly be seen the marks of the feet of earlier worshippers' (or possibly, we may suggest, the marks of the *knees*, as in the Trinity Chapel in Canterbury Cathedral round the site of Becket's shrine).

After another long interval, in 1827, the coffin was again opened and re-examined. The body was found wrapped in ancient robes, there being no less than six of such coverings. There was a tenth-century stole and other vestments, from the condition of which as well as from the state of the bones (as was certified by two skilful anatomists) it seemed certain that the body and the other contents of the coffin could never have been exposed to damp. The Centry Garth being very damp, either no such substitution of a body taken thence could ever have occurred, or else when the danger was past the original body of the Saint was replaced and the substituted body removed. But it will be remembered that in 1542 those who

---

[1] 'Centry Garth.' This word is spelt either as 'centry' or 'sentry.' In Murray's *Dictionary*, s.v. 'sentry,' it is said to be a contracted form of 'sanctuary,' compare French 'sanctuaire'; and also a quotation (1590) is given from Nashe's 1*st Pt. Pasquil's Apol.* C 4, ' He hath no way now to slyppe out of my handes, but to take *sentrie* in the Hospitall of Warwick.' Sir James Murray also quotes from *Rites of Durham* : 'Att yᵉ easte end of the said Chapter howse ... is a garth called yᵉ centrie garth, where all the priors & mounckes was buryed.' In Gostling's *Walk about Canterbury* it is stated that ' a centry gate' parted the cemetery of the laity from that of the monks. This is in fact the arch now forming the entrance to the bowling-green of the old monastery.

[2] A monk of that name is recorded as having been buried in the cemetery in the fifteenth century. If the traditional substitution of another body for that of the Saint from 1537 to 1542 ever took place (which we shall see reason strongly to doubt), it might perhaps be suggested that this was the monk whose bones were employed for this purpose.

witnessed the reinterment saw no change in the appearance
of the contents of the coffin. It seems evident therefore that
at any rate the several wrappings had never been disturbed
at the time of their removal a few years before. This would
explain what might at first sight seem surprising, viz. that
the cross, the comb, the tenth-century stole, and other objects
found hidden among them escaped the notice of Henry's Commissioners. But the cross is a very small one, only 2⅜ by
2½ inches[1], and it was hidden under three of the six coverings
in which the body was enwrapped. The Commissioners were
perhaps satisfied from a cursory examination that there were
no treasures of importance contained in the coffin. Henry and
his emissaries would no doubt regard any of its contents from
the burglar's point of view, in reference to their market value,
rather than from their artistic or antiquarian interest.

Further, it was observed that one of the thigh bones of the
skeleton was missing. This was probably that which was
broken when the coffin was so roughly opened at the Commissioners' visit in 1537.

It should be added that the objects above mentioned correspond with those recorded as having been in the coffin at the
time of the reburial in 1104[2]. Most of them, together with
the fragments of the original coffin, were deposited in the
Cathedral Library, where they are now to be seen. The
remains were then placed in what is described as 'a rough
box of deal planks,' like (as we may note) the rude receptacle
in which the bones of Dante were found.

It may be mentioned in passing that in 1867 notice was
directed to two documents of the seventeenth and eighteenth
centuries which stated definitely that the 'treasure' of
St. Cuthbert was his body, and, further, described with some
variations the spot where it was hidden. Relying on this,
the Dean and Chapter in that year undertook excavations in
three different places in the Cathedral which seemed to be
indicated, but they found nothing. The Benedictines informed
them that they had not gone to the right spot. But this the
Dean and Chapter had discovered for themselves, and it was
unfortunately all that they had discovered.

But more recently, in 1899, the search was renewed, and

---

[1] The cross is said to be of a type of workmanship well known to be of about
the seventh century.

[2] Here we have two points of resemblance to the evidence of identity in the
case of the sarcophagus of Dante. A bone was missing from the skeleton,
which was accounted for by its being found in the sarcophagus. Also there
were found in the sarcophagus the withered laurel or bay leaves which were
recorded as having been buried with him.

there can, I think, be little doubt that it was then rewarded at any rate by the discovery of the body of St. Cuthbert. Whether that be the 'treasure' of the Benedictine tradition or not, we are not in a position to assert. But the circumstantial evidence as to the discovery of the body itself scarcely (as I think) leaves any room for doubt.

The examination of the contents of the box, and especially of the skeleton itself, was much more thorough than in 1827. This led to the discovery of some important additions to the evidence of identification. The most remarkable of these was as follows. Bede relates that St. Cuthbert for a long time after his narrow escape from death by the plague *c.* 664 suffered from a tumour which, at first external, afterwards took an internal direction, and troubled him much for the rest of his life. Now the doctors present in 1899 observed in the breast-bone a well-marked deep cavity, which appeared, as they said, to have been eaten out by a prolonged and obstinate tumour[1]. It was also noted that the skeleton was that of a man about 5 ft. 8 in. in height. Now St. Cuthbert is described by contemporaries as 'neither very tall nor very short.' Further, the apparent age of the remains was that of a man of about fifty-five years, which would at least not be inconsistent with the supposed age of St. Cuthbert. The *Dictionary of National Biography* says that as he became a monk at an early age and continued to be one for thirty-seven years 'he was probably not sixty at the time of his death.'

Finally, as to St. Oswald's head. William of Malmesbury writes that it is said to be held between the arms of the blessed Cuthbert in his tomb. In the translation of 1104 it was restored to its place as thus described. In 1899 a second skull was actually found in the coffin, and on this skull was a tremendous cut, as of a sword. Now St. Oswald was killed in the battle of Maserfelth in 642 A.D.

Surely circumstantial evidence could scarcely go further.

---

[1] The actual statement of Bede referred to in the Victorian history is not quite so pointed and definite as I was led to expect. In Bede's *Vita Sancti Cudbercti*, c. ii, it is related how that the Saint in his youth suffered from a tumour in his knee which caused extreme pain and at last entirely incapacitated him from walking. From this he is stated to have been miraculously cured by an angel. In c. viii we read that in later life he was again attacked by a tumour in the thigh (femur) which took an internal direction, but it is not definitely stated to have centred itself in the breast-bone. The words are : 'Sed quia tumor, qui in femore eius parebat, paulatim a superficie detumescens corporis, ad viscerum interiora prolapsus est, toto paene vitae suae tempore aliquantulum interaneorum non cessabat sentire dolorem.' This does not so precisely localize the seat of the internal pain as I was led to suppose, but it is not inconsistent with such a phenomenon. For at any rate the two passages together show the liability of the sufferer to attacks of this kind.

We cannot indeed say whether we have discovered the 'treasure' of the Benedictines, but if that be the body of the Saint, as is generally supposed, there can scarcely remain any doubt that *that* treasure is now in our hands.

As to the conflicting traditions respecting the disposal of the body in the years 1537–1542, whether it remained in the 'revestry,' or whether it was removed elsewhere in the Cathedral; also whether another body or skeleton was, as a measure of precaution, temporarily substituted for it or not in the coffin—all this seems to me to be quite immaterial. For in any case it was not that other body which was found there in 1899. This is clear from the absolutely undisturbed condition of the six successive coverings of the skeleton, and also of the various articles (cross, comb, stole, portable altar, &c.) found distributed in different places among them. Thus if the original body was ever moved it was moved together with its coverings, as indeed would naturally be the case, even independently of the evidence of those who witnessed the reburial in 1542, as above referred to.

Another case of the abstraction of sacred relics to save them from the threats of Henry VIII occurred at Lichfield. The bones of St. Chad were deposited in two spots in the Cathedral. Part were in the shrine or behind the High Altar, and the rest in the Chapel of St. Chad's Head. Some of them were hurriedly removed by one of the prebendaries about 1537, at the threat of the visit of Henry's Commissioners, and after various vicissitudes a few of them are now deposited at the Roman Catholic Cathedral of St. Chad at Birmingham.

I mention this as a parallel case to the action of the monks at Durham, to show how natural it would be to suppose that the monks of Canterbury would have had recourse to a similar precaution with the bones of Becket at the same date and under precisely similar circumstances.

The following extracts from Dr. Selby Plummer's medical examination of St. Cuthbert's remains in 1899 may be found interesting.

Numerous indications that age was *c.* 55, and height 5 ft. 8 in. or 5 ft. 9 in. ('No signs, however, of wisdom teeth ever having erupted.')

'On sternum and adjacent clavicle on right side, distinct traces of erosion and many perforations due to some ulcerative process.' 'On the right lower border and about the situation of sterno-clavicular joint, immediately below the eroded upper border, is an almost circular perforation, *c.* ½ in. in diameter with rough edges. No sequestrum in the cavity.'

(The left *tibia* absent.)

This extensive disease of sternum and clavicle would probably have given some visible evidence in life, but not necessarily more than a small sinus; no prolonged accumulation of pus to attract attention. It would not entail lameness, or loss of the use of one limb; could be attended to without assistance; and not necessarily either known, or shown, to others. At any rate it gives indubitable evidence of a disease similar to that from which St. Cuthbert is known to have suffered.

Besides the reference in Bede's Life, c. 2, to an acrid humour in the knee in his youth ('cured by an angel'), Cuthbert nearly died of the plague *c.* 664 (æt. *c.* 30), and one consequence of this was a tumour on the thigh which gradually sunk beneath the surface (Bede, c. 8) and caused pain in his inward parts almost all the rest of his life (see p. 105 n.). It is referred to in c. 37 as his 'vetus infirmitas' and his 'quotidiana paene molestia'.

The same report gives details of the skull found in the coffin (presumably that of St. Oswald). Reginald of Durham [Simeon Dunelm.; Rolls Ed., vol. i] describes minutely the injuries to the skull as seen by him when it was deposited in Cuthbert's coffin in 1104. This is stated in the Report to agree so closely with the wounds found in this examination in 1899 as to leave no doubt as to this being the head of St. Oswald.

SECOND APPENDIX NOTE TO ESSAY III

I propose now to describe the very interesting discovery made in the crypt of Canterbury Cathedral in January 1888. In the process of clearing the crypt of the accumulated rubbish of some centuries, a wooden coffin was found, about three inches only below the pavement, very near to the position of the tomb in which Becket was buried immediately after his murder in 1170, and where his body lay for fifty years until, in 1220, the solemn translation of his remains to the shrine in the new Trinity Chapel took place, which is still commemorated on July 7. There they remained till 1538—note the date in connexion with the visit of the King's Commissioners to Durham, mentioned in the preceding Appendix Note—when Henry VIII ordered the shrine to be destroyed and the bones within it to be burned and scattered to the winds.

Let us endeavour to realize the actual circumstances with which the monks were then confronted.

It has been commonly stated that Henry held a mock trial at Westminster, at which Becket was formally summoned to appear, on April 24, 1538. As he naturally did not do so, he was condemned in contumacy, and the sentence was pronounced on June 10 that his bones should be burned and his shrine destroyed. I believe it is now generally admitted that this story of the mock trial was an effort of the imagination[1], but I am not aware of any reason to doubt the date of the formal sentence of condemnation. Let us observe, however, that the King's Commissioners for the execution of this sentence did not appear at Canterbury till September. The monks therefore had three clear months' notice of what was coming. It is hardly conceivable that some of them should not have profited by this interval to remove the saint's bones and substitute others in their place. It would be an enterprise of great danger and difficulty, and would probably be known to two or three only, and it would need to have been carried out by them with the utmost secrecy. The actual removal, however, might have been accomplished both rapidly and secretly by means of either of the staircases still existing both in St. Andrew's and in St. Anselm's Chapels, leading down from the neighbourhood of the shrine to the crypt immediately below it. This would be a spot pointed out by pious sentiment as being that of Becket's original grave, as well as by its convenient proximity to the shrine. Now would not the monks almost undoubtedly have acted just as their brethren at Durham are said to have done, exactly at this same time, in reference to St. Cuthbert, and at Lichfield in the case of St. Chad, and as the Franciscans of Ravenna certainly did in the case of the remains of Dante, as precious to them as the relics of a canonized saint? Would not the neglect of such an obvious precaution during the respite of three whole months be truly amazing?

This at any rate is a pertinent inquiry quite apart from any question of the identity of the remains discovered in 1888. The fact that such action appears to have been an instinctive resource of monks whose treasured relics were threatened with danger, supplies an important link in the cumulative or circumstantial evidence beyond which in the case now before us we cannot hope or pretend to advance. It is also interesting to observe that this would not have been the first occasion when Becket's bones had been removed for a similar reason. For, as in the

---

[1] See Dixon, *History of the Church of England*, vol. ii, pp. 71, 72.

case of the early panic-prompted removals of the body of St. Cuthbert in the ninth and tenth centuries, so in the case of Becket it is recorded by a contemporary monk named Benedict, an eyewitness of the murder, who afterwards became Prior, that on one occasion, very shortly after the martyrdom, the body was temporarily removed into a wooden chest and hidden in fear of an assault from some of Becket's old enemies, who were thought to be lurking about the church with some malicious purpose.

Now let us carefully note the following points in reference to the bones found in this coffin.

1. The coffin or chest was far too small both in length and width for the skeleton found in it. The remains must therefore have been placed there, not as a body, but as a skeleton. The bones were those of an exceptionally tall man. Mr. Pugin Thornton [1] calculated that he was probably 6 ft. 2 in. in life, or not improbably 6 ft. 3 in. He adds that the arms and legs were those of an unusually powerful man (*op. cit.*, pp. 7, 13), and also that the measurements of the head showed that it was much above the ordinary size.

2. The bones are said by some eyewitnesses, from one of whom I have heard it, to have been arranged in an orderly and artificial manner, compared by one of them to the way in which we arrange swords and spears on the walls of museums, the long bones lying across one another. This, I know, has been disputed by others, and, most unfortunately, they were not photographed *in situ*.

3. There was no trace of the remains of a shroud or covering of any kind.

4. The coffin was immediately under the level of the floor of the crypt, not more than three inches below it.

5. It was found very near to the spot where the remains of Becket rested for fifty years after his martyrdom, until their translation by Archbishop Stephen Langton on July 7, 1220, as mentioned above.

6. There was a deep cut, about six inches long, on the left side of the skull, 'such (it was remarked) as might be made by a heavy, sharp cutting instrument like a two-handed sword.' It should, however, be added at once that no injury whatever was apparent on the crown of the skull.

Now it is quite evident that some of the details just mentioned oblige us to conclude that this was a case, not of burial, but of reburial. Also that most of them would be naturally

[1] *Becket's Bones*, 1901, p 13.

accounted for by the supposition of a hurried removal by the
monks of the bones of Becket to this receptacle, under the
alarm created by the sentence pronounced against him and
his shrine by Henry VIII.

It has indeed been ingeniously suggested that the bones
thus discovered were those of a certain William de Andeville,
Abbot of Evesham, who died in 1159 when on a visit to
Canterbury, where he had formerly been a monk. He is
known to have been buried on, or very near, the spot where
this coffin was found. The memory of this fact has been preserved by a curious legend. The chronicler of Evesham[1] records
that the Abbot, before leaving for Canterbury, had a dream that
after his death the sun would be buried at his feet. His monks
saw the fulfilment of this dream—whether an *ex post facto*
or not, we need not inquire—in the fact that eleven years later
Becket was laid in a grave a little further eastwards, in point of
fact near the space between the present two graceful pillars
of the English William's beautiful vaulting of the crypt
beneath his new Trinity Chapel. It was just on the very spot
indicated as the tomb of the Abbot of Evesham that these
bones were found in 1888. Yes, but what is the inference?
Surely not that these were his bones. How could he have
been buried in a chest much too small for his body? Again,
why should he be buried without a trace of any shroud or grave-
clothes? Again, why only three inches below the pavement?
Above all, why should the Abbot have a deep cut in his
skull?

I should rather infer that when the monks were seeking for
a suitable place of concealment for their 'treasure,' and when
they saw a grave close to the very spot known to be that of
Becket's original interment, nothing could be more natural or
obvious than that they should 'requisition' for their purpose
the bones there found, for it would, of course, be necessary
to supply some in substitution for those of the Saint, in order
to satisfy the expectations of the emissaries of Henry when
they opened the shrine. The bones of William de Andeville
may very possibly (I suspect) have been those which they
triumphantly 'then and there brent,' while those of the Saint
were lying all the time in safe concealment hard by.

Nothing can be more certain than that the bones found
in this coffin were not those of its original occupant. It has
in fact been also pointed out by Mr. Pugin Thornton that the
so-called coffin was not a completed or 'properly constructed

---

[1] See Rolls Series, No. 51, 1863, 'Chronicon Abbatiae de Evesham,' p. 99.

one . . ., and certainly was not intended for a proper burial.'[1]
If the bones were really those of William de Andeville, then
he must certainly have been at some time transferred from
his own coffin to some other receptacle. If so, *cui bono?* In
whose interest? or for what purpose?

The fact that the coffin was only just covered up, instead of
being deeply buried in the ordinary way, may perhaps point
to some hope or expectation on the part of the monks that this
concealment would not be a permanent one. Such a hope was
realized (as we have seen) in the case of their more fortunate
contemporaries at Durham, when 'the tyranny was overpast.'

Let us consider next three serious objections that have been
made to the identification of these bones with those of Becket.

1. There is the large amount of more or less contemporary
evidence distinctly asserting that the bones of Becket were
removed from his shrine and publicly burnt. There is no
reason to doubt that *some* bones found in the shrine were
burnt. But if the bones of the Saint were furtively removed,
beyond all doubt the monks would have substituted others,
'fearing the wrath of the King.' Such a precaution was
obvious. Again, I say, it was exactly what the monks at
Durham are said to have done in regard to the body of
St. Cuthbert at this precise date and under similar circumstances.

Observe too that it would obviously be to the interest of such
monks as were in possession of the perilous secret to support
and confirm the belief that Becket's bones were actually
burned, and were safely out of the way of any further
inquiry.

In particular, much importance has been attached to an
apparently very circumstantial statement by Stowe[2] about
1560. He is describing the construction of Becket's shrine,
the upper part of which was of wood overlaid with gold.
This he says 'conteyned the bones of Thomas Becket, skull
and all, with the wound of his death, and the piece cut out
of his skull layde in the same wound.' He adds, 'These
bones by commandment of the Lord Cromwell were then
and there brent.' But observe that this statement as to the
bones occurs in a general description of the shrine itself ex-
ternally and internally, a description which may be compared
to that of the contents of the two tabernacles in the opening
verses of Hebrews ix. For, as in that case, Stowe is merely

---

[1] *Becket's Bones*, pp. 4, 5.
[2] *Annals or General Chronicle of England*, p. 576, ed. 1631.

repeating long afterwards details commonly received and believed respecting the shrine and its contents. Observe that he never says that the bones thus described were seen or verified on the occasion of the destruction of the shrine. All that he states is that 'these bones were then and there brent.'

In other words, that this was the fate of the bones then found in the shrine; as to which there need be no doubt whatever. It may be added that Stowe was only thirteen years old, and living in London at the time of the outrage, and that these words were written nearly thirty years after the event. The details do not involve any personal knowledge, and would be as easily supplied as astronomical observations suitable to a visit to the North Pole.

2. Secondly, the absence of any wound on the top of the skull, such as would have been caused by the complete severance of the crown, which is a prominent feature in the traditional story of the martyrdom, is *prima facie* a very formidable objection. But we must not fail to remember in the first place the scene of wild confusion in which the murder took place. It was at the time of Vespers, in the dimly lighted church, on the evening of one of the darkest days of the year, December 29. There are several contemporary, or nearly contemporary, accounts. Indeed, no less than five are from actual eyewitnesses. These have been gathered and collated by Dr. Edwin Abbott[1], and the numerous divergences in respect of almost every one of the details are simply amazing. There is no agreement as to the number, or the successive order of the wounds, the different persons by whom they were inflicted, or the words that were spoken either by the Archbishop or by the knights. After reading these strangely conflicting narratives one is almost tempted to adopt the cynical dictum of Lord Palmerston that there is nothing more deceptive than figures except facts![2]

And, indeed, it would be impossible to expect a minutely accurate and circumstantial account of the details of the tumultuous scene of the martyrdom from the monks, excited almost to frenzy with terror, and with minds, as all contem-

---

[1] *St. Thomas of Canterbury, His Death and Miracles*, 2 vols., 1898.

[2] Thucydides in a well-known passage (i, c. 22) describes the difficulty he has experienced in obtaining an accurate account of events even when the evidence of eyewitnesses was available : ἐπιπόνως δὲ εὑρίσκετο διότι οἱ παρόντες τοῖς ἔργοις ἑκάστοις οὐ ταὐτὰ περὶ τῶν αὐτῶν ἔλεγον, ἀλλ' ὡς ἑκατέρων τις εὐνοίας ἢ μνήμης ἔχοι. And he adds another possible source of error : καὶ ἐς μὲν ἀκρόασιν ἴσως τὸ μὴ μυθῶδες αὐτῶν ἀτερπέστερον φανεῖται. Compare with this what is said, on the next page, as to attractiveness of details lending themselves to symbolical treatment.

porary records and chronicles show, always apt to exaggerate, and always specially on the look-out for anything of a marvellous or symbolic character.

Now let this point be considered in relation to this traditional feature of the complete severance of the crown.

The infliction of such a wound might seem to have a special significance in relation to the sacred rite of the priestly tonsure. It is noteworthy that one of the narratives describes this blow as 'shearing away the top of the crown [1] consecrated to God by holy unction.' Also this thought is in similar language insisted on by almost all the narrators [2]. There was beyond doubt a predisposition to make the very most of any incident so significant and symbolical.

This also is worth noting. Becket was troubled by not a few dreams which were fulfilled, or for which an appropriate fulfilment was apt to be found, in later events. Archdeacon Hutton [3] mentions a very remarkable one which is said to have occurred to him when he was driven by the persecution of Henry from his refuge at Pontigny in 1166, just four years before the martyrdom. As he rode away, his silence and sadness so impressed his companion that he asked the reason of it. Becket reluctantly confessed that it arose from a vision which he had seen. He had seen himself in a church pleading his cause before the Pope, when four knights came in, dragged him forth and slew him, *by cutting off the crown of his head where he was tonsured.* May not the recollection of this dream have been one of the convergent streams of thought which imparted a special significance and an exaggerated form to the incident of which we are speaking.

Another detail which may excite some suspicion is this. The very first blow that was struck (either by Fitzurse or Tracy), after severely wounding the uplifted arm of an attendant monk, fell with spent force, 'slantwise' as one writer says, upon Becket's head, and grazed his crown, causing only a flesh wound, and it cast down his cap. Another narrative says that first of all and before any wound was actually inflicted, the archbishop's cap was insultingly struck off, and fell upon the ground. (The cap, it may be noted in passing, is in some accounts raised to the dignity of a mitre; a cap, as Dr. Abbott remarks, not lending itself to picturesque martyrology.) How easily might either of these incidents be

---

[1] Abbott, *op. cit.*, i, pp. 128, 152.
[2] *Ibid.*, i, pp. 128, 152, 157.
[3] *Becket*, p. 175.

magnified into the complete removal not only of the tonsured scalp, but of that portion of the skull itself. Thus the Saint might be artistically represented as carrying the cup-like fragment of the skull in his hand just as St. Denis is represented similarly carrying his whole head, or just like poor Bertram de Born in the eighth Circle of the *Inferno*. It scarcely seems likely that while the Saint was still standing upright an upward slanting blow could be delivered with such force as to remove cleanly the actual cap of the skull, it having been already intercepted by the arm of the wounded monk.

But another narrative of the eyewitnesses [1] states that the blow which thus sliced off the top of the skull was a *fourth* stroke inflicted by Richard le Bret standing over Becket, who was then prostrate on the ground, and that the blow was aimed with such violence that ' the scalp or crown of the head was severed from the skull,' and the sword was broken as it fell upon the pavement. Note particularly that expression, 'the *scalp or crown of the head was severed from the skull.*' Besides this, it has been doubted whether a blow thus delivered, with the sword breaking as described, *could* have severed or sliced off the cap of the skull itself. It certainly seems that the deep cut on the left side of the skull that was discovered in 1888 would be a more natural result of a strong downward blow thus delivered by one standing upright over the prostrate victim.

In connexion with this wound it is interesting to note that one narrator says that Becket had fallen on his right side, ' being on his way to God's right hand.' [2] Though we may gather from such a statement as this that the writer was hardly in a frame of mind to be (as Thucydides says) ἀκριβὴς ὥσπερ λογογράφος, yet if we accept the fact without adopting the explanatory comment, it would well account for this gash that was conspicuous on the left side of the skull.

Another point of considerable importance in estimating the value of the evidence of the supposed complete severance of the crown of the head is this. The word *corona* in mediaeval Latin (as well as *couronne* in French) was quite commonly used as a synonym for the tonsure itself. Any one can see ample illustrations of this in Ducange. Thus *Coronam facere*, or *dare*, is equivalent to *tonsurare*. *Coronati* stands for *Clerici*, and hence *Corona* is sometimes used in the abstract for the clerical dignity. Thus ' Corona vestra ' occurs in formal corre-

---

[1] Abbott, p. 169.　　　　　　　　　　　　*Ibid.*, p. 151.

spondence with Church dignitaries, just as we should use 'Your Reverence,' 'Your Lordship,' or 'Your Grace.' Indeed, the Roman form of tonsure [1] (as distinguished from that of the Eastern Church) was considered to suggest an imitation of 'the crown of thorns.' All these considerations seem to me to leave the actual evidence of this picturesque and significant feature of the martyrdom extremely uncertain.

3. But thirdly—and this is perhaps the most serious difficulty, and one that for some time seemed to me almost insuperable—how was it that in the reign of Queen Mary some one did not come forward and earn immense glory, and no doubt very substantial rewards, by proclaiming a secret which would have been hailed throughout the country, and in the Roman Church at large, as revealing a providential and even miraculous preservation of these most precious relics?

But here we must remember :—

(i) The visit of Henry's Commissioners was in 1538, and Mary did not come to the throne till 1553, after an interval of about fifteen years.

(ii) The monastery was suppressed and the monks scattered. Probably very few monks even at the time of the removal of the bones took part in it, or were admitted to the knowledge of it. It was a most dangerous secret, the discovery of which at any time during Henry's reign would have had disastrous results to those cognizant of it, and also probably to the sacred relics themselves. The scattered possessors of the precious secret may have died, without access to any faithful brother to whom it might be safely confided. Those few (six or seven, I believe) who remained at Canterbury as prebendaries, even if they were among those in the secret, being themselves in a sense 'lapsi' or 'traditores,' would probably have had their mouths sealed. What more natural, in the absence of any carefully guarded plan, like that of the Franciscans in the case of Dante (though even that did not avail), and of that of the Benedictines in the case of St. Cuthbert, what more natural, I say, than that the secret should have entirely perished in those fifteen years, while the persistently repeated story of the public burning of the (supposed) bones of Becket

---

[1] The more complete Eastern form is attributed to St. Paul, probably on the strength of his vow at Cenchrea, Acts xviii. 18. The Roman form claims the authority of St. Peter, I know not on what grounds. Robertson, *Church History*, ii. 65, mentions that the consecration of Theodore of Tarsus as Archbishop of Canterbury was delayed until his hair had grown sufficiently to qualify him for receiving the Roman form of tonsure.

would exclude any suspicion that the question could ever be reopened?[1]

(iii) It is stated by Canon Routledge, that this portion of the crypt was walled off from the rest in 1546—observe that date, still in Henry VIII's reign, and seven years before the accession of Mary—and it was never reopened until about 1840, when the Prebendal Houses then abutting on the Cathedral were removed, and the crypt was no longer required to provide them with the convenience of wine cellars!

(iv) It is very remarkable (as Canon Routledge again has observed) that throughout England, with the single exception of Edward the Confessor, no attempt was made in Mary's short reign to restore the bones of the many saints that had been hidden away in Henry's time, though in several cases—some of them in Canterbury itself—the whereabouts of their hiding-place was well known. This omission may seem hard to explain, but it appears to have occurred in fact.

(v) Such seemingly unaccountable omissions lead one finally to remark how many things occur which appear to us inexplicable, and how utterly untrustworthy is the often employed *argumentum e silentio*. Truly indeed did the old Greek poet Agathon declare, 'It is likely that many things should occur which are unlikely.' Humboldt gives three remarkable instances from actual history where the silence of contemporary records is utterly inexplicable, and would *a priori* be thought inconceivable. The archives of Barcelona are entirely silent as to the triumphal entry of Columbus; those of Portugal are entirely silent as to the voyages of Amerigo Vespucci; Marco Polo in his record

---

[1] We in Kent have a very striking object-lesson of the way in which a tradition can be entirely lost under circumstances in which we should conceive such a loss to be quite impossible. In the church at Hythe there is an extraordinary collection of about 6,000 skulls, a large number of them showing marks of violence and almost all of them of *men*. The obvious inference is that they represent the slaughter of some great battle. They also appear to be bleached in a manner which suggests long exposure to the atmosphere either on the shore or in some similar situation. At some time or other they were collected and moved to the underground part of the church, and there carefully arranged in several piles. Yet there is no record or tradition as to when this was done or where they came from. Yet this must have been known to hundreds of people at the time, and it seems inconceivable that among their thousands of descendants the knowledge of such a unique and locally interesting incident should have entirely disappeared. For fifty years and more there must have still been living witnesses of the strange scene of the deportation and deposit of these remains; and the sight of them was continually before the eyes of every one to provoke wonder and inquiry, and to keep alive the tradition. Yet it has entirely perished! A writer, two centuries ago (*c.* 1700), says that 'how or by what means they were brought to this place the townsmen are altogether ignorant and can find no account of the matter.' See further *Archaeologia Cantiana*, xviii, pp. 333-6.

of his travels in China, where he spent several years and left a minute record both of what he saw himself and what he gathered from inquiry and report, never so much as mentions the Chinese Wall! Another surprising instance of *silentium* is that in all Shakespeare's play of *King John* there is not the faintest allusion to Magna Charta. (This is noticed by Pollard in his *Henry VIII*, p. 35.)

In the case now before us (besides other points noted already) how can we be sure of all the details and circumstances and motives and accidents by which the action of the few monks in the secret (if indeed any were still surviving in Mary's reign) may have been influenced? In such a case as this, and still more in the application of such an 'argument from silence' to many similar difficulties raised in regard to higher and sacred subjects, why are we so confident that others would have acted just exactly as we ourselves should have acted under similar circumstances, or rather as we *suppose* that we should have acted under certain *supposed* circumstances, many of the details and surroundings of which are themselves very imperfectly known to us? A brilliant modern writer goes so far in the opposite direction as to ask, ' Do you ever find people do what (you think) you would have done if you had been in their place?'[1]

In such doubtful cases as this it is very natural to exaggerate the difficulties of yielding belief or assent, and to overlook those of withholding it. How constantly is this the case in matters of religious belief! Now suppose we reject the theory that these bones are probably those of Becket; it seems very difficult to suggest or contrive any other which explains so many of the conditions of the problem. We have to account for an obviously hurried burial or reburial, barely below the surface of the ground, of a body that was already a skeleton, and in a coffin that could not have been originally intended for it; also of one who evidently died a violent death ; a burial too in no ordinary spot, but one hallowed by very special associations in connexion with Becket. Moreover, we have also an adequate *motive* for the supposed action, which is always held to be an important element in circumstantial evidence; and the action itself is supported by other historical examples. Can any one suggest a theory which explains so many of the facts? After all, we cannot get beyond probability, but, as Bishop Butler says, ' probability is the guide of life,' and if we make it a condition of assent that no difficulty remains unexplained, and no possible objection

[1] M. Cholmondeley, *Red Pottage*, p. 145.

unanswered we are likely to remain in a state of chronic agnosticism as to things in general. I would venture to say, then, in the familiar words of Horace,

> ' Si quid novisti rectius istis,
> Candidus imperti ; si non, his utere mecum.'

The three incidents which I have thus brought together surely present several interesting features of resemblance.

There is in them all similarity in a threatened danger, similarity in the means adopted (or probably adopted) to escape from it, similarity in the oblivion which ultimately settled upon the transaction. There is a curious gradation of probabilities also in these reputed discoveries. In the case of Dante, the proof of identity is assuredly complete ; in that of St. Cuthbert the strength of the circumstantial evidence is all but irresistible ; in that of St. Thomas, the conclusion remains, and ever must remain, doubtful. In my own mind the balance inclines very strongly to the side of its probability. Others will no doubt come to the opposite conclusion. I certainly do not think them unreasonable in so doing. I hope they will not think me unreasonable if I am disposed to come down with some confidence on the other side of the fence.

IV

INTRODUCTION TO THE STUDY OF THE PARADISO[1]

THE *Paradiso*, though for obvious reasons the least generally popular of the three great Cantiche of the *Divina Commedia*, is in some sense the crown of Dante's poetic work, the highest achievement of his genius. Many have thought it to be so, even on its own merits, apart from any consideration of the peculiar difficulty of the task. Thus Ruskin, whose panegyrics never suffer from understatement, goes so far as to say:— 'Every line of the *Paradiso* is full of the most exquisite and spiritual expressions of Christian truth, and the poem is only less read than the *Inferno*, because it requires far greater attention, and, perhaps, for its full enjoyment, a holier heart.' Thomas Carlyle expresses a similar opinion as to the unapproachable eminence held by the *Paradiso*, and Shelley declared that it embodied 'the most glorious imagination of modern poetry[2].' But if we further regard the supreme *difficulty* of the subject, there can be no doubt as to the relative greatness of Dante's achievement in this *Cantica*. In the *Inferno*, the materials available for the poet's imagination or invention were practically unlimited. In the *Purgatorio* they were scarcely less abundant. But in the *Paradiso* the task before the poet was, by comparison, like 'making bricks without straw.' For is not his whole subject that which 'eye hath not seen, nor ear heard, neither hath it entered into the heart of man to conceive?' Selden, in his brilliant *Table-Talk*, has drawn this striking contrast between the relative definiteness of the popular conceptions of Heaven and Hell:—

[1] Originally delivered as a Lecture.
[2] These three quotations come from Dinsmore, *The Teachings of Dante*, p. 164.

P

'The Turks tell their people of a Heaven where there is a sensible pleasure, but of a Hell where they shall suffer they do not know what. The Christians quite invert this order. They tell us of a Hell where we shall feel sensible pain, but of a Heaven where we shall enjoy we cannot tell what.'

A very striking illustration of this may be taken from the homiletical literature of Scotland in the eighteenth century. We find the torments of Hell described with the most astonishing variety of ghastly detail; but as to the joys of Heaven, when it has been certified that they consist in an ideal Scotch Sabbath, immeasurable and interminable, the subject is pretty well exhausted. Bishop Boyd Carpenter, in his delightful lectures on *The Spiritual Message of Dante* (p. 80), gives another illustration of this contrast from paintings in the Jeypore Court at the Indo-Colonial Exhibition in 1886. 'The Jains believe that there are many compartments in Heaven and in Hell. The former are usually represented as somewhat monotonous in character, while in the latter no complaint can be made of want of variety, for each individual is represented as being tormented by demons in a fashion appropriate to the sins he has committed in the world.'

Who else but Dante would have ventured to describe in a poem of nearly 5,000 lines a subject so vague, so monotonous, so barren in detail as (to use Selden's words) 'the enjoyment of we cannot tell what?' We might well apply to the *Paradiso* the enthusiastic appreciation of Calderon's *Autos sacramentales* by Archbishop Trench:—'We are filled with endless admiration and astonishment at the skill of the poet in conquering the almost unconquerable difficulties of his theme'—in pursuing with such unflagging success

'Things unattempted yet in prose or rhyme[1].'

---

[1] So Keble (*Prael. Acad.* xxxiii), after pointing out several beauties of the *Paradiso*, adds :—' Ex quibus effectum est ut qua materia turpissime labi soleat vulgus scriptorum solus ferme recte se habuerit Dantes. Cum enim illis plerumque moris sit crassa et terrena transferre in Elysia sua ac Paradisos, hic ne hortorum quidem amoenitates, neque castissimam formarum pulchritudinem ullo tempore admittit in suum aethera, tribus illis, ut dicebam, ferme contentus, *Luce, Motu, Cantu.*'

The difficulties of such a task would seem *prima facie* more hopelessly insuperable than those which are plaintively alleged by a now forgotten Italian poet of the seventeenth century named Andreini. This is what he says in apology for his unsatisfactory execution of a *drama* (!) which he had undertaken on the unpromising subject ' Adam '. I borrow this amusing passage from Prof. Raleigh's *Essay on Milton* [1]:—

'The poor dramatist pathetically complains of the uneventful monotony of Adam's life in Paradise; also that (as a natural consequence) he is himself deprived of introducing into his drama any allusions to history, sacred or profane, because nothing had yet happened ; or any experiences of adventure, such as shipwrecks, battles, conflagrations, and sports; nor, while Adam himself speaks, or discourse is held with him, can any reference be made to bows, arrows, hatchets, arms, knives, swords, spears, trumpets, drums, trophies, banners, torches, theatres, bellows, funeral piles, and many other such things which have been introduced by the necessities of sin.'

Though Milton professes to have selected his great subject after the consideration of 108 rival themes that suggested themselves, of which sixty were scriptural, and thirty from English history, he has chosen one in *Paradise Lost* that is beset in some, though in a much lesser degree, by difficulties such as Dante had to face in the *Paradiso*. But this is by no means the case throughout the whole of Milton's poem. It is only in the later Books that his task can be at all compared with that of Dante in the *Paradiso*. And in that very part of his poem, by the confession of even admiring critics, Milton's work exhibits a conspicuous falling off. ' The contrast (says one) between the incomparable majesty of the opening, and the flagging which begins when he enters into heaven, makes itself felt in spite of the continued dignity of style [2].' No one could say this of the *Paradiso* of Dante. No one can complain of any lack of variety of incident, or of definiteness of conception in detail, or of any trace of failure of power, in that glorious *Cantica* which contains such splendid scenes or episodes as those associated with the names of Piccarda, Justinian, SS. Francis and Dominic, Cacciaguida,

[1] pp. 95, 96.   [2] *Quarterly Review* for July, 1901, p. 117.

the three chief Apostles, St. Bernard, and many others. With
sublime μεγαλοψυχία, as Aristotle would say, Dante, though,
like Milton, fully conscious of the supreme difficulty of his
task (as we see by his admissions in *Par*. i. and ii.), was no
less entirely confident in his full power to accomplish it. One
could imagine Dante's resenting the suggestion of any doubt
on this point as emphatically as Dr. Johnson did in reference
to his Dictionary. 'You little knew (said some one) what
a work you were undertaking.' 'Sir (replied Johnson, with
characteristic emphasis), Sir, I knew very well what I was
undertaking;—and very well knew how to do it;—and have
done it very well [1].' At any rate *we* may ourselves confidently
say this on behalf of Dante.

I cannot help recurring for a moment to a passing expression of Ruskin in the passage which I quoted at the
outset, viz. that one condition for the full enjoyment of
the *Paradiso* is 'a holy heart.' I heard Dr. Liddon once
say that he scarcely knew any better or more profitable book
for devotional reading than the *Paradiso* of Dante. The
reason no doubt is that the poet did not regard his work as
a literary exercise, or a field for the display of brilliant feats
of inventive or imaginative power. It was the expression, the
very offspring of his whole spiritual being. What a brilliant
modern writer has said of all true and good poetry is peculiarly
applicable to the *Paradiso* of Dante. The very 'image of the
poet himself (says Aubrey de Vere) is stamped on all great
poetry, and stamped the more deeply the less the poet
intended that it should be so expressed. It is not a single
faculty of the mind that originates a true poem, though the
imagination is specially needed for that end; it is the whole
mind, and not the whole mind only, but the whole moral and
emotional being, including those antecedent habits and experiences which fitted that being for his task. In this respect
the highest poetry bears some analogy to religious faith.'
Then the writer proceeds to apply these thoughts to Wordsworth (of whom he is mainly speaking) in language which
seems to me to be peculiarly forcible in reference to the

---

[1] Boswell, vol. iii. p. 405 (ed. G. B. Hill).

Paradiso of Dante. 'It is this (that we have described) which gives to great poetry, and especially to Wordsworth's [and here I would say, for Wordsworth's read Dante's], its extraordinary influence over as many as enter into *vital* relations with it. They find in it more than beautiful thoughts, vivid images, valuable conclusions, melodious cadences; they find these things and many more, not apart and isolated, but fused into a living and personal union . . . It is their whole being that is challenged by a brother man, and to that challenge they respond[1].'

Or, once more, in the words of Niebuhr:—'We should read great authors with reverence, not with a view to making them themes of aesthetic criticism, but with a resolve to assimilate their spirit.'

Let us approach the study of the *Paradiso* in this spirit. Let us feel that we are being admitted to communion with one of the master-minds of humanity at a time when his supreme energies are wholly concentrated on the great problems that concern us all, the great problems of the spiritual world and human life. He is one of those who speak to us (to use a beautiful expression of his own in reference to Prayer) in that language which is common to all. Those spiritual realities, it is true, present themselves in different aspects of detail to different ages; and this constitutes one of the chief difficulties presented by the study of the *Paradiso*, wherein beyond doubt are 'many things hard to be understood.' Dante was (to use a phrase of his own) 'one of the Christians of the thirteenth century.' Naturally, therefore, nay inevitably, his ideas are expressed in terms of *their* thoughts and not *ours*. The outward forms of the theological and philosophical problems dealt with in the *Paradiso*, often, as it seems to us, with wearisome minuteness, are those which were vitally urgent *then*, but which in many cases have ceased to have any reality, scarcely indeed any interest for us now. We must be prepared for this. The same is true of all great writers in poetry, in philosophy, in religion. They must be in the fullest and best sense repre-

[1] From Aubrey de Vere's *Essays*, p. 320.

sentative of their own age. It is a condition of their greatness. Otherwise they would but 'speak into the air.' The mould and form of the thoughts of one age necessarily differ from those of another, as much as their manners and customs and fashions. But we must seek to go behind the dry technicalities of scholastic disputation ; to go behind also the crude outward imagery by which (as necessarily in all Apocalyptic writings) the inward emotions of joy and blessedness are figured and symbolized ; and so come into touch with the creative heart and mind itself that is at the centre of all. For, as Coleridge has well said, 'The grandest effects of the Imagination are when it leaves with us not a distinct form, but a strong working of the mind . . . the substitution, in fact, of a sublime feeling of the unimaginable for a mere image.'

Now in one of the extant Epistles of Dante we have the unique advantage of a declaration by himself of the manner in which he desired his whole work, and the *Paradiso* in particular, to be studied and interpreted. Further, in this most interesting document we have a sample of the actual application of this method of interpretation to a portion of his own poem. It is unfortunately but a very small portion, only the first thirty-six lines of the first Canto of the *Paradiso*. After this it breaks off abruptly with a promise, never fulfilled, of its subsequent continuation. The Epistle is that usually numbered as 'X.' It purports to be a dedication by Dante of the Cantica of the *Paradiso* to his friend and patron, Can Grande of Verona. Its genuineness has of course been disputed, like that of almost everything else of Dante except the *Divina Commedia*, by the perverse ingenuity of modern critics. One might say the same of many others besides Dante, when their works are of sufficient importance to make it worth while, if they have not been caught in the act of writing. And if evidence amounting even to something like this were forthcoming, it would be thought judicious to cast doubt on the capacity or the veracity (or both) of the alleged witness to such an act. After a long and careful study of the controversy respecting this Epistle [1] I am firmly convinced of

---

[1] See *Studies in Dante*, third series, pp. 284-369.

the genuineness of this precious document. That, however, is a subject which cannot be now discussed. I will only ask attention to two points in this Introduction and Commentary, which have a special interest for us at present.

(1) First, it is important to notice the several different *principles of interpretation* which Dante (in common with many others before him) declares are to be applied not only to his own writings, but also to any other work of serious import. These are in brief (1) *literal*, and (2) *allegorical* or *mystical*. But further, *allegorical* interpretation is subdivided into (*a*) *allegorical* proper, (*b*) *moral*, and (*c*) what was then commonly known as *anagogical* or *mystical*. He proceeds to exemplify these four methods by a definite example. He takes the words 'When Israel came out of Egypt,' &c. (Ps. cxiv. 1). If we look (he says) at the *literal* meaning only, it signifies to us the departure of Israel from Egypt in the time of Moses : if the *allegorical*, it signifies to us our redemption wrought by Christ ; if the *moral*, it signifies to us the conversion of the soul from the grief and misery of sin to a state of grace : if the *anagogical* or *mystical*, it signifies the departure of the sanctified soul from this 'bondage of corruption' to the liberty of eternal glory. And in a very similar passage in *Conv.* II. 1, Dante declares that all writings of real value *can* be understood, and *ought* to be expounded, in these four senses. Unless then a work of serious purpose has been viewed under these several lights, its full meaning has not been sounded, nor its didactic purpose fully exhausted. An elaborate example of this process is given us by Dante himself in his Commentaries on some of his own Canzoni, which form the subject of the *Convivio*. There we find, in constant relation and contrast, the *literal* meaning side by side with what he describes as the *allegorical and true* meaning of the poems commented on. (See e.g. III. c. 10.)

Applying then this method (as Dante's Epistle directs us) to the *Divina Commedia as a whole*, we find that it is at once a *vision* and an *allegory*. To borrow the words of Mr. Gardner, in his admirable work, *The Ten Heavens*, the *Divina Commedia* as a whole purports to be 'a *vision* of the unseen world beyond the grave ; and, based upon that vision, an *allegory* of the nature of vice and virtue.'. . . It is a *vision* of the state of souls after death ; it is an *allegory* of how man *while still in this life* may use his free will for good or for evil, and so receive reward or punishment at the hands of Divine Justice. When we limit our view to the *Paradiso in particular* (so Dante himself proceeds) it is a *vision* of the state of the blessed after death, and it is an *allegory* of how man by a meritorious use of his free will (I am quoting Dante's words in § 11) 'becomes subject to that Justice which *rewards*,' and so, as we may say, can experience the Kingdom of Heaven to be 'within him' even here on earth. Thus then, while the *Purgatorio* is an allegory of the *real* life of man upon earth, painfully treading the path of contrition and self-reformation, so the *Paradiso* is an allegory of the *ideal* life upon earth, so far as it can be attained to, either in the field of *Action*, or, still more, in the higher field of *Contemplation*.

The *Divina Commedia*, then, *as a whole*, is in the mind of its author a veritable 'Pilgrim's Progress.' We follow this 'Christian' from his initial repulse at 'the Hill Difficulty' which he was prepared to assail 'with a light heart' in the first Canto of the *Inferno*. He is first made to realize the true nature and appalling results of sin by his passage through the *Inferno*. Then he treads the path of penitence and remedial discipline in the *Purgatorio* ; and finally he is brought safely to the City of God, and is vouchsafed a foretaste of the Vision of 'the innumerable company of the Angels,' of 'the general assembly and church of the firstborn which are written in Heaven,' and at last (in the glorious concluding Canto of the poem) even of God Himself.

(2) One other salient point in this Epistle X calls for special notice, and it seems naturally to follow from what has been already pointed out. It is the emphatic declaration of Dante as to the *practical* aim and character which pervades the whole work and each part of it (see § 15). That purpose he declares to be 'to remove those who are still living in this life from a state of misery, and to lead them to a state

of happiness.' His purpose then, throughout the whole poem, is strictly a *moral* or *ethical*, or *practical* one (§ 16), and he insists further (*l. c.*) that this is never absent from his mind, even in passages which may seem at first sight to be purely technical, abstruse, and speculative. We know (if I might venture to say so) to our cost that there are many such passages in the *Paradiso*. It is a matter then not only of profound interest that we should bear this emphatic declaration of the author in mind, but also of essential importance, if we would undertake the task of comment or interpretation as Dante would have it to be done. And here it is right once more to warn those who wish, as Dante says, to follow his ship in their 'piccioletta barca,' that they should be prepared to face some extremely arid and abstruse discussions of theological, and especially of scholastic-theological, doctrines and problems, which are no longer enkindled by any living interest for us. The reason why this is so has been already explained. The nature of such scholastic disputations generally has been described by Bacon as consisting in 'particular confutations and solutions of every scruple, cavillation and objection; breeding for the most part one question as fast as it solveth another,' and he quaintly compares them to the 'fable or fiction of Scylla'; for (he says) 'the generalities of the School-men are for a while good and proportionable; but then when you descend into their distinctions and decisions, instead of a fruitful womb for the use and benefit of man's life, they end in monstrous altercations and barking questions.' [*Adv. Learning*, I. iv. 6.]

Such are some of the subjects which Dante does not hesitate to embody in his poem, and critics have often blamed him for so doing. Further (as has been said of Lucretius under similar circumstances), we must admit that 'the graces of poetry are never for one moment allowed to interfere with the full development of an argument[1].' Perhaps, however, we may venture, with a distinguished recent apologist for Dante, to claim that 'Dante could be philosophical without ceasing to be poetical, much as Plato approached Poetry without

[1] Mackail's *Latin Literature*, p. 42.

ceasing to be philosophical[1].' And there is another interesting point in which Lucretius resembles Dante, who (as we have seen) claims for himself that there is a never absent *moral* purpose underlying even passages where it might least be suspected. For the critic above quoted has similarly remarked of Lucretius—'The joy and glory of the art of Lucretius come second in his mind to his passionate love of truth, and the deep moral purport of what he believes to be the one true message for mankind[2].' Another modern critic is struck with the same characteristic: 'No poet' (he says) 'could be more honest than Lucretius in his confession that he is seeking for charm of language, but what makes this quest unique [in his case] is its entire subordination to the main purpose in hand[3].' It seems to me that every word of these quotations, though their authors are thinking only of Lucretius, might have been written with conspicuous truth of Dante, and especially of the *Paradiso*. He pointedly (as we have seen) claims this pervading moral purpose to be the most distinguishing feature of his own work[4]. So, once more, Lucretius, like Dante, is often very difficult and for the same reason. It is because the matter which each of them deals with is difficult, 'sometimes too difficult for his verse, or any verse.' The difficulty is due to the subject, not the style, for that in both cases is transparently simple and direct. In both poets 'the simplicity of genius' is conspicuous[5]; and if there is obscurity, it is 'such obscurity' (as Coleridge says of

---

[1] E. Caird, *Essays*, p. 6.

[2] Mackail, *op. cit.*, p. 43.   [3] Glover, *Virgil*, p. 61.

[4] One more point may be noticed. In the great poem of Lucretius as in that of Dante, and, we might add, in 'the great prose-poem of Bunyan,' the poet's own experience of life may be distinctly 'read between the lines,' though no such conscious purpose is proclaimed. Thus 'the impression of a personal presence is stamped visibly and permanently on the poems, though this has been done quite unconsciously.'

[5] It is interesting to find Keble in the Lecture already quoted (*Prael. Acad.* xxxiii) following out at some length points of resemblance between Lucretius and Dante. Both are described as distinguished by their skill in handling the most abstruse subjects in the simplest language. (As he says of Lucretius, 'Vix quemquam invenias tam parca supellectili contentum' (p. 672, ed. 1844, *init.*); and again, 'Simplicissimo gaudet apparatu' (p. 673 *ad fin.*). On the other hand, both delight to depict in exquisite detail the simple beauties of natural scenery.

Milton) ' as is a compliment to the reader, not that vicious
obscurity which proceeds from a muddled head.'

Leaving then now the subject of this most valuable introductory Epistle X of Dante, I pass on to give a brief account
of the general plan of the *Paradiso* itself. This shall be very
brief, as it must be already familiar to those who have read
even a moderate amount of it ; and besides it can be found in
almost any of the numerous works existing on the subject.
Still it cannot be wholly dispensed with, in order to make
intelligible some of the remarks which I have to offer
presently.

Suffice it then to say that the general plan of the *Paradiso*
is based on the Ptolemaic system of cosmogony, viz. that the
Universe consisted of nine material heavens, or spherical shells,
revolving round the motionless Earth as a centre. But above
and beyond those Nine Heavens of Ptolemy, corresponding to
the Sun, Moon, five Planets, Fixed Stars, and 'Primum
Mobile' (to be explained presently), which together make nine,
there is a tenth Heaven whose existence (as Dante teaches in
Conv. II. 4) has been discovered to us by Revelation, on the
pages of which we read that ' God has set *His* glory *above* the
Heavens.' Consequently (argues Dante) *above* those nine
Heavens which observation reveals to us, we *must*, on the
strength of these words, believe that there is another or Tenth
Heaven, which is the abode of God Himself, and of His Saints
and Angels who dwell in His immediate presence. This Tenth
Heaven is called by Dante the 'Empyrean,' and it does not
revolve like the other nine, but is ever motionless and tranquil.
Neither is it (like the others) *material*, nor has it any 'local
habitation'; it exists (says Dante) in the Primal Mind alone,
in the Mind of God. But we believe in its existence from the
express declaration of Revelation, and ' the teaching of the holy
Church which cannot lie' (*Conv.* II. iv. 31). Into these ten
Heavens in succession Dante, in the *Paradiso*, represents himself as being carried or ' caught up.' These therefore at once
represent the divisions into which the plan of the poem falls.
The nine lower Heavens in the order of relative proximity to
the Earth are as follows :—(1) the Moon, (2) Mercury,

(3) Venus [notice this curious transposition, which was common to the ancient astronomical systems[1]], (4) the Sun, (5) Mars, (6) Jupiter, (7) Saturn, (8) the Fixed Stars, (9) the 'Primum Mobile.' This last was assumed as the cause of the Diurnal Revolution round the Earth (as was supposed) which was common to all the other eight Heavens. In each of these Heavens, or at any rate in the first eight—the ninth being reserved for a vision of the nine Orders of Angels—Dante meets with certain glorified human spirits, or classes of such spirits, separated and distinguished according to the degree or quality of saintly life to which they attained upon Earth.

Such being Dante's *general plan*, the following are some of the principal points, problems, or difficulties upon which some preliminary explanation may not be out of place.

1. The first is this :—

If the Empyrean or Tenth Heaven be rightly described as ' the abode of God and of His Saints,' how is it that so many of these appear to Dante as if located in the lower Spheres or Heavens, from that of the Moon upwards?

Dante has himself anticipated and answered this question.

It *is* true that all the Blessed alike have their abode with God in the Empyrean. Their appearance to Dante in the lower Heavens is a temporary concession to his understanding of the same character as the anthropomorphic language applied to God in Holy Scripture. Note that this is Dante's own illustration (see *Par.* iv. 40–48). It was in order to exhibit to him by a sensible sign ('per far segno,' as he says), the different degrees of Beatitude for which the soul becomes qualified by different types and degrees of saintly life here on earth. At the same time the fact that all alike have their *permanent* abode in the presence of God in the Empyrean is a proof that to every one in Heaven belongs supreme and perfect happiness so far as his spiritual nature is capable of receiving it.

The striking passage to which I am referring is in *Par.* iv. 28–42, where in answer to a supposed doubt in the mind of Dante on this subject the following explanation is given :—' Of the

---

[1] See this explained in *Studies in Dante*, third series, p. 28 n.

Seraphim, that one which is most absorbed in God, Moses, Samuel, and that John whichever of the two thou wilt take, I affirm, even Mary, have not in any different heaven their seats from those spirits which anon appeared to thee (i.e. in the lowest Heaven, that of the Moon), nor have they in their existence more years or less. But all of them adorn the First Sphere (i. e. the Empyrean) and in different degrees possess a blessed life, through feeling more or less the eternal breath or Spirit of God. *Here* (i. e. in the heaven of the Moon) they showed themselves, not because this sphere is allotted to them, but to be a sign of the celestial condition which is least exalted. In such wise it is needful to speak to your intelligence, since only from an object of sense does it learn that which it afterwards renders meet for the understanding. For this reason Scripture condescends to your faculties, and attributes feet and hands to God, but means otherwise.'

In connexion with this explanation there is another point of some interest, which harmonizes with it. The spirits, though able to communicate in some mysterious way with Dante, and to make themselves known to him, yet do not ever appear to him *in human form* in those lower Heavens, never in fact until he sees them in their own true abode in the Empyrean, or Tenth Heaven. But there is a further curious and interesting distinction to notice. Dante held, in accordance with the calculations of the astronomers of his time, that the conical shadow cast by the earth into space reached so far as to come to a point or focus within the orbit of Venus. Consequently the Moon, Mercury, and Venus were liable at times to fall under the shadow cast by the earth. This physical fact, or supposed fact, is noticed by Dante in *Par*. ix. 118, 119. But for him it was something more than a physical fact. He imparted to it a moral significance. It seemed to follow that the three lower Heavens were not wholly liberated from the taint of earthly imperfection, since the shadow of earth was still liable to fall upon them at times. Consequently the spirits manifested to him in those three lower spheres were those in whose virtue or merits there had been some alloy of such earthly imperfection. Thus in the heaven of the Moon are those who had failed to keep fully their vows of monastic life under various degrees of compulsion or difficulty. In that of Mercury are men of active public life, among whom the Emperor Justinian is conspicuous, whose beneficial activity was prompted by, or not unmixed with, personal ambition and the love of fame. In the heaven of Venus are those who had yielded in an inordinate degree to the seductions of earthly love. Dante has another subtle way of symbolizing to us this taint of defect. In these three lowest Heavens, and in these only, is there any reference to the survival of any trace of human lineaments in the appearance of the spirits. In the Moon, beneath the veil of added beauty, Dante is just able to discern, but with an effort, and after Piccarda had already revealed her personality, some trace of her former semblance [1]. But the appearance of the spirits is so faint that Dante takes it for a reflection, not a real object [2]; so indistinct that he likens it by an exquisite simile to the appearance of a pearl on a fair maiden's brow, 'Debili sì che perla in bianca fronte' (iii. 14). In the next Heaven, that of Mercury, there is no reference to any such human form, but in one passage he refers to the glowing of the eyes, and to the appearance of a smile as indications of the exuberant joy of the spirit who is in his presence (v. 125, 126). Observe that this is the last allusion in the *Paradiso* to the *features* of any glorified spirit. In the last of these three Heavens, that of Venus, a spirit tells Dante that his joyousness keeps him concealed from view, like (as he adds by a homely simile) a creature that is swathed in its own silk. This at least would imply that human features were still existent, though thus rendered invisible, being (in Miltonic phrase) 'dark with excessive light' (viii. 52–54). But after this, the Spirits are invariably described as Lights, Splendours, Flames, Torches, Stars, and so on, but without any trace of bodily form. This point also Dante has, after his manner, called our attention to, in xxii. 58–60, where he represents himself as praying St. Benedict to manifest himself to him in his real form—'con imagine scoperta'—and thus he elicits the explicit statement that only in the Tenth Heaven, the

---

[1] *Par.* iii. 58–63.　　　　　[2] *Ibid.*, ll. 7–18.

Empyrean, can this be the case. The promise thus given is afterwards fulfilled. To avoid misconception, I should add that this does not apply to Beatrice herself. The frequent allusions to the increasing radiance of her eyes, and the increasing beauty of her smile, as each higher sphere is reached, are a conspicuous feature in the *Paradiso* and have a symbolical significance into which we cannot enter now [1]. Dante has not attempted to explain the manner of personal recognition hereafter, as he *has* attempted, somewhat fancifully, to explain the nature and origin of the disembodied spirit in Purgatory, and how it yet retains the capacity for physical or corporeal suffering (see *Purg.* xxv. 88 *seqq.*). But (as Bishop Creighton has observed) 'Dante has, for himself at least, solved the problem of personal recognition with the survival of personal interest, personal communion, and personal affection, yet without any admixture of mere earthly love—*that* is indeed transfigured, but not destroyed.' Yet 'they marry not, nor are given in marriage, but are as the angels of God in heaven.' Love there is still, but it is (in the language of Wordsworth)—

> 'such love as spirits feel
> In worlds whose course is equable and pure.'

2. So much for the first question or difficulty. A second question that may be raised is this. How is it that the inferiority of condition, symbolically indicated (as we just now saw) in the case of so many of the glorified spirits, is compatible with the 'perfect consummation and bliss' of all? The answer that Dante would give, or rather that he has given, is twofold. In the *first* place, each spirit *does* enjoy the utmost degree of felicity which his nature is capable of. Note what Dante says in *Conv.* III. xv, ll. 100-104. 'This is the reason why the Saints have no envy of one another, because each attains to the utmost limit of his desire, and that desire is measured by the nature of his goodness.' Or, as the same thought is expressed by Pope, *Essay on Man*, i. 286, 287 :—

> '[Each is] in this or any other sphere
> Secure to be as blest as he can bear.

[1] Note especially the difficult passage in *Par.* xiv. 130-139.

Dr. Johnson very acutely illustrates this :—' Sir, a peasant and a philosopher may be equally *satisfied*, but not equally *happy*.' A peasant has not the capacity for having equal happiness with a philosopher (Boswell, i. p. 315). And again (ii. p. 208), 'A pail does not hold as much as a tub ; but if it be equally full it has no reason to complain. Every saint in heaven will have as much happiness as he can hold.'

Further, and secondly, Dante declares that ideal and supreme beatitude consists essentially in this—that the individual Will is in complete harmony with the Will of God, and in the consciousness that the Will of God is being completely carried out in the condition, whatever it be, which is assigned to each individual Soul. This is set forth in one of the most exquisitely beautiful passages even in the *Paradiso*, viz. iii. 64–90, where Dante, as is his wont, raises the difficulty in order to elicit the authoritative solution :—

'But tell me, ye who are happy *here* [i. e. in the *lowest* heaven], do ye desire a higher place, for fuller vision, or to make to yourselves more friends ? With those other shades first she smiled a little ; and thereupon she answered me with such gladness that she seemed to be glowing in the first fire of love. Brother, our will is set at rest by the power of Love, which makes us wish for that only which we have, and let us not be athirst for aught beside. Should we desire to be more exalted, our desires would be discordant with the Will of Him who separates us here, which thou wilt see can have no place in these spheres, if to exist in Love be here a necessity, and if its nature thou dost well consider. Rather is it essential to this blessed existence to hold oneself within the Divine Will, whereby our wills themselves are made one. So that as we are from station to station within this realm, to all the realm is it pleasing, as it is to the King who inwills us to His Will [i. e. makes our wills to be one with His]. And His Will is our peace. This is that sea whereunto all is moving, both what It [i. e. God's Will] creates, and what Nature forms.'

'Clear was it then to me how everywhere in Heaven is Paradise, and even so the Grace [or favour ?] of the Supreme Good is not showered there in one measure.'

Compare with this *Par.* vi. 118–126, and xxxii. 58–66.

3. A third point—the *principle* on which different individuals are allotted to different Heavens or Stars—indicates in Dante's view something more than merely poetic or artistic propriety. In common with all his contemporaries he firmly believed,

and over and over again in his several works asserts, that our different characters are actually formed by the influence of different stars or planets, although that influence is not such as to interfere with the Freedom of the Human Will and our consequent responsibility (see especially a very important passage in *Purg.* xvi. 67–81). Hence those spirits who are revealed to him in the Heaven of a certain star are those who, by the time or place of their birth, have had their lives moulded, and their characters formed, by the peculiar influence assigned to that star in common belief. Thus Dante in the Eighth Heaven, that of the Fixed Stars, represents himself as located in the constellation Gemini, to whose influence he believed himself to owe whatever gifts of genius he might possess. (See *Par.* xxii. 112–117.)

'O glorious stars, O light impregnate with mighty power, from which I acknowledge all my genius, whatever it be ; with you was rising and with you was setting He who is the parent of every mortal life [i. e. the Sun] when I first felt the Tuscan air.'

In other words, the Sun was then in Gemini ; and so Dante was born in late May or early June—not improbably, as I believe, about, or perhaps on, May 30. See *infra*, pp. 249, 250.

It was believed that poets especially, as well as others distinguished for intellectual gifts, were born under the constellation Gemini, just as warriors owed their qualities especially to Mars ; those of a still and contemplative disposition to Saturn ; statesmen and legislators to Jupiter (see especially *Par.* xviii. 115–117) ; and so on.

4. Fourthly, another current belief in Dante's time, fully endorsed and inculcated by himself, and holding considerable prominence in the *Paradiso*, is this. The several Heavens or spheres were believed to be moved and regulated by the Angels ; the Nine Heavens being allotted each to one of the nine Orders of Angels, though as to the manner and order of this allotment different opinions prevailed. Dante, in the *Convivio*, explains the manner of operation of these 'Angeli Movitori,' or ' Celesti Motori ' [see especially *Conv.* II. ii. 62, 63 ; v. 4 *seqq.*; vi. 151–159 ; III. xii. 82], this being, in his words, 'solo

intendendo,' by thought alone, and without any bodily touch or impulse on their part [1]. He is also careful to insist that to *them* is really due the influence which in popular parlance is attributed to the Heavens or the Planets and Stars themselves [2]. These Angels are in their turn merely the agents or instruments by which God's will is carried out in the Universe (*Par.* viii. 97–111 ; xviii. 115–120 ; *Ep.* V. viii. 134, &c.). This was indeed the main purpose of the creation of the Angels and their special function, when created. Dante, in fact, in *Par.* xxix. 43–45, argues from this (as against St. Jerome) that the creation of Angels and of the Universe must have been simultaneous, since otherwise these 'motori,' or Movers of the Heavens, would have been for a long time without any functions, and consequently in a state of imperfection, which is not to be conceived. The opinion of St. Jerome thus refuted is that the Angels were created a long tract of centuries before the rest of the Universe was brought into being.

5. A fifth point to be briefly noticed is the manner in which Dante believed the Nine Heavens to be allotted to the nine Orders of Angels, and the distribution of those Orders under the three Hierarchies. This subject has a special interest, because Dante takes pains in the *Paradiso* to correct the view on this point which he had formerly maintained and justified in the *Convivio* [3]. It is curious to note that in adopting that system in his earlier work he seems simply to have followed his so-called 'Master,' Brunetto Latini [4]. Later, when he came to study the subject for himself, he would find the authorities divided between the two Systems of Angelic Hierarchies—both considerably differing from that of B. Latini —which were advocated by St. Gregory and by (the supposed) Dionysius the Areopagite respectively. He would also find the subject discussed at length by that author to whom, after Aristotle, he paid the most supreme deference, St. Thomas

---

[1] Vide *supra*, pp. 140 *seqq.*

[2] Cf. *Par.* ii. 127–129 ; *Conv.* II. vii. 100 *seqq.*; III. vi. 66-68.

[3] The reference to the *Convivio* is II. vi, and that to the *Paradiso* is xxviii. 97 *seqq.*

[4] See B. Latini, *Trésor*, I. pt. i. c. xii.

Aquinas.[1] He would learn that, after a careful comparison of the rival systems of St. Gregory and St. Dionysius, St. Thomas is inclined to think the latter preferable, though he admits that 'parum vel nihil differunt si *ad rem* referantur.' It is mainly a question of the significance of names, and the only outstanding difference after all is the transposition of the places of two Orders, viz. the 'Virtues' and the 'Principalities,' as will be seen in the lists below. The preference thus indicated by St. Thomas may probably have been the reason for the adoption by Dante of the system of Dionysius in the *Paradiso*, and for the 'Retractation' of his earlier opinion in which he had followed B. Latini. He rejects, however, the system of St. Gregory much more decidedly than St. Thomas had done. This is rather quaintly indicated in *Par.* xxviii. 133–135, by the statement that as soon as St. Gregory opened his eyes in Heaven he smiled at his own error.

It may be added that among other authors read and admired by Dante, who also adopted the system of Dionysius, were Richard of St. Victor, Hugh of St. Victor, and St. Bernard.

The order then as finally adopted by Dante is this :—

1st Hierarchy : Seraphim, Cherubim, Thrones.
2nd   „   Dominions, Virtues, Powers.
3rd   „   Principalities, Archangels, Angels.

The order of Gregory was :—

1st Hierarchy : Seraphim, Cherubim, Thrones.
2nd   „   Dominions, Principalities, Powers.
3rd   „   Virtues, Archangels, Angels.

The principal passages in Scripture from which the titles of these orders are derived are :—Eph. i. 21, vi. 12 ; Col. i. 16, ii. 15 ; Rom. viii. 38.

6. Sixthly, and lastly, it should be observed that (as Mr. Gardner has pointed out) the Nine Heavens, which represent, as we ascend, higher and higher types of saintly

---

[1] *Summa*, I. cviii. 5 and 6, and especially 6 r_4. The probably guiding principles of the two systems are suggested in 5 r.

life, themselves fall into three well-marked groups of three in each, just as the nine Orders of Angels fall into three distinct Hierarchies.

In the lowest group—the Moon, Mercury, and Venus—as we have already pointed out [1], are found those of the redeemed in whom some flaws of character in the conduct of their earthly life yet remained uneradicated.

In the next group of three—the Sun, Mars, and Jupiter— we find (1) Theologians and Doctors, whose teaching has been 'a light unto the world,' appropriately associated with the Sun; (2) Warriors and Crusaders in Mars; (3) Legislators and Statesmen in Jupiter.

In the final group of three we find (1) those who have attained to the highest type of life upon earth, viz. that of the Contemplative or Recluse, in the planet Saturn, which was the highest or most distant of the planets in the Ptolemaic system [2]. After that, we do not meet with any class of human spirits as associated with the remaining Heavens. (2) The Eighth, that of the Fixed Stars, is occupied by a Vision of the Triumph of Christ, who descends surrounded by an ' innumerable com- pany of angels' and saints. This glorious pageant is suitably displayed in that Heaven of the Fixed Stars, which, as Dante says, 'ha tante vedute,' 'has so many objects of sight;' 'il ciel, cui tanti lumi fanno bello,' 'that heaven, which so many lights adorn' (*Par.* ii. 115, 130). Out of that vast company there come forth to speak with Dante the three great Apostles, Peter, James, and John, examining him severally as to his possession of the three supreme Virtues of Faith, Hope, and Charity. Last of all comes forward Adam, as the father of the whole human race. He expounds to Dante some curious speculations respecting the Fall. Then they are all (so to speak) 'caught up again into Heaven.'

(3) In the Ninth Heaven, that of the *Primum Mobile*, there are no more human spirits. But Dante enjoys from it a distant vision of the whole Court of Heaven beyond in the Empyrean or Tenth Heaven, with the nine Orders of Angels for ever circling round the throne of God, who appears to him, thus

---

[1] Vide *supra*, pp. 221, 222.　　　　[2] Comp. *Conv.* II. xiv. 230.

seen from afar, as a point of the most intense and over-whelming brilliancy.

Finally, in the last and Tenth Heaven, Dante sees the whole company of the redeemed in their own forms, and in their proper seats, appearing like the petals of a vast rose. In this there are still some gaps to be filled, waiting till God shall ' be pleased to accomplish the number of His Elect.'

I will now in conclusion give some description of a remark-able picture by Sandro Botticelli, himself, as we know, the author of a large series of very striking illustrations of various scenes in the *Divina Commedia*. This picture is in our National Gallery, and therein is represented, after the manner of Dante, though not by any means merely reproducing his details, a Vision of the Court of Heaven, with the throne of God surrounded by Saints and Angels in nine concentric groups. The whole scene is associated with the Coronation of the Virgin. As in respect of many other points, I owe it to the excellent work of Mr. Gardner on ' *Dante's Ten Heavens*' that my attention was first called to this interesting picture. I have since examined it for myself more than once, not without difficulty, owing to the unsatisfactory light in which it is placed, and the small scale of its multitudinous figures.

In the three highest Orders, i.e. Seraphim, Cherubim, and Thrones, the Angels are all in the form of Cherubs with six wings. The first two Orders, the Seraphim and Cherubim, are enveloped in their wings, no doubt in recollection of the Vision of Ezekiel. The wings are crimson in the case of the Seraphim, and blue in that of the Cherubim. These colours are appropriate, since crimson is the recognized emblematic colour of love, and blue (as explained by Mrs. Jameson [1] in her *Sacred and Legendary Art*), being the colour of the firmament, symbolizes light, truth, and knowledge. We may all be familiar with the characteristic distinction of Seraphim and Cherubim from the corresponding distinction which Dante

[1] Mrs. Jameson, *Sacred and Legendary Art*, i. pp. 36, 47, 49.

draws between St. Francis and St. Dominic in *Par.* xi.
37–39 :—

> ' L' un fu tutto *serafico* in *ardore*,
> L' altro per *sapienza* in terra fue
> Di *cherubica* luce uno splendore.'

[One [i. e. St. Francis] was all *seraphic* in *fervency* ; the other [i.e. St. Dominic] for *wisdom* was upon the earth a splendour of *cherubic* light.]

Mrs. Jameson adds, as a further illustration of the significance of these two colours, that the Blessed Virgin has usually a red tunic and a blue mantle, combining in herself both heavenly *love* and heavenly *truth*. She says also that, by the accepted conventionalities of Sacred Art, the Seraphim always are, or ought to be, glowing *red*, and the Cherubim always *blue*, and that this rule was regularly observed till late in the fifteenth century.

Coming next to the third Order, that of the ' Thrones ' in Botticelli's picture, the upper part of the body is seen in flesh, the wings—which are blue—not enveloping the figures as completely as in the case of the two higher Orders. It is noticeable that there are no human spirits among the ' Thrones.' Naturally there are none such among the Seraphim—the highest Angelic order of all ; but among the Cherubim there are a few, as e.g. St. Peter, St. John the Evangelist, St. John the Baptist, and St. Mary Magdalen. The reason is probably this. There was a singular, but generally accepted, mediaeval belief that mankind was created in order to fill the gaps occasioned in the ranks of Heaven by the expulsion of the Rebellious Angels. This appears, for example, in St. Augustine [1], and in Peter Lombard [2], who boldly asserts that it is occasionally found in Scripture ! [' in Scriptura interdum reperitur ']. Also in Hugh of St. Victor [3], and in St. Thomas Aquinas [4]. It is very prominent in the *Cur Deus Homo* of St. Anselm [5]. These are all writers mentioned, or quoted, by Dante. Milton, again, refers to this

---

[1] *Enchir.* c. xxix.
[2] *Sentt.* II. Dist. i. § 9. See, however, also II. ix. §§ 8 and 9.
[3] *De Sacr.* I. pars v, cap. 31.   [4] *Summa,* I. lxiii. 9
[5] I. cap. 16–18.

belief in *Par. Lost*, vii. 150, when he speaks of the creation
of Man as a means to 'repair The detriment of the dispeopled
Heaven[1].' As to Dante himself, he refers to this belief in
Conv. II. vi. 98. He there, however, states that from *all*
ranks of the Angelic Hierarchy some fell, and *that* as soon
as they were created ('tosto che furono creati'), or, as he
quaintly puts it in *Par.* xxix. 49, 'before you could count
twenty!' He further suggests that possibly it may have been
to the number of one-tenth part of each Order, and adds:
'to restore which number mankind was then created' (compare
Par. xxx. 131, 132). Dante therefore held (at any rate when
he wrote the *Convivio*) that *all* orders of the Hierarchy lost
some of their numbers. Aquinas speaks doubtfully on this
point in I., Q. 63, Art. 9. He discusses the question whether
the majority of Angels fell or remained faithful. In favour of
the former view an opponent is represented as quoting the
Vulgate in Ecclus. i. 15, 'Stultorum infinitus est numerus,'
'The number of the foolish is infinite.' [This is probably
a mistranslation, as both EV. and RV. are quite different.]
The opponent then argues that if this is true of mankind,
the same may be inferred by analogy to be true in respect
of the foolish or fallen Angels! St. Thomas then confidently
refutes this not very formidable antagonist by quoting—with
rival inappositeness—2 Kings vi. 16, 'Plures nobiscum sunt
quam cum illis,' 'They that be with us are more than they
that be with them.' The reference is to the vision of the
angelic host surrounding Samaria, which was vouchsafed to
Elisha and his servant. That point settled, St. Thomas
next proceeds to consider the two opposite views: (1) that
some Angels fell from every one of the nine Orders, as
Dante held in the passage above quoted; and (2) that all
that fell were from the lowest Order only, viz. 'Angels.'
Without positively deciding the question, he argues for the
probability of, at any rate, the two Orders of Seraphim and
Thrones having been exempt from any defection. His two
reasons are: (1) because these two titles are never applied

---

[1] See also *Par. Lost*, ii. 830–835.

to evil angels in Scripture, whereas 'Cherubim,' 'Powers,' and 'Principalities' sometimes are so; and (2) 'quia haec nomina sumuntur ab *ardore Charitatis*, et ab *inhabitatione Dei*, quae non possunt esse cum peccato mortali,' i.e. 'These two names are connected respectively with the ardour of Love [i.e. Seraphim] and the abiding presence of God [i.e. Thrones], and these qualities cannot consist with mortal sin.' Further, as to the 'Thrones,' he says that they are the very emblem of stability.

I suppose that when Aquinas here says that the name of Cherub is sometimes applied to Evil Angels he is probably thinking of Ezek. xxviii. 12–17:—

ver. 12. 'Son of man, take up a lamentation upon the king of Tyrus, and say unto him, Thus saith the Lord God; Thou sealest up the sum, full of wisdom, and perfect in beauty.

ver. 13. Thou hast been in Eden the garden of God; every precious stone was thy covering, the sardius, topaz, &c.

ver. 14. Thou art the anointed cherub that covereth; and I have set thee so: thou wast upon the holy mountain of God; thou hast walked up and down in the midst of the stones of fire.

ver. 15. Thou was perfect in thy ways from the day that thou wast created, till iniquity was found in thee.

ver. 16. . . . therefore I will cast thee as profane out of the mountain of God: and I will destroy thee, O covering cherub, from the midst of the stones of fire.'

Note especially the occurrence twice of the word 'Cherub,' 'the anointed cherub' in ver. 14, and 'the covering cherub' in ver. 16. The whole passage is very difficult and obscure; but it was a commonly received mediaeval interpretation that 'the king of Tyrus,' who is described as 'the anointed cherub' of ver. 14, here represents Satan. This certainly seems to be supported by several of the expressions occurring in the context, e.g. vv. 12–14, 'Thou sealest up the sum, full of wisdom, and perfect in beauty.' [Compare *Inf.* xxxiv. 18, 'La creatura ch' ebbe il bel sembiante,' and again *Par.* xix. 47, 'Che fu la somma d' ogni creatura.'] Then in ver. 13, 'Thou hast been in Eden the garden of God.' Note in particular that this very passage of Ezekiel is quoted by Dante in *Epist.* X. xxvii. (*fin.*) with the words, 'dicitur contra Luciferum per Ezechielem.' It is probably also on the strength of this passage that another statement of Aquinas is founded, viz. that Satan himself was an Angel of the Order of the Cherubim (I. lxiii. 7 r₁).

Now it is this theory of Aquinas concerning the exemption of the two exalted Orders of Seraphim and Thrones from any defection that appears to be symbolized by Botticelli when he represents those two Orders without any admixture of human spirits; since they would have no gaps in their ranks thus needing to be filled up. This theory was not, as we have seen, adopted by Dante in the *Convivio*, nor in the *Paradiso*, so far as relates to the Order of Thrones, for this corresponded with the Heaven of Saturn, in which are found St. Peter Damian, St. Benedict, and other monks and hermits, who attained to the Contemplative Life on earth. There are, as we might expect, no human spirits in the Ninth Heaven, which would correspond with the Order of the Seraphim and would be under the guiding superintendence of that Order of Angels. Nor indeed are there any allotted to the Eighth.

I need not pursue the description of this interesting picture of Botticelli into further detail, but one or two points may be added quite briefly. In the remaining six lower Circles, Angels and Saints are freely mixed together. The Angels too in all these Orders have full-grown human forms, no longer that of Cherubs, and they are all distinguished by stars on their breasts as well as by the usual addition of wings. There is a clearly marked distinction, however, between the Angels of the different Circles by the employment of different combinations of colours for the dress and for the wings. In one Circle the Angels are represented with Censers. This Circle is that of the Archangels. It may be added that among the Angels of the Fifth Circle St. Thomas Aquinas is prominent, and also an aged Cardinal, who is probably St. Jerome. This would be the Order of δυνάμεις or 'Virtues.' In this Order blue is the prevailing colour of wings and dress, though some red occurs in the wings. By this would probably be indicated some pre-eminence in Knowledge or Learning, which certainly would be appropriate to St. Jerome and

St. Thomas.　The nine Orders are, as usual, divided or distinguished into three Hierarchies.

There is also a picture somewhat similar to this in the Accademia of Venice by Jacobello del Fiore (d. 1439) which I regret not having had time to study in detail, but I saw enough of it to note that there is no such elaborate plan as this to be traced in the arrangement of the multitudinous figures represented.

V

STA. LUCIA IN THE DIVINA COMMEDIA

THE prominence given to Sta. Lucia in the *Divina Commedia*, both in the actions attributed to her and the exalted position assigned to her in Heaven, has scarcely, I think, been sufficiently explained. It is often taken for granted that she represents God's illuminating grace, regard being had, no doubt, to the significance of her name. But I do not think that either this species of grace is so prominent in theological writers, or that Sta. Lucia herself is so prominent in the annals of hagiology as to make this quite an adequate explanation. Another very common theory is that Sta. Lucia represents the 'gratia cooperans' of God in contradistinction to the 'gratia operans' or 'praeveniens,' which latter is thought to be typified by the 'Donna gentil nel ciel' mentioned in connexion with Sta. Lucia in *Inf*. ii. 94 *seqq*. To this I shall return presently.

It will be desirable, however, first to set out the facts with which we have to deal. At two important crises in Dante's progress in his mystical journey Sta. Lucia plays a highly important part. First in his initial deliverance from the dark forest of error and from his fruitless efforts to help himself, even when he had escaped from it. This is set forth in *Inf*., Canto ii. Virgil comes to his aid in C. i, 61 *seqq*., but when Dante despairs of his sufficiency to undertake the terrible journey through Hell, even with Virgil's guidance, Virgil reassures him by telling him that he is but the agent of three heavenly beings who are deeply interested in Dante's salvation. First (see l. 94) the 'Donna gentil nel ciel,' who I cannot for a moment doubt is the Blessed Virgin, who is so full of pity for him that she bends the stern judgement of Heaven in his

favour. We may compare with this the language of *Par.*
xxxiii. 13–18 in the sublime hymn of praise and prayer
addressed to the Blessed Virgin Mary by St. Bernard, 'Lady,
so great art thou and so great is thy power that he who wishes
for grace and has not recourse to thee, wishes that his desire
may fly without wings. Thy goodness not only succours him
who asks, but oftentimes freely precedes the asking.' So
again in *Purg.* xxvi. 59, 'There is a Lady above, who secures
for us grace.' From these and similar passages we may surely
infer that the Blessed Virgin Mary is for Dante both the symbol and also the appointed medium of God's 'prevenient grace,'
that grace which in the first instance 'puts into our minds
good desires.' The Blessed Virgin having thus interested herself in Dante, the first step she takes is to summon to herself
Lucia in these words :—

> 'Or ha bisogno il tuo fedele
> Di te, ed io a te lo raccomando.'

'Now thy faithful one hath need of thee, and I commend him to thee.'

The expression 'il tuo fedele' may be compared with that
employed by St. Bernard to describe his own devotion to the
Blessed Virgin Mary :—

> 'Perocch' io sono *il suo fedel* Bernardo' (*Par.* xxxi. 102),

and again to describe Dante's own devotion to Beatrice :—

> 'Volgi, Beatrice, volgi gli occhi santi ... *al tuo fedele*'
> (*Purg.* xxxi. 133, 134.)

It may evidently therefore be taken to express some peculiar
and special kind of interest or service as existing between
Dante and Sta. Lucia. On this also I shall have more to say
later.

Next, in ll. 100 *seqq.*, Lucia betakes herself to Beatrice,
urging her, on the grounds of Dante's deep affection for her,
and of the elevating influence which she had exercised upon
him when on earth, to go to his help in his present dire distress. Beatrice then finally sets Virgil in motion, entreating
him to help Dante, as he well can, so that she may be com-
forted by his escape from peril (see especially ll. 67–69).
There is evidently a very elaborate allegory conveyed by the

several steps here set forth as precedent to Dante's deliverance. Before speaking of this, I will complete the references to the part played by Sta. Lucia in the *Divina Commedia*. We turn next to *Purg.* ix. The first day of Dante's sojourn on the mountain of Purgatory was occupied in traversing Ante-Purgatorio, where were detained, in exclusion from Purgatory, which they desired earnestly to be permitted to enter, those who from various causes (four distinct classes being enumerated) had delayed any act of repentance till the last hour or moment of life. At the close of the day occurs the famous scene of the Valley of the Kings in Canto vii, and the celebrated passage describing the 'parting day' at the beginning of Canto viii.

Then in *Purg.* ix, l. 10, towards the rising of the Moon—so beautifully described (if, as I hope, we may assume this[1]) in the much disputed passage in Canto ix. 1–9—Dante lays him down to sleep in company with Virgil, Sordello, Nino, Visconti, and Currado Malaspina, the last three having been gathered to him in his progress through the Ante-Purgatorio. Then he has a vision towards dawn, at the hour when dreams are true (as Dante, following classical antiquity, holds. See *Inf.* xxvi. 7, as well as ll. 16–18 of the present passage). This experience is repeated on each of the three mornings during his stay in Purgatory. On this first morning he seemed to see hovering above him in the sky an Eagle, who wheeling about for a time presently swooped down upon him and carried him away he knew not whither, like Ganymede. He was borne through the sphere of fire, the heat of which seemed to consume both the eagle and himself, and so vivid was the impression, that the heat of the consuming fire awoke him and he arose and shook himself. He found the sun had been already up two hours and the place was strange to him, and Virgil alone was standing by his side. What had really happened was afterwards explained to him by Virgil. Just before dawn a Lady appeared who said, 'I am Lucia. Suffer me to take him who is sleeping. So shall I help him on his

[1] See this fully discussed in the author's *Time-References in the Divina Commedia*, pp. 77–98.

way' (ll. 55–57). 'Here she laid thee down after first showing
to me with her beautiful eyes this open entrance (i. e. the
entrance leading to the Gate of Purgatory), and then she and
sleep together departed from thee' (ll. 61–63).

It should be remembered that the base of the mountain of
Purgatory was little above the sea-level; also that the whole
of Purgatory itself was lifted above the reach of storms or
earth-born vapours. See *Purg.* xxi. 43 :—

'Libero è qui da ogni alterazione.'

And the passage then goes on to explain that no heated
vapours rise above the three steps at the entrance-gate (l. 52).
The 'heated vapour,' 'secco vapore,' is obviously the
ἀναθυμίασις ξηρά of Aristotle's *Meteorology*, which is the
common cause of wind, lightning, thunder, and earthquakes,
and which rises to the highest region of the atmosphere.[1]
Thus the 'help upon his way' contributed by Sta. Lucia
must have been very considerable. Now the common explanation is that Lucia is the type of God's 'co-operating
grace.' In this ancient and modern Commentators are
pretty generally agreed. I will say a few words as to the
distinction here implied between 'gratia operans' and 'gratia
cooperans,' or, as they are often described, prevenient and
co-operating grace. It is a distinction commonly found in
theological writers of all periods. We are familiar with this
from our Articles, which speak of 'God's grace *preventing* us
that we may have a good will, and *working with us* when we
have that good will.' Or, again, from our Easter Collect, in
which we refer to God's 'putting into our minds good desires,
and giving us continual help that we may bring the same
to good effect.' So also in many other places in the Prayer
Book[2] which I need not further quote. This distinction
would be familiar to Dante (among other sources) from
St. Thomas[3], who identifies *gratia operans* and *gratia prae-*

---

[1] See *Studies in Dante*, i. pp. 131, 132, and passages of Aristotle's *Meteorology*
there quoted.

[2] e.g. Collect of Fifth Sunday after Easter, and several others quoted in
Hook's *Church Dictionary*, s.v. 'Grace.'

[3] *S. T.* I². cxi. 2.

veniens on the one hand, and sets it, or them, in contrast
with *gratia cooperans* or *subsequens* on the other hand. He
would find the same in Peter Lombard[1], who very clearly
defines *gratia operans* as that 'quae praeparat hominis voluntatem ut velit bonum . . .' and *gratia cooperans* as that
'quae adiuvat ne frustra velit.' And still earlier in St. Augustine[2], who says: 'Deus cooperando perficit quod operando
incipit,' and there are many other passages of the same
import. The same twofold distinction is repeated here by
most of the old Commentators on Dante. Boccaccio, indeed,
commenting on this passage, distinguishes four kinds of grace,
operante, cooperante, perseverante, salvificante, and the last three
of these he considers to be typified here by Virgil, Lucia,
and Beatrice. We need not discuss this notion of Boccaccio
further, but it is obvious to remark that Virgil as the type of
God's co-operating grace seems singularly inappropriate, and
also that these three persons intervene in *Inf.* c. ii. in the
wrong order for this theory, the order not being Virgil, Lucia,
Beatrice, but Lucia, Beatrice, Virgil. In regard to the theory
that Lucia represents illuminating grace, or *gratia illuminans*,
I must observe that I cannot find in early theological writers
any recognition of this as a special kind or type of grace.
That it was a general result of any sort of grace is of course
recognized, as when St. Augustine speaks of 'illuminatio
gratiae[3],' but I do not find (with the help of indexes) any such
definite expression as 'illuminating grace' in any writers that
Dante would be familiar with ; not, for instance, in St. Augustine, St. Thomas Aquinas, St. Bonaventura, Peter Lombard,
Hugh or Richard of St. Victor, &c. It is not likely therefore
to have figured in his system of theology in such a way as
to demand a prominent type like Sta. Lucia. On the contrary,
the familiar distinction of *gratia* '*operans*' and '*cooperans*'
is found conspicuously, as I have stated already, in most of
the writers just named. I think then we may take it for
granted that in some sense these two kinds of grace are

---

[1] *Sentt.* II. dist. xxvi (headed 'De Gratia Operante et Cooperante') and
xxix. Comp. II. dist. v. 4.

[2] *De Gratia et Libero Arbitrio*, c. xvii, § 33.   [3] *Annott. in Job*, c. xxxvii.

typified by the ' Donna gentil nel ciel' and by Lucia respectively. This is in fact the opinion of all the old Commentators, with the exception of Boccaccio, as just explained.[1] But though they are in almost complete agreement about this, they differ considerably as to their explanation of the person intended by the ' Donna gentil nel ciel,' who thus by common consent typifies ' prevenient' grace or *gratia operans*. Most strangely, as it appears to me, not one of them, except, I believe, Castelvetro, thinks of identifying her with the Blessed Virgin Mary.

The majority consider her to be a mere abstraction. Pietro contents himself with saying: ' Nobilis domina pro gratia operante primaeva intelligitur.' And in this he is followed by the Ottimo, Landino, Vellutello and Daniello.

2. In the unpublished Commentary of Guido Pisano (a copy of which is in the British Museum) the writer maintains that the ' Donna Gentil' who symbolizes ' prevenient grace ' is intentionally left anonymous because we can never tell of such grace ' whence it cometh.' The commentator proceeds to identify Lucia with ' gratia illuminans ' (as is signified by her name), and Beatrice with ' gratia cooperans sive consummans,' the last two, however, being generally distinguished as two different kinds or degrees of grace. And these three kinds of grace, ' praeveniens,' ' illuminans,' and ' cooperans sive consummans,' he says are needed by every sinner for his complete conversion to God ('ut ad Deum totaliter se convertat ').

---

[1] To this exception I must add two of the latest who would perhaps rank among ' old Commentators,' viz. Talice da Ricaldone, whose Commentary was completed in 1474, who very strangely supposes the ' Donna gentil nel ciel' to represent ' Predestination ' ! ' Et sciendum quod mulier, que non nominatur, est predestinatio. Ista non nominatur quia predestinatio est nobis incognita ' (note on *Inf.* ii. 94). I observe too that, in the recently published (1891) Commentary of Serravalle, Talice has been anticipated in this curious suggestion. ' Ydea vero representans Dantem in Deo salvandum, potest quodammodo dici electio, vel predestinatio, ipsius Dei de Dante. . . . Hanc ydeam Virgilius vocat unam dominam, cui nomen non imponit.' The Commentary of Serravalle was undertaken at the instance of his patrons Bishops Bubwith and Hallam whom he accompanied to the Council of Constance. It was finished in 1417. The special interest attaching to it is that it is the sole authority for the statement that Dante ever visited Oxford. See *Supplementary Note*, p. 255.

The idea that the Donna Gentil is *intentionally* nameless for the reason above given is maintained also by Benvenuto da Imola, who notices, without accepting it, the alternative suggestion of predestination. But it is surely an intolerable supposition that this related series of four aids to Dante should consist of one abstraction and three real persons ; and, again, that this one should be just the one to whom the supreme position and the most exalted functions are assigned. If then the ' Donna Gentil be a real person at all, all considerations of fitness point unmistakably to her being the Blessed Virgin Mary. I have already quoted the language applied to her elsewhere by Dante, ascribing to her precisely the position and functions implied in this passage. We may confidently say that to no one else *could* Dante have assigned them. And on this point most *modern* Commentators are, I think, agreed.

But to return from this digression to Sta. Lucia, and the theory that she is a general type of God's co-operating grace. It appears to me that this is only partially true. The particular point which I wish to develop is this—that Sta. Lucia probably plays the part of Dante's own *patron saint*, and that so far as she typifies co-operating grace it is as the special medium of that grace *to Dante himself*, as other saints might be in a similar special sense to other persons, but that she is not a general type of co-operating grace to humanity at large, as the Blessed Virgin Mary is of prevenient grace [1]. I thought I had found some recognition of this idea in the *Ottimo Comento*, but so far as it *is* recognized it is not applied to Sta. Lucia. Commenting on *Inf.* ii. 94 the writer says: ' Here we should note that it is an excellent thing (" ottima cosa ") that every mortal should have supreme devotion towards God, and hope in God ; and after that, that he should have

---

[1] This may be illustrated by St. Bernard's Sermon *De Nativitate Virginis*, §§ 4–7 (ed. Migne, vol. 183, col. 440). The Sermon is headed ' De aquaeductu,' and the Virgin is spoken of at length under this metaphor in reference to the prevenient grace of God. She is ' aquaeductus, qui plenitudinem fontis ipsius de corde Patris excipiens nobis edidit illum . . .' Of the ages before Christ he goes so far as to say, 'tanto tempore humano generi fluenta gratiae defuerunt, quod necdum intercederet is, de quo loquimur, tam desiderabilis aquaeductus.' Again (col. 441), ' Sic est voluntas eius, qui totum nos habere voluit per Mariam.'

R

some saint, male or female (*alcuno Santo o Santa*), as a special advocate in the presence of God.' The following context, however, shows that this remark is made, not in reference to Sta. Lucia, but rather to the 'Donna Gentil,' the special medium for the 'dono d' intelletto' which is 'spezialissimo ed a pochi dato, lo quale l' Autore riconosce singularmente in sè.' (He is probably thinking of such passages as *Inf.* xxvi. 21-24, *Purg.* xxx. 115-117, *Par.* xxii. 112-114.) But at any rate the Commentator distinctly recognizes the office and help of a patron saint for each individual.

In the first place I find, as indeed the passage just quoted would show, that there is not any anachronism in the supposition that Dante would naturally have *some* patron saint. For in the Western Church, at any rate, where the Roman relation between patron and client was familiar, the term 'patronus' is applied from very early times to a saint under whose special protection either cities or individuals placed themselves. In the Greek Church the idea and practice were equally common, though the relation was expressed by various terms or metaphors in the absence of any familiar institution corresponding to that of the Roman *patronus* and *cliens*. The special aid sought and expected from the patron saint was mainly twofold: (1) To back up (if I may use the expression) the prayers of their votaries, and so obtain spiritual aid (and often temporal also) which those prayers without such aid might have failed to secure. Thus they were (as St. Gregory says) 'adiutores orationis.' (2) To intervene with help in any special danger or difficulty in which their votaries might at any time be involved. I take these two points from the article in the *Dictionary of Christian Antiquities, s.v.* Patron Saints, and it will be seen how well they describe (or at any rate the latter) the special services rendered to Dante by Sta. Lucia.

1. For, first, I would observe that her interventions involve very definite acts of personal service under circumstances of special difficulty. And from this point of view I should attach considerable weight to the expression already noted, 'il tuo fedele,' which Dante applies to himself in relation to Sta. Lucia in *Inf.* ii. 98. This seems to me to have no meaning if

Sta. Lucia be the general type of God's co-operating grace for mankind at large, but to have a very suitable significance if she were the special and conspicuous, though not exclusive, medium of such help for Dante himself; in other words, if he regarded himself as under her special protection as his patron saint. As we have seen (p. 236 *med.*), Dante applies the same expression to himself in reference to Beatrice (*Purg.* xxxi. 134), and to St. Bernard (*Par.* xxxi. 102) in reference to the Blessed Virgin Mary, and in both cases it implies the relation of one person to another person *as such*, and not as a symbol or type.

Secondly, I would ask by what authority (if I may so say) could Dante take a saint whose position and functions were already fully recognized in current hagiology, and attribute to her so new and so singular a pre-eminence as to be the type of God's co-operating or illuminating grace for humanity at large? Observe, there is no such liberty implied in his treatment of Virgil as representing Human Reason, especially if we remember the current mediaeval conception of him; nor in his selection of Beatrice as representing Revelation or the Church (or whatever it be), since he had an entirely free hand in his treatment of this creation of his own. But Sta. Lucia being already known to his readers, and known with very different associations, it would surely be rather startling and almost unintelligible to them to find her in this wholly new character and position, as the general type of a special and well-recognized kind of grace. Dante in dealing with γενόμενα ὀνόματα (as Aristotle calls them in the *Poetics* [1]) would be bound by some such limitations as Horace, in the *Ars Poetica*, says must control a poet's treatment of Achilles, Ino, Ixion, and other characters already familiar in history or tradition.

This objection wholly disappears if she bears this symbolical character of patron saint for Dante individually, but not for mankind generally.

I would even go further and say that no individual saint whatever, not even 'colui che più s'india,' could appropriately typify God's co-operating grace in this general sense. They are all collectively the ministers of it, and to some individuals

---

[1] c. ix. § 6.

more and to some less, in virtue of personal choice and special personal devotion.

3. It appears to me further that the interventions of Sta. Lucia in the *Divina Commedia* are too special and occasional, and extraordinary in their character, for her to represent fittingly the assistance which man generally derives from God's co-operating grace. That is needed not only in great crises or singular emergencies, but, as we may say, continuously. It will, of course, be understood that the ministry of patron saints or any other saints was always held to be merely instrumental and intermediary. So even the Blessed Virgin Mary, to whom Dante (as we have maintained) reserves the special distinction of being the type and also the medium of God's prevenient grace, occupies the same relative position in regard to *it*. The prayers of the saints, or their influence, or (as some would say) their merits, might call forth a special bestowal from God of His grace, which in this sense they may be said to 'minister' or communicate to those that are 'heirs of salvation.' The idea of a patron saint (somewhat like that of a guardian angel) is that of a saint who has a peculiar interest in one who has devoted himself specially to the cult of that saint, or who has committed himself to his, or her, special protection. Thus to that person a saint thus voluntarily chosen would be the channel, 'aquaeductus,' to use the metaphor of St. Bernard, *op. cit.*, respecting the Blessed Virgin Mary, through which God's helping grace would flow to him in a peculiar (though, as I said before, far from exclusive) sense; and this helpful service would be specially realized, or sought for, or expected, in the great crises and emergencies and turning-points of life. I cannot but think, for reasons which I will explain presently, that Dante did regard Sta. Lucia as standing in that special and peculiar relation to himself. If he did so regard her, it certainly seems to explain the parts she plays in the action of the *Divina Commedia*.

4. It may be noticed that there is no other recognition of the office of a patron saint in the *Commedia*, as contributing to Dante's guidance and protection. The belief in such a special advocate or guardian for each pious Christian was

so common that Dante would surely have shared it. If so, there seems to be, so to speak, an empty niche in the *Divina Commedia* which I cannot but think Sta. Lucia was intended by Dante to occupy.

Thus, to return once more to the interpretation of *Inf.* ii and to sum up briefly its significance. The Blessed Virgin Mary, the source of grace and compassion for mankind generally, arouses Dante's own special patron saint to go and 'minister to this heir of salvation' in his distress, and to be the medium to him of God's assisting or co-operating grace. This she does by bringing him under the influence of Divine Revelation or of the teaching of the Church (i.e. Beatrice). This influence, however, cannot take immediate effect, and not until the guidance of Human Reason (= Virgil) has led him to realize the vileness and folly and inevitable consequences of sin.

In this, and elsewhere, Dante is 'for us a sign,' and his experience is the typical experience of other human souls. Or, as he says himself in his Epistle to Can Grande, 'Si vero accipiatur opus allegorice, subiectum est *homo*, prout merendo et demerendo per arbitrii libertatem Iustitiae praemianti aut punienti obnoxius est.'

We next ask whether any reasons can be suggested for the choice of Sta. Lucia by Dante as his special patron.

Now (1) it is well known that the Syracusan martyr Lucia who suffered under Diocletian *c.* 300 was the special patron saint of those who suffered from their eyes. This we know to have been the case with Dante, as he has twice referred to it, the causes being, first, excessive grief, and afterwards excessive study. The former is mentioned in *Vita Nuova*, *c.* 40, ll. 30-39 : 'It often happened that by the long continuance of weeping there came a purple colour round my eyes, such as is wont to appear after any torment ("martirio") that one may suffer, whence it seems that they were worthily rewarded for their vanity [i.e. for gazing too intently at the Donna Gentile (or Philosophy) who threatened to supplant Beatrice], so that from that time forward they could not gaze at any one who so looked

at them as to be able to draw them to return the look
(i.e. they were too weak to maintain a fixed gaze).'

The other passage occurs in *Conv.* III. ix, where Dante is
discussing the Theory of Vision, especially in reference to
the rival views of Aristotle and Plato on the subject. He
says that a disordered eye may cause dimness or false
colouring to affect the appearance of external objects, and
especially the stars, to which the language of the *Canzone*
then under consideration referred. Dante adds (l. 147): 'And
I had experience of this the very year which saw the birth
of this *Canzone*, because through much weariness of my eyes,
through study, I so enfeebled my visual spirits that the stars
all appeared to me dimmed with a sort of white haze. And
through prolonged rest in shady and cool places, and by
cooling the body of the eye with pure water, I reconquered
the power that had been dissipated, and returned to a good
condition of sight.' Thus one condition was present which
might have turned the thoughts of Dante to Sta. Lucia.
There seems, too, to be at least one definite allusion to the
beautiful eyes which were traditionally characteristic of
Sta. Lucia, viz. in *Purg.* ix. 62:

> 'pria mi dimostraro
> *Gli occhi suoi belli* quell' entrata aperta.'

(2) Dean Plumptre suggests that the Parish Church of
Beatrice in the Via dei Bardi was dedicated to Sta. Lucia,
and adds that it was perhaps in that church that Dante
saw Beatrice at her prayers, as recorded in *Vita Nuova*, c. v.
This is pretty and ingenious, but, I am afraid one must add,
fanciful, at any rate in reference to the latter part of the
suggestion. Beatrice cannot be imagined to have been married
at the time of that incident, and it would only be as 'Frau
Bardi' (as some German writers love contemptuously to term
her) that this can have become her Parish Church.

(3) A much more ingenious and interesting suggestion is
one made by Dr. Witte in the second series of his 'Dante-
Forschungen': viz. that Dante may have had also in his
mind another Sta. Lucia, not instead of, but as well as, the
better-known Syracusan martyr, viz. Sta. Lucia degli Ubaldini,

a sister of 'Il Cardinale' who is mentioned with honour, though in Hell, in *Inf.* x. 120 :—

> 'Qua dentro è lo secondo Federico,
> E il Cardinale, e degli altri mi taccio.'

She was a nun in the Convent of Monticelli at Florence, which was founded by Sta. Agnese, sister of Sta. Chiara d'Assisi, the companion of St. Francis. This Sta. Chiara (d. 1223) is referred to in *Par.* iii. 97–99 as a Donna in a still higher sphere of Heaven than that in which Dante then was:—

> 'Donna più su, mi disse, alla cui norma
> Nel vostro mondo giù si veste e vela.'

Sta. Agnese, as I say, founded this Convent of Monticelli at Florence in 1219, and on her death in 1253 was succeeded as Abbess by another Sta. Chiara, viz. Sta. Chiara degli Ubaldini, the aunt of 'Il Cardinale' and of his two sisters Lucia and Giovanna. This Sta. Chiara with her two nieces were original members of the Convent, and they were all three canonized, or rather beatified. The Abbess Sta. Chiara died on Feb. 27, 1264, but both her nieces, Sta. Lucia and Sta. Giovanna, died long before her, viz. *c.* 1225–1227 [1].

Another point of interest in this Convent for Dante may be found in the fact that his kinswoman, Piccarda Donati, was an inmate of it, and it was from hence that she was forcibly carried off, as is narrated in *Par.* iii. 103–8, by her brother Corso Donati in order that she might be forced to marry according to his wishes. This unfaithfulness to her vows, being involuntary, did not exclude her from Heaven,

---

[1] I cannot find anywhere the date of their beatification, but Wadding, *Annales Minorum*, II. p. 228 (under the year 1261), says a good deal as to the sanctity of *this* Sta. Chiara, and of the miracles performed by her dead body. He speaks also in general terms of the holy life of Giovanna and Lucia, her nieces. Speaking of them and others whose bones were transferred when the Convent was moved, he says: 'Virginum virtutes magno probavit Deus prodigio,' which is further described. There is nothing in Stadler (*Heiligen-Lexikon*) as to the date of canonization, nor in Hueber's *Menologium*, to which he refers, nor in Arturus de Monasterio (p. 221 b), who is cited by Dr. Witte. Nor again is there anything whatever about Sta. Giovanna and Sta. Lucia (beyond their names) in the *Acta Sanctorum* under May 30.

but caused her to occupy the lowest sphere therein with the great Empress Constance, 'la gran Costanza' (see l. 118), who under similar circumstances was compelled to marry the Emperor Henry IV, and so became the mother of the celebrated Frederic II.   See ll. 50, 51, where Piccarda says of herself:—

> 'Posta qui con questi altri beati,
> Beata sono in la spera più tarda.'

It is also perhaps to be noticed that this was a Franciscan convent, and Sta. Lucia a beatified Franciscan nun.   There is, at any rate, a strong tradition that Dante was at one time attached to the Franciscan order as a tertiary, though he never proceeded further.   So says Buti in a note on *Purg.* xxx. 42.   The difficult passage about the 'corda' in *Inf.* xvi. 108 is often thought to refer to this.   We know that he was buried in the Franciscan Church at Ravenna, and one tradition says that before his death he caused himself to be clothed in the Franciscan habit [1].   This, however, is regarded by Ricci [2] as apocryphal, but it is perhaps only the historical adornment of an authentic tradition, asserting Dante's connexion at one time or another with the Order.

So far we have been dealing with recognized facts or traditions, though the value which may be assigned to them in this connexion may be matter for individual opinion.   We come now, under the guidance of Dr. Witte, to the region of conjecture, but it is, I think, both ingenious and attractive conjecture. The commemoration day of this Sta. Lucia is May 30.   Now we know that Dante's birthday was late in May or early in June, for he tells us that he was born when the Sun was in the sign Gemini, i.e. according to popular belief between about May 20 and June 20.   For this see *Par.* xxii. 112 *seqq.*, 'O glorious stars, O light impregnate with mighty power, from which I acknowledge all my genius, whatever it may be ; with you was rising and with you was setting He who is the father of every mortal life when I first felt the Tuscan air [3].'

---

[1] Pelli, *Memorie*, p. 144.   [2] *Ultimo Rifugio*, p. 156, n. 1.

[3] It may be noted in passing that this description of the Sun as 'padre d'ogni

It seems to me that we can fix even more closely the limits within which Dante's birthday probably fell. There is happily preserved by Boccaccio in Lezione II of his Commentary on the *Inferno* a very interesting anecdote relating to the last hours of Dante's life. He declares that he had it from Pier Giardino of Ravenna, who was one of the most intimate and devoted friends of Dante in Ravenna [1]. It is the fashion nowadays to treat Boccaccio as an idle romancer, and to think apparently that any statement made by him is *prima facie* more likely to be false than true. It is therefore worth while to state that recent researches have discovered ample documentary evidence of the presence of this Pier Giardino at Ravenna at this very time, as well as of the fact of frequent visits of Boccaccio himself later to Ravenna, where he had family connexions [2]. There does not seem the faintest ground for doubting the authenticity of this anecdote, which is as follows :—'Ser Piero di messer Giardino da Ravenna . . . assured me that he had had it from Dante, as he lay in that sickness whereof he died, that he had passed his fifty-sixth year by the amount of time that there was from the month of May last up to that day, "tanto . . . quanto dal preterito maggio aveva infino a quel dì".' In other words, that his birthday was at the very end of May, in fact on one of the last two or three days of the month, and it was very probably therefore on May 30, the actual day on which Sta. Lucia degli Ubaldini was commemorated.

I cannot help adding a very curious and singularly ingenious argument constructed by Dr. Witte. He says that in three or

mortal vita' is derived directly from Aristotle (*Phys.* II. 2 *fin.*). Also there is a passage in the *Canzoniere* which may be quoted in illustration. In *Canz.* xv. 1–3 Dante describes midwinter by saying that it was that season when the sign Gemini rises as the Sun sets : i. e. the conditions of the present passage are just reversed, and the Sun is opposite to, or six Signs distant from, Gemini   Thus he would be in Sagittarius, and the time according to the current astronomy would be Nov.–Dec. Other features of the wintry season are further described in the *Canzone*.

[1] See the Author's *Dante and his Early Biographers*, p. 52.

[2] See Ricci, *Ultimo Rifugio*, pp. 212–217 ; Guerrini e Ricci, *Studi e Polemiche*, pp. 23, 38, 53, 59.

four MSS. the scribe has appended a statement that the number of *days* in Dante's life was 22,506. On what authority such a statement is made there is no evidence, but it is clearly false as it stands, for the day of his death, Sept. 14, 1321, being perfectly well known, it is possible to work out the calculation, and these figures would place his birth in 1259. So palpably a false statement is not likely to have been deliberately made by any one. Dr. Witte therefore ingeniously guessed that an accidental transposition of the figures might perhaps have taken place. After trying two or three combinations of them without arriving at a satisfactory result he found that the figures 20,562 instead of 22,506 gave for his birth the precise day, May 30, 1265! This calculation (duly allowing for leap-years) is absolutely correct[1]. This is surely a very striking and significant coincidence.

Let us now gather up the threads of these several indications.

1. This less-known Sta. Lucia was one of a family to which Dante's attention at any rate was directed along more lines than one.

2. She was an inmate of a convent in which Dante had several points of interest, and which must have been itself well known to him at Florence.

3. She was not improbably one of the saints commemorated on Dante's birthday.

4. She was a nun of the *Franciscan* order.

5. Her name corresponded with that of the saint to whom his physical infirmity would naturally cause him to turn.

The fact that they were two different persons presents no difficulty. The interchange of the attributes and functions of saints bearing the same name is extremely common in mediaeval hagiology. The result is to form a sort of composite or 'conflate' sanctity under some one revered name.

---

[1] Thus :—   56 years (including 14 leap-years)   20,454
                108 days, May 30 to Sept. 14, 1321   108
                                                      20,562

I am not for a moment supposing that Dante confused
or combined the two saints of this name. But having chosen
Sta. Lucia of Syracuse as his special patron, he would feel that
his choice was enforced and accentuated by the fact that
another Sta. Lucia had so many curious links of connexion
with himself. She was associated with his own birthday;
with a family in several members of which he had a special
interest; with a convent familiar to him through several
of its inmates; and with the Monastic Order with which he
was possibly himself connected. Mediaeval minds, and among
them certainly that of Dante, were moved much less by
logical rules of inference than by shadowy analogies and
striking coincidences. Nor would these be regarded as mere
'coincidences.' Nay, rather, it would be felt:—

> 'Non haec sine numine divûm
> Eveniunt.'

The very fact that different lines of association in connexion
with his own personal history converged upon a Sta. Lucia
would seem to Dante to lead him with twofold force to place
himself under the special protection of that sainted name.

I admit that we are largely in the region of conjecture and
hypothesis. No other arguments or evidence are available.
But if we combine these *antecedent* considerations of probability with the *fact* that the supposition of Sta. Lucia being
regarded by Dante as his patron saint seems entirely to fit
the position and actions attributed to her in the *Commedia*,
the suggestion seems at least worthy of some consideration.
Once more I repeat that I do not wish to repudiate altogether
the commonly received view that Sta. Lucia represents the
'co-operating grace of God;' but I hold that she represents
it in a peculiar sense for Dante himself, owing to his special
devotion to her as his patron, but not as a general type of it
for humanity at large.

In conclusion, there are two other references to Sta. Lucia
which should not be left wholly unnoticed—both implying for
her a high degree of preeminence in the mind and system of
Dante—beyond anything that is found in the current hagiology.

We have dealt with the notices in the *Inferno* and *Purgatorio*. She also appears in the *Paradiso*, and again as occupying a far more prominent position than would have been expected. The heavenly Rose, it will be remembered, is divided into two parts, comprising respectively those who lived before and after the coming of Christ (see *Par.* xxxii. 22–27). The seats dividing these two parts at opposite poles are occupied by the

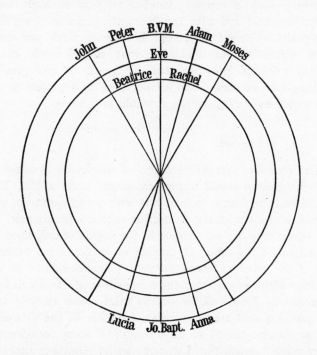

Blessed Virgin Mary and St. John the Baptist. On the right and left of the Blessed Virgin Mary are St. Peter and Adam, and opposite to each of these and consequently on the right and left of St. John the Baptist are Sta. Anna and Sta. Lucia. In the second row, at the feet of the Blessed Virgin Mary, is Eve, and immediately below her, in the third row, are Beatrice and Rachel. See *Inf.* ii. 102, where Beatrice says—

‘Che mi sedea con l’ antica Rachele.’

When this position in Heaven of Sta. Lucia is indicated, the service she rendered to Dante in *Inf.* ii. is specially recalled. If it be thought an objection to my theory that one whose prominence was mainly a personal one in the eyes of Dante himself should have such a conspicuous position assigned to her, I think it would be a sufficient answer that the prominence given to Beatrice is due to the same cause. For himself, and in regard to their action in the poem, they did hold such a precedence. This was the idea which Dante had pictured to himself of Heaven and its inmates. Under this aspect it presented itself to his imagination. It is not of course seriously meant that this represents the final decision of God as to who should 'sit on His right hand and on His left in His Kingdom'. Else were the preeminence assigned to Beatrice a still greater anomaly. In her case and in that of Sta. Lucia, Dante represents them in the relative position they held in his mind and thoughts, and in the work of his salvation.

One other mention of the name Lucia by Dante remains to be briefly noticed. It occurs in that very strange, half astronomical, half geographical, discussion in *Conv.* iii. 5. Dante wishes to describe the apparent motions of the Sun through the changing seasons to a spectator situated at the Poles of the Earth. He imparts a certain amount of vividness to his description by imagining two cities existing at the North and South Poles respectively, and proceeds to describe the phenomena which their inhabitants would witness. He further gives names to his imaginary cities and calls that at the North Pole *Maria* and that at the South Pole *Lucia*. This does not bear upon our present subject except as confirming the prominent position which Sta. Lucia held in Dante's mind and thoughts.

Before concluding, I should like to add a few words as to the difficult expression which occurs in *Inf.* ii. 100:

'Lucia nimica di ciascun crudele.'

The old Commentators, and indeed the moderns also for the most part, throw very little light upon this, and treat it as a sort of paraphrase for 'full of mercy or pity.' Perhaps it may be so, but it seems to me that the choice of the word *crudele* needs a little further explanation. Is it not possible, as so very often elsewhere, that the language of the *Summa* may throw some light on it? There is a good deal about *crudelitas* in one place, and its comparison with other related vices and contrasted virtues. St. Thomas *defines* 'crudelitas' by saying 'importat excessum in puniendo,' and adds that (in the words of Seneca) 'crudeles vocantur qui puniendi causam habent, modum tamen non habent.' In this they are contrasted with 'saevi' and 'feri' 'qui in poenis propter se delectant[1].' Further, he says[2] that the precise opposite to 'crudelitas' is 'clementia'—the former is 'asperitas in poenis inferendis,' the latter 'lenitas in poenis remittendis vel mitigandis.' Again, he adds that 'clementia,' 'mansuetudo,' 'misericordia,' and 'pietas' often agree in their effect, viz. 'prohibere mala proximorum. Clementia vero hoc facit ex animi lenitate in quantum iudicat *aequum esse ut aliquis non amplius puniatur*[3].' Would not this almost exactly describe the action of God's grace as administered here by Sta. Lucia to Dante? He had in some way gone astray (in what precise sense we need not now enquire) so that he had come under the stern sentence of God's condemnation; he was, to use his own words, 'Iustitiae punienti obnoxius,' and, as we read in *Purg.* xxx. 136—'He had fallen so low that all other means were inadequate to effect his salvation, short of seeing with his own eyes the sufferings of the lost.' In his case 'Judgement was rejoicing against mercy.' But, thanks to the intervention of the 'Donna Gentil,' the stern decree of judgement above was mitigated—'sì che duro giudizio lassù frange' (*Inf.* ii. 96). It was a congenial task to Lucia to be the medium of conveying this message of grace and clemency, Lucia, the foe of all harshness or severity, or of every one that is pitiless. I do not of course mean to imply that Dante here applies the term *crudele* either to God Himself, or even to his judgements. Still 'duro

---

[1] *S. T.*, II², clvii. 1. r₃.   [2] *ib.* clix. 1 and 2.
[3] *ib.* clvii. 4. r₃.

giudizio,' in l. 96, may have suggested the more general statement that all that are harsh and severe are odious to her who represents Divine grace or clemency. He does, however, call it ' duro giudizio,' and in much the same sense he applies to it the epithet 'severo' in *Inf.* xxiv. 119. It may be noted that in the Vulgate the very word *crudelis* is applied to the vengeance of God. In Isa. xiii. 9 we read ' Ecce dies Domini veniet, *crudelis* et indignationis plenus et irae.' And in Jer. xxx. 14 God's punishment is described as ' castigatio crudelis,' 'a pitiless infliction:' ' I have wounded thee with the chastisement of a cruel one.' St. Thomas, at any rate, considers the fundamental conception of *crudelitas* to be the infliction of punishment which is harsh, severe, pitiless, but not necessarily unjust. It seems to me that that is the spirit, wherever found, to which Lucia as representing and conveying Divine clemency and grace is said to be utterly opposed.

SUPPLEMENTARY NOTE FOR P. 240.

IT should be added that Barbi (*Bullettino*, N. S., xv, pp. 213 *seqq.*) has recently shown that the so-called Commentary of Talice da Ricaldone is little more than a réchauffé of the Lectures of Benvenuto da Imola. Benvenuto himself gives ' praedestinatio' as an alternative explanation, but he does not adopt it.

VI

THE 'BATTIFOLLE' LETTERS
ATTRIBUTED TO DANTE [1]

IT will be within the knowledge of all students of Dante that about twenty-four or thirty years ago there broke out a kind of epidemic of scepticism in regard to his works, and also (as we might add) to the authorship of many of the Books of the New Testament. It became a kind of fashion [2] to raise ingenious critical objections which often represented merely subjective impressions of the writer dogmatically propounded. These, being often as incapable of formal refutation as of formal proof, were claimed by their authors to be unanswered, and therefore unanswerable. It is quite notorious that the tide has turned in the field of theological criticism, but of that we have nothing more to say now. It has also turned very remarkably in respect of the works of Dante. It is not surprising that such negative criticisms as those of Dr. Prompt now only provoke a smile, when we find him boldly enumerating not only the *Quaestio* and the Epistles, but even the *De Monarchia* among 'Les œuvres apocryphes de Dante,' and describing the author of the last-named work as 'the personage who composed this barbarous and abominable book.' So again a certain Canonico Moreni is quoted as rejecting, in addition to all the works above mentioned, also the *De Vulgari Eloquentia*, as 'stuff (*roba*) written in a barbarous style, and including words not even found in Ducange'! It is difficult now to imagine how such criticisms

---

[1] Reprinted from the *Modern Language Review*, vol. ix, No. 2, April 1914.

[2] It has been well characterized by a recent writer as 'quell' *andazzo* di una ventina di anni fa.'

could ever have been taken seriously. They are scornfully, but aptly, described by Novati as 'incredulità aprioristica, e scetticismo elevato a sistema.'

But in regard to the genuineness of the Epistles there are some special considerations to be borne in mind and admitted. It must not be forgotten that the external evidence for the minor works of an author of distant date, especially those of a local, personal, or ephemeral interest, such as his letters, is liable to be slender, and often can scarcely be otherwise. Thus the field is left open for the display of literary and critical ingenuity on grounds of internal evidence. It is a very cheap and easy exercise. It is scarcely possible to imagine any process of argumentation more perilous and untrustworthy, unless it be the much-abused *argumentum e silentio*, which is indeed but one familiar form of it. At the period to which I am referring, the defence of all but three of the Epistles commonly ascribed to Dante was very generally abandoned. This wholesale 'slaughter of the innocents' was confidently insisted on as altogether necessary by (among others) Bartoli and Scartazzini. A reservation was indeed generally made in favour of Epistles VI, VII, and VIII, on the ground that they were attested by Villani. But even here Scartazzini saw a possible way of escape by suggesting that the mention by Villani may have itself prompted the ingenuity of a forger to compose those which have come down to us, the original letters known to Villani, together with others that he mentions, having probably been lost!

The total number of letters attributed at one time or another to Dante is fourteen. One of these, written in Italian, and professing to be addressed to Guido da Polenta, is still, I believe, universally rejected. But there would probably be no strong protest raised now against admitting as many as ten to be at least within the possibility, not to say probability, of genuineness. In some cases there is indeed little or no evidence beyond a vague prevalent tradition; yet on the other hand positive adverse evidence on internal grounds is in no case strong enough to justify the unqualified rejection of any of them.

We may be content to admit them at any rate as ἀντιλεγό-
μενα, remembering that that term when applied to several
Books of the New Testament did not involve their exclusion
from the Canon.

There remain then the three so-called ' Battifolle ' letters,
which have generally been rejected unhesitatingly. But when
we find so distinguished a Dante scholar as Prof. Novati
demanding a reconsideration of the question we can scarcely
regard it as finally closed. It should also be noticed that the
probable genuineness of these letters was vigorously maintained
by Corrado Ricci in his elaborate work *L'Ultimo Rifugio di
Dante*, published as long ago as 1891 (pp. 17, 18). I have
lately found that earlier still, in 1882, Scheffer-Boichorst
expressed a very strong opinion in favour of the Dantesque
authorship of these letters, ' ich muss mich durchaus für
Dantes Autorschaft erklären.' He even goes so far as to say
' sowohl *Sprache* wie *Gedanken* lassen mir keinen Zweifel [1].'

At the same time they have been so almost universally
rejected by editors of Dante's works that they are rather
difficult of access. They have been very rarely printed : only,
so far as I know, by Torri in 1842 (a work now out of print
and very difficult to obtain), and by Giuliani in 1882. We
have now, however, the advantage of the MS. text published
diplomatically by Dr. Toynbee, but this is at present only to
be found in *The Modern Language Review* for January 1912.[2]
But it appears necessary to reprint the Letters here, since the
discussion which follows would be quite unintelligible to any
readers without the actual text before them. The following
is Dr. Toynbee's text, but with the orthography of the MS.
modernized, and punctuation supplied, as is usual in the
printed editions of Dante's Epistles and other Latin works.

LETTER 1.

Gloriosissimae atque clementissimae dominae, dominae .M., divina providentia Romanorum Reginae et semper Augustae, .G. de Battifolle Dei et
adiuvalis magnificentiae gratia Comitissa in Tuscia Palatina tam debitae
quam devotae subiectionis officium ante pedes.

[1] *Zeitschrift für romanische Philologie*, vi (1882), p. 645.
[2] *Modern Language Review*, vii, pp. 19–24.

Gratissima regiae benignitatis epistola et meis oculis visa laetanter et manibus fuit assumpta reverenter ut decuit. Cumque significata per illam mentis aciem penetrando dulcescerent, adeo spiritus lectitantis fervore devotionis incaluit, ut numquam possint superare oblivia, nec memoria
5 sine gaudio memorare. Nam quanta vel qualis ego? Ad enarrandum mihi de sospitate consortis et sua (utinam diuturna) coniunx fortissima Caesaris condescendat? Quippe tanti pondus honoris neque[1] merita gratulantis neque dignitas postulabat. Sed nec etiam inclinari humanorum in graduum dedecuit apicem, unde velut a vivo fonte sanctae
10 civilitatis exempla debent inferioribus emanare. Dignas itaque persolvere grates non opis est hominis, verum ab homine alienum esse non reor pro insufficientiae supplemento Deum exorare quandoque. Nunc ideo regni siderii iustis precibus atque piis aula pulsetur, et impetret supplicantis affectus quatenus mundi gubernator aeternus condescensui tanto praemia
15 coaequata retribuat, et ad auspitia Caesaris et Augustae dexteram gratiae coadiutricis extendat, ut qui Romani Principatus imperio barbaras nationes et cives in mortalium tutamenta subegit, delirantis aevi familiam sub triumphis et gloria sui Henrici reformet in melius.

LETTER 2.

Serenissimae atque piissimae dominae, dominae .M., coelestis miserationis intuitu Romanorum Reginae et semper Augustae devotissima sua .G. de Battifolle Dei et Imperii gratia largiente Comitissa in Tuscia Palatina flexis humiliter genibus reverentiae debitum exhibere.
Regalis epistolae documenta gratuita ea qua potui veneratione recepi, intellexi devote. Sed cum de prosperitate successuum vestri felicissimi cursus familiariter intimata concepi, quanto libens animus concipientis arriserit, placet potius commendare silentio tamquam nuntio meliori:
5 non enim verba significando sufficiunt ubi mens ipsa quasi debria superatur. Itaque suppleat regiae celsitudinis apprehensio quae scribentis humilitas explicare non potest. At quamvis insinuata per literas ineffabiliter grata fuerint et iucunda, spes amplior tamen et laetandi causas accumulat, et simul vota iusta confectat. Spero equidem, de coelesti
10 provisione confidens, quam numquam falli vel praepediri posse non dubito, et quae humanae civilitati de principe singulari providit, quod exordia vestri regni felicia semper in melius prosperata procedent. Sic igitur in praesentibus et futuris exultans de Augustae clementia sine ulla haesitatione recurro, et suppliciter tempestiva deposco, quatenus me sub
15 umbra tutissima vestri culminis taliter collocare dignemini ut cuiusque sinistrationis ab aestu sim semper et videar esse secura.

LETTER 3.

Illustrissimae atque piissimae dominae, dominae Margaritae, divina providentia Romanorum Reginae et semper Augustae fidelissima sua .G. de Battifolle Dei et imperialis indulgentiae gratia Comitissa in Tuscia

[1] MS. *atque.*

Palatina cum promptissima recommendatione se ipsam et voluntarium ad obsequia famulatum.

Cum pagina vestrae serenitatis apparuit ante scribentis et gratulantis aspectum, experta est mea pura fidelitas quam in dominorum successibus tam[1] subditorum fidelium collaetentur. Nam per ea quae continebantur in ipsa, cum tota cordis hilaritate concepi qualiter dextera summi regis vota Caesaris et Augustae feliciter adimplebat. Proinde gradum meae fidelitatis experta petentis audeo iam inire officium. Ergo ad audientiam vestrae sublimitatis exorans et suppliciter precor et devote deposco quatenus mentis oculis intueri dignemini praelibatae interdum fidei puritatem. Verum quia nonnulia regalium clausurarum videbatur hortari ut, si quando nuntiorum facultas adesset, celsitudini regiae aliquid per-optando de status mei conditione referrem, quamvis quaedam prae-sumptionis facies interdicat obedientiae, tamen suadente virtute obediam. Audiat ex quo iubet Romanorum pia et serena maiestas quoniam tempore missionis presentium coniunx praedilectus et ego, Dei dono, vigebamus incolumes, liberorum sospitate gaudentes, tanto solito laetiores quanto signa resurgentis imperii meliora iam saecula promittebant.

Missum de castro Poppii xv. Kalendas Iunias faustissimi cursus Henrici Caesaris ad Italiam anno primo.

The problem of these three ' Battifolle' Letters is quite different from that of the others. The evidence for them is extremely slender. It really amounts only to this, that they are found in a single MS. (Vat. Palat., 1729), which contains six of the commonly received Epistles of Dante, in the midst of which, not after or before them, these three ' Battifolle' Letters are found embedded. The MS. is a fairly early one, dated 1394, and so just within the limits of the fourteenth century, and only about seventy years after Dante's death[2]. The nine Epistles or Letters occur in the MS. in the following order : (1) Epist. VII (to Henry VII); (2) Epist. VI (' Scelestis-simis Florentinis intrinsecus'); (3) (4) (5) the three Battifolle Letters ; then the four Epistles usually numbered II, III, I, and

---

[1] There is evidently some corruption here. It looks as if a short-sighted copyist, mistaking the meaning of *quam*, thought to emphasize the antithesis of *dominorum* and *subditorum* by inserting *tam*. Somehow the subject of *col-laetentur* seems to have dropped out. *Pectora*, *corda*, and *animi* have been suggested *e conj.*, but none of them seems to have any relation to *tā*.

[2] The whole contents of the MS. are as follows (*auct.* Witte, *de Monarchia*, p. lviii. See also *Dante-Forschungen*, 1, p. 474) :—

1. Twelve Eclogues of Petrarch.
2. *De Monarchia*.
3. Nine Epistles attributed to Dante.

V, in this order. Now observe (*a*) The three Letters in question are introduced without note or comment, but from the position they occupy, and the company in which they occur, the copyist evidently had no doubt they were to be attributed to Dante. (*b*) There is nothing in any of the Letters to suggest any connexion with Dante as their author, or any relation to anything in his life or history. (*c*) Further than this, the writer of the Letters distinctly professes to be some one else. They are written in the name of the Countess Gherardesca di Battifolle, not Catarina, as printed by Giuliani, since the initial letter, which alone is found in the MS., is clearly a G. (There were two Counts Guido di Battifolle, the wife of one was Gherardesca, and the wife of the other Catarina.[1]) The Letters are addressed to Margherita di Brabante, the wife of the Emperor Henry VII.

All this makes the insertion of these Letters in the MS., without note or comment, in the middle of six others indubitably presented as written by Dante, very surprising. How came this about in the teeth of such very strong *prima facie* evidence to the contrary presented by the Letters themselves? It seems only accountable on the supposition of the existence of a strong backing of tradition, though we have no other trace of this. Indeed, the greater and more obvious the *prima facie* difficulties, such as we have already pointed out, the stronger is the case for the existence of such a tradition to overbear them. Its existence must be presupposed as has been that of an unknown and invisible planet to account for some otherwise unexplained action of other visible bodies. This consideration at least contributes something to reinforce the scanty evidence otherwise adducible for these Letters. For, after all, *any* tradition, however weak, is an asset to be reckoned with, as far as it goes. It is not to be summarily dismissed as worthless without some reason appearing against it beyond its weakness. It at least holds the field till it is overthrown. Tradition is not itself a zero, or still less a minus quantity, as would seem to be assumed by the practice of some critics, which has been thus characterized by Bishop Creighton:—

---

[1] Ricci, *Ultimo Rifugio*, p. 17.

'We have been taught (he says) by a long series of sceptical inquiries to take almost for granted that, if according to an ancient tradition a famous event happened in some particular spot, it must really have happened somewhere else ; unless, indeed, it never happened at all.'

The problem presented by these Letters then is a very peculiar one, and indeed unique in another way. There is no question of deliberate forgery, for they do not claim or pretend to be written by Dante. The circumstances under which they were written by him (if at all) are thus explained. In the spring of 1311 Dante was in Tuscany, following with eager anxiety the progress of Henry VII in Italy. That, at any rate, is certain. Also, more definitely, that he was in the Casentino is proved by the colophons to his Epistles VI and VII, both of which are stated to have been written 'sub fonte Sarni' in March and April of that year. That he was there definitely as a guest of a branch of the Battifolle family, is also assigned to tradition by some writers.[1] But I have not been able to trace the existence of such a tradition independently of these Letters· His probable hostess, the Countess Gherardesca di Battifolle, having the privilege of writing on friendly terms concerning her family affairs to the Empress, naturally desired that her communications with so exalted a personage should be couched in the most respectful and formally correct terms. She is thought therefore to have availed herself of the help of her distinguished guest in the composition of these Letters. Some writers have sneered at the idea of Dante acting as 'secretary' to this lady [2], as though it were altogether *infra dignitatem* for so great a man ; as if he were to be imagined as a sort of Hercules spinning wool for Omphale. But to him the task of writing these Letters would be no piece of literary drudgery, but rather a congenial work, as bringing him into some kind of relation with the great Emperor, for whom his adoration was so profound that, as we know, he addresses him in

---

[1] e.g. Witte, *Dante-Forschungen*, 1, p. 487.

[2] Dr. Toynbee kindly reminds me that Flavio Biondo records that Dante composed letters for Scarpetta Ordelaffi, which were transcribed by Scarpetta's secretary, Pellegrino Calvi. *Bull. Dant.*, O. S., viii, pp. 21, 22.

language that we can scarcely conceive to have been applied
to any merely human being without profanity (see Epp. V,
VI, VII). We may also be allowed to suppose that the good
Countess would not be so familiar with Latin composition
(which was naturally to be employed in a Letter to such high
quarters) as to be indifferent to such a unique opportunity of
getting the work executed in the best possible style. We
remember how in the *Vita Nuova*, § 25, ll. 45 *seqq.*, Dante
attributes the habit of writing love poetry in the Volgare
instead of Latin—a practice (he adds) not yet a hundred and
fifty years old—to the consideration that the language had to
be intelligible 'a donna, alla quale era malagevole ad intendere
i versi Latini.' Besides it was not only a question of writing
in Latin, but also in the courtly language and style required
in addressing royalty. There would probably be, in the quaint
language of Bishop Latimer, 'a plentiful lack' of any such
'ready writers' in the recesses of the Casentino. For in the
language of Dante:—

> 'Non era impresa da pigliare a gabbo.'

The question now arises whether there is anything in the
internal evidence of the Letters themselves either favourable or
adverse to the tradition of their Dantesque authorship.

It is obvious to remark at once that if these Letters were
composed in the manner and under the conditions already
described we cannot expect much help from internal evidence
either favourable or adverse. Let us take first the considerations commonly urged as adverse.

In regard to general objections such as these, viz. (*a*) that
there is nothing to connect these Letters as they stand with
Dante in any way whatever; and (*b*) further, that they
definitely profess to be written by some one else, we may point
out that the former objection would apply precisely to the three
Epistles numbered I, II, and III ; and indeed both would apply
to Epistle I, which is addressed to the Cardinal Nicholas of Ostia
in the names of Alexander, the ' Captain,' and the Council and
general body of the party of the Bianchi at Florence.

But more definitely it is urged :

(1) That the style is pompous and fulsome and the expres-

sions of the writer almost grovelling in their humility. But in regard to this and all similar objections it is obvious to reply that Dante here is not supposed to be speaking for himself, but writing ' to order,' and expressing 'by desire' the feelings and sentiments of another. Further that he is bound (as we said) to adopt the conventional and artificial language of a courtly document. But it is not uninteresting to observe that the same criticism has been urged with a view to the rejection of Epistle X. There Dante is confessedly speaking in his own name and describing his own feelings towards his patron Can Grande. Now Can Grande with all his greatness, and however highly Dante estimated both his public services and his private friendship, stood on a much lower level than the Emperor and his Court. Yet there is not much to choose between the humble language of these Letters and that of the first four sections (the dedicatory portion) of Epistle X. Courtly language is as artificial and conventional as that of literary dedications, so that we might take refuge, if necessary, in the defence made by Dr. Johnson of the recognized style of dedications—' Sir, the known style of a dedication is flattery, it professes to flatter.'

(2) It is objected that the occasion and contents of the letter are altogether trivial and commonplace and unworthy of the pen of Dante. The same answer as before might suffice for this too, but as the objection has also been urged with more force against others of the Epistles purporting to be written by Dante, and in his own name (notably No. III, that addressed to Moroello Malaspina), one may say a few more words about it.

There must be large tracts of commonplace in the most exalted lives in all the paths and positions of life, even for the greatest names in politics, religion, literature. Sydney Smith once made the calculation of the months or years occupied in any life of about seventy years in sleeping, dressing, eating, walking, gossiping, and even, as he added, in his own case, shaving. It is curious to find this argument from triviality or commonplace in details urged in early Christian ages (and noted, though of course not accepted, by St. Jerome) against the admission to the Canon of the second and third Epistles of St. John and the Epistle to Philemon.   Also some passages in the Pastoral Epistles were subjected to a similar censure ; such as ' Prepare for me a lodging '—' Bring the cloak which I left at Troas '—or again, ' Use a little wine for thy stomach's sake,' &c.   Nor, in the last-mentioned instance, is the difficulty removed, perhaps it is even increased, if the teetotal lecturer's exegesis be accepted, that the word ' use ' implies that it was to be limited to ' external application only ' !   We may readily then grant that even in his own ordinary correspondence and familiar intercourse with friends Dante could not be expected (or desired) to have maintained the *Divina Commedia* level of style, or what we might perhaps call the ' Ercles' vein.' Indeed the context of that expression contemplates the possibility of even the lion ' roaring like a sucking-dove.'

Still (3) it is somewhat absurdly asked, why or how should such trivialities have been preserved ?   The obvious answer is, By pure and blind chance.   We are all familiar with the survival of scraps of what we call utter rubbish among our possessions, just as we know only too well the capricious freaks of our memory both in ' what it takes away, and what it leaves behind.'   We know too how some of ' the treasures of Egypt ' consist of ὄστρακα, whose interest both for their writers and recipients was so transient that they were deliberately thrown away.   Yet after 2000 years and more they have an interest which has no relation to their intrinsic value at any time.

There is unhappily no ' Natural Selection ' or ' Survival of the Fittest ' to be looked for in regard to the letters of Dante.   There was never any attempt at collecting or editing, much less at selecting from, his correspondence, which on the authority of his biographers was somewhat copious.   Boccaccio states that several of his letters were still extant, and Lionardo Bruni, who died in 1444 (as much as fifty years later than the date of this MS.), says he had seen several autograph letters of Dante and he describes minutely the character of his handwriting.   It is quite likely that, among so many, some of little value or interest should have chanced to survive.   It must be confessed that in some modern biographies of great

men letters are published, even after the power of selection
has been, or may be supposed to have been, exercised, where
a similar estimate of the value of their contents might incline
the enlightened critics of future generations to dispute their
genuineness.

The contents of the MS. in which these letters are found
appear to be the nearest approach to a ' collection ' of Dante's
correspondence extant. The copyist seems to have had access
to a packet or bundle of letters attributed to Dante, for there
are gathered here as many as nine. No other MS. existing
has more than three, viz. one in the Laurentian Library
(marked xxix. 8) which contains those numbered IV, VIII,
and IX, none of them corresponding with any in this Vatican
MS. or indeed in any other existing MS. There is happily
a prospect of this Laurentian MS. being published in a photographic facsimile very shortly, but only in fifty copies. It
has been proved to be in the handwriting of Boccaccio, and
the reproduction now promised is in honour of the sixth
centenary of his birth, which occurred in the year 1913 [1].

To return now to the question of internal evidence. Here
again we cannot expect much help if we seek for positive
traces of Dante's style, though I think we may confidently
say that it yields no adverse evidence of any relevancy. The
' native hue' of Dante's writing is disguised by the admittedly
conventional style (as we have noted already) of complimentary
and official Court language, the adoption of which was almost
as much *de rigueur* as the technicalities in the composition
of a legal document. We can scarcely imagine even a Ruskin
betraying the characteristic richness of his style in drafting
a lease or a legal bond. But there are some small touches
even here in which we may perhaps detect echoes of Dante's
language, just as even in a purposely disguised handwriting
some peculiarities of the writer often betray themselves. And
at any rate there are, I think, at least three arguments of

---

[1] Since the above was written the photographic reproduction has been
published under the title of *Lo Zibaldone Boccaccesco*. A veritable ' medley' or
' miscellany' it is, comprising seventy-six folips, of which the three Epistles
occupy less than one folio.

a somewhat substantial character: (1) from the titles of the three Letters; (2) from the colophon of the third Letter; (3) from a clear reminiscence of a passage of Virgil in the first Letter.

I would first notice that for some unexplained, and to me unintelligible, reason Torri (who is followed by Giuliani) alters the order of the Epistles as found in the MS., the only MS., it will be remembered, in which they have been preserved. Instead of the MS. order 1, 2, 3, they are printed in the order 3, 1, 2. They have been given above (pp. 258–260) in the order in which they occur in the MS.

(1) It should be observed that in the case of all the Epistles of Dante the titles are of two kinds. First, those which are in the language of the author of the Epistle itself, and secondly those which are obviously prefixed by the scribe. The former have an authority equal to that of the Letter to which they are attached: the latter have none, any more than the subscriptions to some of the Epistles of St. Paul.

The titles to the three Letters before us belong to the former class, and so also do those which introduce the following among the Epistles as usually printed:—Nos. I, IV, V, VI, VII, and X. But Nos. II and III clearly belong to the latter. Epistle VII is preserved in three MSS.[1], of which two have the author's title, and the third, viz. this Palatine MS., only a scribe's title. Now let us refer to the title of the first Letter. It ends with the words 'officium ante pedes,' without any verb. The omission of a main verb in such epistolary formulae is extremely common. (It occurs for instance in the three Pastoral Epistles in the New Testament.) We find such an omission in all the titles of the three Letters now before us. So it is again in the title of Epistle IV of the *Oxford Dante*, and in fact also in that of Epistle VII, when the reading of the two MSS. in which that Epistle occurs is restored, as it should be, viz. 'osculum ante pedes,' instead of the arbitrary alteration of editors, 'osculantur pedes.' But further, with this corrected reading, we have a very close parallel to the title of this first Battifolle Letter. In

[1] Viz. 'Vat. Palat. 1729,' Rome; 'Pantaleo,' Bibl. Vitt. Em., Rome; 'Marciana, Cl. Lat. xiv Cod. 115,' Venice.

Epistle VII we have 'osculum ante pedes,' in this Letter 'officium ante pedes.' Reasons may easily be suggested for the variation 'officium' in this very humble and dutiful address of the Countess. Also *osculum* in the other case corresponds with ll. 42, 43 in the body of that Epistle.

(2) Next as to the colophon attached to the last of these three Letters.

We have already referred to the colophons of Epistles VI and VII as evidence of the presence of Dante in the Casentino at this date. They are dated March 31 and April 17 respectively[1]. Now the third of the Battifolle Letters is dated May 18. So not only do these three dates very closely correspond, but it is remarkable that the date of the *year* is given in precisely the same terms in all these three cases, viz.: 'faustissimi cursus Henrici Caesaris (or divi Henrici) ad Italiam anno primo.' We may note that 'felicissimus cursus' occurs also in the body of Letter II *sub init.* Indeed the similarity of the terms of the colophon is the only direct correspondence in these Battifolle Letters with a recognized Dantesque formula. Now if the question of forgery were at issue, such a marked correspondence would clearly be liable to a suspicion, which cannot be held to attach to it when the motive for any such imitation is entirely absent. But if Dante were composing a Letter in set terms on behalf of, and in the name of, his hostess the Countess, it does seem quite natural that he should suggest, instead of the prosaic date, the formula which he had adopted in two other Letters written in the previous few weeks by himself. It was expressed in terms relating to the stirring events by which his own mind and that of his hostess were entirely obsessed, and which are conspicuous in the subject-matter of the Letter itself. It was a formula that would appeal both to the sender and

---

[1] In the case of Ep. VII this MS. (Palat.) has no colophon. Codd. Ven. and Pant. have distinctly xv (and not xiv) for the day of month, and there is no numerical date for the year, which would be clearly superfluous. (Frat. and Giul. have such a date, and also 'xiv' as *supra*. Witte, who omits the date of the year, reads 'xi.') I have already noticed that in *this* MS. Ep. VII has only a scribe's title, so that the regular title and colophon are for some reason both absent from this MS. in the case of Ep. VII.

receiver of the Letter as being most appropriate. The date is given as though it had relation to a new Anno Domini, starting from the Advent of him whom Dante elsewhere, with questionable reverence, greets as a new Messiah. The date was the inauguration of 'meliora saecula,' as we read in the last words of the Letter. We are reminded how with similar hopes the French Revolutionists in 1793 began to date their years from the inauguration of the new régime. Now this identical formula for the date could not possibly have occurred to any other writer, unless to one who was consciously endeavouring to imitate or personate Dante, of which there is no trace or motive here discernible.

(3) Another passage of even greater weight—since there can be no possible suggestion here of any deliberate copying of a definite formula existing elsewhere—is found in the first of these Letters (ll. 10–15). Indeed I may say that it was the occurrence of this passage that first made me suspect that these Letters might perhaps after all be genuinely attributed to Dante. After describing in flattering terms the honour done and the extreme condescension shown by the Empress to the writer in her friendly communications, she proceeds : ' Dignas itaque persolvere grates non opis est hominis, verum ab homine alienum esse non reor pro insufficientiae supplemento Deum exorare ... quatenus mundi gubernator aeternus condescensui tanto praemia coaequata retribuat.' Who can fail to recognize here the familiar Virgilian passage in *Aen.* i. 600–605 :—

> ' Grates persolvere dignas
> Non opis est nostrae, Dido, nec quidquid ubique est
> Gentis Dardaniae, magnum quae sparsa per orbem.
> Dî tibi, si qua pios respectant numina, si quid
> Usquam iustitia est, et mens sibi conscia recti,
> Praemia digna ferant.'

Now we can scarcely imagine that such a classical allusion should have occurred spontaneously to the Countess. On the other hand, we do know that this passage was very familiar to Dante, for it is quoted, or distinctly recalled by him in at least two, and I think we may say three, places in his works. They are these :—

Ep. I. ii, ll. 39–44: Quis vobis dignas grates persolvere attentabit? Nec opis est nostrae, pater, nec quicquid Florentinae gentis reperitur in terris: sed si qua coelo est pietas quae talia remunerando prospiciat, illa vobis praemia digna ferat.

This is quite a complete and explicit quotation slightly adapted.

Then again *Par.* iv. 121–123:—

> Non è l' affezion mia tanto profonda
> Che basti a render voi grazia per grazia;
> Ma quei che vede e puote a ciò risponda.

Naturally here the verbatim reproduction is less precise, but in both cases the twofold divisions of the original passage are clearly marked: (1) the inadequacy of the speaker's expression of gratitude; (2) the pious wish that a Higher Power would supply that deficiency.

But besides these two passages we may notice yet a third in which the expression 'praemia digna' occurs, viz. in Epistle II, l. 8, where Dante says of the lately defunct Alexander Count of Romena, 'super astra nunc affluenter *dignis praemiis* muneratur [*or* remuneratur].'

Returning to the passage in this first Battifolle Letter, the indirect reminiscence of the Virgilian passage seems to me even more significant than a formal quotation. The writer's mind was so familiar with the words that his own thoughts tended spontaneously to express themselves in its terms. And this, as we have shown by other references, would certainly be characteristic of Dante. We may also perhaps note that the other most explicit reproduction of the passage occurs in that Epistle I, which, just like the present Letters, has been traditionally ascribed to Dante though written in the name of others. Thus there can be no suspicion in either case of the quotation possibly serving the purpose of a forger.

Next there are several words or expressions which seem to me to have a Dantesque flavour, but I hesitate to lay too much stress upon them as I am not sufficiently familiar with the style of contemporary Latin writing to know whether they are at all distinctive. But if not distinctive, they are at least such as would be natural to Dante, as appears from their occurrence in the other writings attributed to him.

These at any rate are some that have struck me:

(1) In the third of these Letters (l. 8) there is a word the meaning of which I at first rendered quite wrongly, and indeed the Italian translation by Torri does the same, viz. 'prae-libatae.' We observe that at the beginning of the Letter the absolute sincerity of the writer's devotion to the Empress is insisted upon; and in the middle of the Letter the subject is reintroduced with the words 'praelibatae fidei puritatem.' I did not at first realize that 'praelibatae' here means simply 'afore-mentioned,' or 'before touched upon.' Dante so uses it in Epistle VIII. 63: 'Quod si de *praelibato* precipitio dubitatur'—'If there is any doubt as to the above-mentioned overthrow.' The word occurs again in this sense in *V. E.* I. iv. 49, 'contra superius praelibata'—'contrary to what has been indicated above': and again in *V. E.* II. viii. 9, 'si bene comminiscimur omnia praelibata.' I observe that Ducange gives 'supradictum' as one meaning of 'praelibatum,' with an example from some formal document, but there is nothing to show whether it was a common usage in ordinary writing. Dante at any rate so uses it three times elsewhere.[1]

(2) Then again the word 'Augusta' for the 'Empress' occurring in all these three Letters. This may not perhaps be uncommon, I do not know. At any rate Dante applies it to the Virgin, as the 'Regina Coeli,' in *Par.* xxxii. 119 :—

> Per esser propinquissimi ad Augusta.

Also 'Augustus' is applied to Henry four times in Dante's Epistles. Note especially V, l. 27: 'Henricus, Divus et Augustus et Caesar.' So here in the third of these Letters we have 'Vota Caesaris et Augustae.'

(3) The expression 'mentis oculis' (Letter 3, l. 8) occurs twice again in the Epistles ascribed to Dante, viz. V. 163 and II. 30.[2] It is also found in *De Mon.* II. i. 17. So that it occurs at any rate three times elsewhere in his reputed works, and we may also add, as similar, *Conv.* II. v. 117, 'soverchia gli occhi della mente umana,' and *Par.* x. 121,

> Or se tu l' occhio della mente trani.

---

[1] Compare also *Par.* x. 23 and Casini's note, *l. c.*

[2] [To which may be added Epist. viii. 147, 'mentales oculos' (according to the MS. reading for which the printed editions substitute 'mortales'.]

The expression perhaps may hardly be considered distinctive, but at any rate it is thoroughly Dantesque.

(4) Next, at the end of Letter 1, we read ' delirantis aevi familiam sub triumphis et gloria sui Henrici reformet in melius.' Compare with this the description of Henry as ' delirantis Hesperiae domitorem ' in Epistle VI, l. 87.

(5) There is a curious expression in the third Letter (l. 9) where the writer, referring to the royal letter already received, says ' nonnulla regalium clausurarum videbatur hortari.' With this we may compare Epistle IX, l. 25, 'literae discretius et consultius clausulatae.'

(6) We may perhaps notice ' quanta vel qualis ego ' in the first of these Letters, l. 5 : for a similar combination is found in *Par.* ii. 65 ; viii. 46 ; xxiii. 92 ; xxx. 120, in the Italian, and in Epistle I, l. 7, and Epistle X, ll. 584, 585, in the Latin works.

(7) At the end of the third Letter we have the words ' signa resurgentis imperii meliora iam saecula promittebant.' Compare with this Epistle VII, l. 20, ' nova spes Latio saeculi melioris effulsit.'

(8) Again we may note the phrase ' humanae civilitati ' in the second Letter (l. 11), and compare *De Mon.* I. ii. 50, ' finis universalis civilitatis humani generis ' ; and again in the following Chapter, l. 2, ' finis totius humanae civilitatis.' Add Epist. VIII. 152. Further not only the phrase but also the sentiment expressed in this passage of the Letter resembles *Conv.* IV. iv. *init.*—' Lo fondamento radicale della Imperiale Maestà . . . è la necessità della umana civiltà.'

(9) The passage last quoted (from Letter 2, l. 11) contains apparently a somewhat strange use of the preposition *de* with ' providere ' : ' humanae civilitati de principe . . . providit.' We may compare *V. E.* I. ii, l. 35, ' Animalibus . . . de locutione non oportuit provideri.' In the previous sentence of Letter 2 (l. 9) we have another rather singular combination : 'de coelesti provisione confidens.' The same construction is found in *V. E.* II. iv, l. 78, ' de solo ingenio confidentes ' ; and in *De Mon.* I. i, ll. 36, 37, ' non tam de propria virtute confidens quam de lumine Largitoris illius.' Possibly we might also note *De Mon.* III. iii. 57, ' de illarum praevalentia . . . sperantes.'

(10) We may compare 'debitae subiectionis officium' at the end of the Title of the first of these Letters with the same words in Epist. VI, ll. 33, 34: and also perhaps the similarity of the thought between l. 13 of the same Letter and Ep. VI, ll. 1–5.

(11) The use of the word *insinuare* which we find in Letter 2 (l. 7) in the sense of 'to set forth' or 'communicate' = ἐμφανίζειν (as Ducange says) may possibly be too common in mediaeval and patristic Latin to lay much stress upon, but at any rate Dante thus employs the word no less than three times in Epistle X, viz. ll. 538, 548, 577 [1].

(12) The same consideration may perhaps have to be applied when *quatenus* is used in the sense of *ut*, as it is in each one of these Letters, viz. in 1, l. 14; in 2, l. 14; and in 3, l. 8. Anyhow Dante so uses it elsewhere at least three times, viz. Epistle I, l. 63; II, l. 38; and *De Mon.* I. i. 6.

(13) Then in ll. 4, 5 of Letter 2 we have some thoroughly Dantesque thoughts, viz. (*a*) the inadequacy of language to express thought; and (*b*) that this is because sometimes the mind is so elevated as to be, as it were, 'inebriated' by the strain put upon it.

For (*a*) see *Par.* xxxiii. 55, 'il mio veder fu maggio che il parlar nostro,' and Epistle X, l. 575, 'multa per intellectum videmus quibus signa vocalia desunt.' Add also *Canz.* ii. 1–18, prefixed to *Conv.* Tratt. III ('Amor che nella mente,' &c.), and the commentary on this in Chapter IV, ll. 16–22; especially l. 38, 'la cortezza del nostro parlare, lo quale dal pensiero è vinto.' The thought is too familiar to need further references; but a remarkably close parallel to the words (Letter 2, l. 4) 'placet potius commendare silentio tanquam nuntio meliori' may be found in *Conv.* IV. v, ll. 140 *seqq.* in the apostrophe to Cato: 'Chi presumerà di te parlare? Certo maggiormente parlare di te non si può *che tacere.*' Then Dante goes on to quote St. Jerome's language about St. Paul, of whom he declares 'che meglio è tacere che poco dire.'

(*b*) As to the metaphor of an 'inebriated' mind, 'mens ..

---

[1] See note on this word in *Studies in Dante*, iii. p. 336.

debria ¹' (Letter 2, l. 5), which Dante probably borrowed from the Vulgate in *Ps.* xxxv. 9, comp. *Conv.* III. viii. 133, 'quivi s' inebria l' anima.' Add also *Inf.* xxix. 2 and *Par.* xxvii. 3. Also *ibid.* ll. 5–6:—

> 'Mia ebbrezza
> Entrava per l'udire e per lo viso.'

(14) Note further the expression 'de principe singulari' in Letter 2, l. 11 for a Universal Monarch, and compare this with the title to Epistle VII, 'Domino singulari, domino Henrico.'

(15) Lastly, we might perhaps notice the phrase 'Romanus Principatus' in Letter 1, l. 16. Compare 'sacratissimi Caesarei Principatus... Vicarius' in the title to Epistle X. 'Principatus' is common in the *De Mon.*, and the actual expression 'Romanus Principatus' occurs there twice. Also Dante appears to use the word 'Principatus' in a sense oscillating between the concrete and abstract, Prince and Princedom, Emperor and Empire. Sometimes too we find the abstract term when the concrete would seem more natural, as distinctly in *Purg.* x. 73–4, 'l' alta gloria Del roman principato' (i.e. Trajan). Here, as might be expected, the inferior and slightly supported variants 'Principe' and 'Prince' are both found as *lectiones faciliores*. There seems to me to be a curious parallel to this in Cowley's *Discourse concerning the Government of Oliver Cromwell*, where the 'strange and terrible apparition' visiting him is made to announce himself thus: 'I am called the North-West Principality, his Highness the Protector of the Commonwealth of England, Scotland, and Ireland and the dominions belonging thereunto.' Ducange does not mention any such use of 'Romanus Principatus' for the Emperor or Empire, nor is the expression apparently to be found in Classical Latin, though 'principatus alicuius' (e.g. Neronis) for *the reign of* is natural enough. The only recognition of the word by Ducange is as the title of one of the orders of Angels. We might perhaps, I think, infer from this that

---

¹ For the form 'debria' comp. St. Bernard, *De diligendo Deo*, x. 27. He there describes one in ecstasy as 'divino debriatus animo, oblitus sui'. Also 'debrius' is noted as a common form by Ducange, *s. v.*

the title ' Romanus Principatus' for the Emperor or Empire was not in ordinary use.

We may now perhaps sum up the arguments so far offered from internal evidence under four heads :—

1. The language of the titles to the three Letters.

2. That of the colophon to the third Letter.

3. The distinct Virgilian reference in the first Letter.

4. The correspondence of words, expressions, and thoughts with those occurring in other works of Dante, or such as are generally attributed to him.

Many of these last parallels, taken separately, may seem weak and inconclusive, but we can scarcely ignore the cumulative force derived from the occurrence of so many similarities of expression within such narrow limits; especially if we take into account that both the subject-matter of the Letters and the conventional character of the composition tend to throw some disguise over the writer's ordinary style. Some of them, it is true, may very likely be nothing more than ' terms of speech commonly used in those days.' But at least they are such as are found elsewhere in Dante, and therefore are quite consistent with his traditional authorship. On the other hand, there is, I believe, nothing that can be pointed out as inconsistent with it, either in language or in sentiment.

The same may be said of the regular observance of the rules of the *Cursus*. For, whether the letters are genuine or not, this is nothing more than was to be expected at that time. It is not a discriminating test, though the disregard of such rules would have formed a serious objection.

It must be regretfully admitted that the Letters, even if genuine, have scarcely any intrinsic value or interest. They throw no light on Dante's history or character. But it is absolutely futile (as Novati protests) to argue ' indegna di Dante e quindi apocrifa.' Their main interest is that which attaches to any personal relic (if such it be) of so great a man. And we know that some other relics are very highly prized by those who are assured of their genuineness, for which no intrinsic value can be claimed, or any scientific interest.

T 2

VII

MISCELLANEOUS NOTES

The Almanac of 'Jacob ben Machir ben Tibbon' (Latinè 'Profacius')[1] c. 1300.

[Reprinted, with revision and additions, from *Modern Language Review*, July 1908.]

ALL Dante students are familiar with the controversy whether 1300 or 1301 is the year indicated by internal evidence as that which was assumed by Dante for the date of the Vision of the *Divina Commedia*. Though there are now scarcely any advocates remaining for the latter date, yet there are some who still maintain that there is at least one of their astronomical arguments which holds the field. It is assumed on both sides that Dante's references to the positions of the planets must correspond with their true places in the supposed year of the Vision. Now it is undeniable that Venus was in point of fact a Morning Star at Easter 1301 and an Evening Star in 1300. And the presence of Venus as a Morning Star is a conspicuous feature in the splendid description of the Easter Dawn at the beginning of the *Purgatorio*. The advocates of 1300 have been obliged hitherto to maintain that this may fairly be considered to be a purely ideal picture, and therefore not necessarily subjected to such matter-of-fact conditions.

But an entirely new light has now been thrown upon this point by the researches of Prof. Boffito.[2] He has discovered the actual Almanac which was in general vogue in the early fourteenth century, and the one which there is little reason to

---

[1] J. Boffito et C. Melzi d'Eril : *Almanach Dantis Aligherii sive Profhacii Judaei Montispessulani Almanach perpetuum ad annum 1300 inchoatum. Nunc primum editum ad fidem codicis Laurentiani* (Pl. XVIII, sin. N. i). Florentiae, apud L. S. Olschki. MDCCCCVIII.

[2] There is a brief note on this (then recent) discovery in *Studies in Dante*, iii. p. 372.

doubt was that likely to have been employed by Dante. When we remember that the scene in *Purg.* i. is entirely imaginary, and that Dante was writing ten or twelve years after the date assumed for that scene, it is evident that, if he desired to conform to the astronomical conditions of the period, he would have to consult an almanac for that purpose. The remarkable point is that in this contemporary Almanac, to which Prof. Boffito has called attention, Venus is in fact (though erroneously) recorded as a *Morning Star* in 1300.

The Almanac was written in Hebrew, but was immediately translated into Latin [1], became very widely known, and seems practically to have 'held the field,' and was therefore almost certainly the Almanac that would have been used by Dante himself. The quasi-Latin name of the author appears in numerous MSS. in fourteen or fifteen different forms (*op. cit.*, Praef., p. v. note). He was born c. 1236 at Marseilles, lived and worked chiefly at Montpellier (Montepessulanum), and was a voluminous writer on Philosophy, Medicine, Astronomy, &c. Prof. Boffito says that the Almanac exists in 'innumeri codices,' many of them of the very beginning of the fourteenth century. (There are as many as six [2] in the Bodleian Library.) It was a 'perpetual Almanac'; i.e. the Tables of the position of all the planets were constructed from 1300 onwards until in each case the number of revolutions of the epicycle brought the Planet back again (approximately) to the position which it occupied in 1300, so that the Tables could (with slight corrections for which rules are given [3]) be used again continuously. The positions of the 'superior planets' are given at intervals of ten days; those of the more swiftly-moving 'inferior planets' at intervals of five days.

The periods of recurrence of the original position are of course very different for the different planets. Thus the Tables have had to be calculated in the case of Saturn for sixty years, in that of Jupiter for eighty-four years; in that of Mars for eighty; and in that of Mercury for forty-seven: while in the case of Venus eight years suffice.

Now it is curious that in the original Hebrew Almanac the Planetary Tables all begin from 1301, while in the Latin Version they all begin from 1300 *with the exception of*

---

[1] There were also in Latin two recensions, one enlarged and the other abbreviated (*op. cit.* p. xiii).

[2] Of the six Bodleian MSS. referred to in the text, two contain Tables for the 'superior' Planets only. In the remaining four the Tables for Venus begin with 1301, and those for the other Planets with 1300.

[3] e.g. in the case of Venus there would be a difference of 2 d. 10 h. 23 m. in the eighth year of recurrence to take account of.

Venus, which still starts from 1301. It is singular, however, that in the 'Preface' both of the Hebrew and Latin Almanacs (and also in both 'recensions' of the latter) it is stated that the Almanac has 1300 for its initial year. The result then is—however the strange difference may have come about— that in the case of Venus *alone* the position given in the first column is that for 1301 and it is correctly given for that year; whereas in all other cases the first column represents 1300. (In some MSS. the year 1300 has been erroneously inserted in the first column for Venus.) What then could be more natural than that any one consulting the Almanac should fall into the error of supposing that the figures which he found in the first column of the Table of Venus represented (as in the case of all the other planets) her position in 1300? If Dante made this mistake, in a perhaps cursory inspection of the Almanac, he would find the position of Venus, say on April 10, to be about 20° within the sign of Pisces, and hence she was

Velando i Pesci ch' erano in sua scorta.

By consequence, as the Sun was in Aries, Venus would be a Morning Star, visible before Sunrise, as Dante has repre-sented her.

If we wished from this 'perpetual' Almanac to find the *true* position of Venus in the year 1300 we must look under 1308, the year of the recurrence (approximately) of her position in 1300, and we should find that she was then about 8° within the constellation Taurus, and consequently *behind* the Sun, or, in other words, an Evening Star.

This interesting discovery not only destroys the supposed surviving argument for 1301, but entirely transfers it to the other side. It affords also an interesting illustration of the importance of interpreting astronomical passages in Dante by contemporary evidence and ideas, rather than by the Nautical Almanac.

I append an examination of Almanacs in Bodleian MSS. for 1300 in reference to the above question.

In the following MSS., 'Ashmole 369,' 'Digby 114,' 'Raw-linson 117,' the Table for Venus runs thus (the first year date omitted) :—

Martius		I	2	3	4	5	6	7	8
		Aquarius							
		gr. m.							
	5	4 40							
	10	10 48							
	15	16 5							
	20	22 17							
	25	27 47							
		Pisces							
	31	3 26							
Aprilis	5	9 2							
	10	14 57							
	15	&c.							
	&c.								

For *all* the other planets, Saturn, Jupiter, Mars, Mercury, as follows :—

Martius		1300	I	2	3	4	5	6	7	8
	5									
	10									
	15									
	&c.									

Observe that in the case of *Venus alone* the year 1300 is not inserted, and this is so in all the three MSS.

Also in ' Savile 25 ' Venus is tabulated *thus* :—

Martius		1301	2	3	4	5	6	7	8
	5	4 40							
	10	&c.							
	15								
	&c.								

but *all* the other Planets begin with 1300 as in the three afore-mentioned MSS.

I have no idea why this curious difference occurs.

Other MSS. containing Almanacs are—

Laud Misc. 594. ⎫ These have only the Tables of the *superior*
Coll. Univ. 41. ⎭   planets.

Cod. Ashmol. 360 has an Almanac, but it seems mainly *Ecclesiastical.*

Also 'Digby 176'—but I find no similar Tables bearing on this point.

Two proposed Emendations in Dante's Epistola VI, § 6.

[Reprinted from the *Modern Language Review*, Vol. V, No. 3, July 1910.]

I.

THE received reading at the beginning of this section is 'O miserrima Fesulanorum propago, et iterum iam *Punica* barbaries.'

Professor Meyer of Göttingen is one of the leading authorities on the comparatively recent science of 'Cursus,' i.e., the study of the recognized euphonic sequences of the concluding syllables of clauses in Prose Composition, both in Classical Greek and Latin, and also in Mediaeval Latin. The Classical and Mediaeval conditions are different, but in each, after their kind, definite rules have with great labour and research been established, especially in reference to terminal clauses. Prof. Meyer has shown[1] how regularly the style of Dante (among others) is controlled by these long unsuspected conditions. He noticed, however, that the termination 'Punica barbaries' does not conform to any recognized type, and he therefore conjectured 'punita barbaries,' which would do so. Practically 'c' and 't' are in many MSS. almost or even quite undistinguishable. In the case of this Epistle there is unfortunately only one MS. extant, which is in the Vatican Library[2]. I have obtained a photograph of this page of the MS., and I am convinced (and in this two eminent authorities on palaeography agree with me) that there can scarcely be a doubt that the word is 'punita' and not 'punica' in the MS.

Now it is very curious that suspicion as to the reading should have been first aroused by this kind of side issue. But the emendation proposed, besides being confirmed apparently by the MS. itself, seems to be fully justified by other considerations.

(1) No such combination as 'Punica barbaries' is known. 'Punica fides' and 'Punica crudelitas' are found, but never 'Punica barbaries.'

(2) But if this is not a recognized phrase, it cannot be said that there is any special propriety in associating Carthage in any way with Florence or Fiesole.

---

[1] See *Bullettino Dant.*, N.s., xiii. 267 n.
[2] Vatican. Palat. Lat. 1729, ff. 57ʳᵒ–58ᵛᵒ.

(3) The Latinity is intolerable, if 'a repetition of Punic barbarism' is intended. 'Iterum' would require a participle, not an adjective. Why not 'altera' (as in l. 50), or 'rediviva' (as l. 104), or 'redintegrata,' &c.?

On the other hand, the application of 'barbaries' to Florence, and to its parent Fiesole, would be thoroughly Dantesque. See *Purg.* xxiii. 94–96, *Inf.* xv. 63, 73. Perhaps compare *Par.* xvi. 49 *seqq.* In Ep. V. 4 *init.* the 'coadducta barbaries' of the Lombards relates to their stubborn resistance (as in this case) to the Emperor.

Then as to 'iam punita,' Dante in familiar prophetic manner speaks of the punishment which is already imminent and entirely inevitable, as though it were already accomplished. Compare in this Epistle ll. 22–25, 73–76, 147–150, and § 4 *passim.*

Finally 'iterum' would be explained in reference to the previous destruction of Florence by Attila (Totila). See *Inf.* xiii. 149.

II.

The second passage which it is proposed to emend is at the end of this same section, viz. 'ut sine retractatione revertatur.' It occurred to me to test the value of the above argument from 'Cursus' by examining all the terminal clauses throughout the Epistle. I found that one or other of the four commonest forms required by the rules of the Mediaeval Cursus was found in every single instance with the solitary exception of the passage here quoted. I was content, under such circumstances, to treat this as 'the exception proving the rule'; though it must be confessed that it would be very surprising if this should occur only in the concluding clause of the whole composition. But I was accidentally informed by a friend to my great surprise that the offending word 'revertatur' was not in the MS. at all, and was nothing but an editorial conjecture. The word in the MS. is corrupt and unintelligible, viz. 'riuantur.' The 'n' at any rate is clearly a blunder, since a singular and not a plural is required. It may easily have arisen from an erroneously superposed mark of abbreviation, either (as sometimes) from pure accident, or possibly from confusion with the cross of the 't,' if it had one in the original MS. So that we may safely take 'riuatur' as a first correction.

But curiously enough (as in the previous case), apart from any considerations of 'Cursus,' a little reflection shows 'rever-

tatur' to be entirely out of place here. The context requires
a word of exactly opposite meaning. Dante is warning the
'scelestissimi Florentini' that penitence now, even if it came,
would no longer be of any avail. 'It is too late to cry for
mercy when it is the time of justice.' Hence to say here that
'the sinner is smitten that he may be converted without falling
back' is just to reverse Dante's meaning.

The next thing that suggests itself is that the words appear,
both from the manner of their introduction and from the
unusual expression 'sine retractatione,' to be a quotation. If
so, it would be natural to suppose the Vulgate to be its source.
Now we find in 1 Sam. xiv. 39 the expression 'absque
retractatione morietur' spoken by Saul in reference to Jona-
than. (In E.V. 'he shall surely die,' i.e. without further
consideration. In LXX. θανάτῳ ἀποθανεῖται.) I cannot therefore
help thinking that 'moriatur' was the word written by Dante.
It would suit the sense exactly; it would conform to the rules
of 'Cursus'; it would fulfil the condition of being a quotation,
thereby also accounting for the somewhat singular expression
'sine retractatione.' The word 'retractatio' is a ἅπαξ λεγόμενον
in the Vulgate. And though three references are given in
Cicero and Livy by Facciolati for 'sine retractatione,' in all
cases the expression refers to an action done by some one
'without hesitation,' or 'with alacrity,' or, as we say, 'without
thinking twice about it.' In St. Augustine's well-known work
'Retractationes' the word seems to mean 'reconsiderations'
rather than 'retractations,' though one naturally leads to the
other. That would also suit the sense of the Vulgate and of
Dante *h. l.*, but the expression is hardly a natural one, except
as part of a quotation.

The chief objection to the suggested conjecture is that
there is no process by which a change of 'moriatur' into
'riuatur' could be explained. But in the archetypal MS. the
word, or part of it, might have become disfigured through
a blot, or a wormhole, or other such defect, or the initial
letters may have faded, and thus even a common word might
become unintelligible.

Since the above was written, my friend Professor Sayce has
suggested to me the ingenious conjecture that 'riuatur' may
be a corruption of 'eruatur,' the 'e' being lost in the termination of the previous word 'retractatione.' This has the
advantage of suiting the sense and of explaining in a recognized
manner the process of corruption. The argument from probable
'quotation' would lose much of its force, though there might
still be a possible 'echo' of the passage in the writer's mind.

Cf. Ep. X. 28 *ad fin.* : ' Nam [*scil.* Deus] . . . . aliquando misericorditer ad conversionem, aliquando severe ad punitionem, plus et minus ut vult, gloriam suam quantumcunque male viventibus manifestat.' The latter alternative is evidently the case here.

DANTE IN NORTHERN LATITUDES.

[Reprinted from *The Academy*, Dec. 23, 1893.]

I VENTURE to suggest the following explanation that has occurred to me of a difficult passage in the *Convivio* of Dante (III. vi. 23-25), which I have long sought in vain to understand.

Dante, when speaking of the inequality of the days and nights at the different seasons, makes the following curious statement :—'Sometimes the day has fifteen hours and the night nine; and sometimes the night has sixteen hours and the day eight.'

Now why should the maximum length of the day and of the night be different, the former fifteen hours and the latter sixteen? Such an inequality clearly could not exist, in fact, at any one place or spot ; yet the definiteness with which this anomalous statement is made seems to stamp it as a phenomenon empirically observed, or ascertained in some way, by its author. An astronomical friend to whom I submitted the above extract replied by asking whether there was not in the context some reference to difference of latitude. There certainly is not, but this seemed to me to give the clue to the interpretation. Such a difference could only be true of two places differing in latitude, the longer day occurring at a more northerly and the longer night (or shorter maximum day) at a more southerly station. I next inquired what places would correspond to the phenomena here described, and the reply I received was:— ' *Rome* : Summer day, about fifteen hours, night about nine hours. *Paris* : Summer day, about sixteen hours, night about eight hours (and, consequently, winter night sixteen hours and day eight hours).' This appeared to me at once to throw a curious sidelight on the traditional story of Dante's wanderings. If he were in Paris (or shall we say at Oxford ?), he would probably be struck by the increased length of the winter night as compared with that with which he was familiar in Italy, and by observation or inquiry he might have ascertained that the difference was about one hour. It would be natural, then, in such a passage as this, that he should record the maximum inequality with which his own experience had made him acquainted. At any rate, unless he had travelled as far north (roughly speaking) as Paris, he could not have personal knowledge of such a length of night or shortness of day as is here described. And unless some personal experience is thus recorded, why should Dante stop short at the limits here given? For the previous chapter shows that he was aware of the day of six months, and the night of the same length, at the poles.

This might be described, in the language of Paley, as an ' undesigned coincidence' tending to establish the truth of the tradition that Dante visited our northern latitudes. I am afraid, however, that the most ingenious advocate could hardly extract from it a new argument for his having prolonged his journey to Oxford.

SUPPLEMENTARY NOTES

ADDITIONAL NOTE ON *Conv.* II. xiv. 120–122
(See above, pp. 57–60.)

FRESH light has been thrown upon this passage in a recent note by Professor A. Marigo in the *Bullettino* for June, 1915, by a reference to a passage in B. Latini, *Trésors* B. iii, Part I, c. 4 (p. 474, Ed. Chabaille). The chapter is headed 'De ij manières de Parler, ou de *bouche* ou par *letre*.' This requires the withdrawal of my statement on p. 59 that the contrast between speech and writing is not a distinctive peculiarity of Rhetoric, since that is precisely the subject of which Brunetto is speaking. Though my interpretation of the whole passage is not necessarily rendered untenable, yet the close resemblance between the language of Dante and that of B. Latini gives a very strong support to the other explanation, which, as I have said in the text, is the one usually given.

The writer is wrong in saying that my text follows Fraticelli, since I have *della lettera* which is strongly supported by MS. evidence, and not *la lettera*, as it were personified, as in Fraticelli.

ADDITIONAL NOTE ON *Conv.* III. ii. 60
(See above, pp. 66–8)

My note on this passage does not appear to me sufficiently clear.

In the text, as it is there proposed to be revised, the chief alterations are (1) to interchange the *della* before *ragione* and the *la* before *divina*. (2) Also, I think, the conjectural insertion of the important word [umana] should perhaps be further guarded by a '?'. But as the subject of the two previous sentences has been l'anima *umana* as it is again the subject of the present sentence, *umana* might possibly be 'understood' to be implied here without its actual insertion in the text. I regret not having examined MSS. here. But I should admit that the word does not occur in either B. or M.

Still as I find it in several Edd., e.g. Edd. Mil., Ped., Frat., Giul., without any comment, or claim (as one would expect) to the credit of supplying a satisfactory conjectural change, one may perhaps suspect that it has some MS. support.

[*Conv.* IV. ix. 118–19

(See below, p. 293)

This passage is not discussed by Dr. Moore. The emendation, which he has marked for insertion in his corrected copy of the third edition (1904) of the *Oxford Dante* (now in my possession by his bequest), was suggested to him by Dr. Jackson, who drew his attention to a note on this passage in Mr. Wicksteed's translation of the *Convivio* (p. 275). (See Dr. Jackson's translation of the *Convivio*, p. 304.)—T.]

Conv. IV. x. 67

[Le divizie] non possono causare [*al.* curare] Nobiltà.

My attention was not directed to this variant in time to collect any collations of MSS. I can only state that B. and M. both have *curare*. But according to the statements of Editors this appears to be the reading of the majority of MSS. I am indebted to Dr. Toynbee for the information that *curare* is found in the *Editio princeps* (1490), the three sixteenth-century Edd. (1521, 1529, 1531), Ed. Biscioni (1723), the Paduan Ed. (1826-7), and the Edd. Milanesi; and that *causare* seems first to have been introduced into the text by Fraticelli, who claims for it the support of three MSS. *Curare* would seem to have the unusual sense of *procurare*, in which case it would be generally accompanied by *di* or *che*. Hence *curare* is, I think, to be preferred, for (1) it would be more likely to be changed to *causare*, as a *facilior lectio*, than the converse change; (2) it has preponderant MS. support; and (3) it agrees more closely with the words in the Canzone with which it corresponds, viz. *dar* gentilezza, than *causare* would do.

The reading *curare* is recognized and explained as above in Diz. Tramater[1], and also in Diz. Tommaseo and Bellini (s. v. *curare*, § 22). I cannot find the passage quoted, or the sense *procurare* (used absolutely), recognized in the new Vocabolario della Crusca[2].

[1] [Tramater says, s.v. *Curare*:

'§ 9. Procurare. *Dante Conv.* 165, Mostro com' elle (*le ricchezze*) non possono curare nobiltà, perchè sono vili.']

[2] [Since the above note was written by Dr. Moore I have come across another

[*Conv.* IV. xxiii. 52–5

(See below, p. 294)

The emendation of the punctuation of this passage was suggested to Dr. Moore by Dr. Jackson. Dr. Moore has not discussed the passage, but he has marked the emendation for insertion in his corrected copy of the *Oxford Dante* mentioned above. (See Dr. Jackson's translation of the *Convivio*, p. 307.) —T.]

'*Battifolle*' *Letters* (p. 270 *fin.*).

I anticipated (*loc. cit.*) that, owing to my imperfect acquaintance with Latin literature contemporary with Dante, some of the words or expressions cited as Dantesque in character might prove to be insufficiently distinctive. I have already found this to be the case, thanks to the kindness with which Dr. Toynbee has given me the benefit of his knowledge, as on so many other occasions. He informs me, in regard to (2) on p. 271, that in the *Acta Henrici VII* (Florence, 1877) the Emperor is commonly addressed as ' Romanorum Rex et semper Augustus,' as part of his formal title. Also that ' Augusta ' is similarly applied to the Empress.

He has also pointed out to me instances of *praelibare* used as explained in (1) p. 271 *supra* from the same *Acta* and also from the correspondence of Innocent III. Doubtless critics may find other similar flaws, as I have already anticipated, but I hope the cumulative evidence for the Dantesque authorship of the letters is still strong enough to bear such losses of details.

instance of the use of *curare* in the sense of *procurare*, namely in the fourteenth-century Italian translation of Benvenuto da Imola's *Romuleon* :

' La plebe, come dice Tito Livio, libro secondo *ab urbe condita*, era molestata e tormentata dalli usurarii : però ricorsono al dittatore, e cercarono aiuto da lui. Lo dittatore curava per la plebe ' (i. e. the dictator procured the desired relief). (Bk. iii. Ch. 14.)

Another MS. of the text reads *procurava* for *curava*. A MS. of the original Latin work is in the Public Library of the City of Boston (U.S.A.). By the courtesy of the Librarian, Mr. Horace G. Wadlin, through the kind offices of Mr. S. C. Cockerell, Director of the Fitzwilliam Museum at Cambridge, I am able to give the Latin text of the above passage :—

Plebs, prout dicit Titus Livius libro secundo ab urbe condita, vexabatur ab usurariis. Ideo recurrerunt ad dictatorem et imploraverunt auxilium eius. Dictator procurabat pro plebe.' There can be no doubt, therefore, as to the sense of *curava* in the translation.—T.]

LIST OF EMENDED PASSAGES IN THE TEXT OF THE *CONVIVIO*

DISCUSSED IN 'TEXTUAL CRITICISM OF THE *CONVIVIO*'
(pp. 23-118)
[COMPILED BY DR. PAGET TOYNBEE]

F. = Fraticelli's text (in *Le Opere Minori di Dante Alighieri*), representing the *textus receptus* prior to the publication of the *Oxford Dante*.
M. = Moore; the addition of an asterisk (M*) indicates that the emendation has been introduced into the text of the *Convivio* as printed in the third edition of the *Oxford Dante* (1904).[1]

I. ii. 20-1 (p. 23)[2].
F. Le quali cagioni rusticamente stanno a fare parlare di sè
M*. Le quali ragioni rusticamente stanno a fare di sè

I. ii. 109 (pp. 23-4).
F. la quale per più vero testimonio
M*. la quale per sì vero testimonio

I. iii. 2-3 (p. 24).
F. tôrre alcuno difetto per sè medesima, e quello induce
M*. tôrre alcuno difetto, e per sè medesima quello induce

I. iii. 64 (p. 24).
F. siccome suo effetto
M*. siccome qui suo effetto

I. iv. 51 (pp. 24-5).
F. veggiono assai pari membra
M*. veggiono a sue pari membra

I. v. 100-4 (pp. 25-6).
F. quello sermone è più bello, nel quale più debitamente le parole rispondono; e ciò fanno più in latino, che in volgare, però il bello volgare seguita uso
M. quello sermone è più bello, nel quale più debitamente rispondono; e più debitamente rispondono[3] in Latino, che in Volgare, però che lo Volgare seguita uso

---

[1] Some of these emendations had already been introduced into the text in the first (1894) and second (1897) editions of the *Oxford Dante*.
[2] The reference in brackets is to the page of the present volume in which the passage is discussed.
[3] In the Oxford text (M*) the words *e più debitamente rispondono* are printed within square brackets as indicating a conjectural interpolation. Dr. Moore subsequently had the satisfaction of finding manuscript authority for them; hence the brackets are now removed.

I. vii. 11–14 (p. 26).
   F. e però era impossibile essere obbediente. Che allo latino fosse stato impossibile, come detto è, si manifesta per cotal ragione.
   M*. e però era impossibile essere obbediente. Che allo Latino fosse stato impossibile essere obbediente, si manifesta per cotal ragione.

I. vii. 58–9 (pp. 26–8).
   F. e l'uomo è obbediente alla giustizia quando fa quello che comanda la legge, e non più nè meno.
   M*. e l'uomo è obbediente alla giustizia quando comanda al peccatore.

I. viii. 110–12 (pp. 28–9).
   F. conviene, acciocchè sia con atto libero, la virtù essere libera, e lo dono dirizzarsi alla parte
   M*. conviene, acciocchè sia con atto libero la virtù, essere libero lo dono alla parte

I. ix. 41–3 (p. 29).
   F. nulla cosa è utile se non in quanto è usata: nè la sua bontà in potenza è essere perfettamente
   M*. nulla cosa è utile, se non in quanto è usata ; nè è la sua bontà in potenza, che non è essere perfettamente

I. xii. 89–92 (pp. 31–3).
   F. Provato adunque, che la bontà della cosa più propia, più in essa è amata e commendata, è da vedere qual essa è.
   M. Provato è adunque la bontà della cosa più propria che più in essa è amata e commendata ; ed è da vedere qual è essa.

I. xiii. 22–4 (p. 33).
   F. E ch' ella sia stata a me di questo essere cagione, brevemente per me si può mostrare.
   M*. E ch' ella sia stata a me di essere, se per me non stesse, brievemente si può mostrare.

I. xiii. 25–7 (pp. 33–5).
   F. Non è una sola la cagione efficiente dello essere delle cose, ma tra più cagioni efficienti una è la massima delle altre :
   M*. Non è secondo a una cosa essere più cagioni efficienti, avvegnachè una sia massima delle altre ?

II. i. 19–23 (pp. 35–6).
   F. L'uno si chiama litterale, e questo è quello che non si distende più oltre che la lettera propia, siccome è la narrazione propia di quella cosa che tu tratti : che per certo e appropiato esempio è la terza canzone che tratta di Nobiltade. L' altro si chiama allegorico, e questo è quello che si nasconde
   M*. L'uno si chiama litterale, e questo è quello che non si stende più oltre che la lettera propria ; l'altro si chiama allegorico, e questo è quello che si nasconde

II. i. 74–6 (pp. 37–8).
   F. conciossiacosachè nelle scritture la sentenza literale (*sic*) sia sempre il di fuori
   M. conciossiacosachè nelle scritture sia sempre il di fuori

II. ii. 19–20 (pp. 38–9).
   F. e così fatti dentro lei, poi fêro tale
   M*. e così fatti, dentro me poi fêro tale

II. ii. 32-8 (pp. 39-40).
F. Perocchè l'uno era soccorso dalla parte della vista dinanzi . . . . contrario a quello che impediva
M*. Perocchè l'uno era soccorso dalla parte dinanzi . . . . comente quello che impediva

II. ii. 41-2 (pp. 40-1).
F. per iscusare me dell' avversità
M*. per iscusare me della novità

II. iv. 28 (p. 42).
F. E questo quieto e pacifico cielo è lo luogo
M*. E quieto e pacifico è lo luogo

II. v. 27 (pp. 42-3).
F. e un' altra tutto l' argento
M*. e un' altra tutte le ricchezze

II. v. 91-3 (pp. 43-5).
F. che alle sustanze separate convegna pure la speculativa vita ; come che pure l' attiva convegna loro.
M. che alle sustanze separate convegna pure[1] la speculativa vita, come pure la speculativa convegna loro.

II. v. 126-7 (pp. 45-6).
F. per un poco di splendore, o come raggio che passa
M. per un poco di splendore,[2] ovvero raggio che passa

II. vi. 24-5 (pp. 46-8).
F. donzella di tredici anni
M*. donzella di quattordici anni

II. vi. 25 (pp. 48-9).
F. da parte del Salvatore celestiale.
M*. da parte del Santo Re celestiale.

II. vi. 137 (pp. 50-1).
F. verso lo suo epiciclo
M*. per lo suo epiciclo

II. vii. 106 (p. 51).
F. quanto è più al mezzo
M*. quanto è fin al mezzo

II. ix. 43-8 (pp. 51-5).
F. dico effetto, in quanto l' anima e 'l còrpo congiunti sono ; e non effetto in quanto quella perpetualmente dura, partita che è, in natura più che umana : e così è soluta la quistione.
M*. Dico effetto, in quanto l' anima col corpo congiunti sono effetto di quella ; chè perpetualmente dura, che è partita, in natura più che umana : così è soluta la quistione.

II. xiii. 14-15 (p. 55).
F. quello, non conosciuto da molti, libro di Boezio
M*. quello da molti non conosciuto libro di Boezio

II. xiv. 15-16 (p. 57).
F. il quale quanto per lo suo movimento non si muove
M*. il quale per suo movimento non si muove

---

[1] See p. 43, n. 1. This is the reading adopted by Dr. Jackson in his translation of the *Convivio* (see pp. 83, 301-2).
[2] The Oxford text (M*) reads 'splendore ;' see p. 46, ad init.

II. xiv. 121-2 (pp. 57-60, 285).
F. quando la lettera, per la parte remota
M*. quando della lettera per la parte remota

II. xiv. 145 (pp. 60-1).
M*. nel primo della [*Meta*]*fisica*
M. nel primo della *Fisica*[1]

II. xiv. 234-5 (p. 61).
F. volge grandissimo spazio di tempo
M*. vuole grandissimo spazio di tempo

II. xv. 135 (pp. 63-4).
F. tutti quelli ricevono e mandano quaggiù la virtù
M*. tutti quelli ricevono quaggiù la virtù

II. xv. 157 (pp. 64-5).
F. il movimento degli astri sarebbe indarno.
M*. il movimento degli altri sarebbe indarno.

II. xvi. 30 (pp. 65-6).
F. liberata nelle condizioni.
M*. libera nelle condizioni.

III. i. 71-2 (p. 66).
F. veggendo me beneficato da lei, mi sforzo di lei commendare
M*. veggendo me beneficato da lei, . . . di lei commendare

III. ii. 59-61 (pp. 66-7, 285-6)
F. perocchè nelle bontadi della natura umana la ragione si mostra della
    divina, viene
M. perocchè nelle bontadi della natura [umana] la ragione si mostra
    della divina, viene

III. ii. 125 (pp. 67-8).
F. nel terzo *dell' Anima*
M. nel sesto *dell'* [*Etica*]

III. ii. 155-7 (p. 69).
F. mente, che è quella fine e preziosissima parte dell' anima
M*. Mente, che è quel fine, e preziosissima parte dell' Anima

III. iii. 118-20 (pp. 69-71).
F. dico che li miei pensieri, che sono parlar d'amore, sono di lei, chè
M*. dico che li miei pensieri (che sono *parlar d'Amore*), *suonan dolce*,
    sì che

III. v. 101-5 (pp. 71-2).
F. e lo spazio, da qualunque parte si tira la corda, sia di dieci mila dugento
    miglia tra l'una e l'altra, cioè mezzo lo cerchio di questa palla,
M*. e di spazio, da qualunque parte si tira la corda, dieci mila dugento
    miglia ; e sì, tra l'una e l' altra, mezzo lo cerchio di questa palla ;

III. v. 152-5 (pp. 72-5).
F. lo suo montare è a Maria quasi tanto, quanto essa monta a noi nella
    mezza terza, ch' è del giorno e della notte eguale :
M*. lo suo montare è a Maria quasi tanto, quanto essa monta a noi
    nella mezza terra [alla mezza terza], ch' è del giorno e della notte
    eguale.

[1] Dr. Moore now reverts to the reading of the *textus receptus* for reasons
explained in his article.

III. vi. 47 (p. 75).
F. conoscendo lui, tutte le cose conosconsi
M*. conoscendo Lui, tutte le cose conoscono

III. vii. 31-2 (pp. 75-8).
F. per multiplicamento di luce in quelli, appena discernibile è lo loro aspetto
M*. per multiplicamento di luce in quelli e 'n lo loro aspetto

III. vii. 116-24 (pp. 78-80).
F. solo quello che veggiono e odono ripresentano siccome la immagine delle corpora in alcuno corpo lucido si rappresenta. Onde siccome nello specchio la immagine corporale, che lo specchio dimostra, non è vera; così la immagine della ragione . . . non è vera.
M. solo quello, che veggiono e odono, si rappresentano. Onde siccome la immagine delle corpora in alcuno corpo lucido si rappresenta, siccome nello specchio; così[1] la immagine corporale che lo specchio dimostra non è vera: così la immagine della ragione . . . non è vera.

III. viii. 35-7 (p. 80).
F. le quali dimostrano de' piaceri, e intra gli altri di que' di paradiso.
M*. le quali dimostrano *de' piaceri* (intra gli altri di quelli) *di Paradiso.*

III. viii. 178-82 (pp. 80-1).
F. del tutto non se ne vanno, quanto al primo movimento ; ma vannosene bene del tutto, quanto a durazione, perocchè la consuetudine è equabile alla natura
M. del tutto non se ne vanno quanto al primo movimento (ma vannosene bene del tutto, quanto a durazione), perocchè la consuetudine non è equabile alla natura[2]

III. ix. 79-80 (pp. 81-2).
F. sicchè la forma, che nel mezzo trasparente non pare lucida, è terminata :
M*. sicchè la forma, che nel mezzo trasparente non pare, lucida è terminata ;

III. xi. 47-51 (pp. 83-4).
F. che tanto vale come in greco *filos*, che a dire *amatore* in latino, e quindi dicemo noi *filos* quasi *amore*, e *sofia* quasi *sapienzia* ; onde *filos* e *sofia* tanto vale, quanto *amore di sapienzia.* Per che veder si può, che questi due vocaboli fanno questo nome *filosofo* che tanto vale a dire, quanto *amatore di sapienzia.*
M. chè tanto vale come in Greco *filos*, ch'è a dire *amatore* in Latino, e quindi dicemo noi *filos* quasi *amatore*, e *sofia* quasi *sapienza* ; onde *filos* e *sofia* tanto vale quanto *amatore di sapienza* ;

III. xi. 159 (p. 84).
F. che chiama Ettore
M*. che chiama Enea

III. xii. 46-8 (pp. 84-7).
F. di cosa intelligibile per cosa non intelligibile trattare si conviene.
M*. di cosa *intelligibile* per cosa *inintelligibile* trattare si conviene.

---

[1] The Oxford text (M*) reads *e così* here ; otherwise the reading of M* in this passage is identical with that of M given above.
[2] This emendation is due to Dr. Jackson (see above, p. 81 n.).

III. xii. 51-2 (p. 87).
F. lo sole spirituale e inintelligibile, ch'è Iddio.
M*. lo Sole spirituale e *intelligibile*, ch'è Iddio.

III. xiii. 93-4 (p. 87).
F. che superata n' è la capacità della nostra natura
M*. che sempre attrae la capacità della nostra natura

III. xiii. 101-2 (pp. 87-8).
F. qui si vede l' umile sua lode
M*. qui si vede l' ultima sua lode

III. xiv. 97-100 (p. 88).
F. e 'l filosofo dice, nel primo della *Metafisica*, che quella cosa è libera ch' è per cagione di sè, e non per altrui.
M. e 'l Filosofo dice, nel secondo della *Metafisica*, che quella cosa è libera, ch' è per sua cagione (dice) [1], e non per altrui.

III. xv. 98-9 (p. 89).
F. e terminato è quanto in quella sapienzia
M*. e terminato *in quanto* in quella sapienza

III. xv. 105-7 (pp. 89-92).
F. conoscere Dio e certe altre cose, come l'eternità e la prima materia, non sia possibile
M. conoscere di Dio, e di certe altre cose, 'quello esso è', non sia possibile

IV. iv. 24 (p. 92).
F. ma sempre desideri gloria acquistare
M*. ma sempre desideri terra acquistare

IV. v. 89-91 (pp. 92-3).
F. li sette regi ... Romolo, Numa, Tullo, Anco Marcio, Servio Tullio e li re Tarquinii
M*. li sette regi ... Romolo, Numa, Tullo, Anco, e li re Tarquinii

IV. vi. 48-53 (pp. 93-4).
F. autoritade vale tanto, quanto atto degno di fede e d'obbedienza ...
Manifesto è che le sue parole sono somma e altissima autoritade.
Che Aristotile sia degnissimo di fede e d' obbedienza, così provare si può.
M*. *Autoritade* vale tanto, quanto *atto degno di fede e d'obbedienza.*
Manifesto è che Aristotile sia degnissimo di fede e d' obbedienza; e che le sue parole sono somma e altissima autoritade, così provare si può.

IV. vi. 79-80 (p. 94).
F. avvegnachè universalmente sieno
M*. avvegnachè universalmente siano uno

IV. vii. 114 (p. 94).
F. negli animali vegetare e sentire e muovere
M*. negli animali vegetare e sentire

[IV. ix. 118-19.
F. siccome nel trebbiare il formento, che l' arte fa suo strumento del caldo
M. siccome nel trebbiare il formento. . . . che l' arte fa suo strumento del caldo] [2]

---

[1] Dr. Moore thinks it possible that the right reading is *ch' è per sua cagione di sè.*
[2] See supplementary note on p. 286.

IV. x. 67 (pp. 286–7).
F. non possono causare nobiltà
M. non possono curare Nobiltà

IV. xii. 123–4 (pp. 96–7).
F. adunque per la distinzione del conseguente
M*. adunque per la destruzione del conseguente

IV. xiv. 62–4 (pp. 98–9).
F. conciossiachè com' è onorata la cosa quanto è migliore, tanto è più
cagione di bene :
M. conciossiacosachè è memorata la cosa che quanto è migliore tanto è
più cagione di bene :

IV. xvii. 125–6 (pp. 99–100).
F. e vedute nell'aspetto di fuori
M*. e unite nell'aspetto di fuori

IV. xviii. 38–42 (pp. 100–2).
F. qui non si procede per necessaria dimostrazione (siccome sarebbe
a dire se il freddo è generativo dell' acqua, se noi vedemo i nuvoli),
bensì per bella e convenevole induzione
M. qui non si procede per necessaria dimostrazione ; †siccome sarebbe
a dire, se il freddo è generativo dell' acqua, e noi vedemo i
nuvoli ; † dice bella e convenevole induzione

IV. xix. 31–3 (p. 102).
F. e non è questo vero e converso, che
M*. e non è questo vero *e converso*, cioè rivolto, che

IV. xx. 84–7 (pp. 103–4).
F. che ad alquanti, cioè a quelli che hanno intelletto, che son pochi, è
manifesto che nobiltà umana non sia altro che seme di felicità
M*. che *ad alquanti* (cioè a quelli che hanno intelletto, che son pochi)
[*lo seme di felicità s' accosta.*] È manifesto che Nobiltà umana
non sia altro che *seme di felicità*

IV. xxi. 24–5 (pp. 105–6).
F. tutta la differenza delle corpora è forma.
M*. tutta la differenza è delle corpora e forme.

IV. xxi. 35–7 (pp. 106–7).
F. la vertù degli alimenti legata, cioè la complessione del seme. Esso
matura
M*. la virtù degli elementi legati, cioè la complessione: e matura

IV. xxii. 11–12 (p. 107).
F. ragionare della dolcezza dell' umana felicità, intendo
M. ragionare [della dolcezza dell' umana felicità], intendo

IV. xxii. 46–7 (p. 109).
F. e non pur ne' biadi, ma negli uomini e nelle bestie.
M. E non pur negli uomini, ma negli uomini e nelle bestie.[1]

[**IV. xxiii. 52–5.**
F. sia causata dal cielo ; . . . si scuopra ; così conviene
M. sia causata dal cielo, . . . si scopra ; e così conviene][2]

---

[1] This is the reading adopted by Dr. Jackson in his translation of the *Convivio*
(see pp. 267, 306).
[2] See supplementary note on p. 287.

IV. xxiii. 74-5 (p. 109).
F. di maggiore tesa, che quello dell' altro, per alcuna morte violenta,
M*. di maggior tesa che quello dell' altro.   Alcuna morte è violenta,

IV. xxiv. 46-7 (pp. 110–17).
M*. ma presso a otto anni
M. ma presso a otto mesi [1]

IV. xxviii. 37-9 (pp. 117–18).
F. alla nobile anima si fanno incontro quelli cittadini
M. alla nobile Anima si fanno incontro, e deono fare, quelli cittadini

IV. xxviii. 45-8 (p. 118).
F. 'A me pare già vedere, e levomi in grandissimo studio di vedere li
   vostri padri, ch' io amai, e non pur quelli ch' io stesso conobbi,
   ma eziandio quelli di cui udii parlare.'
M*. 'Levomi in grandissimo studio di vedere li vostri padri, ch' io
   amai, e non pur quelli, ma eziandio quelli, di cui udii parlare.'

[1] This is the reading of Fraticelli, which Dr. Moore now adopts for the
reasons given in his article.

INDEX

Academy, vi, 283.
Academy, British, 61.
Accademia Arcivescovile di Ravenna, 188.
Accademia at Venice, 234.
Accademia della Crusca, *Vocabolario*, 39 n, 50, 286.
Achilles, 243.
Acta Sanctorum, 247.
Adam, 252.
Agnese, Sta., 247.
Albertus Magnus, 41, 62, 76, 77, 78, 112, 138.
Alexander of Romena, 263, 270.
Alfraganus, 42, 50.
Almanac of Profacius, 276-9.
Andreini, his *Adam*, 211.
Angels, Dante's theories as to, 44-5, 49, 89, 134, 140, 146-56, 225-34.
Anna, Sta., 252.
Anselm, St., 50, 148 n, 153.
— *Cur Deus Homo*, 50, 146, 153 n, 230.
Antwerp, 116 n.
Aquinas, St. Thomas, vii, 30, 31, 41 n, 49, 52, 60, 61, 68, 97, 113, 116, 138, 142, 144, 145, 146, 147 nn, 148 nn, 149 n, 150 n, 151 n, 153, 155, 156, 161, 163 n, 226, 227, 230, 231, 232, 233, 234, 238, 239, 254.
Aretino, Lionardo, *Vite di Dante e del Petrarca*, 122.
Aristotle, slip of memory, 84.
— *Antiqua Translatio* of, 46, 60, 63, 68, 97, 152, 158.
— his theory of vision, 246.
— *Ethics*, 24, 30, 37, 44, 53, 63, 68, 84, 88, 89, 92, 97, 114.
— *De Anima*, 30, 62 n, 67, 68, 151, 152.
— *De Coelo*, 41, 62.
— *Metaph.*, 44 n, 46, 60.
— *Phys.*, 60, 62, 63, 249 n.
— *De Gen. et Corr.*, 62, 157.
— *Poet.*, 91, 243.
— *De Gen. Anim.*, 106.
— *Hist. Anim.*, 111.
— Περὶ μνήμης, 155.
— *Meteor.*, 238.
Ashburnham, Earl of, his MS. of *Convivio*, 119.

Astrology, Dante's belief in, 163.
Augusta, as title of the Empress, 271, 287.
Augustine, St., 113, 114, 145, 148 nn, 150 n, 153 n, 155, 156, 230.
— *Enchir.*, 50, 116.
— *De Genesi*, 59, 136, 137 n, 148 n.
— *Comm. in Ioan.*, 113.
— *De Trin.*, 113, 154 n, 163 n.
— *Civ. Dei*, 116 n, 135 n, 137 n, 148 n.
— *Lib. Imperf.*, 137.
— *Conf.*, 137, 143, 148.
— *Enarr. in Psalmos*, 147 n.
— *De Gratia et Lib. Arbit.*, 239 n.
— *Annott. in Job*, 239 n.
— *Retractationes*, 283.
Augustus, Emperor, 93.
— as title of Emperor, 271, 287.
Averroes, 52, 113, 144.
Avicenna, 61, 62 n, 113.

Bacon, Francis, quoted, 217.
Bacon, Roger, 61.
Barbi, Prof., edition of *Vita Nuova*, 128.
— establishes relations between the two versions of Boccaccio's *Vita di Dante*, 189 n.
— article on commentary of Talice da Ricaldone, 255 n.
Bardi, Via dei (Florence), 246.
Bartoli, Prof. A., 257.
Batines, Colomb de, *Bibliografia Dantesca*, 178, 179 n.
Battifolle, Gherardesca di, 261, 262, 263, 268, 269.
Battifolle, Guido di, 261.
Battifolle Letters attributed to Dante, 256-75.
Beatrice, 39, 52, 69, 115, 135, 139, 185, 223, 243, 245, 246, 252, 253.
Beatrice di Dante, 175.
Becket, history of his remains, 191, 197-208.
Bede, 83.
Bembo, Bernardo, restores Dante's tomb, 171, 173, 174, 176, 177, 178, 181.
— epitaph on Dante, 174.
Bentley, Dr., 13.

DATE DUE

GAYLORD			PRINTED·IN U.S.A.